Thinking and Writing in College

Thinking and Writing in College

Tom Anselmo
New York City Technical College
City University of New York

Leonard Bernstein
Herbert H. Lehman College
City University of New York

Carol Schoen
Herbert H. Lehman College
City University of New York

Little, Brown and Company
Boston / Toronto

Library of Congress Cataloging-in-Publication Data

Anselmo, Tom.
  Thinking and writing in college.

  Includes index.
  1. English language—Rhetoric.   2. College readers.
I. Bernstein, Leonard.   II. Schoen, Carol.   III. Title.
PE1408.A618   1985   808'.0427   85-19831
ISBN 0-316-04335-4

Library of Congress Catalog Card No. 85-19831

ISBN 0-316-04335-4

9 8 7 6 5 4 3 2 1

HAL

Published simultaneously in Canada
by Little, Brown & Company (Canada) Limited
Printed in the United States of America

Credits and Acknowledgments

*The authors and publisher would like to thank the following sources for granting permission to
use their material:*

"Closing in on Cloning." Copyright 1981 by Time Inc. All rights reserved. Excerpted by
permission from *Time*.

  "Key to Trees in Leafy Condition" from *A Field Guide to Trees and Shrubs* by George A.
Petrides. Copyright © 1958, 1972 by George A. Petrides. Reprinted by permission of Houghton
Mifflin Company.

  "My Papa's Waltz" from *The Collected Poems of Theodore Roethke* by Theodore Roethke.
Copyright 1942 by The Hearst Magazine, Inc. Reprinted by permission of Doubleday & Company.

  "Rapid Transit" by James Agee from *Forum* (February 1937, p. 115). Reprinted by permission.

  "Nothing Gold Can Stay" from *The Poetry of Robert Frost*, edited by Edward Connery Lathem.
Copyright 1923, © 1969 by Holt, Rinehart and Winston. Copyright 1951 by Robert Frost.
Reprinted by permission of Holt, Rinehart and Winston, Publishers.

  "Pennsylvania Station" by Langston Hughes. Copyright © 1963 by Arna Bontemps. Reprinted
by permission of Harold Ober Associates Incorporated.

  "There Will Come Soft Rains (War Time)" from *Collected Poems* by Sara Teasdale. Copyright
1920 by Macmillan Publishing Company, renewed 1948 by Marnie T. Wheless. Reprinted with
permission of Macmillan Publishing Company.

  "Opportunity Cost" from *Microeconomics* by Bronfenbrenner, Sichel, Gardner. Copyright ©
1984 by Houghton Mifflin Company. Reprinted by permission.

(Continued on page 441)

Preface

The difficulties students currently face in reading and writing for their college courses are too well known to need repeating here. Over the years, the authors of this text, like most composition instructors throughout the country, have devised a variety of curricula, struggled over student papers alone or in conference, and discovered, more often than not, that the problems encountered involve the basic issue of developing the students' ability to think. Recent developments in theoretical knowledge about the writing process have been an inestimable source of help to us — inspiring new approaches, modifying old ones, and generally providing standards against which we could test our ideas. As writing teachers with over 70 years of combined experience, we are attempting to provide here a text that makes practical use of this burgeoning new knowledge of how people learn, but that, at the same time, includes those approaches we have found to be successful in the classroom.

We know, for instance, that the aims of a liberal arts education, however obvious they may seem to the college faculty, often seem to the students merely a bewildering array of distribution requirements in which their composition course is simply another discrete element. In this text we hope to show some of the unifying factors of learning that can be integrated with the composition course. We also believe that students learn best when they discover ideas for themselves rather than memorize formulae. To achieve this goal, we have arranged the elements of this text so that students actively develop strategies as they work through the book. These strategies will, we believe, provide a basis for competency in all college-level study.

A fundamental concept governing this text is that students need a systematic approach in order to develop the thinking necessary for college-level work. The strategy we concentrate on is a carefully controlled questioning process. We know that our students can and do think in their everyday lives, but their efforts are often random and haphazard. We are also aware that the use of questioning as a technique is hardly new. What is needed now, we believe, is a method that will give students some clear guidelines for using the questioning process. We have therefore developed the concept of a "controlling question" as the primary tool for focusing inquiry. To discover what questions would be most useful for this purpose, we read exam questions and term-paper assignments from professors in a wide range of disciplines, and asked them about the kinds of responses they looked for. Reviewing our findings, we noticed that four patterns seemed to predominate — definition, process, comparison/contrast, and cause/effect. The fact that these patterns conformed to familiar rhetorical modes substantiated the belief that they mirror the thought processes through which knowledge is discovered, as well as the writing patterns by which it is presented. These four questioning patterns thus become the models for the "controlling questions."

Controlling questions provide a necessary first step, but techniques are also needed to probe more deeply into the issue under consideration. One way to achieve this is by a second level of questioning using the four basic patterns combined with other sorts of questions that they suggest. But since we are aware of the fact that much of the best thinking grows out of non-logical, free-associational, and intuitive leaps of the mind, we provide a wide range of techniques for tapping these resources such as free-writing, brain-storming, and feedback from fellow students. Organizing information in order to produce clear, coherent writing is equally vital and this process grows organically from the questioning strategies. It is not a superficial structure imposed on the data. Bringing order out of the chaos depends on creating suitable categories.

While the concerns of the disciplines play a significant role in determining categories, the controlling question is essential. For example, it can suggest either a classification system based on the steps needed to describe a process or the significant elements necessary for a comparison.

As you can see, the basic philosophy that underlines this text is a belief in the unity of investigating, understanding, and writing in all fields of knowledge. While there are a range of forms, such as case studies and lab reports, that are specific to a particular discipline, they are not the crucial element; they are easily mastered once the students have developed the thinking and organizing strategies that provide a basic understanding of the issue at hand. All too often we have seen how easily students mimic the form of an academic essay yet still fail to comprehend the problem that they are discussing. In this text we try to show students that the same kinds of questions can be asked in any field of knowledge, the same techniques can be used to probe further, and the ways of organizing data are a natural outgrowth of the method of investigation. We believe that students may thereby begin to understand the significance of inquiry to their college education.

The opening section of the book consists of two chapters. The first chapter considers the idea of controlling questions and the ways subsidiary questions and other strategies can be used to investigate an issue further. The second chapter shows how the principles of organization grow out of the questioning patterns being used. A summary at the end of the section provides a handy reference that students may use as they work through the text. Part Two of the book contains five chapters, one on each of the four controlling questions, and one on the application of our approach to research papers. Materials from a wide variety of disciplines, including readings from actual textbooks used in introductory-level courses, are presented in each. Although one subject is used as a focus for the development of an essay in each chapter, such as the use of art history for comparison/contrast, there is sufficient material in the anthology at the end of the book so that instructors may alter assignments to suit their own needs. Part Three provides an application of our approach to research papers and a substantial anthology for additional or alternative assignments.

Many people have been instrumental in helping us develop this text, and to them we offer our heartfelt thanks and gratitude: our students whose responses helped us develop our ideas; our colleagues at our respective colleges who were generous in their suggestions, especially Elaine Avidon, Flavia Bacarrella, Juliana Bassey, Phyllis Cash, Nila Ganhhi-Schwalto, James Vaughn, and Eve Zarin at Lehman College, and John Bell and Joyce Buck at New York City Technical College; our friends at other colleges and universities, Janet Saunders, Ann Spector, Elizabeth Stone, and Debra Tannen, who offered helpful criticism; the staff at Little, Brown whose encouragement kept us going, Joe Opiela, Barbara Breese, Ellen Kennedy, Nancy DeCubellis, and Dorothy Z. Seymour; and the reviewers whose knowledgeable suggestions guided the book, Gerald Belcher and Janice Haney-Peritz, Beaver College; Patricia Bizzell, College of the Holy Cross; Robert Dees, Orange Coast College; Toby Fulwiler, University of Vermont; Diana Hacker, Prince George Community College; Louise Smith, University of Massachusetts–Boston; Judith Stanford, Merrimack College; and particularly Robert A. Schwegler, University of Rhode Island.

A very special thanks is due to Leslie Goldstein-Anselmo who suffered through endless hours of shop-talk without complaint.

To the Student

Now that you are in college, you are probably taking a number of introductory courses in several disciplines. You will be required to absorb a great deal of new information, you will be asked to think about issues from the particular perspectives of those disciplines, and you will be expected to express your understanding of the material in writing. Whether you answer essay questions on examinations, prepare reports on some aspect of a broad subject, or produce research or term papers, you must think about, interpret, and organize data and present it in clear prose. To help you live up to these expectations, you are now enrolled in a college composition course and your instructor has selected this text so that you can acquire the skills necessary to accomplish this task.

As composition teachers in a large, urban university, the authors of this text were struck with the difficulties many of our competent students faced when writing for their other courses. When, for our classes, they wrote papers comparing and/or contrasting the personalities of two people they knew or had read about in a short story we were considering, they managed these assignments quite well. Some of these same students, however, would question us about how to approach a similar assignment in an economics course, for example, when they were asked to compare and/or contrast how goods and services are distributed in capitalist and socialist societies. These students were certainly familiar with the material covered, but they were not automatically making the vital connection between what they were doing with comparison/contrast in our writing classes to other situations. We therefore decided to revise our approach to the writing courses we taught in two essential ways.

We first reasoned that in addition to using selections such as short stories, poems, and essays on general topics of interest as a stimulus to writing, we would incorporate materials from introductory courses in a broad range of academic disciplines into our writing classes. If students could write about subjects they might be called upon to respond to in the actual courses they were or would be taking, an immediate and practical connection might be made between what we were teaching students about writing in our classes and the demands of the larger academic community. Most students take writing courses during their freshman year and an exposure to some of the basic concepts in the disciplines would certainly serve as an orientation to college and would, hopefully, help them see at the beginning of their college careers that the issues raised by all areas of scholarship are significant to an understanding of the human experience. Using readings from the several disciplines would also allow students greater flexibility in selecting writing assignments.

Second, we decided to make it clear that the way to think about, plan, and write essays is approximately the same in all disciplines. College students often face difficulty because they constantly have to shift intellectual gears. One hour they learn how cells reproduce, and in the next hour they absorb information about the American Civil War. The content of these courses seems so radically different that students fail to realize that both the biologist and historian think about their specific areas of expertise in much the same ways. They both systematically *define* terms, investigate *why* something occurs and *what the outcomes* might be, *enumerate* a sequence of events, and make judgments about the *similarities* and *differences* between phenomena. The focus, of course, is different, but the thought patterns are the same for the biologist and the historian. Although we are probably less systematic when we confront the issues of our daily lives, don't we all use the same strategies? Once students understand this similarity in the thinking process, they will become better writers in college.

As we introduced and refined these notions, we found that students not only reported greater success in writing for their other courses, but also that they were doing better in our composition classes. And so we decided to write this book which would reach a greater audience than the students we personally teach.

The text is divided into three parts. The first part deals broadly with how systematized thinking can be translated into coherent writing. The second and largest section takes each of the thinking strategies in turn — defining, comparing and contrasting, describing processes, and discovering causes and effects — and illustrates how to think about and write essays when these strategies are the central focus of an essay. Also included in this section is a chapter on how to do research. Throughout the text you will find readings in many disciplines and follow student writers as they develop their essays in these disciplines. You will be asked either to write papers in these disciplines or to choose from assignments that appear after the selections in the anthology, the third part of the text. These selections are also taken from a broad range of subjects, and we expect that you will be intellectually stimulated writing about the many issues they raise.

We hope you enjoy using this book and certainly hope that, as a result, the writing you do in college and beyond will be easier and more meaningful for you.

Contents

1

Strategies for Thinking and Writing

It is the beginning of the semester. You have just come from your first class, a history course on the Roman Empire. You are hunched over a table in the cafeteria, poring through the introductory notes you took in class, the course outline the instructor handed out, and the required textbook you bought. The topics on the course outline seem interesting, but you are somewhat concerned about all the work you will have to do.

For example, the instructor is asking for several short essays in response to questions found at the end of each chapter in the text under the heading "To Think About." He is also requiring a long library paper on some aspect of the political, social, or cultural life of the Romans, due at the end of the semester. You think to yourself, "What a lot of writing!"

Since you are curious about the questions, you thumb through the text and find several challenging ones, like the meaning of "republic" versus "empire," the development of Rome's military power, the difference between Greek and Roman philosophies, and the reasons for the decline and fall of Rome. They seem thought-provoking, but how do you organize your thoughts to write good answers?

To add to your concern, the choice of topic for the library paper is left up to you. You know that you will need to decide on a topic in a few weeks. What should you write about? How do you get started?

You are considerably overwhelmed, worrying not only about the writing requirements for this history course, but also about the possible writing assignments you may get in Sociology 101 and Biology 201, classes that have not met yet.

This degree of apprehension is common to most students faced with the prospect of writing papers for their courses. Such a level of anxiety, however, can be greatly lessened if students develop common thinking and composing strategies for all their writing assignments, whether they are in history, sociology, biology, or marketing. Such overall strategies will be described in this part of the text.

1

Questioning

ACADEMIC DISCIPLINES: A FOCUS ON UNDERSTANDING

One of the most striking aspects of college for you as new students is the broad number of courses offered in a wide range of disciplines. Some of these fields, like history and biology, are probably familiar to you; others, like sociology, art history, and philosophy, may be totally unfamiliar. Although you will need to understand the differences among the disciplines, you should also realize that scholars and teachers in different fields share the common aim of understanding the world we live in. They also share a common strategy for arriving at understanding: using questions to explore events, ideas, objects, and people.

From Questions to Insights

The mutual concern of scholars and teachers for understanding and interpreting our world can be seen in the way they respond to the momentous events of recent history. Take, for example, the atomic bombs dropped over the Japanese cities of Hiroshima and Nagasaki by the United States in 1945.

Historians, studying the past, inquired about the chain of events that led to the blasts in order to explain how and why they happened. Biologists, exploring animal life (zoology) or plant life (botany), were concerned about the long-range effects of the explosion on living things. Political scientists, researching the structure and operation of governments on the local, national, and international levels, were interested in the way the various agencies of the American national government worked together to develop the bomb and finally decided to drop it. Psychologists, considering how living things interact with the environment and thus interested in sensory perceptions, drives, and behavior, examined the emotional reactions of both Japanese and Americans to this disaster. And economists, wanting to learn how human beings allocate scarce resources, were interested in the way these blasts affected the supply and distribution of goods and services and the way possible future nuclear explosions would influence the economy.

PRACTICE

List the other courses you are currently taking and in a sentence or two indicate what concerns an expert in each of those fields might have about a nuclear explosion.

This common concern may also be seen if we consider a momentous advance made by scientists in their ability to clone — that is, to derive a group of new organisms from an individual organism by asexual reproduction. A discussion of cloning appeared in *Time* magazine on January 19, 1981.

Closing in on Cloning

In the book and movie *The Boys from Brazil,* a demented Nazi doctor uses blood and tissue cells from Adolf Hitler to clone dozens of copies of the German dictator in the hope that at least one of them will seize power and conquer the world. Though the cloning of human beings is likely to be confined to fantasy for decades — perhaps forever — other kinds of cloning have long been possible. The Greek word *klon* means twig, and the simplest kind of vegetable cloning consists of cultivating cuttings from a plant. By the mid-1950s scientists had succeeded in cloning amphibians, producing frogs that were generally identical to each other and carried the inherited characteristics of only a single parent. Most animal cloning has been done by transplanting nuclei into egg cells to produce an entire organism from a single cell. But the cloning of higher forms of life, like mammals, is hard to achieve. Mammal eggs are microscopic, ten to 20 times smaller in diameter than frogs' eggs, and vastly more difficult to manipulate. Consequently, the barriers to cloning laboratory mice had, until now, proved insurmountable.

But last week the word was out that biologists had successfully done just that.

The work was carried out in Switzerland by Karl Illmensee of the University of Geneva and Peter Hoppe of the Jackson Laboratory in Bar Harbor, Me., both veteran researchers in cell biology.

If biologists can clone mice, can they some day clone humans? Scholars in a wide number of fields are already beginning to ponder the implications of this advance in biological science, and the insights they can provide from their individual perspectives are vital to our understanding. We therefore asked instructors in several academic departments at our colleges to prepare a number of questions they might want to consider if cloning were to be a topic in their introductory courses.

Among the many responses we received were the following questions:

From a biologist:

What is cloning?

Describe one technique that might be used to clone humans.

How does cloning differ from sexual reproduction? Are there any similarities?

From a political scientist:

What effect would cloning have upon democratic institutions in the United States?

From a sociologist:

How would the socialization process of a clone differ from the socialization process of a sexually produced individual?

Define the roles of men and women in a world of clones.

From a philosopher, teaching a course in ethics:

Why does cloning (genetic engineering) raise moral problems now or for future generations?

Should limits be imposed upon the gaining of scientific information?

From a psychologist:

Compare and contrast the emotional stress factor in the human clone with that in the sexually produced individual.

From a historian:

Imagine the events that might lead a society to adopt cloning as a means of human reproduction.

From an economist:

> What steps are necessary to determine the cost of labor in a society of clones?
>
> Would cloning benefit or hinder the distribution of goods and services?
>
> How would goods and services be distributed in a society of clones?

From a literary scholar:

> In the novel *Brave New World,* Aldous Huxley describes an "ideal" society of clone-like people. Why does Huxley feel that such a society would be less than perfect?

From an art historian:

> Since cloning would eliminate art as I understand it, I cannot supply you with any questions on the subject.

The art historian obviously felt strongly about her position, but her statement raises yet another set of questions:

> Why does an art historian believe that art would disappear in a society of clones?
>
> What does the art historian mean by *art?*

PRACTICE

Examine the following list of current issues and either in groups or in general class discussion determine what questions the instructors in different academic disciplines you have studied or are studying might contribute to your understanding of the issues involved.

1. Television commercials

2. Violence in sports

3. Private automobiles vs. mass transportation

4. Society's responsibility toward the elderly

5. The consequences of technological advancement

6. Higher education vs. on-the-job training

7. The punishment of crime

Four Basic Questioning Patterns

Not only do the same issues concern scholars from different disciplines, the questions they ask fall into a few basic patterns, four of which will be discussed in this text. Take a closer look at the questions about cloning.
The biologist asked:

> What is cloning?

and one question that the art historian's comment generated was:

> What does the art history professor mean by *art*?

Examine the other questions and write another one that requires a similar way of looking at an issue.

Can you discern a common element in these three questions? Both the biologist's question and the question asked about the art historian's note require that you respond by *explaining the meaning* of a term or idea. If you examine the sociologist's question about the "roles of men and women in a world of clones," you will see that answering that question requires you to *explain the meaning* of the word *role* as sociologists use it, as well as to enumerate the various categories that might be included under the term. You would need to show that sociologists are talking about "the customary functions of individuals in a society of clones" and then detail the different sorts of roles involved, such as sex roles, occupational roles, and cultural roles, and would perhaps need to go even further to divide each of these categories into specific groups.

Questions that ask for an explanation of the meaning of a term or idea are labeled *definition* questions.

The biologist also asked:

> Describe one technique that might be used to clone humans.

and the historian asked:

> Imagine the events that might lead a society to adapt cloning as a means of human reproduction.

Examine the other questions and find another one that requires a similar way of looking at an issue.

Can you discern a common element in all these questions? The biologist's question asks that you list the steps included in one method of cloning. The historian's question requires that your response relate a sequence of events (steps) that would result in a society adopting cloning as a method of reproduction. If you examine the economist's question — "How would goods and services be distributed in a society of clones?" — you will discover that it also calls for a step-by-step analysis of a method. In each case a process must be traced.

> Questions that call for a sequence of steps are *process* questions.

The biologist asked:

> How does cloning differ from sexual reproduction? Are there any similarities?

and the sociologist asked:

> How would the socialization process of a clone differ from the socialization process of a sexually produced individual?

Examine the other questions and find one that calls for a similar way of looking at an issue.

Can you discern a common element in all these questions? The first part of the biologist's question requires that two systems of reproduction be contrasted; the second part of the question asks that these two systems be compared. The sociologist's question asks that the two systems of reproduction be contrasted with respect to the socialization process. And the psychologist's question also asks for both a comparison and contrast.

> Questions requiring us to identify and explore similarities, differences, or both are called *comparison/contrast* questions.

Examine the political scientist's and the philosopher's questions.

> What effect would cloning have upon democratic institutions in the United States?

Why does cloning (genetic engineering) raise moral problems now and for future generations?

Examine the list to find those questions that call for a similar way of thinking.

Can you discern a common element in all these questions? The political scientist's question asks that the result of an event or action (cloning) be investigated, and the philosopher's question asks *why* an event or action (cloning) may cause problems. Do all the questions you selected above ask for reasons (causes) and/or results (effects)?

Questions that ask for reasons (causes) and/or results (effects) are called *cause-effect* questions.

Why did the questions the instructors asked about cloning fall into a number of patterns? Simply because these types of questions represent several strategies of thinking that the human mind uses to probe for an understanding of the world. To interpret a phenomenon, we usually explain what it is by *defining* it, we establish *causes* for its existence and examine the *effects* it might have, we *compare and/or contrast* it with what we already know, and we trace the *process* by which it appears. For example, even when writing the brief excerpt from "Closing in on Cloning" on page 4, the author used these four patterns of thought, as represented by the questions below.

1. What is cloning? (definition)

2. How was most animal cloning achieved prior to 1981? (process)

3. What is the difference between cloning amphibians and cloning mammals? (comparison/contrast)

4. Will it be possible to clone humans in the future? (cause-effect)

PRACTICE

Choose any problem you experienced in the recent past (this morning will do). It could be a problem in getting an assignment done; it could be some difficulty at home; it could be some disagreement with a friend; it could be a financial problem. In small groups, identify the pattern of thought (definition, cause-effect, comparison/contrast, and process) you might have used to understand and analyze the problem and possibly to arrive at a solution.

The rest of this chapter will introduce a number of thinking and writing strategies that can be used in developing an essay. To illustrate, we will be using the first topic in the practice on page 14, "Television Commercials." You should, however, choose one of the other topics and, by following several of the techniques discussed, write your own essay.

Since this may be your first attempt, and since you are probably making it during the first or second week of the semester, you will not be expected to write as well as you will by the end of your composition course. This chapter only touches upon issues in writing that will be considered fully in later portions of the text. It is, however, important early on for you to get a sense of what writing for college is about. After all, we begin to learn to swim by getting into the water and begin to learn to drive by getting behind the wheel, obviously knowing that there is a trustworthy and competent person around to prevent disasters. The swimming or driving instructor avoids judging you in these initial stages, but is concerned only with helping you gain sufficient confidence to proceed with the task. Remember, however, that unlike learning to swim or to drive, you have been using language for most of your life, and you have been writing for as long as you have been in school. You are, therefore, not in deep water for the first time. Many of you are doubtless anxious to try your hand at college-level writing, and for those of you who are a bit hesitant we remind you that you are not at this point being judged as you would later be, and that the rest of the book will delve into a great deal of specific detail about how to improve your writing ability.

THE CONTROLLING QUESTION: CONNECTING THINKING AND WRITING

After reading the discussion of questioning presented above, you may be tempted to ask, "So what has all this to do with writing? There is an important connection between the two processes. The patterns of thinking and questioning we have just discussed will form the basis of much of your investigation and to a large degree control the way you present your ideas. Often in introductory college courses your writings are responses to questions your instructors ask, and these questions are based to a large extent on the four patterns: definition, process, comparison/contrast, and cause-effect. If, for example, the question calls for a definition, the major thrust of your answer would be to supply that definition. It is vital, therefore, that you determine the type of question an instructor is asking you and the kind of critical thinking required for an appropriate response. Despite the demands of the different assignments you may be given — an essay question in an exam, a report, or a term paper — it is the question that mainly provides the focus for the thinking to be done.

> A question that expresses the overall purpose of an inquiry and therefore limits that inquiry is called a *controlling* question.

Discovering a Controlling Question

Applying the Four Basic Patterns

When your instructor gives you an assignment in the form of a controlling question, he or she provides you with a focus for your thinking. Instructors do not, however, always ask specific questions; sometimes they provide a general topic for you to explore, such as, for an introductory course in sociology, "Discuss the socialization of teenagers in modern urban societies." They leave it up to you to establish the limits of your inquiry. This is, most often, not a deliberate tactic to confuse you on the part of your instructors, but rather an attempt to stimulate your thinking about the issues raised in your courses. By leaving it up to you to pinpoint the direction of your essay, they are challenging you to focus on pertinent matters that interest you. Establishing your own limits means that data you have acquired are used creatively and indicate both to your instructors and, more significant, to you that you have truly absorbed the material.

You will, in this case, need to ask yourself what the overall purpose of your essay should be. If you fail to do this, you will find yourself floundering as you write. One way to establish a focus for your essay is to create questions in as many of the four patterns as you can and choose one as the controlling question. Thus, if your instructor asks you to discuss the socialization of teenagers in modern urban societies, you might ask yourself, "What are the major differences between the socialization patterns of teenagers in rural and urban areas?" a comparison/contrast question, or "What are the effects of living in a densely populated area upon the socialization of teenagers?" a cause-effect question. You could then organize your thoughts around one of these questions.

"Television Commercials" is certainly a broad topic whose parameters need to be limited in order to think and write with any degree of clarity about the many issues involved. By creating the following controlling questions in the four patterns, a student begins to restrict the topic.

Definition

How would I define a good television commercial, and what aspects of commercials — sound, color, scenario — need to be included?

Process

How is a typical television commercial produced?

Trace the steps by which an effective television commercial might lead the viewer to make a purchase.

Comparison/contrast

Compare and contrast the television commercial with another advertising medium (radio, print).

Cause-effect

Are television commercials necessary for a healthy economy?

What effects do commercials have on the buying habits of young children?

Would the fact that most TV programs are paid for by commercials influence the content of those programs?

When you create controlling questions in these patterns, you are trying to establish a focus for your own writing. You should, therefore, choose a question that would be of interest to you and your potential audience. You should also choose one you are equipped to answer with the information you already have or can acquire. Not all the questions you create would necessarily fulfill these criteria.

PRACTICE

Choose one of the topics listed on page 6 (not "Television Commercials") and create as many controlling questions as you can in the four basic patterns. If you cannot think of one for all the patterns, do not worry. When you finish, select one that you think would be significant and interesting enough for you to pursue. It should be one you would be able to answer given the knowledge you now have or are easily able to acquire. If you find that the topic fails to yield a good question for you, you need not stick to it; you may choose another topic and create new controlling questions.

Freewriting

Imagine the predicament of the columnist in your daily newspaper who several times a week has to write a commentary on some aspect of current local events. She has a deadline; she may not be personally interested in, or may not initially have much to say about, the event she has to interpret for her readers; she has other obligations that distract her from the task at hand. She may have tried the questioning process, but it seemed to yield no idea worth investigating. In order to create a focus for her column, to establish a controlling question, she might use the alternative of freewriting.

Freewriting is nothing more than putting down on paper all your thoughts exactly as they occur to you when you start thinking about writing a paper. And, as you know from having listened closely to your own thoughts, while your mind is working it jumps from idea to idea with little apparent order. Nor do the ideas come out as complete sentences. Nevertheless, there is value to committing this jumble of thoughts to paper despite their apparent randomness. Many writers, including professionals, use freewriting not only because they find it helps them to discover ideas about the topic that they did not know they had, or to make connections that had not previously occurred to them, but also because it helps clear out any minor annoyances that may be blocking their creativity. It is also useful because it provides a starting point on a project that seems, at first glance, too complex to organize coherently. In freewriting you begin with whatever is on the top of your mind and let your thoughts go where they choose. At this point, you forget about organizing, forget about correcting, forget about revising, since in this initial stage these concerns will only interrupt the free flow of your ideas.

The freewriting process is based on the premise that your heads are filled with a great deal of information that you are not consciously aware is there. The ideas and information in what is called your long-term memory bank are not always retrievable through logical approaches.

Freewriting is not, of course, the same as writing the paper itself, not even the equivalent of writing a first draft. Its value lies in uncovering ideas, information, and relationships that might be valuable when you start the actual writing.

One student, trying to discover a controlling question on television commercials, produced the following freewriting:

> Got to write about television commercials. don't know where to begin. what's that song on the radio? nice beat. Only three days to do it. gross . . . grossly unfair. Had to break date with Mary. Love to be over at Aldo's right now. Should have at least 3 days just to watch TV before doing this. The real bitch is having to get involved this way with TV. that's just for relaxing. actually, though, its hard to relax with all those stupid commercials. Buy this, buy that . . need a new oil pan where'll I get money. phooey. you'd think we're made of money. boy were my parents mad when I used to want them to buy all those stupid things. Bozo the Clown, what'd he say Be happy something like that. the moveable monster, the star wars stuff, and they weren't cheap either. got me in the habit of expecting to see TV in order to see what I could buy. kind of a training, daily lessons in how to spend money. say that might be useful . . . tv commercials as training to be a buyer, to be a consumer . . that sounds better . . .

As you can see, the student's mind wandered from one thought to another, but she was able to move from her complaints about being given the assignment to recognizing that she could fulfill the assignment by writing about a process question she genuinely felt interested in: "How do TV commercials train young people to become consumers?"

Below is another example of a student's freewriting on television commercials:

> Everytime a commercial comes on, the volume goes up, and I'm forced to pay attention or leave the room, usually to go to the refrigerator. If I keep doing this, I'm going to burst my seams. Anyway, that program about abortion last night really got me mad. It didn't take a position one way or the other. I guess I should be grateful that the program was on a serious issue, but I wonder if the network hedged because they were afraid they wouldn't get a sponsor?

This freewriting contains the germ of a cause-effect question about the effects of commercials on television programs themselves, another interesting idea that could be developed into a paper.

While freewriting, many people find it helpful to probe their feelings about the writing process. If you are tense about what you are writing, it is often a good idea to express what is bothering you. Do you resent your instructor? Are you competing with your friend for a grade? Is it too late at night to think logically? Is your toe itching? Are you worried about your roommate? Certainly, you could let these thoughts remain unwritten, but putting them down on paper frequently clears them from your mind while allowing you to start on the task of writing.

PRACTICE

Using the topic you have chosen and without any further thought, write for ten minutes completely freely, putting all your thoughts down without any conscious attempt to censor or correct. Keep writing steadily. If your mind seems to be blank, write the alphabet, or the words "I can't think" until some ideas emerge (they always do if you stick to it long enough). If necessary, repeat the process an hour or two later. Then read over your paper and see what questions seem to recur and what aspects of the issue seem most prominent.

Brainstorming

Working with others can frequently help you develop ideas that might not have occurred to you while working alone. In the process called *brainstorming*, a group of people concerned with a similar topic simply list the ideas that occur to them individually or in response to the words of the other members of the group. One person acts as a recorder, writing down a phrase or two to capture each idea. Many of the phrases may seem dull or silly, but sometimes even these stimulate other members of the group to think of better ideas. A group of students asked to brainstorm about television commercials might produce a list like this:

Television Commercials

Interrupt programs

Hunger

Purchase

Gives me time to call Mary

Want to see movie advertised

Fast talkers

Sexy girls, silly housewives

Lots of laundry

Why cars in the desert

"Coke Is"

"Where's the Beef"

Buy, buy, buy

"Call 800–000–0808, call 800–000–0808"

Truck drivers' school

Louder than show

When you reread the list, you might discover that a pattern of concern emerges, indicating a possible topic for exploration. In this case, one such topic is that television commercials effectively convince people to spend their money, and the student might want to write an essay investigating the controlling question, "How do commercials convince people to buy the products advertised?"

PRACTICE

Work with a group of three or four students in a brainstorming session and see if you can come up with a controlling question on your topic.

Using a Controlling Question to Probe a Topic and Develop Ideas

Once you have an idea for a controlling question, you have made a valuable start toward writing your paper. Your next step is to discover what you will need to include in order to discuss the issue intelligently, to explain it clearly to others, and to provide a valid response to the question. These ideas do not spring automatically to mind; they need to be found. Even experienced writers do not sit at their desks and begin immediately writing beautifully shaped and well-substantiated essays. They struggle to find pertinent information, to decide on a proper arrangement, even to get themselves started on their projects. And in the course of writing a paper, they frequently need to find new ideas for particular sections, to delete others, or even to modify the controlling question itself. The methods they use can, fortunately, be taught and learned.

Below are some of the techniques that writers have found useful in developing their ideas and in getting themselves started.

Generating Subsidiary Questions

One way to get started is to derive other questions from the controlling question. Think of this method as a secondary, a subsidiary, level in the questioning process. Suppose you were going to write an essay in response to one of the controlling questions about TV:

> What effects do television commercials have on the buying habits of children?

What questions come to mind that would help you start to think about the many facets of this topic? Below is a running account of one student's thinking that led to a number of questions for possible exploration.

Mental Notes	*Subsidiary Questions*
"Well, first thing that must be established . . ."	a. Are children asking their parents to buy the products they see on TV?
"Need data . . . may have to research this — or are observations enough? . . . If children are asking for these products . . ."	b. What kinds of commercials are children responding to most?
"I wonder . . . how does it work?"	c. At what time slots are these commercials most effective?
	d. How does the TV commercial do it?
"Maybe a better way to ask this . . ."	e. What emotions are the TV ads appealing to most?
"Reminds me . . ."	f. Are certain kinds of children more prone to buying products advertised on TV than others?

"Maybe should classify cer- ──────── boys/girls?
tain groups"

young/old?
from professional homes?
from non-professional
homes?

rural/urban?

"m . . . m . . . this question is
an interesting topic by itself . . .
wonder if controlling question
may be too broad to tackle . . .
well, continue and see . . .   g. Why did I ask this control-
but . . . :   ling question?

"Was this meant to be a ques-   h. What is responsible
tion about morality in   advertising?
advertising?"   or
                                    i. What is the difference be-
                                        tween proper and improper
                                        ads?

"Might consider this for the
conclusion . . . could possibly
pursue this during the discus-   j. Are TV ads creating exagger-
sion part also . . . Here's a   ated needs in children? Why
tougher question.   or why not?

"That's good! And . . ."   k. If so, what kinds of prob-
                                        lems are these exaggerated
                                        needs causing parents?

"Of course, the follow-up . . ."   l. What can parents do to off-
                                        set these ill effects?

"This last set of questions could
be a separate topic also! . . .
Good idea to take a look at an
opposing view."   m. What benefits are derived
                                        from persuading children
                                        to buy? for children? for
                                        parents? for the general
                                        economy?

Using these questions is an excellent way to open up the topic. They are different from the controlling question in that they help the writer to gather material for support.

> Questions derived from a controlling question are called *subsidiary* questions.

Given the controlling question,

> Compare and contrast the TV commercial with the commercials of another advertising medium (radio or print).

the following questions in the four patterns could serve as subsidiary questions:

Pattern	*Example*
Definition:	What is a commercial?
Comparison/contrast:	Compare the impact of the visual and aural experience of television commercials with those of the exclusively aural radio.
Process:	A short story usually has three major stages: beginning, middle, and end. Show how typical TV and radio commercials follow these steps.
Cause-effect:	What effects are lost or gained when a commercial is on the radio rather than on television?

PRACTICE

Take your own controlling question and reflect on it in the same manner; see how many questions you can generate. Try to create subsidiary questions in the four basic patterns — definition, comparison/contrast, cause-effect, and process — that would warrant exploration. Of course, your final essay may not answer all these subsidiary questions, but by creating them you have begun to probe the controlling question. When you actually begin to write, you can select those you think most useful.

In addition to using these kinds of subsidiary questions, you can add another questioning technique to your repertoire. By asking questions that begin with *Who, Where,* and *When* you can provide avenues of inquiry that may previously have been ignored. These questions ask you to determine, for example,

Who:	the different people or groups of people who might be involved;
Where:	the different locations that might be relevant;
When:	the different time periods that might be considered.

In continuing the probe of the topic, comparing and contrasting TV and radio commercials, the following subsidiary questions can be generated.

Who	*Where*	*When*
children?	at home?	at one's leisure?
teenagers?	at work?	on the run?
adults?	in a bus? in a T?	early morning?
senior citizens?	in a tavern?	late at night?
executives?	in a diner?	in prime time?
professionals?	in an automobile?	interrupting TV or
white-collar workers?	at the beach?	radio program?
blue-collar workers?		
men? women?		
the sponsor?		

More subsidiary questions can be generated by seeing these two types of question patterns in conjunction with each other. You might, for instance, expand your list of questions by combining the *who* question form with *comparison/contrast* to produce the following:

What similarities and differences are there between the responses of adults and children to TV commercials?

What similarities and differences are there between the responses of men and women (rural and urban viewers; professionals and blue-collar workers; teenagers and senior citizens) to TV commercials?

Combining *when* questions with *cause-effect* produces the following questions:

What causes a sponsor to advertise a product on a daytime soap opera?

What are the effects of interrupting a TV show with a commercial?

If the two kinds of questions are listed in columns side-by-side, you may be able to generate even more questions by crossing from one column to the other.

Some of the questions that one student created from such a crisscrossing are:

1. What do young children think commercials are?
    (Definition — *Who*)

2. Compare and contrast the claims made for a product with its actual performance in the home. (Comparison/contrast — *Where*)

3. What are the differences between the kinds of commercials presented at prime time and those presented late at night? (Comparison/contrast — *When*)

4. What steps are necessary in producing a commercial to gain the attention of a woman busy in her home? (Process — *Where*)

5. What motivates a sponsor to decide to invest in a TV commercial? (Cause-effect — *Who*)

6. Why are most of these children's shows and commercials on during early morning and early evening? (Cause-effect — *When*)

A diagram of this student's questions would look like this:

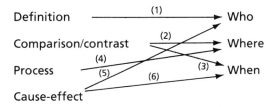

When a student probes the controlling question by creating questions, he or she may discover that one of the subsidiary questions emerges as a more interesting focus of inquiry and could become the controlling question for an essay. The subsidiary question number 5 above, "What motivates a sponsor to decide to invest in a TV commercial?" for example, could easily be the basis for an entirely new approach.

PRACTICE

Using the topic that is of interest to you, create as many *Who/Where/When* questions as you can. Then, crisscrossing from the basic question patterns to the *Who, Where, When* questions, see how many additional questions you can create.

Listing

Listing is like brainstorming, only this time you are working alone, responding to a specific controlling question. If, for example, you were asked to write an essay answering the question, "Are TV commercials necessary for a healthy economy?" a list might begin like this:

Create artificial demand

Make people waste money

Poor eating habits

Over-medication

Bought record advertised on TV

Many records sold

More jobs

More money

Other products bought

More jobs

Learn about new products

Learn new uses for existing products

Better informed

Point up flaws in competition

This particular list suggests how commercials can stimulate the economy and indicates some problems they raise. Once you have established these positive and negative aspects of commercials, you will be better equipped to consider the issue of whether TV commercials are useful or not.

Charting

Certain controlling questions lend themselves to creating charts. If you were answering the controlling question of definition, "How would I define a good television commercial?" you might create a chart with some commercials you consider excellent listed across the top and some common characteristics of the commercials listed down the side. You would then fill in the boxes by describing how each commercial exhibits the characteristics, as in Table 1.1.

Focused Freewriting

Focused freewriting is similar to freewriting in having no conscious organizational structure and in being unconcerned with editing. Unlike freewriting, however, it is committed to investigating a particular aspect of an issue. A writer about to start a paper on television commercials would need to have a sense of the controlling question to be answered before engaging in focused freewriting. Using this strategy the writer can find information to support a position, sort out categories that might be considered, and see relationships that might clarify the data. Focused freewriting is thus used at a point in composing different from the point at which freewriting is used. You use freewriting when you are trying to find a direction, a controlling question; you use focused freewriting when you have a sense of direction and want to find material to develop your idea.

The same considerations, however, apply to both freewriting and focused

TABLE 1.1   Television Commercials

	Commercial A	*Commercial B*	*Commercial C*
Music	A lot of brass to stir patriotic feelings	Full string orchestra	Hard rock
Color	Primary colors — red, yellow, blue	Muted to create romantic mood	Purples and orange
Pace	Rapid	Serene	Jagged
Plot	Fourth of July	Boy meets girl	Surprise ending

freewriting: you are unconcerned with orderly thoughts; you will often find yourself writing off the topic; the grammar, spelling, and punctuation may be incorrect.

Below is an example of a student's initial response to the controlling question, "What effects do TV commercials have on young children?"

> Well, when I was a kid I would watch the cartoons on Saturday morning and be really fascinated by the commercials. They would always make me feel that I must have what they were selling. After all, Crunchies were being eaten by the athlete, the Olympic star — and since I wanted to be big and strong and play tennis at Wimbledon, I'd better get some real quick. Or they'd make me feel that the toys my parents gave me were already outdated — after all, Johnny down the block had the latest computer game and I should have one too. By the time my parents got up, I was ready to press them for whatever new gimmick the television had convinced me I must have.

This student, through focused freewriting, began to investigate two possible subjects that the essay could discuss: the erosion of parental authority and the tendency of commercials to devalue thrift.

Must you use all of these techniques? Of course not. They are simply strategies that might help you get started with your essay. What you will use depends on what makes you comfortable as a writer. A few writers can establish in their heads a focus for an essay and feel comfortable when they start writing their first drafts, knowing that the plan in their heads is sufficient to carry them through. Most apprentice writers, however, need to develop a repertoire of techniques that will permit them to investigate a topic far more carefully than their previous experience has allowed. Even if you think you know exactly what you want to say and how you want to say it, it is advisable to use several of these invention techniques to discover any additional lines of thought that might improve your papers.

PRACTICE

If you have not as yet established a controlling question for the general topic you have chosen, or if you feel that the topic you have begun to explore is now unsuitable, generate a focus for an essay by questioning, freewriting, or brainstorming.

Once you have established a focus for your paper, generate additional ideas on that subject by asking subsidiary questions, creating lists or charts, or engaging in focused freewriting.

Using a Controlling Question to Guide the Writing and Revising Process

Whatever pre-writing techniques you have chosen to use, you should, before you start writing the first draft, have in some written form a body of information that you will want to use in your paper. The problem now is to decide how to organize your data.

Before you begin, however, you need to make clear to yourself who the audience of your paper is.

Visualizing an Audience

The audience for your college essays generally will be made up of your instructors and your fellow students. Occasionally, your instructors may ask you to imagine that you are writing for some other particular group, but in the absence of such directions you will need to consider what your peers and your teachers must have in order to appreciate your paper. Most students in college visualize their instructors only as examiners, the givers of grades, and to a certain extent the papers and exams you write in college are assigned in order to see how well you have absorbed the material in the course. Limiting your perception to that purpose, however, creates more than a little anxiety and tension for you the writer, and, more importantly, destroys the possibility of other approaches. Your instructors have chosen to be teachers because they are interested in the intellectual growth of the people in their classes, and, as experts in their fields, they want their students to appreciate the insights that their disciplines can offer for understanding human problems.

Students often disregard their fellow students as a potential audience. Yet frequently student papers are read aloud in class or shared in some way. These students are, like you, apprentice investigators in the field and are interested in seeing how your thinking can illuminate for them the subject matter of the course. Although some of them may be friends outside the classroom, you need to address them in your papers in the more formal manner of colleagues in a joint enterprise.

What do these two groups, instructors and students, look for in a paper? Both expect you to stay as closely as possible to the subject at hand, to take a stand on the issue or offer an interpretation, to provide enough explanation so that they can see why you hold the position you have chosen, and to fill in any special information that is needed. Some students believe that there is no need to fill in the material from the course, since both audiences are already familiar with the information, but both groups need to know the aspects of concern to you and are interested in understanding the uniqueness of your position. In writing your paper, you will want to use this somewhat more formal view of your audience. You do not, however, have to reject your own voice. Unless your instructors direct you otherwise, you can inject yourself into your essay by judicious use of such expressions as "I believe that . . ." and by explaining your position through the use of incidents from your own life or from those you know. Your personal observations and experiences will frequently be asked for directly, but even indirectly your personal vision will form the paper.

Planning the Parts

Just because a writer has collected all the information for a paper and has decided what direction to take in presenting it, all problems are not automatically solved; in fact, some of the most difficult decisions still lie ahead. A student whose progress we have been following felt confused as she sat at her desk and tried to figure out how and where to begin. She was even annoyed that her instructor had given her no formula to follow in writing the paper. Although she realized that her teacher was interested in having her develop her own style and thought, she stared at the blank sheet of paper in front of her, feeling angry and frustrated. But the instructor had said this version was only a first draft and she would be able to revise it. Reassured by that knowledge, she reviewed her notes, confirming that the controlling question she wanted to focus on was:

What are the effects of TV commercials on children?

Her answer would be:

The effects are harmful.

She studied the rest of her notes and gleaned from them the following subsidiary questions she thought she could answer and bits of information she might be able to use.

From using basic question patterns:

What benefits are derived from persuading children to buy (for children, parents, general economy)?

From crisscrossing with *Who, When, Where* questions:

Compare impact of TV on children vs. impact on adults.

How do commercials get children to want a product even though parents have said no?

Why are most of these children's shows and commercials on during early morning and early evening?

From freewriting:

TV commercials train a child to become a consumer, Olympic star endorses candy, computers.

From listing:

Poor eating habits, artificial demand.

From focused freewriting:

Erosion of parental authority, commercial pressure, devaluation of thrift.

The only thing left to do now, she thought, was to start writing.

PRACTICE

Review all the notes you have made from questions, lists, freewritings, and so on, and decide what controlling questions you want to answer. List the ideas you might use to explain your position. Then attempt a first draft.

After several false starts and much rewriting, the student described above produced the following first draft:

It's 5:00 p.m.; do you know where your children are: In front of the TV set, that's where. From one end of the country to the other, when its just before dinner time, you can be sure that most American kids are huddled in front of the boob-tube, out of Mom's way while she's getting dinner ready. And what are they watching? fights, killings, impossible rescues by supernatural powers flying through the air. The level of these children's shows are not just stupid, but downright dangerous. Some children have even thought they were Superman and have jumped out of windows five stories above the ground. The injuries and even deaths that have resulted are the fault of the TV producers and the stations.

But bad as the shows are, the commercials are even worst. These innocent children sit their night after night being told that should have, must have. They are told all sorts of things. That candy bars will make them Olympic heores. The new computer game will make them the happiest kid on the block. That the new doll will solve all their problems.

The kids in America are turning into miniature buying machines. Every night, night after night, they are bombard with these ads that make them believe that life would not be complete without another new something or other. There mothers can say over and over again that candy isn't good for you because it ruins your teeth or spoils your appetite or make you fat, but does that stop them? No. They just keep nagging and nagging until Mom breaks down and gets them what they want. Or else they take their allowances and go spend it on candybars instead of saving it for more important or more useful things.

And some of the things advertised on television are really expensive. The new computer games are made to seem exciting. Blobs of colored lights going on and off, crazy space music filling the air, all the kids in the neighborhood want to play with the kid who owns it. But the game itself might cost 20 or $30.00. And in order to play it you have to have a computer, and that's going to cost hundreds of dollars. It don't do Dad any good to shout that "we don't have that kind of money!" The kids see it on television and they want it. So then the TV ads tell them that they'll do better in school if they have a computer, so now what can the fathers do? They all want their kids to do good in school so that they finally give up, spend more than they can afford.

It used to be that kids decided among themselves what made another kid a good friend — someone who was fun to be with, who liked doing the same things you liked to do. Now, though, the popular kid is the one who owns the latest gimmick advertised on TV.

The TV commercials are a menace. They ought to be banned.

Revising

This student's instructor gave the students several suggestions for revising their drafts independently, but since this student felt that her paper represented her best effort at this stage of writing, she could find nothing to change. The instructor then assigned her to a group of three other students who read and discussed their papers together. All the students felt nervous about this procedure, but they soon discovered that everyone tried to be as kind as possible, and that the comments were far more helpful than anything they could have thought of by themselves. After reading the draft printed above, the students in the group said that they were confused by the transition from the opening paragraph about TV programs to the next paragraph about TV commercials. In fact, they were not sure until near the end of the paper whether she was writing about the harmful effects of TV programs or just of the commercials. They also felt that she had a lot to say about parent-child relationships, but that it was scattered throughout the paper. These comments made the writer realize that her controlling idea — the dangers of TV commercials — had not been clearly stated soon enough. Their remarks about the amount of material dealing with parents was a surprise, for she had been unaware of how much her thinking had been geared to urging parents to do something to protect their children. The discovery was rather exciting and made revising a less onerous task. She resolved to make the following changes:

- Put a statement about the dangers of TV commercials into the early part of the paper. (She liked the idea of having it at the end of the paper and decided to keep it there as well.)

- Make the point that parents are the ones who need to do something about these commercials.

- Do something about the section on TV programs. (She liked that part, even though it had caused some confusion. She believed it was a good way to get the readers' attention. She thought she might shorten it, and if the answer to the controlling question came early enough, the confusion would disappear.)

Here is the student's revised version:

It's 5:00 p.m.; do you know where your children are? In front of the TV set, that's where! From one end of the country to the other, when it is just before dinner time, you can be sure that most American kids are huddled in front of the boob tube, out of Moms way while shes getting dinner ready. The programs themselves are bad enough, but even worst are the commercials. Night after night these innocent kids sit there and are told that candy bars will make them Olympic heroes, that the new computer game will make them the happiest kid on the block, or that the new doll will solve all their problems! These commercials are a danger! Parents should realize what these commercials are doing lasting harm to their children and should do something about it!

Shortened version of section on TV programs

Answer to controlling question

Focus on parent/child relationship

A major problem these commercials create is the way they make children disregard their parents ideas. There mothers can say over and over again that candy isn't good for you, that it ruins your teeth or spoils your appetite or makes you fat, but does that stop them? No. They see an Olympic star telling them to buy Mounds bars, so they do. But as bad as those results might be, its even worst that the children stop listening to their parents advice at all. They go on nagging their parents to get them things there parents think are bad, and if that don't work, they take their allowances and go buy the things they want, like candybars.

Focus on parent/ child relationship
These commercials also make the children force the parents to buy things they can't afford. The kids see the new computer games and they are made to seem so exciting. Blobs of colored lights go on and off, crazy space music fills the air, all the kids in the neighborhood want to play with the kid who owns it. The game itself might cost $ 20. or $30.00, but in order to play it you have to have a computer, and that's going to cost hundreds of dollars. It doesn't do Dad any good to shout that we don't have that kind of money! The television is more important than what Dad says, especially when they are told that the computers will make them smarter in school.

The TV commercials are a menace and they ought to be banned. Parents should do something about it because they are losing control of their kids.

Answer to controlling question

The student paper presented here is not perfect, but as a first attempt by an entering freshman it is adequate. Although she did not follow her notes precisely, the writer has a clearly-stated answer to her controlling question, and her sense of purpose in writing gives her work vividness and immediacy. Her decision to restrict her arguments to those that have to do with parental authority gives a unified focus to the paper, and the examples she cites are both interesting and relevant.

The excessive militancy in the tone of the paper and the exaggerations, particularly in the following sentences, should be avoided:

> Night after night these innocent kids sit there and are told that candy bars will make them Olympic heroes, that the new computer will make them the happiest kid on the block, or that the new doll will solve all their problems! These commercials are a danger! Parents should realize what these commercials are doing lasting harm to their children and should do something about it!

The student has failed to take into consideration the sophistication of many children or even the reasons commercials exist, as well as the possibility that there would be much less variety of programming for children without them. Such a blanket condemnation needs to be modified by showing some awareness of the place of commercials in the economics of the television industry. While each of the paragraphs contains a statement on the aspect of the problem she is discussing, her final sentences in each of the two central paragraphs seem to trail off rather than complete the thought. This is particularly true at the end of paragraph 2:

> They go on nagging their parents to get them things there parents think are bad, and if that don't work, they take their allowances and go buy the things they want, like candy bars.

This student also made errors in sentence punctuation, verb forms, and spelling, which will be considered when we discuss editing.

The very word *revise* can bring panic even to professional writers, so it is no wonder that you, like the writer of the draft printed above, may feel uneasy about what is expected of you at this stage. In the first place, many students are unaware that the word *revise* does not mean correcting spelling and grammatical errors. Those steps are important, but the current term used for that aspect of writing is *editing*. Revision means more than that; *re-vision* literally means "seeing again," a total thinking-through of the draft. In revision you can add new information, delete irrelevant or unnecessary information, rearrange parts of the essay, or discard the entire draft and start again.

How do you know what you need to do for your particular draft? The following suggestions will guide you through the process.

Since the draft you have written represents your best thinking at the time, you may be dismayed at the prospect of having to improve it on your own. There are some helpful questions you can ask yourself, however. The first one is **"Can I summarize or outline my paper?"** That is, can you state the controlling question and your answer to it, tell what your main points are and what illustrations you gave? Putting the information into a form like the one below may help.

```
┌─────────────────────────────────────────────────────────┐
│                                                           │
│   Question and answer:    _____     │
│                                                           │
│                           _____     │
│                                                           │
│   First point:            _____     │
│                                                           │
│        Illustration:      _____     │
│                                                           │
│   Second point:           _____     │
│                                                           │
│        Illustration:      _____     │
│                                                           │
│   (and so on)             _____     │
│                                                           │
└─────────────────────────────────────────────────────────┘
```

Be sure you can actually locate the information in your paper before you add it to the form. Not infrequently, writers think they have written on paper some information that they merely had in mind, and so it has been inadvertently omitted. If you find gaps in your form, you know where you need to add more information.

Another helpful question to ask yourself is, **"In what order did I present the information?"** If you think you have an order, check to see if it follows the pattern you had in mind. Did you move from least important to most important reasons? Or the reverse? Have you included answers that respond to the basic question patterns?

A third helpful question is **"Who will be reading my paper and will they understand what I am talking about?"** It is particularly difficult to step outside yourself and pretend you are someone else reading your paper, but the better you can do that the better your paper will be. Who are the students in your class? If your paper deals with the finer points of professional football, for instance, and your class consists mainly of students who seem uninterested in spectator sports, you might need to supply some additional information to explain your points. Asking yourself, "Will they understand it?" at each step will force you to consider this issue.

Although you will undoubtedly notice and correct misspellings, punctuation faults, and other errors as you reread, your main focus at this point is not on editing; you should concentrate now on the organization and content of your paper.

However useful and necessary it is to attempt to revise your paper independently, it is no substitute for getting responses from a few other people. Because professional writers are aware of the limitations of their own view of their works, they often read their works in progress to a group of writers. The responses are invaluable for pointing out confused spots and for suggesting alternative ways of approaching the subject.

Student writers who would probably benefit the most from this kind of feedback are often the most reluctant to try it. They are convinced, even before they start, that other students will criticize their papers unmercifully, or that they are the only ones who have problems. The overwhelming number of students, however, are all too aware of the effort needed to produce even a first draft and, rather than being too critical, are frequently too kind in their acceptance of the effort.

To avoid either of these pitfalls, you can set up a few steps to guide the discussion. Instructors often organize reading groups in their classes; if yours does not, find a group of two or three students with whom you feel comfortable. Students in your class who are involved in the same study as you and who know what effort goes into a first draft are better readers than friends or family.

Next, set up a series of questions to guide the comments of members of the group. Some suggestions are:

1. What sentences or phrases do readers remember most vividly?

2. Where would they like to have more information?

3. What controlling idea do they get from the paper?

4. Do they see the connection between the explanations and the idea they believe is being stressed?

5. What significant issues have been omitted?

The group should, however, avoid questions that ask readers to say whether or not they generally liked the paper. While their approval may be flattering, it gives none of the needed concrete suggestions. And a negative response is not only difficult to accept, it may also discourage students from taking any action at all.

PRACTICE

Working by yourself or with a small group of students, read and revise your draft.

Editing.   Although you will automatically correct your sentence structure, grammar, spelling, and punctuation as you proceed with your writing, you should try to avoid halting your momentum by doing so. What is more important in the initial steps of writing is to get your ideas down on paper, organize them properly, and detail them adequately. You can make corrections later when you edit the draft you are considering for submission.

Editing before you submit your paper is essential. Many writers know what is correct, but because they have not read there copy carefully or they have read to quickly, the submitted manuscript contains errors they could of avoided. Stop! Did you discover any errors in the last sentence? What are the three that it contains? The following techniques might help you correct what you have written.

1. Read each sentence in isolation. Start at the capital and read to the period, question mark, or exclamation point. Stop! Consider! Is it a complete sentence? Is it really more than one sentence, a run-on, and should it therefore be divided?

2. Reread the sentence word for word — very slowly — and be sure to read what you see and not the correct word or expression that might be in your head.

3. A useful proofreading device is to read the paper backwards — the last sentence first, the next to the last, next, and so on. Because the sentences are now out of context, you can examine them for corrections rather than for meaning.

PRACTICE

Using the above techniques, proofread the final version of the student's paper on p. 29. When you are finished, compare your corrections with those made by other students in your class. Then proofread your own revised draft.

By now you must realize that good writing does not spring full-blown from the brain in one burst of creativity but is developed slowly with much trial and error through many steps of questioning and thinking as well as writing. Some of the major steps have been explained in this chapter: finding a controlling question; developing ideas through such techniques as subsidiary questions, focused freewriting, brainstorming, listing, and charting; and revising either by yourself or in a group. These steps have been presented in the order in which they commonly occur, but in actual practice you will find that you will frequently skip back and forth among them. All of these steps actively involve you both as a thinker and as a writer, and it is important for you to realize that both are necessary.

We have, however, in this chapter focused on only one part of the thinking process: the one that provides you with ideas and information you can use in your papers. In the next chapter we will be concerned with the part of the thinking process that involves organizing your material. Although for the purposes of clarity we have separated these elements, they are, as you will soon discover for yourself, closely interconnected. With both thinking approaches, questioning and organizing, you will be able to tackle the writing of assignments in your college courses.

Writing means thinking, and your success as a writer will grow as your ability to use thought effectively increases.

2

Organizing

It has been said that "life is organization." Certainly, human society is highly organized. A nation, a city, a corporation, a department store, a supermarket, your college — all are highly-organized systems. Like it or not, we live in a world that demands we be aware of these organized systems; otherwise life becomes unmanageable. Asking for Nurse Alice Simmons at the information desk of a vast hospital complex without identifying the medical section and ward she works in can result in undue frustration. Without organization our daily lives could be filled with little annoyances, like those exasperating moments when looking for an unpaid bill on a cluttered desk or fumbling for a lost key in a mass of cosmetics, pharmaceuticals, and stationery at the bottom of a purse. With clenched jaws, we make the familiar resolution, "I've got to get organized!"

Getting organized is also a necessary requisite of a student's life, not only in dividing the day into times for attending class, reading, and studying for maximum efficiency, but also, more important and elementary, in shaping thinking.

The demand for orderly thinking is the same for the academic professional. We three authors working together to write this textbook represent a prime example of this demand. In our early meetings, the three of us grappled with what was perhaps the most challenging part of the project: deciding upon the place of the thinking strategy in writing. If you had been able to tape our first discussion sessions — literally several hours of elaborating upon ideas, getting exasperated with ourselves or with each other for not communicating well, and, of course, relieving the professional tension (and thereby saving our friendship) with timely coffee breaks — you would have noticed that we were struggling to develop an organizational scheme for the initial chapters of the text that would deal with the thinking strategy. As a result of our discussions, we finally concluded that two major features of the thinking strategy would be *questioning* and *organizing,* and that they would be dealt with separately, the questioning element in Chapter 1 and the organizing element in Chapter 2.

As you saw in the first chapter, we broke down questions into controlling and subsidiary questions, and we further broke down these categories into sub-categories, such as process and cause-effect questions. For this second chapter we decided to separate the organizing process into two elements: dividing into parts and creating groups. Let's first look at dividing.

DIVIDING INTO PARTS

A prime example of dividing is what we have just described: breaking down the thinking strategy into parts, and still further breaking down the questioning and organizing processes. A general definition is in short:

Dividing into parts is separating a whole into its funda-mental elements or component parts.

A concrete example you come across every semester that displays dividing is the college catalog. This catalog generally lists its courses by disciplines, not only to show the range of subjects it is possible to study on a particular campus, but also to mirror the many ways the total sum of human knowledge can be approached. At most colleges, the entire curriculum is divided into three major groupings. At one college, these courses are grouped under three categories: humanities, natural sciences, and social sciences. These broad groupings are further subdivided into the various departments. The breakdown does not stop there; the offerings of each department are further divided by groupings of courses, and finally by the courses themselves. For example, the History Department is one of the several departments included in the Humanities Division at Lehman College, but within the History Department the courses are grouped according to specific regions, such as History of Europe, History of Asia, History of Latin America, and so on. A diagram of this resultant division and sub-division would look like the one in Figure 2.1.

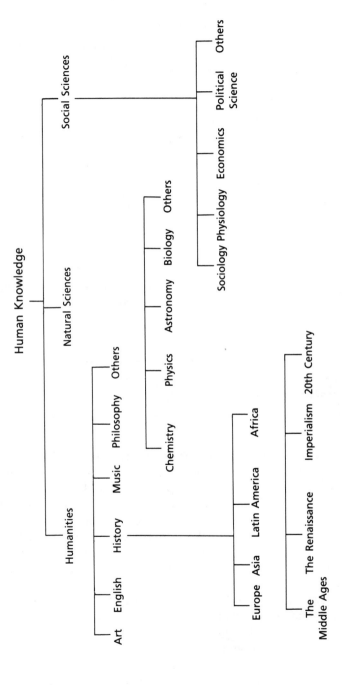

Figure 2.1 *Categories of a College Curriculum*

In all disciplines, dividing is a necessary component of thinking. In analyzing you will be asked to break down key ideas into their fundamental elements. From a study of literature, for example, you might answer the question, "What are the forms of literature?" with the breakdown shown in Figure 2.2.

Did you notice the duplication in Figure 2.2 of the concept of drama, with its appearance both as a form of literature and as a kind of poetry? Such overlappings can occur with surprising frequency, for classification systems are not rigid, fixed entities; they are flexible tools through which varying points of view can be expressed. One scholar concerned with human expression, for example, might regard music as one of the humanities, while another scholar concerned with the physical properties of sound might list it with physics, one of the natural sciences. In *marketing,* an economist might break down the question into "What are the variables that can be controlled by the marketing manager?" as in Figure 2.3. In *physics,* a scientist might analyze the question "What phenomena did Einstein attempt to bring together in his 'unified field theory'?" as in Figure 2.4.

PRACTICE

The writing class you are now a part of is a unit that can be divided in a wide variety of ways. The most obvious breakdown is by gender, but many other kinds of division are possible. Is there a range of ages in your class? Do you represent a number of ethnic groups? Or just consider the range of physical size — can members be classified as short, medium, or tall? The categories suggested here merely scratch the surface of possibilities.

Working with a small group of students, list as many ways as you can

Figure 2.2 *Forms of Literature*

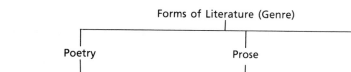

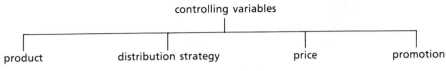

Figure 2.3   *Controlling Variables in Marketing*

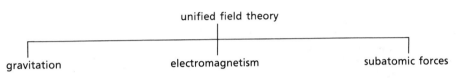

Figure 2.4   *Phenomena Resulting in the Unified Field Theory*

to divide your class. Then, working with the class as a whole, select the most interesting divisions and physically separate the class into those categories.

CREATING GROUPS

Organizing has one other major component. In Chapter 1 you saw that after listing the questions instructors asked regarding the subject of cloning, you discovered that they fell into several patterns: definition, process, cause-effect, comparison/contrast. This process of finding patterns is called *grouping.* In short,

> *Grouping* is placing units (items) into categories.

Generally, grouping requires that the subject matter be such as to lend itself to categories. Almost every academic subject has particular names for groups that students must learn.

Sorting is a type of classifying that assumes that groups are already known. In zoology, for example, where the categories are pre-established, animals are sorted into families: The lion, leopard, jaguar, wildcat, and so on are combined into one family, or genus, called *Felidae.* All kinds of domestic cats — Siamese, Angora, Persian, and so on — are one part of the same family, grouped together under the sub-category, or species, *Felis catus.*

Often you will be required to discover categories from a list of items. To help you discover the question patterns in Chapter 1 of this text, we used an example of this process of discovering categories. We could easily have told you what the question patterns were at first and then had you sort the number of questions the instructors asked. We thought, however, that requiring you to discover the patterns would increase the chances of your realizing their importance. You would then remember them better and apply them in the pre-writing stages.

PRACTICE

In stores the merchants categorize their wares so that people can easily find them. Below is a list of a bookstore's new acquisitions. If you were the manager, how would you separate these books into groups? There are many possible groupings. Discuss in class which ones would be most useful for a bookstore.

New Budget Landscaping by Carlton B. Lees

The Case of the Poisoned Eclairs by E. V. Cunningham

Shanghai, a novel by Wilham Marshall

Earl Warren, The Judge Who Changed America by Jack H. Pollock

The Complete Beginners Guide to Tennis by Rex Lardner

How to Hit a Golf Ball by Arnold Palmer

The Compact Edition of the Oxford English Dictionary

The Times Atlas of World History

The Story of Civilization by Will and Ariel Durant

Darrow, A Biography by Kevin Tierney

Franklin Roosevelt and American Foreign Policy 1932–1945 by R. Dallek

Feed Your Kids Right by Dr. Lenden Smith

Food Power by George Schwartz, M.D.

The French Garden 1500–1800 by W. H. Adams

The Complete Scarsdale Medical Diet by H. Tanower

The Complete Book of Running by James F. Fixx

The Women's Dress for Success Book

Crockett's Victory Garden by James Underwood Crockett

The Vegetarian Epicure by Anna Thomes

The Stories of John Cheever by John Cheever

COURSE NUMBER CODE	SEC. NO.	COURSE TITLE / DAYS	START-END TIME	BLDG. & ROOM	CREDITS, HOURS, CR. REF. INSTRUCTOR
ITA 101 60 101	01	ELEMENTARY ITALIAN 1			05.0 05.0 SAN FILIPPO
		T	900 950	CA249	
		W,F	900 1050	CA249	
	02	M,T,W	1000 1050	CA228	PERSICO
		H	900 1050	CA235	
	03	M,H	1100 1250	CA235	TRAPANESE
		T	1200 1250	CA235	
FRE 101 42 101	01	ELEMENTARY FRENCH I			05.0 05.0 VAN VOORHIS
		M,H	900 1050	CA247	
		T	1000 1050	CA247	
	02	M,H	1100 1250	CA249	POUCHARD
		T	1200 1250	CA247	
	03	M	100 150	CA247	VAN VOORHIS
		T	200 350	CA247	
		H	100 250	CA247	
ITA 322 60 322	01	ITA DRAMA 16-18TH CENT			03.0 03.0 PICCOLOMINI
		T,W,F	100 150	CA251	
SPA 204 93 204	01	ELEM CONTEMP SPAN II			03.0 03.0 MORAN
		T	1000 1050	CA249	
		W,F	1000 1050	CA247	
	02	T,W,F	100 150	CA247	BASTOS
	03	T	100 150	CA247	LERNER
		W,F	100 150	CA228	
SPA 320 93 320	01	DEV LIT FORMS-LAT AMER			03.0 03.0 MONTERO
		M,T,H	1200 1250	CA245	
Meets with LAC 320-01.					
ITA 330 60 330	01	RENAISS CHIVLRC POETRY			03.0 03.0 PICCOLOMINI
		T,W,F	1000 1050	CA251	
FRE 102 42 102	01	ELEMENTARY FRENCH II			05.0 05.0 MEDEOT
		M	1000 1050	CA233	
		T,W	1000 1050	CA235	
		H	900 1050	CA235	
	02	M,H	1100 1250	CA247	VAN VOORHIS
		T	1200 1250	CA247	
	03	M,H	1200 150	CA228	FURBER
		W	200 250	CA228	
SPA 102 93 102	01	ELEMENTARY SPANISH II			05.0 05.0 PINA
		M	800 950	CA237	
		T,W,H	800 850	CA237	
	02	T			RODRIQUEZ
		W,F	900 1050		
SPA 203 93 203	01	ELEM CONTEMP SPAN I			03.0 03.0 PINA
		M,H	1100 1150	CA251	

COURSE NUMBER CODE	SEC. NO.	COURSE TITLE / DAYS	START-END TIME	BLDG. & ROOM	CREDITS, HOURS, CR. REF. INSTRUCTOR
	02	W	1200 1250	CA251	PINA
	03	M,T,H	1200 1250	CA251	ESTEVES
	81	T,W,F	100 150	CA237	VIVERO
		T,H	615 730	CA251	
	03	T,F	900 1050		CANEPA
		W	1000 1050		
	04	T,W,F	1000 1050		ESTEVES
		H	900 1050		
	05	T,F	1100 1150	CA235	DOYLE
		W	1100 1250	CA235	
		H	1100 1150	CA239	
	06	M,H	1100 1250		HABOUCHA
		W	1200 1250		
	07	M	100 150	CA235	MONTERO
		T	200 350	CA235	
		H	100 250	CA235	
	08	M,H	100 250	CA239	BRUZZI-COSTAS
		W	200 250	CA239	
	92	M,W	700 915		FABRE
Meets at Helen Keller School in Co-op City.					
SPA 340 93 340	01	SPA LIT OF MIDDLE AGES			03.0 03.0 HABOUCHA
		M	1000 1050	CA245	
		H	1000 1050	CA245	
ITA 102 60 102	01	ELEM ITALIAN II			05.0 05.0 PICCOLOMINI
		T,W,F	900 950	CA247	
		H	900 1050	CA	
	02	M,T,H	1100 1250	CA228	GAYE
	03	M,T	1200 150	CA228	GAYE
		H	1200 1250	CA228	
SPA 342 93 342	01	20TH CENT SPA STUDY II			03.0 03.0 GOTTLIEB
		T,W,F	1000 1050	CA245	
FRE 450 42 450	01	ADVANCED SEMINAR			03.0 03.0 FURBER
		M	200 450	CA251	
SPA 306 93 306	01	ADV SPA COMPOSITION			03.0 03.0 LERNER
		T,W,F	1100 1150	CA217	
FRE 234 42 234	01	INTRO FRENCH CINEMA			03.0 03.0 FURBER
		M	200 450	CA251	
ITA 265 60 265	01	INTERMED STUDIES-ITAL			03.0 03.0 PICCOLOMINI
		T,W,F	1100 1150	CA251	
SPA 201 93 201	01	INTERMED SPA GRAMMAR			03.0 03.0 RUIZ
		T,W,F	900 950	CA239	

Figure 2.5 Courses in Romance Languages at Lehman College

The Art of French Cooking by Julia Child

Pat, A Biography of Daniel Patrick Moynihan by Douglas Schoen

---

PRACTICE

Figure 2.5 is a random listing of all the courses offered by the Romance Language Department at Lehman College. What other groupings and subgroupings could you create?

Grouping for Different Purposes

The same subject matter may be grouped in different ways. You could, for example, categorize trees by observation in one of several ways, as in Figure 2.6.

By their shape:

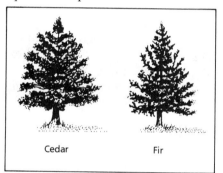

| Cedar | Fir |

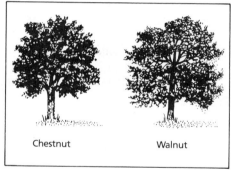

| Chestnut | Walnut |

By their height:

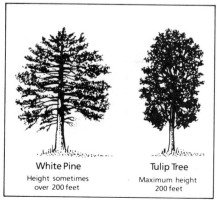

| White Pine | Tulip Tree |
| Height sometimes over 200 feet | Maximum height 200 feet |

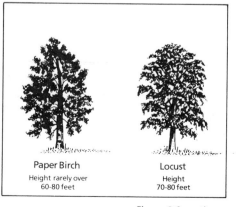

| Paper Birch | Locust |
| Height rarely over 60-80 feet | Height 70-80 feet |

Figure 2.6 continues

By their leaves:

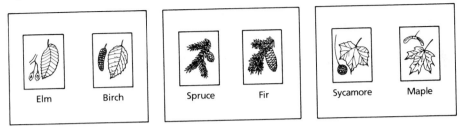

Figure 2.6 *Tree Shapes*

Trees could also be grouped by their barks, by their flowers, and even by their use—for making pianos and furniture, for shade, and for decorative purposes.

Botanists, the scientists of plant life, take most of these groupings into consideration, making scientific decisions that create major categories under which are included other sub-groupings. Within their major categories, the "family of trees," are such divisions as those in Figure 2.7.

A guidebook on trees will use many, if not all, the categories used by botanists, but its major concern is that readers identify trees easily. They would need to group trees by some distinguishing feature. Most use leaf type as their major category, a so-called tab for simple identification, as in Figure 2.8.

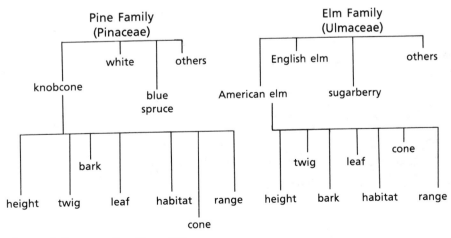

Figure 2.7 *Two Families of Trees*

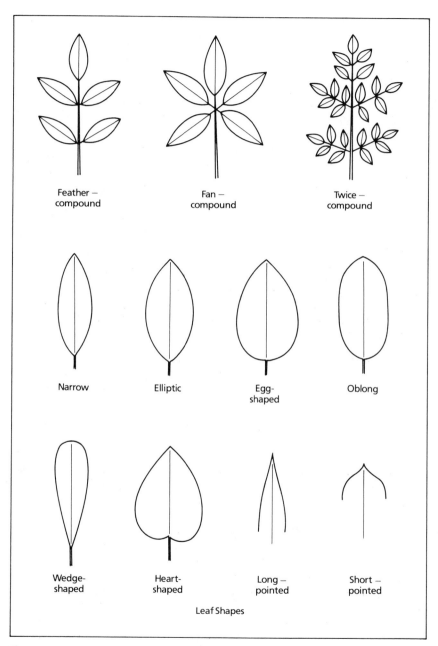

Feather —
compound

Fan —
compound

Twice —
compound

Narrow

Elliptic

Egg-
shaped

Oblong

Wedge-
shaped

Heart-
shaped

Long —
pointed

Short —
pointed

Leaf Shapes

Figure 2.8   *Leaf Shapes*

Key to Trees
in Leafy Condition

For use only in identifying specimens at least 25 feet tall, thus excluding shrubs.

Name

1. Leaves needlelike or very small and scalelike; mostly cone-bearers:
   2. Leaves long, needlelike:
      3. Needles in bundles or groups along twigs   **PINES, LARCHES**
      3. Needles occurring singly:
         4. Needles blunt, flat   **FIRS, etc.**
         4. Needles sharp:
            5. Needles 4-sided, neither in opposing pairs
               nor in whorls of 3   **SPRUCES**
            5. Needles 3-sided, either in opposing pairs
               or in whorls of 3   **JUNIPERS**
   2. Leaves very small and scalelike, hugging twigs:
      6. Leaves blunt; conifers   **WHITE CEDARS**
      6. Leaves sharp; a flowering tree   **TAMARISK**
1. Leaves broad; flowering plants:
   7. Leaves opposite:
      8. Leaves compound:
         9. Leaves with only 3 leaflets, or twigs
            large, pithy   **BLADDERNUT, etc.**
         9. Leaves with 5–11 (rarely 3) leaflets;
            twigs if large, not pithy:
            10. Leaves feather-compound:
               11. Twigs neither densely velvety nor white-
                   powdered   **ASHES**
               11. Twigs either densely velvety or white-
                   powdered   **ASHES, etc.**
            10. Leaves fan-compound   **BUCKEYES**
      8. Leaves simple:
         12. Leaves not toothed:
            13. Leaves not heart-shaped:
               14. Leaves with veins that strongly
                   tend to follow leaf edges   **DOGWOODS**
               14. Leaves with veins only slightly if
                   at all following leaf edges:
                  15. Leaves thick, leathery   **DEVILWOOD**
                  15. Leaves thin, not leathery   **FRINGE-TREE**

Notice that the one major characteristic, the type of leaf (not height, bark, habitat, or family name), identifies the tree.

Besides having fun identifying trees, some nature lovers and landscape architects want to experience trees more esthetically: They pay attention to their shapes, their silhouettes against the horizon. They would describe such features as volume, height, angle, and extent of branching. Figure 2.9 has excerpts from a student paper on "The Shape of Trees" using images as the major groupings. It seems natural to group according to what one sees.

As one textbook on the animal kingdom phrased it:

> ... let us separate out the ones that swim in the sea (barracudas, whales, sharks) from the ones that fly in the air (vultures, bats, sparrows), and from the ones that walk on the land (horses, mice) ... Are the above categories satisfactory?[1]

The authors of that text, being experts on the animal kingdom, realized that other factors needed to be considered. They answered their own question and explained why the most obvious, observable features were inadequate:

> Not entirely. Biologists point out that while whales swim like fishes and bats fly like birds, the most significant thing about them, at least to the biologists, is that both bear their young alive and nurse them — just like horses and mice — and so the biologists prefer to classify all of these four together as mammals, however different they may look to us.[2]

Biologists claim that mere appearances are superficial and that other important scientific criteria have to be used in the grouping of animals, such as how creatures bear their young, the structures of the heart, the ability to regulate body temperatures, bone structure, and so on. All of the animals in Figure 2.10 swim and certainly look like fish, but they are grouped differently, as fish, reptile, and mammal.

Some categories appear static, unchanging, like the grouping of trees by botanists and the grouping of the animal kingdom by zoologists. Yet even in the physical sciences different groupings are possible for two reasons: (1) because of different theoretical interpretations and (2) because new discoveries necessitate new groupings.

Linnaeus, the great Swedish naturalist, who lived in the eighteenth century, had great influence on the groupings of animals and plants. Naturalists from all over the globe still employ his Latin names. Yet there has been a major change in the categories he presented. He grouped animals into a linear arrangement, from the highest order to the lowest, known in the

---

[1] Morton Klass and Hal Hellman, *The Kinds of Mankind* (Philadelphia: J. B. Lippincott), pp. 13–14.
[2] Ibid.

Fan:

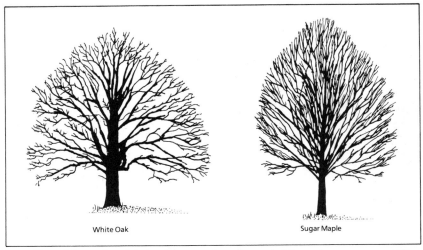

White Oak

Sugar Maple

   The white oak, with its short trunk and gnarled branches, spans out like a ragged, broken fan; the sugar maple spreads out like a symmetrical, delicate fan.

Tight-Rope Walker:

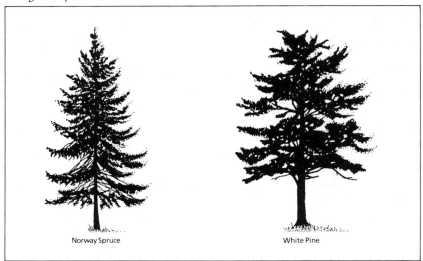

Norway Spruce

White Pine

   The drooping, upturned branches of the Norway spruce seem like the steady outstretched arms of a balanced tight-rope walker; the horizontal limbs of the white pine jut out in an ungainly manner like the wavering arms of an unbalanced tightrope walker.

Figure 2.9 *Tree Silhouettes*

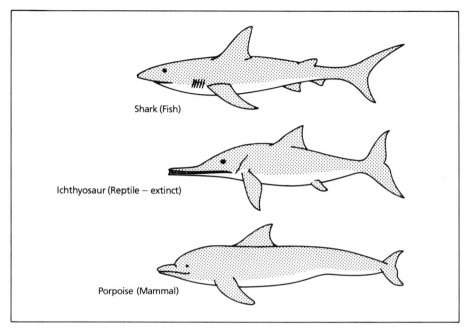

Shark (Fish)

Ichthyosaur (Reptile – extinct)

Porpoise (Mammal)

Figure 2.10   *Look-alike Animals*

eighteenth century as the "Scale of Being." His primary groups are charted on the left side of Table 2.1. At the turn of the nineteenth century, Cuvier, another naturalist, reorganized the animal kingdom by other criteria.

> Cuvier's Four Branches: By extended studies in comparative anatomy, he came to the conclusion that animals are constructed upon four distinct plans or types: the vertebrate type; the molluscan type; the articulated type, embracing animals with joints or segments; and the radiated type, the latter with a radial arrangement of parts, like the starfish; etc. These types are distinct, but their representatives, instead of forming a linear series, overlap so that the lowest forms of one of the higher groups are simpler in organization than the higher forms of a lower group. This was very illuminating, and, being founded upon an analysis of structure, was important. It was directly at variance with the idea of scale of being, and overthrew that doctrine.[3]

---

[3] William A. Locy, *Biology and Its Makers* (New York: Holt, Rinehart and Winston), p. 136.

TABLE 2.1   Classification of the Animal Kingdom

Linnaeus		Cuvier
Mammalia	(man and all other animals that nourish their young with milk)	Vertebrata (embracing five classes: Mammalia, Aves, Reptilia, Batrachia, Pisces)
Aves	(birds)	
Amphibia	(frogs, toads)	
Pisces	(fish)	Mollusca
Insecta (including Crustacea, etc.)	(insects)	Articulata (animals with joints or segments)
Vermes (including Mollusca [snail] and all lower forms)	(worms)	Radiata (starfish)

Cuvier had turned his attention more to the internal structure of living beings. Although his chart on the right side of Table 2.1 is an improvement, other biologists who followed him have modified and remodified it. All disciplines continually evaluate their set of criteria for grouping.

Problems in Grouping

Poems for Grouping

Imagine that an English instructor has asked his class to read the poems below. As a start toward answering the question, "What are some universal themes of poetry?", he wanted his students to group the poems in some way and to write a short essay discussing the system they discovered. As you read these poems, think of possible categories that might be useful.

My Papa's Waltz

The whiskey on your breath
Could make a small boy dizzy;
But I hung on like death:
Such waltzing was not easy.

We romped until the pans
Slid from the kitchen shelf;
My mother's countenance
Could not unfrown itself.

The hand that held my wrist
Was battered on one knuckle;
At every step you missed
My right ear scraped a buckle.

You beat time on my head
With a palm caked hard by dirt,
Then waltzed me off to bed
Still clinging to your shirt.
                     — Theodore Roethke

On My First Son

Farewell, thou child of my right hand,[4] and joy;
My sin was too much hope of thee, loved boy:
Seven years thou wert lent to me, and I thee pay,
Exacted by thy fate, on the just day.
O could I lose all father now! for why
Will man lament the state he should envy,
To have so soon 'scaped world's and flesh's rage,
And, if no other misery, yet age?
Rest in soft peace, and asked, say, "Here doth lie
Ben Jonson his best piece of poetry."
For whose sake henceforth all his vows be such
As what he loves may never like too much.
                     — Ben Jonson

Death Be Not Proud

Death be not proud, though some have cálled thee
Mighty and dreadful, for thou art not so;
For those whom thou think'st thou dost overthrow
Die not, poor Death, nor yet canst thou kill me.
From rest and sleep, which but thy pictures be,
Much pleasure; then from thee much more must flow,

---

[4] Literal translation of the son's name, Benjamin.

And soonest our best men with thee do go,
Rest of their bones, and soul's delivery.
Thou art slave to Fate, Chance, kings, and desperate men,
And dost with Poison, War, and Sickness dwell;
And poppy or charms can make us sleep as well,
And better than thy stroke; why swell'st thou then?
One short sleep past, we wake eternally
And death shall be no more; Death, thou shalt die.

— John Donne

Ozymandias

I met a traveler from an antique land
Who said: Two vast and trunkless legs of stone
Stand in the desert . . . . Near them, on the sand,
Half sunk, a shattered visage lies, whose frown,
And wrinkled lip, and sneer of cold command,
Tell that its sculptor well those passions read
Which yet survive, stamped on these lifeless things,
The hand that mocked them, and the heart that fed:
And on the pedestal these words appear:
"My name is Ozymandias, King of Kings:
Look on my works, ye Mighty, and despair!"
Nothing beside remains. Round the decay
Of that colossal wreck, boundless and bare
The lone and level sands stretch far away.

— Percy Bysshe Shelley

How Do I Love Thee?

How do I love thee? Let me count the ways.
I love thee to the depth and breadth and height
My soul can reach, when feeling out of sight
For the ends of Being and ideal Grace.
I love thee to the level of every day's
Most quiet need, by sun and candlelight.
I love thee freely, as men strive for Right;
I love thee purely, as they turn from Praise;
I love thee with the passion put to use
In my old griefs, and with my childhood's faith.
I love thee with a love I seemed to lose
With my lost saints — I love thee with the breath,
Smiles, tears of all my life! — and, if God choose,
I shall but love thee better after death.

— Elizabeth Barrett Browning

Western Wind

Western wind, when wilt thou blow,
The small rain down can rain?
Christ, if my love were in my arms
And I in my bed again!

— Anonymous

One student noticed that the poems seemed to discuss a few particular topics. He divided them into three groups: those that dealt with death, those that talked of love, and those that discussed family. He made the following chart:

Love	*Death*	*Family*
Western Wind	Death Be Not Proud	On My First Son
How Do I Love Thee?	Ozymandias	My Papa's Waltz

Can you detect the problem with his scheme? Excerpts from two of his paragraphs are given below to highlight the difficulty:

Paragraph #3

Poets frequently use death as the subject for their poems. In "Ozymandias," Shelley describes an ancient statue of a dead king which has fallen apart, but which the king thought would proclaim his ability to conquer death . . . . In "Death Be Not Proud," on the other hand, the faith in an after-life is seen as the way to conquer death . . . Both of these poems on death deal with the problem of loss and the ways people try to cope with this inevitable event . . .

Paragraph #4

Another subject that often is used for poetry is family relationships. The poems in this group which treat this subject are particularly concerned with fathers and sons. Ben Jonson's misery over the death of his son breaks through the carefully controlled, formal lines of the epitaph. The inevitability and the finality of the event, and the way Jonson faces it, makes this poem reach beyond the specific loss of a son to a sense of how the loss by death affects us all . . . In Theodore Roethke's poem "My Papa's Waltz," the emotions are those of love and terror. . . .

The repetition of the idea of death in each paragraph is a problem that resulted from a faulty scheme of organization. While the categories *death* and *family* appear to be distinct, the particular poems in this collection blur that distinction. Ben Jonson's poem does indeed deal with his son, but it is especially concerned with his death and would easily fit with the ballad and the sonnet on that topic. In the same way, Roethke's poem might easily fit with poems on love. In this particular situation, the category *family* overlaps with the categories *love* and *death.*

For practice in placing items in an appropriate category, the instructor presented the students with several other poems, printed below, and asked them to create appropriate groupings. What categories can you find? As you read the poems and experiment with grouping them, you might want to use some of the pre-writing techniques you learned in Chapter 1, such as focused freewriting or listing. Among the possibilities you might consider are: poems with a positive message versus those with a negative message; hopeful poems or despairing ones; poems about people or poems about nature. Place the poems in the categories you have chosen and compare your arrangement with those of your fellow students.

Rapid Transit

Squealing under city stone
  The millions on the millions ran,
Every one a life alone,
  Every one a soul undone.

There all the poems of the heart
  Branch and abound like whirling brooks
And there through every useless art
  Like spoiled meat on a butcher's hooks.

Pour forth upon their frightful kind
  The faces of each ruined child:
The wrecked demeanors of the mind
  That now is tamed, and once was wild.

— James Agee

"There Will Come Soft Rains"
(War Time)

There will come soft rains and the smell of the ground,
And swallows circling with their shimmering sound;

And frogs in the pools singing at night,
And wild plum-trees in tremulous white;

Robins will wear their feathery fire
Whistling their whims on a low fence-wire;

And not one will know of the war, not one
Will care at last when it is done.

Not one would mind, neither bird nor tree
If mankind perished utterly;

And Spring herself, when she woke at dawn,
Would scarcely know that we were gone.

— Sara Teasdale

Nothing Gold Can Stay

Nature's first green is gold,
Her hardest hue to hold.
Her early leaf's a flower;
But only so an hour.
Then leaf subsides to leaf.
So Eden sank to grief,
So dawn goes down to day.
Nothing gold can stay.

— Robert Frost

Pennsylvania Station

The Pennsylvania Station in New York
Is like some vast basilica of old
That towers above the terrors of the dark
As bulwark and protection to the soul.
Now people who are hurrying alone
And those who come in crowds from far away
Pass through this great concourse of steel and stone
To trains, or else from trains out into day.
And as in great basilicas of old
The search was ever for a dream of God,
So here the search is still within each soul
Some seed to find that sprouts a holy tree
To glorify the earth — and you — and me.

— Langston Hughes

War Is Kind

Do not weep, maiden, for war is kind.
Because your lover threw wild hands
    toward the sky
And the affrighted steed ran on alone,
Do not weep.
War is kind.

   Hoarse, booming drums of the regiment,
   Little souls who thirst for fight,
   These men were born to drill and die,
   The unexplained glory flies above them,
   Great is the battle-god, great, and his
                           Kingdom —
   A field where a thousand corpses lie.

Do not weep, babe, for war is kind.
Because your father tumbled in the yellow
    trenches,
Raged at his breast, gulped and died,
Do not weep.
War is kind.

   Swift blazing flag of the regiment,
   Eagle with crest of red and gold,
   These men were born to drill and die.
   Point for them the virtue of slaughter,
   Make plain to them the excellence of killing
   And a field where a thousand corpses lie.

Mother whose heart hung humble as a button
On the bright splendid shroud of your son,
Do not weep.
War is kind.

                              — Stephen Crane

To Lucasta, Going to the Wars

   Tell me not, sweet, I am unkind
      That from the nunnery
   Of thy chaste breast and quiet mind,
      To war and arms I fly.

   True, a new mistress now I chase,
      The first foe in the field;
   And with a stronger faith embrace
      A sword, a horse, a shield.

Yet this inconstancy is such
As you too shall adore;
I could not love thee, dear, so much
Loved I not honor more.
— Richard Lovelace

One woman in the class created three groups: poems on war, poems about the city, and poems about nature. Her categories looked like this:

War	City	Nature
To Lucasta, Going to the Wars	Rapid Transit	Nothing Gold Can Stay
War Is Kind	Pennsylvania Station	There Will Come Soft Rains

Below is an excerpt from a paragraph in her essay:

The enduring quality of the natural world is emphasized in Teasdale's poem. The spring rains, the blossoms on the fruit trees, the birds and the frogs — all of these return every spring and bring a sense of renewal. This natural world is not even aware, Teasdale says, of the destruction and death that mankind inflicts on itself through war . . .

We must stop here. The placement of Teasdale's poem with poems of nature has created a problem. While it is true that the poem deals with the natural world, the poem's main thrust is to condemn humanity for making war. The student writer recognized this aspect of the poem as she was writing her essay and should have moved the poem from the category *nature* to the category *war*.

PRACTICE

As you read the above categorizations, you may have objected to many of the placements. It is one of the marks of a good poem that it defies such simple breakdowns. Nevertheless, it is often useful to set up some sort of grouping when you are considering a number of poems together. There are obviously many more ways to group these poems. In discussion with your class or in small groups, see which category system you would like to work with. Among the possibilities you might consider are: (1) poems that emphasize the permanence of our world versus those that emphasize the impermanence; (2) poems that present a positive viewpoint and those that present a negative view. Place the poems in the categories you have chosen and compare your arrangement with those of your fellow students.

How Dividing and Grouping Work Together

Figure 2.1 on page 38, "Human Knowledge," is an example of the way the *dividing* process works. The illustration on trees on page 43 shows the way the *grouping* process works. Yet the charts are similar: they are both marked by divisions and sub-divisions, or categories and sub-categories. In such charts, both operations, dividing and grouping, are present.

The relationship between the two can be seen more clearly if you look at the poetry illustration again. When the English instructor asked, "What are some of the universal themes of poetry?" a good answer would break down the overall idea into its component parts — that is, dividing:

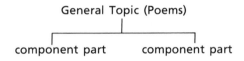

The arrow in the right-hand margin represents the direction of the process of dividing. When the students were categorizing the poems, they were grouping:

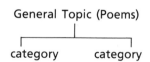

The arrow in the left-hand margin represents the direction of the process of grouping.

These two processes are interrelated. For convenience, every time we present such charts we shall refer to the process as a *classification system*. The discussion connected with such charts will make it clear whether dividing or grouping, or both, is involved.

USING THE ORGANIZING PROCESS

Let us see how our familiarity with the dividing/grouping process can help us examine a given topic as perceived in two different academic disciplines. And since we have stressed the importance of purpose in dividing and grouping, let us complicate matters and see how the thinking strategies are utilized by two different groups — by lay people and experts — in response to the same controlling question.

Is a College Education a Good Investment?—the Economic Perspective

You might have asked yourself whether a college education was a good investment for you. An economics instructor and a lay person would approach the cost of a college education in dissimilar ways. Most people would probably attempt to write an answer to this question by using the same approach they use in figuring their weekly budgets; their system would involve two categories: expenses and income. Under expenses, they would list the subheadings of tuition, books and supplies, transportation, and so on; under income they would list whatever they might expect to earn from part-time or summer jobs, or any other sources they might have, such as family contributions. They would then try to estimate their potential income in the career of their choice at some future time, whether immediately at graduation or, more likely, five or ten years later. A chart based on this sort of classification system might look like Table 2.2.

Economists, however, would view the problem from quite another

TABLE 2.2   College as an Investment

Cost of College		Potential Income At Graduation
Expenses	*Income During College*	
Tuition	Job	Five years after
Books	Family contribution	Ten years after
Transportation		

perspective. The following reading will give you a brief explanation of their approach.

OPPORTUNITY COST

Since resources are scarce, the decision to use them for one thing means that something else will be given up. Suppose that a company could manufacture either 100 chairs or 30 tables using the same resources. The opportunity cost of using its resources to produce 100 chairs is the benefit that could have been obtained from producing 30 tables (the best alternative) with the same resources. Thus, **opportunity cost** is the true cost of choosing one alternative over another. With limited resources, people cannot "have their cake and eat it too." Opportunity cost recognizes the fact that when resources are employed in a certain way, there is a simultaneous choice made not to use those resources in some other way. That which is given up, then, is the opportunity cost of what is actually chosen. If, instead of producing one chair, we might have produced three dresses or five taxi rides or seven hours of leisure, the opportunity cost of one chair is whichever of these would yield the most benefit. It is certainly *not* the sum of all three.

Opportunity Cost in Consumption

Opportunity cost applies to both consumption and production. In discussing consumption, we consider how consumers spend their income, wealth, and time and how governments spend the resources that they have at their disposal.

The Individual. Since people have only so much income and hold a limited amount of wealth, they are continually faced with buying decisions. When consumers decide to spend their dollars for one item, those dollars are not available to them for some other item. The opportunity cost of buying a blue sweater may be the green sweater that was therefore not bought. Taking a trip to the Caribbean might mean forgoing, or giving up, a new car.

To get a better understanding of the opportunity cost involved in consumer choice, consider the following example. Suppose that you are having dinner in a seafood restaurant and that you select the combination shrimp and scallop plate shown on the menu for $5. This restaurant allows you to choose the particular mix of shrimps and scallops that you want. Shrimps, however, are twice as expensive (50¢ each) as scallops (25¢ each). Thus, the opportunity cost of each shrimp is two scallops, and the opportunity cost of each scallop is one-half shrimp.

People also face opportunity costs in allocating their time and their effort. This choice may be between work and leisure, between one kind of work and another kind of work, or between one leisure activity and another leisure activity. If a particular Saturday night offers a college student both a party and a basketball game, and if these are the best alternatives available, the event that the student doesn't attend is the opportunity cost of the one that he or she does decide to attend. A student who decides to attend a summer session may experience three kinds of opportunity costs. The first is the goods and services that the student forgoes so that he or she can pay for tuition and books. A second includes the goods and services that the student could have bought with the money he or she would have earned had the student spent the summer on a job. Third is the extra leisure time that the student would have enjoyed, since school is more time-consuming than a job would have been.

A classification system based on the economists' approach would take all the items that the lay person had listed under expenses and use the total amount as money that could have been invested in some other way, such as in a savings bank account from which interest could have been earned. With this approach, the time spent going to college, which lay persons would usually ignore, would also be seen as an investment that might have been used in another way, such as getting a full-time job. As you can see, economists would use the same category of potential income that others use, but they would be more precise in determining the probable amounts of income for specific time periods. A chart based on the economists' approach would look like Table 2.3.

Is a College Education a Good Investment? — the Sociological Perspective

Suppose you considered the same question from a sociological point of view:

Is a college education a good investment for me?

TABLE 2.3   College as an Investment

Cost of College		Potential Income At Graduation
Interest Not Earned	Salary Not Earned	
(Money for expenses invested in savings bank at 5½%)	(Earnings at full-time job minus earnings at part-time job)	5 years after 10 years after

TABLE 2.4 College as a Social Investment

Costs	Potential Gains
Less time for family	Increased prestige from being a college grad
Loss of high school friends	Higher-status job
Less money for material things	More money

The idea that a college education has social costs might come as something of a surprise to people unused to thinking in sociological terms. If pressed on the matter, they might list under the social costs of college such items as less time for family functions, loss of high school friends, and possibly less money for clothes and records. Against these costs they would list the increased prestige and money they expect would result from a college education. A classification system based on this approach would look like Table 2.4.

Sociologists have a more complex view of the matter. *Social* means much more than being with friends and family; for sociologists it means all the powerful forces that bind people together in groups that control many aspects of human behavior. The following brief excerpts from a sociology textbook explain some of the issues that would be significant for this perspective:

VALUES

Values are ideas shared by the people in a society on what is important and worthwhile. Our values are the basis of our judgments about what is desirable, beautiful, correct, and good as well as what is undesirable, ugly, incorrect, and bad. Most values have both positive and negative counterparts, which are reciprocally related. If you place a high positive value on fighting for one's country, for example, you probably place a high negative value on those who refuse to fight. If you value marital sexual exclusiveness, you probably disapprove of those who engage in extramarital sexual relationships. Values are often emotionally charged because they stand for things we believe to be worth defending.

Most of our basic values are learned early in life from family, friends, the mass media, and other sources within society. These values become part of our personalities, and because we learn them from society, few people possess unique sets of values. They are generally shared and reinforced by those with whom we interact. Placing a high value on God, money, honesty, cleanliness, freedom, children, education, or work serves as a general guide for our behavior and the formation of specific attitudes. Since values indicate what is proper or improper, they tend to justify certain types of behavior and forbid others.

When basic values are in conflict, we usually place them in a hierarchy of importance and behave in ways consistent with those defined as most important. During a war, for example, the value of patriotism may overcome the value that human life is precious. When it is impossible to place our values in a hierarchy to resolve a conflict, we may feel guilty or suffer mental stress.

To give another example of value conflict, consider the case of a husband who enjoys spending time with his family. If job demands take him away from his family for extended periods, he is likely to feel stress. To avoid stress, he could quit his job, take the family along on job trips, justify the job demands as in the best interests of the family, compromise on both family and job demands, or leave the family. Some of these choices may be impossible, however. Quitting the job or taking the family along may not be realistic alternatives, and divorce may conflict with social and religious values. Mental stress is likely to result when choices are impossible. The alternative courses of action, as well as the choice selected, will generally be consistent with the values of the society and those most important to us.

Sometimes our stated values and our behavior are inconsistent. We may place a high value on freedom of the press but want to censor communist writings. We may place a high value on individualism but want to punish people whose behavior is inconsistent with our definition of appropriate behavior. Our true values are often reflected more by what we do than by what we say. If we say we value education but have no interest in attending classes, or if we say we value simplicity but spend money conspicuously to display our wealth, it is our actions that expose our real values.

Since values are learned cultural products, they differ from one society to another. One society may value political independence, another may place a higher value on political conformity and obedience. One society may value individual achievement, another may emphasize family unity and kin support. In the United States, despite the tremendous diversity of our population, certain value patterns tend to be shared by almost everyone. Robin M. Williams, Jr., in a sociological interpretation of American society (1970), described fifteen major value orientations in our culture. These included a belief in *achievement and success,* stressing personal achievement, especially secular occupational achievement; *external conformity,* emphasizing the adherence to similarity and uniformity in speech, manners, housing, dress, recreation, politically expressed ideas, and group patterns; and *democracy,* advocating majority rule, representative institutions, and the rejection of monarchical and aristocratic principles. It must be kept in mind that these are general themes in American values, which change constantly. They are often in conflict, and they are not all exhibited in a single person's behavior.

It is rare to find a society that has a single culture shared equally by all its members. This could happen only in small, isolated, nonindustrial societies, but most societies include groups who share some of the cultural complexes of the larger society yet also have their own distinctive set of cultural complexes. These units of culture are called *subcultures.* Although subcultures exist within the confines of a larger culture, they also have their own norms, values, and lifestyles. They often reflect racial or ethnic differences such as those found among Black, Polish, or Chinese Americans. Other subcultures develop around occupations: athletics, the military, medicine, or factory work. The Mormons, Amish, Hutterites, and other groups form religious subcultures; some are based on geography, such as those found in the South and New England; others are based on wealth and age. There are also drinking, drug, disco, and homosexual subcultures. Every society that has diverse languages, religions, ethnic or racial groups, or varying economic levels has subcultures.

All subcultures participate in the larger, dominant culture but possess their own set of cultural elements: symbols, languages, values, norms, and technologies. In heterogeneous societies, a person may be a member of several subcultures at any one time or at different times in his or her life. In the United States, a Black adolescent male living in poverty may speak a black dialect, have an Afro haircut, wear African dress, enjoy "soul" food. ... An Amish adolescent male living on a Pennsylvania farm might speak a form of German, wear a black suit and hat, part his hair in the middle cut to shoulder length, enjoy sauerkraut and potatoes, be forbidden to dance or go to movies, and turn all earnings over to his father. Both the Black and the Amish adolescent are required to abide by the laws of the dominant society, however.

At times, the dominant culture and the subculture may conflict to such a degree that tremendous stresses occur and a crisis results. Members of the subculture may be required by the dominant culture to register for the military even though they value pacifism. The subculture may value the use of certain drugs but be forbidden by the dominant culture to obtain them, or speak a language not used in the public schools. It is important to realize that, in addition to the differences among cultures, there are great variations within cultures as well.

With this reading in mind, you can see that the generally-accepted benefits of a college education might involve some conflicts with the particular sub-culture to which an individual belongs. For some men, the preference for action and practical skills that their sub-group extols might conflict with the introspection and intellectual goals of higher education; for some women, the cultural values of marriage and motherhood might conflict with the independence and nonfamily-oriented direction of college and career. Immigrants could experience a sense of conflict between the need to retain the

TABLE 2.5   College as a Social Investment

Costs (possible conflicts)		Potential Gains		
With personal values	With values of the subculture	Respect	Prestige	Leadership

mother tongue that would convey the warmth and sense of their community and the opposing need to be part of the English-speaking community. Members of particular religious groups might even find that college interferes with particular customs, such as observing holy days. Sociologists allow for these possible variations by constructing a different sort of classification system, illustrated in Table 2.5 above.

Although both lay persons and sociologists are dealing with the problem of the social cost of a college education and its potential gain, they deal with it in different ways and construct different kinds of classification systems. The experts' approach usually allows for a more thorough investigation.

ORGANIZING: CONNECTING THINKING AND WRITING

Dividing/grouping, as you have seen, is the process of either breaking down an idea into its fundamental elements or placing data into discernible patterns. Without the ability to do this, we would find life chaotic, and without it most communication, written or oral, would be, at best, disorganized and unclear. This section of the chapter illustrates how dividing/grouping is used to organize and develop college-level essays.

PRACTICE

Figure 2.11 contains some headlines reproduced in no apparent order. Try to create as many different sets of categories and sub-categories for them as you can.

Several classifications were possible. You could have classified the headlines into *significant/nonsignificant*. After all, when we scan a newspaper, we

Figure 2.11   *Newspaper Headlines*

usually read only those news stories that interest us. But it would be more useful to have created the categories *international, national,* and *local news* and placed the headlines under these headings. Or you might have placed the items under military and social issues and then further sub-divided the social issues into crime, nuclear power, pollution, and so on. Scholars in each discipline would approach data from their own perspectives and thus create categories appropriate to those disciplines. Political scientists, for example, would be particularly interested in the issues raised by these items of news because all of them must in some way be dealt with by governmental institutions. Political scientists divide and group data in order to make sense of governments' complex roles.

Classification is a vital part of the writing process. As an example, the following section illustrates one important classification system in political science and shows how to use that system to write essays for a political science course. You should understand as you read these pages, however, that even though they focus on one particular discipline, the methods presented here can be applied to the writing of essays in any field. Once you have established appropriate categories for your exploration, you can then proceed to write your paper in a logical and well-organized manner. As you read the following pages, think about how the strategies developed here can be applied to any essay you might be asked to write. An essay in political science is assigned in this section, but your instructor might give you another option. The information in this chapter will help you no matter what is assigned.

Choosing an Appropriate Organizing Strategy

As an ordinary citizen who follows the news and who views issues from a political perspective, you are probably aware that in the United States there are two major political organizations (categories): the Republican and Democratic parties. That is one useful pair of categories, and depending on your party affiliation or your position on various issues, you might favor a particular Republican for governor and/or a Democrat for the United States Senate. Do these categories tell you enough, however, about the overall political outlook of the candidates? Two Republicans might, for example, differ about defense spending, and a Republican and a Democrat might agree about who should receive social security benefits. For complex historical reasons, each of the two parties represents a variety of views on many issues. Many political scientists in their analysis of the American political system therefore group politicians in another way, into *conservatives* and *liberals*.

These categories, as developed by experts in the discipline, allow the citizen to evaluate candidates from a different perspective. Using this set of categories, you might arrive at a different appraisal of a candidate's political stance and possibly make different choices in an election.

Taking Notes

You might have only a vague notion of what conservatives and liberals believe, but let us assume that in your political science course a series of class discussions were held in response to the questions, "What do conservatives believe?" and "What do liberals believe?" By pooling the responses of your fellow students, you came up with a surprisingly long list of ideas. The lists below represents your notes on the conservative and liberal positions.

Conservatives Believe That:

1. Reducing the minimum wage for teenagers would combat youth unemployment.

2. The right of citizens to bear arms is guaranteed by the Constitution.

3. The death penalty is necessary to combat violent crime.

4. Taxation limits the development of corporate investment and growth.

5. The deep religious values of our nation should be fostered by prayers in schools.

6. The payment of welfare reduces individual initiative and is inefficient and expensive.

7. The dangers of the expansionist tendencies of communism require the highest level of military expenditures to protect our way of life.

8. The free workings of the marketplace provide the best possible protection for consumers.

9. Industrial growth is endangered by federal attempts to protect the environment.

10. Medical treatment and its costs are the private concern of citizens.

11. People who have lost their jobs or who have been temporarily laid off are discouraged from seeking other employment if they receive unemployment compensation.

12. Citizens who fail to prepare themselves adequately for the job market must live with the results of their own decisions.

13. People who have not made payments for old-age insurance or who have other means of support should not receive money from the government when they retire.

Following are your notes on the liberal position.

Liberals Believe That:

1. To protect citizens from criminal violence, the possession of handguns must be strictly regulated or banned outright.

2. Criminal behavior can be changed through rehabilitation.

3. Regulation of business is necessary to protect consumers against faulty or dangerous goods.

4. It is the duty of the government to support those who are unable to feed, house, and clothe themselves.

5. Corporations should contribute to the general welfare through taxes.

6. All workers should be guaranteed an adequate wage necessary to support a decent life.

7. The separation of church and state is a basic principle of our system of government.

8. Government regulation is necessary to protect the public.

9. Unemployment insurance is a necessary cost that businesses and the government must assume to help workers during periods of economic decline.

10. Social security is a basic right for all those who have contributed to it or who need it.

11. The national government should assure all citizens of adequate health care.

12. Federal job training programs are a useful way to decrease unemployment.

13. The ecological balance of our land is threatened by uncontrolled incursions of businesses.

Charting

The notes the student took are helpful for understanding the views of conservatives and liberals on particular issues. It would be even more useful, however, if the student reorganized these lists by creating a chart pairing the items. In this way, the student could see them at a glance, and compare and contrast the two positions.

PRACTICE

Reread the lists, and for each item that indicates a conservative position, find a comparable statement that reflects the liberal view. Then complete the chart below. Consider each statement carefully before you include it on the chart, since the pairing is not always immediately obvious. The first pairing has been included. Write in a one- or two-word name for each topic and indicate the conservative and liberal position by writing *pro* or *anti* in the appropriate box. Then check the accuracy of your work by discussing your pairings in class.

			Position	
Conservatives	Liberals	Topic	Cons.	Lib.
The right of citizens to bear arms is guaranteed by the United States Constitution.	To protect citizens from criminal violence the possession of handguns must be strictly regulated or banned outright.	Handgun Control	Anti	Pro

The chart you created is not only a good way to contrast the conservative/ liberal positions on issues but is also helpful if you are interested in investigating your own political attitudes. Do your views generally coincide with one or the other of these categories? It is important to know how you feel now in order for you to keep an open mind as you continue to study any discipline. All too often, students have difficulty viewing a discipline objectively because of their particular bias. If you consciously know your own position, you should more readily be able to understand another point of view. In addition, understanding the opposition can better equip you to argue for your own beliefs and even allow you to revise your judgments as a result of considering new information.

PRACTICE

Using the chart you have created, engage in focused freewriting to answer the controlling question, "On the basis of conservative and liberal positions on issues, do I consider myself a conservative, a liberal, or a bit of both?"

Answering a Controlling Question

You have investigated the way conservatives and liberals stand on a number of current issues, but would you be able to determine the essential differences between conservative and liberal approaches to politics? Not knowing the basic principles of liberal or conservative thought, you would not be able, for example, to answer the questions, "Why are liberals in favor of gun control?" and "Why do conservatives support the death penalty?" For this kind of information, you would have to rely on the judgment of experts in the field of political science.

Below is an article entitled "What Is Conservatism?" that categorizes conservative thought into some basic beliefs. It answers the controlling question, "What are the fundamental principles of conservative philosophy?" To guide your reading, it would be useful in advance to formulate some subsidiary questions.

PRACTICE

Create as many pertinent subsidiary questions as you can think of that are suggested by the controlling question, "What are the fundamental principles of conservative philosophy?" The techniques of questioning described in Chapter 1 might help you here.

1.   What is the difference between principle and practice?

2.   _____

3.   _____

4.   _____

5.   _____

Read the following article, keeping the subsidiary questions in mind.

WHAT IS CONSERVATISM?

Conservatism and Republican Candidates
(*National Review*, December 12, 1967)

Although I do not quarrel with the spirit of political realism that has matured conservatives over the past few years, I think there is some danger of carrying that realism so far as to lose sight of conservative ends. Thus, while it is surely correct not to expect the Republican candidate to be a model of conservative purity, some conservatives go off the deep end in the other direction and talk as though the victory of any Republican would be a victory for conservatism.

When conservatives flirt, as I have heard them do during the past year, with the idea of Charles Percy as Republican nominee or with that ultimate monstrosity in cynicism, a Rockefeller-Reagan ticket, they are making Republicanism per se, instead of conservatism, their end. It seems to me that to deserve conservative support, a candidate should hold broad views which are in general consonant with the conservative consensus in America today. Such consonance does not demand agreement on every specific issue but only a broad outlook that is conservative in its essence.

For want of a better definition of the conservative consensus, I offer a summary of my own definition of it, which I presented a year or two ago in a paper on conservatism for the Public Affairs Conference Center. It may serve as something of a rough test for conservatives in their consideration of candidates.

The following attitudes, I maintained, outline the American conservative position.

1) Conservatism assumes the existence of an objective moral order based upon ontological foundations. The conservative looks at political and social questions with the assumption that there are objective standards for human

conduct and objective criteria for political theories and institutions, which it is the duty of human beings to understand as thoroughly as they are able and to which it is their duty to approximate their actions.

2) Within the limits of an objective moral order, the primary reference of conservative political and social thought and action is to the individual person. There may be among some conservatives a greater emphasis upon freedom and rights, as among others a greater emphasis upon duties and responsibilities; but, whichever the emphasis, conservative thought is shot through and through with concern for the person. It is deeply suspicious of theories and policies based upon the collectivities that are the political reference points of Liberalism — ''minorities,'' ''labor,'' ''the people.'' It rejects the ideological concept of associations of human beings as collective entities and the collectivist politics based upon this ideology.

3) Conservatism is profoundly anti-utopian. While it recognizes the continuing certainty of change and the necessity of basic principle being expressed under different circumstances in different ways, and while it strives always for the improvement of human institutions and the human condition, it rejects absolutely the idea that society or men generally are perfectible. It is perennially suspicious of the utopian approach, which attempts to *design* society and the lives of human beings.

4) On the basis of concern for the individual person and rejection of utopian planning, conservatives believe in a strict limitation of the power of government. They are firmly opposed to the Liberal concept of the state as the engine for the fixing of ideological blueprints upon the citizenry. They stand for freedom of social and personal action as against government-directed action, and for a free economic system.

5) From these positions American conservatism derives its firm support of the Constitution of the United States as originally conceived — to achieve the protection of individual liberty in an ordered society by limiting the power of government. Conservatives support the preservation of the elements of the structure thereby created: restriction of government to its proper functions; within government, tension and balance between local and central power; within the Federal Government, tension and balance between the coordinate branches. They strive to reestablish a federal system of strictly divided powers, as far as government itself is concerned, and to repulse the encroachment of government, federal or state, upon the economy and the individual lives of citizens.

6) In their devotion to Western civilization and their firm American patriotism, conservatives are deeply aware of the danger of Communism as an armed and messianic threat to the very existence of Western civilization and the United States. They believe that our foreign and military policy must be based upon recognition of this reality. As opposed to the vague internationalism and the wishful thinking about Communist ''mellowing'' that characterize Liberal thought and action, they see the defense of the West and the United States as the overriding imperative of public policy.

There is nothing here on specific issues — no conservative ''party line'' on urban questions or tax structure or the detailed strategy and tactics of Vietnam. Nor will any candidate politically likely under current circumstances present himself as the philosophical exponent of such a theoretical conservative position. But in the minds of conservatives that position can act as a criterion by which men and their stand on issues may be adjudged — not only positively as to whom a conservative might most desire as a candidate, but negatively also as to who must be opposed at all costs.

Although the article might have seemed difficult, notice that the author has helped you by numbering the basic conservative principles, thus enabling you to consider one item at a time. It would be helpful to reread each item several times and attempt to explain in writing in your own words what the author is saying.

For the first principle of conservative thought, a student might have rephrased the second sentence to read, "Conservatives believe that there is only one standard of conduct that applies to all of us, no matter who we are or where we come from. Not only must individuals follow this 'law,' but the society as a whole must follow it as well." This process of rephrasing an author's exact words is called *paraphrasing*.

Paraphrasing when dealing with written materials helps you test your understanding of difficult concepts. Often, a writer will even incorporate a paraphrase into the essay itself in order to translate a complex idea for readers.

Through careful reading of the article and possibly through paraphrasing, you probably have arrived at the following list of conservative beliefs:

1. There is a universal moral order.

2. The rights of the individual must be emphasized.

3. Man is imperfect by nature.

4. Government should interfere as little as possible with the individual or society.

5. The Constitution should be interpreted strictly.

6. Communism as an economic or governmental system is suspect.

A useful way to see how conservative positions reflect basic conservative principles would be to make another chart, combining the two lists you have worked out. Table 2.6 places the basic conservative principles along the horizontal and the issues along the vertical line. In effect, the horizontal coordinate is the result of dividing, breaking down the principles into their

TABLE 2.6   Conservative Principles and Positions

	I *Universal Moral Order*	II *Emphasis on Individual*	III *Imperfec- tibility of Man*	IV *Non-government Interference*	V *Strict Interpre- tation of Constitution*	VI *Fear of Communism*
1. Handguns		✓		✓	✓	
2. Health care		✓		✓		
3. School prayer						
4. Social security						
5. Welfare						
6. Job training						
7. Death penalty						
8. Consumer protection						
9. Limits on corporate taxes						
10. Environmental protection						
11. Unemployment insurance						
12. Defense spending						
13. Dropping of minimum wage for teenagers						

fundamental elements, and the vertical coordinate is a list that provides the raw material for grouping.

Table 2.6 can be used in several ways. It is useful because it will highlight some key approaches. By reading the chart horizontally — dividing — you can see how the conservative stance on particular issues is determined by certain basic principles. By reading the chart vertically — grouping — you can see how one basic principle influences the conservative stance on a number of issues. The horizontal list is equivalent to the *down* arrow mentioned on page 58; the vertical equals the *up* arrow.

PRACTICE

Taking each issue in turn, check off the principles you think reflect the conservative stand on that issue. Several have already been done for you.

Below is part of a political science instructor's lecture that answers the controlling question, "What are some principles of liberal thought?"
Create several subsidiary questions to guide you as you read, for example:

1. How are the liberal principles different from the conservative ones?

2. _____

3. _____

4. _____

5. _____

LIBERALISM

After some fifty years of a liberal cast to American politics in which the social reforms of the thirties and the civil rights legislation of the sixties were enacted, there has been a decided shift toward a more conservative attitude. To understand this trend, it is first necessary to define what is meant by liberal thought in America.

Liberals have traditionally believed that a significant function of government is to protect and perfect freedom. They have maintained that all people have the right to govern themselves, to be able to express themselves freely, to make their feelings known in peaceful public assembly, to own property, and to be free to pursue their own interests. Government, liberals have felt, must guard these civil liberties.

Whereas conservatives have historically thought that government intervention hinders individuals from fulfilling their potential, liberals have maintained that government can and should assist citizens in realizing their goals. Thus liberals have supported legislation and programs which will aid people otherwise unable to help themselves. Not only have liberals believed in government aid from a humanitarian point of view, but they support it as a basis for building a stable society.

Liberals have felt that since economic security is necessary for the freedom of the individual, government should provide appropriate assistance to ensure it. Men and women, they have argued, who cannot get an education or afford decent housing are not free to pursue their own interests, nor can they contribute to the greater good of society. It is the obligation of government, therefore, to create social and economic programs which ensure the economic security necessary for freedom.

Liberals, finally, have felt that change is necessary for progress. Without advocating revolution, they have favored constant modification within the established political, legal and economic structures. Change must be welcomed for society to move forward.

Although the lecture does not list the principles numerically, each paragraph after the introduction deals with a separate liberal belief:

1. Government must guard freedom. (paragraph 2)

2. Government must help men to fulfill their potential. (paragraph 3)

3. Economic security is necessary for freedom. (paragraph 4)

4. Change is essential to progress. (paragraph 5)

PRACTICE

Create a chart that will show how the liberal positions on several issues reflect the basic principles of liberalism. Use the conservative chart (Table 2.6) as a model.

1. Taking each issue in turn, check off the principles you think reflect the liberal stand on that issue. (Read the chart horizontally.)

2. Taking one liberal principle, list all the issues to which it is relevant. (Read the chart vertically.)

PLANNING AND WRITING AN ESSAY

So far, you have seen how questioning can generate several interesting and useful classification systems that can help you understand complex material. Now we will focus on the way the questioning process along with appropriate classification systems can help you plan and write essays in college.

Not only did the classification charts given above grow out of the instructor's original questions, but the charts themselves suggest further topics of investigation. In examining the charts, one finds that the following controlling questions, among others, are possible.

1. Why is the position on one issue a reflection of conservative or liberal philosophy?

2. How does the conservative or liberal position on several issues reflect the principles of conservatism or liberalism?

3. Taking one basic principle of either conservative or liberal thought, can you show how it affects the conservative or liberal position on several issues?

It was the classification system, as illustrated in the charts, that helped generate this list of questions. Each of these questions is a possible examination or essay question that a political science instructor might ask. In fact, one instructor gave these questions to his class, asking them to select one as the basis for an essay of from 350 to 500 words.

Use of the questioning and the dividing/grouping processes in this interrelated manner has produced the clarity of thinking necessary for the preparation of an essay on the topics above. In the following chapters, these two major processes make up the common thinking strategy for all essays as well. We shall also see that the general nature of an essay — the pattern of the written essay — is determined by the controlling question and by the classification system the writer designs.

Essay Form: Introduction, Body, Conclusion

The following pages provide three model essays and analyses. The first two essays below are final drafts in the complicated process of essay writing. They are provided in order to supply a basis for explaining the organization and development of an academic essay. The third model, however, illustrates the entire process of writing an academic essay, from techniques of getting started to final draft. Your instructor may ask you to write an essay on one of the controlling questions in political science provided above or may give you another writing assignment. Whatever the case, be aware of the basic organizational principles that are illustrated in the following pages labeled the *introduction, body,* and *conclusion.* In this book we will use this three-part division as the basis for writing essays in college. It is our belief that it provides the clearest method for presenting information to others. The basic skeleton it provides is no more restricting to composing than the human skeleton is in creating the infinite variety of human shapes.

There are, of course, particular forms such as lab reports or case studies used in particular disciplines that students learn to write in their chemistry or psychology classes, for example. On the surface they may seem different, but these specialized forms all announce an intention of the matter to be discussed in an *introduction,* develop that intention in a *body,* and provide a wrap-up of the findings through a *conclusion.* In any case the three-part essay form will give you a foundation for college writing which you will be able to elaborate upon, vary, or modify as your skills as a writer develop.

Read the model essay below written by a student. See if you can divide it into three sections. Even though the paper has more than three paragraphs, it has only three main sections: introduction, body, and conclusion.

IMPOSING THE DEATH PENALTY: A CONSERVATIVE APPROACH

Paragraph 1

[1]Americans perceive violent crime to be dramatically on the rise. [2]They see themselves as vulnerable to attack on their streets and in their homes. [3]The elderly, urban poor hesitate to venture forth from their apartments. [4]The rich make their homes virtual fortresses, barricading themselves with sophisticated electronic alarm systems. [5]This fear of crime revives the issue of what society's response should be to anti-social behavior. [6]One aspect of the issue being debated in the political arena, whether at party conventions or in state legislatures, is the death penalty. [7]Although proponents of capital punishment are found across the political spectrum from left to right, a rationale for this position can be found in several of the tenets of conservative doctrine. [8]It is a belief in the existence of an objective moral order, a rejection of the idea that men and women are perfectible, and a suspicion of government intervention.

Paragraph 2

[1]According to most conservatives good and evil are absolute values; standards of morality do not vary from society to society or from class to class within societies. [2]An action is either universally right or universally wrong. [3]This idea implies a single standard of justice. [4]If, as the Ten Commandments caution, ''Thou shalt not kill'' then it is the duty of all citizens to abide by that dictum. [5]If they do not, they are subject to an even-handed system of justice. [6]The death penalty for murder is justifiable

because the law against murder is applicable to all men — and those who do not abide by it must be willing to suffer the consequences of their actions. [7]To argue, as liberals do, that socio-economic circumstances make it difficult for individuals to function in a law-abiding manner and that the criminal justice system must weigh these factors in judging criminals is to defy what conservatives feel is the moral basis for all human conduct. [8]That a particular individual might have lived in poverty or might have had abusive parents does not mean that he or she is not subject to the extreme penalty of the law.

Paragraph 3

[1]In addition, conservatives do not believe that innate human weaknesses of character are capable of change. [2]Those who break the law are doing so because of their essential wickedness. [3]Reeducation of the killer is doomed because the inherent urge to violence cannot be eliminated from a person's basic behavior pattern. [4]What purpose, therefore, is served by punishment other than the death penalty for murder? [5]Society would be safer from further attack if the killer were summarily eliminated through capital punishment. [6]Why bother trying to change human nature when it cannot be accomplished?

Paragraph 4

[1]How does the death penalty conform to the conservative philosophy that government should, as much as possible, not intervene in the lives of the individual? [2]After all, by eliminating the murderer, government is guilty of the ultimate interference. [3]This must, however, be viewed from another perspective. [4]Maintaining the killer in jail — feeding, clothing, sheltering and trying to rehabilitate him or her — is an economic burden on society. [5]Who pays for this care, if not individual taxpayers? [6]Citizens should have the right to keep as much of their hard-earned money as possible. [7]Therefore, taxing citizens to support what conservatives feel are inefficient and wasteful programs is to deprive citizens of their right to benefit from their labor and their economic investments. [8]Obviously, it is the responsibility of government to maintain law and order so that citizens can go about their business — but beyond that other demands upon the citizen's pocketbook are infringements. [9]Maintaining a violent murderer in jail is an unnecessary economic burden that the government should not impose on its citizens who are law-abiding taxpayers.

Paragraph 5

[1]Americans feel that the very basis of their society is being threatened by violent crime. [2]Something must be done. [3]Americans should seriously consider the death penalty as a generally accepted punishment. [4]As conservatives maintain, it will, with the least government interference, protect society from those who cannot by their very nature abide by a universal code of morality.

In reading the essay, you probably discovered that in the middle section the student chose to discuss the three principles of conservative philosophy that he felt applied to the conservative stand on the death penalty. Which are they? These principles (categories) were selected from the chart that grouped the data from the lecture notes and the reading (Table 2.6). His choice of categories was determined by the controlling question, however, because he had to ask himself which of the six principles applied to the question he was answering. The controlling question caused him to choose three and eliminate the others.

Introduction

The overall purpose of any essay is to answer the controlling question that you may have been asked or a controlling question you have asked yourself. The introduction indicates the idea to be investigated and it provides a general answer to the controlling question in a brief statement. This is called the *thesis statement*. The thesis statement for this essay is found in sentences 7 and 8.

> Although proponents of capital punishment are found across the political spectrum from left to right, a rationale for this position can be found in several of the tenets of conservative doctrine. It is a belief in the existence of an objective moral order, a rejection of the idea that men and women are perfectible and a suspicion of government intervention.

The thesis statement did two things: it presented the main idea of the paper in sentence 7, and it listed in sentence 8 the three topics (the classification system) to be investigated. If the thesis statement had been limited to sentence 7, it would certainly have been adequate in that the overall purpose of the essay would have been established. Including the specific topics to be discussed, however, provides both the writer and his potential audience with a map of the rest of the paper, an indication of the way the essay will be developed. This helps the writer stay within the confines of the classification system and provides the reader with a guide. Neither the introduction as a whole nor the thesis statement in particular specifies the way the three principles reflect the conservative position on capital punishment; they simply mention them. All the details of proof are provided later in the body.

Body

The body of the essay specifically answers the controlling question by supporting the claims of the thesis statement. If, for example, the thesis provides categories for a claim, the body will discuss each one in a separate paragraph or section. A useful way to signal each category would be to supply a sentence that indicates the particular concern of that section or paragraph of the body. This is called a *topic sentence.*

In the first paragraph of the body, the first sentence is the topic sentence.

> According to most conservatives good and evil are absolute values; standards of morality do not vary from society to society or from class to class within societies.

The idea of this sentence is derived from the classification system the student created, and it follows from the first topic indicated in the thesis statement: that conservatives believe in an objective moral order.

The second topic sentence beginning paragraph 3 is derived from the second category of the expanded thesis statement, the imperfectibility of man.

And the third topic sentence, sentence 8 in paragraph 4, derived from the third part of the expanded thesis statement, refers to the third category, suspicion of government intervention. Unlike the previous body paragraphs, it is placed near the end. Variety is one reason for placing the topic sentence elsewhere. Another reason is that the nature of the argument calls for some explanatory remarks first. The student writer has anticipated a question a reader may have had in mind: "Isn't the death penalty a form of government intervention?" The student thought that the paragraph would have more impact if he addressed this question first and followed it with the topic sentence.

Sometimes a writer may want to use more than one paragraph to develop a single topic. Examples of this will be illustrated later. For now, the model student essays will use only one paragraph to develop a single aspect of the body.

Must you provide topic sentences in your essays? Not necessarily; however, they make your organization clear to your readers and, again, they help you stay within the limits of your sub-topics, your categories. Without them, some writers tend to wander off the subject and thus confuse the reader. A confused reader will not be convinced that what you are saying is so, nor will he or she necessarily understand what you are trying to say. For the purposes of this text, you will be asked to provide these useful indicators in your writing.

Conclusion

If you want to avoid leaving your readers in a suspended state, you must supply a conclusion to your essay. Your readers should not be forced to review the entire paper in order to be reminded of your intentions. In its simplest form, a conclusion restates the thesis. The thesis now has added weight, however, because it has been developed in the body. In essence, this restatement says to the reader, "If you have followed what I have written, you will now understand that what I claimed in the beginning is so." In the model essay, the statement that performs this function is sentence 3 of the last paragraph:

> As conservatives maintain, it [the death penalty] will, with the least government interference, protect society from those who cannot by their very nature abide by a universal code of morality.

This sentence indicates again why the conservative position in favor of the death penalty is a reflection of three of the basic tenets of conservative philosophy.

If you put all this together by filling in the outline below, you will see at a glance the basic organization of the model essay.

The Death Penalty: A Conservative Approach

I.   Introduction
     Thesis Statement

     _____

     _____

     _____

II. Body
     A. Topic Sentence 1

     _____

     _____

     _____

     B. Topic Sentence 2

     _____

     _____

     _____

     C. Topic Sentence 3

     _____

     _____

     _____

III. Conclusion
     Concluding Statement

     _____

     _____

     _____

In examining this outline you should be able to see that the answer to the controlling question — in this case, one of cause-effect — provides the overall plan, and that the classification system used is indeed a reflection of that controlling question.

Developing an Essay

If all there was to writing an essay was to create the skeletal pattern illustrated above, it would be a relatively simple task. Obviously, however, the model essay accomplished much more. It used the pattern as a basis for developing a cohesive and detailed answer to the controlling question. Although a major purpose of the rest of this text will be to help you flesh out your answers to the four basic question patterns, you should be aware even now of what can be done. Read the following analysis of the model essay. Assume that before the student writer planned and wrote his essay, he asked himself several subsidiary questions.

Controlling Question

Why is the conservative position in favor of the death penalty a reflection of conservative philosophy?

Subsidiary Questions:

1. Why is a discussion of one issue more profitable than a discussion of several issues?

2. Why is the issue of the death penalty a current one?
   A. What groups in society are most affected?

3. Which of the six conservative principles apply to this issue?

4. In what way is the objective moral order pertinent to the issue of the death penalty?
   A. What is meant by the objective moral order?
   B. Does it apply uniformly to all murderers?
   C. Are there other factors, such as environment, that should be considered?

5. In what way are each of the other principles pertinent to the issue of the death penalty?
   A. _____
   B. _____

See if you can finish the questioning process.

Taking another look at the three major parts of the essay — the introduction, the body, and the conclusion — see how the student, using these questions and other techniques, expanded each of these sections.

Introduction.   First let us examine and discuss paragraph 1. Besides including the thesis statement, introductions can also include opening remarks that engage the reader's attention and introduce the general significance of the subject.

There are several items that may be included in order to capture the reader's attention. Among them are: (1) an anecdote (personal or otherwise), (2) an appropriate quotation, (3) a startling statistic or description, and (4) a bold statement (that is, one not generally known or accepted). The choice will depend on the writer's knowledge of the subject and on the tone the writer wants to create. How did the writer capture the reader's attention in this introduction?

The writer of this essay probably wanted to establish a sense of urgency in the introduction through a startling description. The subsidiary question (2A), "What groups in society are most affected?" may have given the writer the idea of describing people of varying status who are affected by the fear of crime.

The writer also used the introduction to establish the tone of the essay — that is, the writer's attitude toward the subject and the reader. The tone of this introduction is somewhat formal, as can be seen from the language used. For instance, the writer says, "They see themselves as vulnerable to attack . . ." rather than saying "They are scared stiff. . . ." Distance between the writer and the audience, another aspect of tone, is maintained by not relating a personal anecdote and by not interjecting the first-person *I.* And yet the introduction is not dull, for the writer's warlike image — *attack, fortress, barricade* — dramatizes the situation.

The writer chose a formal approach, and certainly it is appropriate for academic and professional audiences. A formal tone does not mean, however, that for all academic or professional writing, personal experience need be eliminated, or that humor could not be interjected, or even that such expressions as "scared stiff" must necessarily be removed. Such elements can and often do arouse reader interest or express the particular personality of the writer. What you must be aware of is that you use these strategies to enhance your overall purpose and not to detract from it. If, for example, you want to elaborate upon a point by using personal experience, you would be unwise to go into great detail and thereby refocus the reader's attention from the point you want to illustrate to the anecdote itself. If you are using an expression like "scared stiff," you should use it with a full understanding of what its effect would be on your particular audience.

At this point, the writer, wanting a lead into his thesis, wrote the next sentences, numbers 5 and 6, as a bridge connecting the description of a life controlled by criminals with the assertion of a need for a remedy, in this case, capital punishment. The student then followed with sentences 7 and 8, his thesis statement, completing the introduction.

Body. To convince the reader of the validity of a topic sentence, a writer must, of course, support it. The questions asked at every step throughout the process provide the students with material to develop the body paragraphs.

Look at paragraph 2. The allied subsidiary questions, 4A, 4B, and 4C, helped the student writer to find the supporting details. Question 4A ("What is meant by the objective moral order?") indicates a need to *define* the term because it may be ambiguous to the reader; 4B ("Does it apply uniformly to all murderers?") suggests either a need to *contrast* different kinds of killers, or to *compare* all murderers, and 4C ("Are there other factors, such as environment, that should be considered?") asks the writer to provide reasons why other mitigating factors should or should not be considered (*causes*). Since all these allied subsidiary questions are developed in the essay, the writer used several methods of development within the paragraph: definition (sentences 2 and 3), comparison (sentences 4 through 6) and cause-effect (sentence 8). A paragraph in the body of an essay may be supported by more than one approach.

Now examine paragraph 3. Cause-effect is the primary method of development used in this paragraph, especially sentences 3, 4, and 5. The argument is: Since criminals are innately wicked (the cause), it is useless to attempt any change through rehabilitation (no effect). The judicious use of the death penalty (the cause) would help make our communities safer (the effect). Sentence 2 uses definition for development by further explaining the meaning of the topic.

Look at paragraph 4. After the first three sentences, which set up a contrast between two possible instances of government interference, the rest of the paragraph provides reasons why maintaining a murderer in jail is an imposition on citizens (causes).

Conclusion. Finally, examine paragraph 5. Certainly the major aim of a conclusion is to (1) reaffirm the idea of the thesis. It can, in addition (2) state the implications of the issue and (3) call for a course of action. In a sense, the student writer has used all three strategies: stating the general implication that violent crimes are a threat; suggesting a course of action, a change in government policy; and reinforcing the thesis by summarizing its ideas.

As for the tone established in the conclusion, it seems consistent with the rest of the paper. It is formal, somewhat impersonal and sympathetic regarding the subject of the essay — that is, conservative principles. The student has attempted to interweave his apparently objective answers with his apparently subjective responses.

Read the second student essay below, keeping in mind the discussion on the previous pages about the organization and development of a college essay. Then study the questions in the practice exercise that follows the model and reread the essay. Then you should be ready to answer the questions. Before you actually answer them, however, you might want to review the discussion on the first essay.

The Right Way

Today, in the decades of the 70's and 80's, we have experienced in America a resurgence of conservatism — President Nixon's election as President for two terms in 1968 and 1972, and most recently President Reagan's election. Therefore, there has been a renewed interest in understanding the philosophy of the "right." An examination of four elements in Frank Meyer's definition of conservatism seems to indicate several major features of the conservative political philosophy: one, it sees man as developing his highest capabilities through individual freedom and initiative; two, it believes the power of government should be limited; three, it emphasizes the role of religion in everyday life; and four, it holds that Communism is a great danger. An analysis of the conservative position on the major issues of the day should make these conservative principles more apparent.

Conservatives believe that the highest good a society can achieve is through each individual exercising the greatest degree of self-reliance and initiative. The proof of this, they claim, is that America has grown from a wilderness into a prosperous and powerful nation in less than three centuries. And it is these traits of personal independence that enabled Americans to endure, even in the worst of times. Any economic and social problems have been solved by individuals or groups of individuals in local communities; relying on others outside the immediate community is not the American way. This is why Conservatives have been dismayed by the attempts of federal and state government programs to provide social and economic aid. For example, they see welfare and unemployment benefits as "handouts." Such programs keep people dependent rather than nurturing their self-reliance.

Another Conservative principle, which is a logical extension of the first, is that the power of government should be limited. Conservatives feel that government intervention in all areas of our lives is out of hand. It is involved in a massive way with education, health, energy, environmental protection, rehabilitation, etc. Conservatives feel the expectation by too many of our citizenry is that all social problems be remedied by the government. Not only is this expectation not good for the American character, Conservatives claim it has led to enormous government programs that are wasteful and costly. For example, they cite the innumerable government regulations required by such agencies as EPA (Environmental Protection Agency) and NHTSA (National Highway Traffic Safety Administration) have crippled business. New plants are not built because of the great costs in meeting unreasonable safety standards, and automobiles are unnecessarily more expensive for the same reason. Why, Conservatives ask, must car manufacturers supply safety belts at great expense if owners don't want one? The arm of government is crippling the potential investor, the potential worker, the potential consumer. The expansion of government influence, they conclude, is a social problem.

Morality is an integral part of the fabric of a healthy, vibrant, civilized society according to conservatives. The strongest supporters of the moral order are the religious groups. As such, religious faith and practice play an important role, especially for the young. For this reason, many conservatives insist that school prayers be allowed in public schools. They are disturbed by the notion that education can be thought of as separate from moral teaching. Another practice that runs counter to the conservative support of a religious moral order is abortion. Many religious groups believe that human life begins at conception. Abortion, therefore, they feel, does not respect the sanctity of human life, and the "miracle" of life: conception.

Conservatives believe in building superior defense systems. They fear that the spread of communist doctrine is an ever-present danger. Its doctrines are contrary to almost every tenet of the conservative creed. Communism believes in a classless society, in a society without religion, in the notion that the state is more important than the individual. The one area which conservatives feel that the federal government should have power is for the defense of the nation and the free world and for deterring Soviet global aggression. They are wary of any SALT agreements (a proposed treaty to ban and/or limit the number of nuclear weapons) with the Soviet Union. With the help of its allies and friends around the world, conservatives believe the American government can prevent those doctrines from spreading by maintaining a strong defense perimeter around the Soviet sphere of influence.

Conservatives believe that their stands on the political issues of the 80's derive from a vital political philosophy. Such principles as allowing the greatest individual initiative, attempting to limit the power of government, giving more recognition to religious values, and establishing a vigilant stand against communism have made America a self-reliant, industrious, and powerful nation. Conservatives are sure that the political "right" is right.

PRACTICE

The Introduction

1. What is the thesis statement?

2. What categories did the author indicate he was going to discuss?

    _____

3. What strategies were used to gain the reader's attention?

    _____

4. How was the significance of the thesis introduced?

    _____

5. What is the tone?

    _____

The Body

1. How many major sections are there?   _____

2. How many paragraphs are there to each section?   _____

3. What is the topic sentence in each of the following:

    Paragraph 2._____

    Paragraph 3._____

    Paragraph 4._____

    Paragraph 5._____

What methods of development (definition, comparison/contrast, process, or cause-effect) were employed in each paragraph, and what subsidiary questions may have helped the student probe the methods to be used?

	Methods of Development	*Possible Subsidiary Question*
Paragraph 2.	_____	_____
Paragraph 3.	_____	_____
Paragraph 4.	_____	_____
Paragraph 5.	_____	_____

The Conclusion

1. What strategies were used in the concluding paragraph?

2. What is the tone?

3. Is the tone consistent with that of the rest of the essay?

The Writing Process: A Student at Work

The two model essays discussed in the preceding pages were presented in order to explain the criteria by which a completed paper should be judged and to provide a goal toward which you should be striving. It is important to realize, however, that the final products were achieved only after several revisions had been written, and that each of the revisions required the writer to think through the entire process — to consider adding new information, to weigh the evidence again, to reorganize the material, and to re-edit for correctness. Below is a description of the way one student worked through the task of writing her essay. As you will see, it was not a simple, straightforward process, but one that required many backward steps in order to move forward. Nevertheless, there were certain guideposts that kept her — and will keep you, if you follow them — from hopeless confusion.

Getting Started

The first problem the student faced was choosing from the list of suggested questions the controlling question she would answer. (See page 78.) She had never been particularly interested in current events and was worried that she would know too little about any of the issues that the instructor had listed. She read over all the questions several times. Then she looked at her charts showing the issues, the liberal and conservative principles, and their application in each case. She noticed one factor that appeared in several situations: the liberal belief in the need for some economic security. Writing about it might, she thought, give her the best chance for finding enough to say. She also felt that she had understood that part of the reading more thoroughly than any other section. Rereading the focused freewriting she had done on whether she was a liberal, a conservative, or a bit of both, she noticed that sentences about economic security cropped up again and again. She realized it was an issue she cared about. She was, she realized through her focused freewriting, quite aware of the way the lack of money had blotted out all other issues in her life and in the lives of people she knew. She now understood that, for her, the liberal concern with economic security was a primary issue in government. She therefore decided to write an answer to the following question:

Can you show how one principle of the liberal philosophy determines the liberal position on at least three of the issues?

The next step, and a vital one, was to create a tentative thesis that would provide a controlling idea for her paper. She knew that she should decide now the topics she would discuss, but she was still unsure of what she could write, and so limited herself to stating her main idea. She also looked at her chart and saw that it would provide the main divisions for the body of her paper, with each issue she discussed serving as a separate section. She took a pencil and circled that section of the chart, as in Table 2.7.

TABLE 2.7   Liberal Principles and Positions

	I Government Must Guard Freedom	II Government Must Help People Fulfill Potential	III Economic Security Necessary	IV Change Is Essential to Progress
1. Handguns	✓			
2. Health care		✓	✓	
3. School prayer				✓
4. Social security			✓	
5. Welfare		✓	✓	✓
6. Job training		✓	✓	
7. Death penalty				
8. Consumer protection	✓		✓	
9. Limits on corporate taxes	✓			✓
10. Environmental protection				
11. Unemployment insurance		✓	✓	
12. Defense spending				
13. Dropping of minimum wage for teenagers		✓	✓	

She made the following notations to herself to guide her writing:

Thesis — Liberal belief, in need for some economic security, influences attitudes on several issues.

Issue 1 —

Issue 2 —

Issue 3 —

Issue 4 —

Getting Words on Paper

Writing the main idea at least made the blank paper a little less empty, but where should she go from there? She went back to the chart and looked at the list of issues, trying to remember the class discussions on them, testing them one by one to see if any ideas came to her head. When she came to the one on lowering the minimum wage for teenagers, she decided to do another focused freewriting on that subject and describe the difficulties some of her friends were having.

> When I think of the possibility of lowering the minimum wage for teenagers, I really see red. When Dolores worked at the hardware store parttime last year for $4.25 an hour, 50¢ more than minimum, she found that she couldn't even cover her expenses without pestering her mom for more bucks — what with getting her clothes clean for work, buying school supplies, paying fees for college applications — let alone a movie once a week. And what about John whose family live on welfare because his dad is disabled? That summer job at $4.00 really came in handy for all of them. And Maggie — she takes babysitting jobs at less than minimum (what a jerk!). She works pretty much every night to keep herself going — and she can't even afford a Big Mac. Where would these kids be if they lowered the minimum wage in these times of rising prices?

It was obviously a subject about which she had something to say; she would begin there. She realized that she had not yet written a full introduction, but decided that could wait till later.

As she wrote, she frequently reread her words, crossing out some, correcting others. She became much involved with the story of her friends, and it was only after she had written almost six sentences that she saw that she had lost sight of the main purpose of the paper. She crossed it all out and substituted just one sentence. She tried, without success, to think of another example. She corrected a sentence error and wondered where to go from there. Her essay up to this point is printed below:

The liberal belief that ~~thexdegxeexofxecon~~
~~xemie~~ people need some economic security ~~was~~ is a
princip~~x~~le that influences the liberal position on a number of issues.

One area where the force of this principle
can be seen i~~s~~ the ~~present~~ current issue of lowering the minimum wag for teenagers. The assumption behind the proposal is that teenager/s
don't need as much mon~~g~~y to live as older ~~peopl~~
workers. But that just isntt true. I have
friends who are married, support families and
have to p~~a~~y rent~~x~~. ^T^ they have to buy food and
clothes just like anybody else. My friends
George and JoAnn got married when they were ~~16~~
sixteen years old. Today they are the ~~preue~~ parents of an el~~t~~ht month old baby boy. George had
~~a/~~ a lot of trouble finding a job at first, but
he finally got ~~xeeex~~ one in a gas station. He
only got the minimum wage and that wasn't enough
to live on with rents so high, so he took a secnd
job ~~asxx~~ at McDonalds. He only makes the miminum
wage there too and the family is really strug-
gleing to mak ends meet. If the minimum wage was
lowered, George and JoAnn just wouldnt have
enough mon~~g~~ay, they'd probably have to move in
with JoAnns parnts and what kind of life is that?
The minimum wag is necessary for teenagers who
have families so they can live a decent life on

once the
baby was
born

there own. Without it they would ave to be de-

pendent on ther parents, or even ~~governwelfare~~

and you cant call that being free.

Then the student remembered the subsidiary questions she had written when she had done her reading. Looking at them, she saw that one of them could be useful here: "What effect will maintaining the minimum wage have?" She finished off the paragraph with a sentence on that topic.

Writing the next paragraph caused a problem. The student tried to think of another issue and seemed only to find a muddle in her head. Instead of looking at her chart, she started thinking about other workers who might have economic problems. She thought of the issue of unemployment compensation, and wrote a few sentences about that. She felt that she had only touched on the edges of the problem, but did not know what was missing. The fifth paragraph was somewhat easier. Again, it was the chart that provided the impetus. She noticed the listing of welfare. She remembered that there had been a class discussion on the topic, and she tried to recapture some of the ideas that had been expressed. The conclusion in a separate paragraph was a simple restatement of the thesis, but this time it included the major points that had been covered in the paper.

Planning Revision: Self-Evaluation and Feedback from Others

Once the first draft was completed, the student reread it. She was not satisfied with it, but she was not sure what was wrong. Putting the paper aside for a few hours, she gave herself a chance to look at it with fresh eyes.

Before the student read the paper again, she read the guidelines developed in the analysis of the first model essay (pages 81–87), looking for ideas on ways to judge her own paper. It was apparent immediately that some very clear standards had been presented in that section. She saw that she had left out the beginning of the introduction and that her thesis had not included the topics she would discuss. She redid the introduction, using a summary of liberal principles as her background information and pasted it to the original.

Judging the body of the essay from this criteria was less clear-cut. She felt that her topic sentences were good, but she was not sure if her explanations were helpful. She added another sentence to the paragraph on teenage wages and one to the paragraph on unemployment compensation, but she could not tell if the meaning was as clear to others as it seemed to her.

She noted that in the conclusion she had restated her thesis, and she added another sentence calling for continued government support of economic security, hoping that it was enough.

The draft of the student's essay is printed below. As you can see, the writer was involved in rethinking, revising, and editing the essay all at the same time. She had stopped and reread her words every few sentences, correcting mistakes, adding new phrases, and cutting out whole sections. Even after she had removed the copy from the typewriter, she thought of additional ideas which she added in pencil. This practice is a common one for all writers; in fact, it is probably impossible to write without constantly rereading what came before. Remember, however, that this sort of editing is not a substitute for a thorough revision and proofreading of the paper before making the final copy.

Liberal and Conservatives have different

ideas about how government should be run. Liber-

als believe that ~~change~~— government must guard

freedom, must help men˄to ful̸fill their
               and women

potential, that change is essentail for progress

and that̸economic security is nec̸essary for
      some

freedom. Of these principles, the influence of

the one requirng ecomonic security can be seen

in the Liberal positions on minumum wages for

teenagers, unemplyment compensation and

welfare.

The liberal belief that ~~thexdegxeexefxeeen-~~

~~xeeie~~ people need some economic security ~~was~~ is

a principä̶le that influences the liberal posi-

tion on a number of issues.

One area where the force of this principle

can be seen is the ~~pxesent~~ current issue of low-

ering the minimum wag for teenagers. The assump-

tion behind the proposal is that teenager̸s

don't need as much mongy to live as older ~~peepl~~

workers. But that just isntt true. I have

friends who are married, support families and

have to pay rentx. T̲they have to buy food and

clothes just like anybody else. My friends

George and JoAnn got married when they were ~~is~~

sixteen years old. Today they are the ~~proud~~ par-

ents of an eitht month old baby boy. George had

~~ay~~ a lot of trouble finding a job at first, but

he finally got ~~somst~~ one in a gas station. He

only got the minimum wage and that wasn't enough

to live on with rents so high, so he took a secnd

job ~~asxa~~ at McDonalds. He only makes the miminum

wage there too and the family is really strug-

gleing to mak ends meet. If the minimum wage was

once the
baby was
born

lowered, George and JoAnn just wouldnt have

enough mongay, they'd probably have to move in

with JoAnns parnts and what kind of life is that?

The minimum wag is necessay for teenagers who

have families so they can live a decent life on

there own. Without it they would ave to be de-

pendent on ther parents, or even ~~gaxonxnelfa-~~

~~x~~eand you cant call that being free. also, if
people don't receive equal pay for equal work, that
limits their freedom.

its belief in

Another area where Liberal policy is influ-

ence by ~~thexLibexa~~l the need for economic se

curity ~~ós~~ ~~unemplexnent~~ the unemployment ~~sxs~~ in-

surance program. When business is slow or if a
corporation goes out of business, it's the workers wh suffer. But it isn't the workers fault if
the executives are making things people dont
want to buy or if the contry is in a recession.
Why should they be the ones to suffer.

B t the most important area where Liberal
philosophy affects ~~praek~~ practice is the liberal
support of welfare. Sometimes people ~~haxexfami-~~
~~iies~~ have children when they cant support them
or they los there jobs and dont have unemployment insurance. Conservatives say they should of
done ~~some~~ something to protect themselves, but
we cant just sit by and watch people starve once
the situation exists. People who are hungry will
do anytning to get something to eat--steal, com-
mitt crimes, even become ~~a~~ prostitutes. And
children who suffer from malnutirition cant do
well in school and seometimes even have permanent brain damage.

The Liberal belief that people need som eco-
some   nomic security in order to be free influences
the liberal support for the minimum wage for
tennagers and the continuance of unemplyment
benefits and the maintenance of wlefare. The
government should continue to support
these programs.

Because she realized that she could not see her paper in the same way
that others could, this student arranged with two other classmates to read

over each other's essays. She was shy about showing them her writing, but calmed down somewhat when she realized they were nervous too. Their comments about the body of the paper were especially helpful. They pointed out that the example in the paragraph on teenage wages was now so long that the idea of the paragraph was obscure. They thought that the paragraph on unemployment compensation was unconnected to the principle of freedom, and that while several issues were raised in the paragraph on welfare, none of them was fully explained.

The most important questions they raised, however, were concerned with the tone and direction of the essay. To them, the paper sounded like a propaganda piece rather than an explanation of liberal principles. Even though she might be a liberal, they pointed out, the essay should not present the liberal position in such a personal way. The assignment, as given by the instructor, called for an objective analysis of a position rather than a defense of that position. They also mentioned that the paper sounded as if she were talking to a friend rather than discussing important problems. They urged her to sound less conversational and to use fewer colloquial expressions.

The student realized that she had been confused about her purpose in writing the paper. Instead of writing an impersonal paper on the subject, she had written a personal argument in favor of certain government actions; the instructor had not asked for her feelings, but that was what she had written. Her personal feelings were, she realized, a vital first step in deciding what to write about and provided her essay with energy and authentic concern; but now she saw the necessity for transferring her emotional statements into more judicious prose.

Although there was still a great deal of work to be done, the student now had a sense of how to revise her paper. She went back to the chart she had made, thought of the class discussions, even read the model essays to see what particular issues they had treated. She had to write two more drafts before she felt she had answered all the questions she and her readers had raised, but at the end she believed she had really begun to understand what a college essay should be like.

Below is her revised essay. Of course, she proofread the essay as best she could.

A Liberal Principle: Economic Freedom

Many arguments start because people have different ideas about how to cope with the problems our society faces. Even Democrats differ with other Democrats, and Republicans argue among themselves. You would think that members of each party would agree with each other. Why don't they? The reason is that within each party there are two major political philosophies; these are liberal and conservative. Certainly liberals and conservatives differ about how much government should be involved in the economic security of citizens. Liberals believe that economic security is necessary in upholding freedom. You can see how this principle applies to the problems of minimum wage for teenagers, unemployment insurance, and welfare.

There has recently been some discussion of lowering the minimum wage for teenagers. The idea behind the proposal is that teenagers do not need as much money as older workers. That is simply not true. I have teenaged, married friends who have to pay for high rents, for rising food prices, and for children's clothing that is as expensive as adult clothing. The guys in each case had to take a second job. Because they are receiving the lowest minimum wages, they are thinking of returning to their parents' houses. If they do that, there go their personal freedoms. Liberals also point out that offering teenagers less money than older workers would violate another basic notion of freedom — equal pay for equal work. The position that liberals hold on these issues shows their belief that freedom requires some sort of economic security.

Another area where the liberal position is explained by liberal philosophy is the issue of unemployment insurance. The changes in the American economy can often cause hardships. Workers are often thrown out of jobs or laid off due to a downswing in the economy. The situation in Detroit is particularly bad. We have read the figures of these poor people laid off in the automobile industry. These workers are not responsible for the recession or for the competition of the Japanese auto industry; yet they are the ones who suffer the most. At least with unemployment insurance they can support their families and they don't have to get an altogether different job. They can hope to return to the same industry and use their special skills again. By providing unemployment insurance, workers do not have to make unpleasant economic choices. Thus, they have more freedom.

The most important area that shows how the liberal philosophy explains liberal positions on issues is in the case of welfare. People who do not have the basic needs of life are not free. People who are hungry will do anything to get something to eat — steal, commit other crimes, even become prostitutes. Their children suffer even more. Studies have shown that when children do not receive proper nourishment they do very poorly in school. Sometimes, in severe cases, there could even be permanent brain damage. If children fail at school, then they miss out on the education that could be their best chance for good jobs. The opportunity of employment means greater freedom in the future. As liberals see it, the welfare programs provide a basic ingredient for the freedom which the American system of government promises.

Liberals believe in the necessity of providing some economic security to insure freedom. This is why liberals support the minimum wage for teenagers, unemployment compensation, and welfare programs. According to the liberal philosophy, these programs should be maintained to preserve our basic freedoms.

What follows is a list of steps that will guide you in writing a college-level essay.

Guide to Writing an Essay

1. Read and study the controlling question, or establish your own.

   1A. If you need to establish a controlling question, use the question and other invention techniques (described in Chapter 1) and the dividing/grouping process (described in this chapter) to help you *establish the major point.*

   1B. Once you have established the controlling question or have been given one by the instructor, use the techniques for probing the question (Chapter 1) and again the dividing/grouping process *to establish major categories.*

2. Write a *tentative thesis statement* to guide your writing. This statement should not only state your position, it should also indicate the breakdown of the paper (your classification system).

3. Using the classification system indicated by the thesis statement, write *tentative topic sentences* to guide you as you write the several sections of the body.

4. Write a *tentative concluding statement* that at the very least restates the thesis.

5. Using these statements as a basis, write your *first draft.* You might find that as you write you want to change the focus of your entire paper, or of some of its parts. Do not hesitate, but remember that you will need to change the thesis as well. You may also find that some, if not all, topic sentences will require revision.

6. *Reread* the entire first draft and determine whether you have proven what you set out to prove. To do this, you might want to read your draft to members of your writing class, or to a friend whose honest and informed opinion you value.

7. *Revise* your draft as many times as you think necessary.

8. When you are finally satisfied with the essay, *edit* your draft carefully.

9. *Recopy* your draft for submission.

PRACTICE

You should now be ready to write your own essay responding to one of the three controlling questions presented on page 78.

Remember that you are to choose aspects of the general questions different from those illustrated in the model essays. Your instructor may give you another assignment.

2

Putting the Strategies to Work in the Academic Disciplines

Part 1 described two major components of the thinking strategy required for college writing: questioning and organizing. Together they help generate the ideas and details that make up an essay and crystallize the form that shapes it. The summary outline at the end of Chapter 2 is a guide to assist you with the thinking strategies necessary to write any college essay.

As you have seen, a major consideration, after establishing a controlling question, is to probe that question to determine what the key elements of an essay will be. This probing, however, is not the same for all types of controlling questions. Indeed, each kind of controlling question suggests a particular way of thinking about a subject. Part 2 examines specific thinking strategies for each of these controlling questions: definition, comparison/contrast, process, and cause-effect. It shows how these strategies evolve into the kind of writing you will be asked to do in college.

chapter

3

Questions of Definition

THINKING

Why Define?

If you are like most people, definition seems like an unimportant matter; if there is a dispute about a word, all that the people involved have to do, you would say, is to look it up in a dictionary. If you have ever used that method to resolve a serious argument, however, you might have discovered that, rather than solving the problem, the dictionary added nothing useful.

The definition of *life*, for example, seems innocent enough in general conversation, but it can become a burning issue. Some people define life as beginning at conception, while others claim that life begins at birth. How might these differing definitions affect attitudes toward legalized abortion? Similarly, defining *death* seems to raise no problems until the question of ending the life of a comatose person is being considered. At what point would a person who favors cutting off life-support systems define the moment of death? When would someone opposed to such an action define that moment?

In academic study, definitions can help you understand the perspective of a particular discipline. Examine the reproduction of a painting by Pablo Picasso in Figure 3.1. What sense do you make of it?

Like many average viewers you may be hopelessly confused by this painting, searching in vain for the real-life images you expect to find in it,

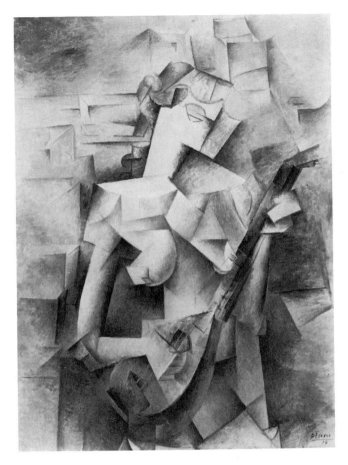

Figure 3.1.   *Pablo Picasso. "Girl with a Mandolin" (Fanny Tellier), early 1910. Oil on canvas, 39½ × 29". Collection, The Museum of Modern Art, New York. (Nelson A. Rockefeller Bequest.)*

and you may dismiss the work as incomprehensible. With the following definition paraphrased from an art history text, however, you may begin to understand the painting and, indeed, to appreciate it.

> Cubism is an art movement that sees the human mind imposing geometrical shapes upon nature — planes and angles on a flat surface — and sees the world in fragments from several points of view.

With this definition you may now be able to look at the painting "Girl with a Mandolin" again and understand why the rearrangement of features, the exaggerated geometric shapes, the doubling of views have been used.

Definitions become the bases upon which further knowledge is acquired. They often summarize what is known in a field of study, and they can then be applied to the investigation of the unknown. When you wear one layer of clothes over another, for example, you may be irritated by the tendency of the two layers to stick together. You are witnessing the phenomenon known as static cling, and to avoid it you might spray your clothes with a product advertised on television. Are you curious about how and why the product works? Reading the first page of an introductory chemistry text, you are introduced to a number of basic definitions of such terms as atom, proton, neutron, electron, and positive and negative charges. When you learn, as part of the definitions of positive and negative charges, that two like charges repel each other and two unlike charges attract each other, you might then figure out that the two layers of clothes have two unlike charges (positive and negative) and therefore attract each other, this attraction causing them to cling. You might then be able to figure out that if you could change the charge of one of the layers, making both layers alike in charge, the clothes would separate. The chemists who created the products designed to accomplish this separation that you see advertised on television must have based their experiments on these fundamental concepts in chemistry, so many of which were incorporated in definitions.

In academic study, definitions not only help you understand the perspective of a particular discipline, they also widen and deepen your knowledge of the world around you.

Creating Precise Definitions

Most of us, most of the time, do not worry much about whether the words we use are exactly right. You might say "Pull over a chair" when only a stool or an ottoman is available. A friend will understand what you mean and will take whatever seat is available. For academic work you need to be more precise. A definition is precise when it is *exclusive* and *true* — that is, the definition applies to one word and no other (exclusive) and it accurately describes what that word represents (true).

The most common way of defining a word or a term is (1) to place the word in its general class and then (2) to distinguish the word from all other words in that class. For example:

A *chair* is a seat.

This definition places the word *chair* in the general class of items that we sit on. The definition is inadequate, however, because it fails to distinguish a chair from a stool, a sofa, or a bench. The definition must, therefore, be expanded to separate the word *chair* from all other kinds of seats. More accurately, then:

A *chair* is a seat for one person, with four legs and a back.

This definition is exclusive in that no other item for sitting is described here. It is true in that it accurately describes the general object. We tend to forget this need for precision because our expectation of general agreement about the class and characteristics of any particular word is so strong that we rarely give it any thought. When the word *automobile* is used, most Americans have a common image in their minds, but for someone from the mountainous regions of Tibet who has never seen an automobile, no such image is created. For that person, it is necessary to give the class and the characteristics, explaining that an automobile is a vehicle used for transporting people and is powered by an engine. By describing it as "a vehicle," we clarify for the Tibetan that it is some kind of conveyance; by saying that it is "used for transporting people," we distinguish it in the Tibetan's mind from conveyances such as wagons, which are used to carry things; by mentioning that is has a device called an engine to power it, we help the Tibetan understand why it needs no ox or horse. And if worse came to worse, and the Tibetan still did not understand, we could produce the object itself, point to it and say, "This is an automobile!"

Look at the following words and their definitions.

	Word	*Class*	*Distinguishing Characteristics*
1.	A **house**	is a **building**	that serves as **living quarters.**
2.	A **church**	is a **building**	that is used as **a place of worship.**
3.	A **school**	is a **building**	that is used for **education.**

As you can probably recognize, defining is an application of the classifying process described in Chapter 2. The term to be defined is first grouped with other items that share similar characteristics. Thus each of the items considered above (house, church, school) was first placed in the general class, *building*, as in Figure 3.2.

Now examine the diagram in Figure 3.3.

Figure 3.2 *Classifying Three Items*

Term being defined: House   Church   School

Class: Building

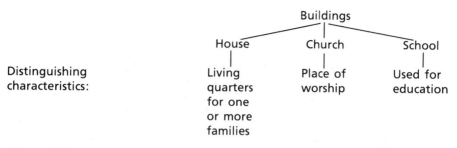

Figure 3.3 *Adding Distinguishing Characteristics to Classified Items*

The distinguishing characteristics should make it impossible to confuse the term with any other term belonging to the same class. After we have provided the distinguishing characteristic "place of worship" for the term *church*, could it be mistaken for any other kind of building, such as a factory, an office building, a concert hall?

Of course, once you define a term, you might discover that the term itself can be further analyzed. It can become the class for definitions of other terms that share some general characteristics, and other *distinguishing characteristics* must be supplied.

PRACTICE

Using the word *school* as the class, complete the definitions of the following terms by supplying the *distinguishing characteristics*.

1. A college is a school   _____

2. A university is a school   _____

3. A music conservatory is a school   _____

Sometimes even a distinguishing characteristic can become the *class* for other terms, whereupon further *distinguishing characteristics* must be supplied.

PRACTICE

Using the phrase "place of worship" as the class, complete the following definitions by supplying further distinguishing characteristics.

1. A synagogue is a place of worship   _____

2. A cathedral is a place of worship   _____

3. A mosque is a place of worship   _____

PRACTICE

Define the following words, supplying the general class and the distinguishing characteristics. Be certain that what you write adds up to the particular term under consideration, nothing less and nothing more. Avoid using the word you are defining in its definition.

1. A dog   _____

2. An ocean   _____

3. A text   _____

4. A poem   _____

5. Detente   _____

6. Neurosis   _____

Part of being precise when defining a term in college courses is to understand how the term is being used by a particular discipline. Imagine the confusion that might occur for a student who is at the same time taking biology, anthropology, and American literature and discovers the same term being used in all three courses. A sentence in his biology text reads:

> The amoeba was grown in a *culture* of agar solution.

Turning to his anthropology text an hour later, he finds this sentence:

> The *culture* of the Arapesh tribe emphasized peaceful coexistence with neighboring tribes while the culture of the Mundugumor tribe emphasized violent behavior.

The next day in his text for American literature, he sees:

> Being a man of high *culture*, the novelist Henry James did not appeal to a mass audience.

Obviously, each of the texts is using the word in quite different ways.

PRACTICE

1. Look up the word *culture* in a dictionary and decide which of the definitions would be used by each of the disciplines above.

2. Look up the word *depression* and decide which definition would be used in psychology, in economics, and in geography. Write a sentence illustrating how each of these disciplines would use the word.

3. Can you recognize some common element(s) in the several definitions of *culture* and *depression* that would explain why the same terms were used by the different disciplines?

The Importance of Context

Most definitions are rarely static entities that, once given, remain the same for all people at all times and in all situations. Like all human activities, they reflect the ever-changing nature of human life, along with the circumstances, the past histories, and the predilections of the people who create them.

If you and your friends were on a beach enjoying a sun-baked day with the temperature in the nineties, one of you might exclaim: "Wow, what a hot day!" Undoubtedly, everyone there would know what you meant. But would all groups of people understand the same thing by the word *hot*? An Indian from Madras, for whom days of 110° Fahrenheit are common, might find the day pleasantly cool, while a Laplander from Northern Finland, where 70° or 75° is unusually hot, might find the day so excruciatingly hot that he would be unable to enjoy it. The *difference in past histories* of these two individuals would play an important part in the way they would define even so simple a word as *hot*.

Changes in perspective also affect the way a term is defined. One of the most revolutionary changes in definition occurred with developments in astronomy that caused new definitions of our solar system to be created and then caused major redefinition of our universe. The following excerpts from an astronomy text illustrate the nature of the redefinition:

Exploring the Cosmos

Even though the spherical shape of the earth was, in general, accepted by the early natural philosophers, they still thought the earth was an immovable and solid globe surrounded by the fixed sphere of the heavens.

Certainly the most immediately obvious and simplest geometrical model was one in which the earth was located at the center of the universe, while between the earth and the heavens was a second sphere, a rotating one, that would account for the stars' daily rising and setting.

However, with this model the problem was to explain the other movements in the solar system — those of the sun, moon, and five planets,[1] all of which seemed to wander among the stars. Never changing their course, the sun and moon move eastward relative to the stars on the celestial sphere, with the planets generally following the same path from west to east. The planets confuse matters, though, because sometimes they temporarily reverse their direction in retrograde motion. They further compound the problem by displaying irregularities in their motions (as do the sun and moon) and variations in brightness.

Explaining the universe with a logical system was a challenge for the natural philosophers of ancient Greece. For centuries various schools of philosophy proposed, debated over, and elaborated on several *geocentric* (earth-centered) theories. With their taste for balance and symmetry, the Greeks reasoned that nature arrayed her celestial bodies in the perfect geometric figure, the sphere, and moved them on flawless circles. Their philosophers, beginning with Plato (427?–347 B.C.) or earlier, thought that planetary movements were accounted for by combinations of uniform circular motions with the earth at the center.

Hellenistic culture spread throughout the eastern Mediterranean world and after about 300 B.C. centered in Alexandria, where a new establishment for science was started. Alexandrian astronomers set themselves to removing discrepancies between the geocentric theory and the motions they observed. Thus geocentric theory maintained its dominance in philosophical thought — except for a brief departure in the third century B.C. — until the sixteenth century.

During the third century B.C. a *heliocentric* (sun-centered) scheme was proposed by Aristarchus (320?–?250 B.C.). He thought it natural to put the largest and only self-luminous body, the sun, at the center of the system. According to Aristarchus, the heavens moved each day because the earth rotated on its axis. Annual changes in the sky and the planets' irregular motions could be explained if they and the earth then revolved about the sun.

Halfway through the thirteenth century, knowledge of astronomy had spread throughout Europe as Greek manuscripts were translated into Latin in the newly founded European universities. The Renaissance blossomed in the next two centuries, ending the dominance of ecclesiastical concerns in medieval thought and beginning the development of a broader range of intellectual considerations, including cosmology. Renaissance scientists proved to be creative in picturing the physical world, not letting themselves

---

[1] The word *planet* is of Greek origin, signifying "wanderer," in contrast with the fixed stars.

be dominated by past dogmas. They prepared the way for a deep change in scientific thought and viewpoint. Cultural ideas, including astronomy, proliferated after the 1430s, when the printing press was invented. Although the Ptolemaic system had been immensely successful in describing general aspects of planetary motion for over 13 centuries, by the fifteenth century easily recognizable discrepancies had arisen in the observed and predicted positions of some planets.

About the time the New World was being discovered, Nicolaus Copernicus (1473–1543), a Polish canon of ecclesiastical law and astronomer, began wondering whether any other arrangement of the planetary system might not be simpler, more reasonable, and more aesthetically pleasing than the Ptolemaic one. He resurrected Aristarchus's heliocentric idea and built a new cosmology based on it. After nearly four decades of study, Copernicus's monumental book *On the Revolutions of the Heavenly Orbs* was published in the year of his death, 1543. Dedicating the work to Pope Paul III, he died without seeing his theory accepted, except by a few friends to whom he had given his manuscript years before its publication. The public reception given at the time to what was much later a revolution in the concept of the universe varied between indifference and open hostility. His system, then, was not much more accurate or simpler than Ptolemy's, but the Copernican system was a tremendous step in cosmological thought for its time. In the next century this change led to acceptance of the concept that celestial physics was not a supernatural matter but only an extension of terrestrial physics.

The hypothesis that our solar system is a heliocentric one was, as you saw from the above passage, under consideration as early as the third century B.C., yet the idea was ignored until Copernicus's time. Partly this was due to the fact that whole philosophical systems — the understanding of who human beings are, what is their place in the universe — depended on the idea that the earth was the center of the universe. The pre-Christian religious communities in ancient Greece and Rome, as well as those in the Near East and Africa, assumed that our world was of central importance, and the early Christian church depended on that view as well.

In order to gain a sense of how revolutionary the new definition of the solar system as heliocentric was, imagine an intelligent person in the sixteenth century trying to adjust his or her thinking to this new knowledge. How does this new knowledge affect the importance we give to the earth? How does it affect the importance we give to human beings? How does it affect the relationship many people believe exists between God and humans? How does it affect our understanding of the place of the stars in the universe? What possibilities exist for better understanding of the planets? What potential does it offer for new studies of the universe?

PRACTICE

Discuss in groups what a person in the sixteenth century might have to say on these subjects.

In the same way that past histories can influence the way terms are defined, so also can *differences in present circumstances* have an effect. The definition of 9 A.M. creates no problem for people living within the same time zone, but think of the trouble you might have if you tried to tune into a particular television program in Los Angeles using a schedule presented in a Philadelphia edition of *TV Guide*! Or imagine the confusion that could result if two friends, one in London and one in Chicago, arranged to call each other "next Wednesday at 9 A.M." without stating precisely whether that meant 9 A.M. in London or in Chicago. Even so simple a word as *school* might produce several different definitions if it were being defined on the basis of present circumstances by a high school student, a college student at an urban university, a college student at a small, rural institution, and a parent of any of the above.

Serious disputes can develop when definitions are applied on the basis of *differing sets of assumptions*. Take the case of the word *pornography*. *The New York Times* reported that at a symposium arranged by *Harper's* magazine to answer the question, "What is pornography?" the participants "never quite managed to answer that question, but their spirited two-hour discussion covered everything from esthetics to censorship, from the causes of violence against women and the meaning of 'sexual liberation' to the shortcomings of 'uptight intellectuals.'"[2] Below are shown some of the answers the members of the group provided:

Participant	*Definition of Pornography*
Susan Brownmiller, the author of *Against Our Will*, a book about rape	"anti-female propaganda"
Erica Jong, novelist, whose *Fear of Flying* contains passages some consider pornographic	"While erotic literature attempts to probe the human soul . . . , pornography has no esthetic value, but only shows the 'ugliness of twisted Puritanism' in Western society"
Midge Decter, a New York writer	pornography provides "a vision of

---

[2] *The New York Times*, August 13, 1984, p. C21.

"identified with new conservative causes"

Al Goldstein, publisher of *Screw* magazine

erotic utopianism, of sex without entanglement" which turns "sex into a 'joyless pursuit, a kind of gymnastic discipline.'"

pornography is "junk entertainment." "Today's pornography is tomorrow's eroticism." Those who argue against pornography are "uptight intellectuals who thought anything that was fun was wrong." [But he felt] "the term remains undefined . . . I don't know what pornography is . . . I haven't a clue."

Here is another case. If two persons in an office were discussing a woman whose purse was stolen from her desk, one might insist the woman was foolish and the other might vehemently deny it. The two persons would not be arguing about the meaning of the word *foolish*, for they would share a general agreement about this particular term as meaning "acting without judgment"; their disagreement would be over the *application of the term* in this particular instance. The first person might feel that leaving a purse on one's desk is an invitation to a thief and hence foolish, while the second person might believe that people have the right to assume the honesty of their co-workers, and thus for this person leaving a purse on one's desk would seem reasonable. Knowing how and where a term is going to be applied is a crucial aspect in understanding its meaning.

A differing set of assumptions can also result in two different definitions for the same term. For example:

1. *Religion* [is] the personal commitment to and serving of God . . . . . (*Webster's Third New International Dictionary*)[3]

2. *Religion* is the opiate of the people (Karl Marx, 1843, in *Critique of Hegel's Philosophy of Right*)

In 1, the class to which the term is put is "commitment," which connotes a serious and thoughtful obligation or pledge; the commitment has the force of one's full being. In 2, the term *religion* is put in the class *opiate*, a narcotic, thus connoting an escape from the pressures of reality. Karl Marx, one of the authors of the *Communist Manifesto*, believed that religion was encouraged by rulers to drug workers into thinking that their lives of toil

[3] By permission. From Webster's Third New International Dictionary © 1981 by Merriam-Webster Inc., publisher of the Merriam-Webster® Dictionaries.

would be rewarded in heaven, making them passive recipients of their rulers' exploitation.

Often, definitions referring to the same idea or practice will use different terms, especially if a word has acquired a negative connotation, as with the word *imperialism*. The generally-accepted definition is "the policy, practice, or advocacy of seeking . . . new territory or dependencies, by the extension of its rule over other races of mankind" (*Webster's Third International Dictionary*). When, however, the United States in its early history was widening its boundaries westward and engulfing native American lands, one American did not call this expansion "imperialism." Instead, he referred to "Our *manifest destiny* to overspread the continent allowed by Providence for the free development of our yearly multiplying millions" (John L. Sullivan, 1845, in *The United States Magazine and Democratic Review*). Whether you think Sullivan's term is warranted depends on how you perceive American history. Definitions, besides helping us to understand physical reality, tell us something about human nature as well.

PRACTICE

Examine the following terms and discuss how the given contexts could alter the application of their definitions, or even the definitions themselves.

Term		*Context*	
1.	rural	a.	farmer
		b.	urbanite
2.	rock 'n' roll	a.	teenager
		b.	his/her parent
3.	adult	a.	19-year-old
		b.	40-year-old
4.	classical	a.	musician
		b.	architect
5.	beauty	a.	Miss America contestant
		b.	Cubist painter
6.	morality	a.	civil libertarian
		b.	dictator

Looking at the issue in yet another context, you can see how particular philosophies often lead to very different sorts of definitions. The American poet Emily Dickinson produced the following imaginative definition of a snake:

A NARROW FELLOW IN THE GRASS

A narrow Fellow in the Grass
Occasionally rides ——
You may have met Him —— did you not
His notice sudden is ——
The Grass divides as with a Comb ——
A spotted shaft is seen ——
And then it closes at your feet
And opens further on ——

He likes a Boggy Acre
A Floor too cool for Corn ——
Yet when a Boy, and Barefoot
I more than once at Noon
Have passed, I thought, a Whip lash
Unbraiding in the Sun
When stopping to secure it
It wrinkled, and was gone ——

Several of Nature's People
I know, and they know me ——
I feel for them a transport
Of cordiality ——

But never met this Fellow
Attended, or alone
Without a tighter breathing
and Zero at the Bone ——

During the same period in which Dickinson was writing, a mechanistic approach to definition was popular. Charles Dickens satirized that school of thought in a novel by having a schoolboy begin to define a horse in the following terms:

"Bitzer," said Thomas Gradgrind. "Your definition of a horse."

"Quadruped, Graminivorous. Forty teeth, namely twenty-four grinders, four eye-teeth, and twelve incisive. Sheds coat in the spring; in marshy countries, sheds hoofs, too. Hoofs hard, but requiring to be shod with iron. Age known by marks in mouth." Thus (and much more) Bitzer.

PRACTICE

Reversing the two approaches above, define a snake the way you think Dickens's schoolboy might have done it, and define a horse the way Emily Dickinson might.

Informed Bias

The basic issues in definition, then, are (1) being as precise as possible, by placing a word in a class to which it fits and by supplying the characteristics that distinguish that word from all other items in that class, and (2) knowing to what extent precision might be threatened when past history, personal circumstances, and the world view of the definer become an integral part of the definition or its application to particular circumstances. In creating definitions, you need to investigate the extent that your personal assumptions have colored your understanding; when you read the definitions of others, you should see if you can recognize any of the unstated assumptions that might have influenced the writer.

Although definitions based on particular points of view are often acceptable, even intriguing and entertaining for conversation or literary purposes, you will find that for college discussion and writing, your instructors will usually prefer definitions in which the personal assumptions of the definer are openly and clearly stated.

Within academic disciplines, there is certainly room for the expression of *informed* personal bias. A scholar may view material in the field from a new perspective that can help other experts and students in the field test and reinterpret information to reevaluate previously-held concepts. In the following introduction to a political science text, entitled *The Irony of Democracy*, the author explains his informed bias. Notice his precision in defining all his terms and his objective tone. To guide your reading, first look at the questions immediately following the selection on page 120.

To the Student

An instructor who has asked you to read this book wants to do more than teach about "the nuts and bolts" of American government, for this book has a "theme": only a tiny handful of people make decisions that shape the lives of all of us, and, despite the elaborate rituals of parties, elections, and interest group activity, we have little influence over these people. This theme is widely known as the *theory of elitism*. Your instructor may not believe completely in this theory but may instead believe that power in America is widely shared among many groups of people, that competition is widespread, that there are checks against the abuse of power, and that the individual citizen can personally affect the course of national events by voting, supporting political parties, and joining interest groups. This theory is widely known as *pluralism* and characterizes virtually every American government textbook now in print — except this one. Your instructor, whether personally agreeing with the "elitist" or with the "pluralist" perspective, is challenging you to confront our arguments and to deal directly with some troubling questions about democracy in America.

It is far easier to teach "the nuts and bolts" of American government — the constitutional powers of the president, Congress, and courts; the functions of parties and interest groups; the key cases decided by the Supreme Court; and so on — than to tackle the question, How democratic is American society? It is easier to teach the "facts" of American government than to search for their explanations. While this book does not ignore such facts, its primary purpose is to interpret them — to provide an understanding of *why* American government works *as it does*.

Pluralism portrays the American political process as competition, bargaining, and compromise among a multitude of interest groups vying for the rewards distributed by the political system. Any individual seeking any portion of such rewards can effectively gain them only by joining (or organizing) such a group. Moreover, pluralists argue, most individuals are members of more than one kind of organized group. Thus the multiplicity of such groups and the overlap of their memberships are believed to be insurance against the eventual emergence of any one group as a dominant elite.

While pluralists highly value individual dignity, they nevertheless accept giant concentrations of power as inevitable in a modern, industrial, urban society. Realizing that the unorganized individual is no match for giant corporate bureaucracy, pluralists hope that countervailing centers of power will balance each other and thereby protect individuals from abuse. It is by organized groups and coalitions of groups (parties) that individuals gain access to the political system and ensure that government is held responsible. The essential value becomes participation in, and competition among, organized groups. Pluralism contends that the American system is open and accessible to the extent that any interest held by a significant portion of the populace can find expression through one or more groups.

Elitist theory, on the other hand, contends that all organizations tend to be governed by a small minority of their membership and that the backgrounds and values of the leaders across all groups tend to be similar — so similar, in fact, that they constitute an American sociopolitical elite. The members of this elite determine the society's values and control its resources. They are bound as much — if not more — by their elite identities as they are by their specific group attachments. Thus instead of constituting, as pluralists see them, a balance of power system within American society, organized interest groups are seen by elitists as platforms of power from which the elite effectively governs the nation. These leaders are more accommodating than competitive toward each other. They share a basic consensus about preserving the system essentially as it is, and they are not really held accountable by the members of their groups. Members have little or nothing to say about policy decisions. In fact, leaders influence followers far more than followers influence leaders. Each of these assertions conflicts with pluralist beliefs.

A generation or more of Americans have been educated in the pluralist tradition. We do not claim that they have been educated poorly (if for no other reason than that we are among them); nor do we argue that pluralism is either "wrong" or "dead," for clearly it contains much of value and commands many perceptive adherents. In short, this book was not undertaken to "attack the pluralists." Our primary concern is to make available to students and teachers of political science an introductory analysis of American politics that is not based on pluralist theory.

The Irony of Democracy explains American political life by means of an elitist theory of democracy. In organizing historical and social science evidence from the American political system, we have sacrificed some breadth of coverage to present a coherent exposition of the elitist theory. An encyclopedic presentation of the "facts" of American government must be sought elsewhere. Nor do we present a "balanced," or theoretically eclectic, view of American politics. Students can find democratic-pluralist interpretations of American politics everywhere.

The Irony of Democracy is not necessarily "antiestablishment." This book challenges the prevailing pluralistic view of democracy in America, but it neither condemns nor endorses American political life. America's governance by a small, homogeneous elite may be interpreted favorably or unfavorably according to one's personal values. Each reader is individually free to decide whether the political system described in these pages ought to be preserved, reformed, or restructured.

PRACTICE

1. Why did the author believe that it was necessary to write this preface?

2. What two essential terms are defined in this article?
   a. Which term is the traditional definition?
   b. Which term is the author's substitute?

3. Locate the places in the article where the definitions of these terms first appear.

4. Why did the author expand on the definition of the first term? Where is the expansion located?

5. Why did the author expand on the definition of the second term? Where is the expansion located?

In college you will more than likely be asked to write definitions expressing your personal bias. In order for that bias to be an informed one, however, you, as an emerging scholar, must use the perspective of the discipline you are studying and the information you have acquired in that field. This chapter offers you practice in doing that.

WRITING

The Extended Definition

Imagine a sociology professor giving his class this briefly-worded assignment:

Define "social control."

Would the following one-sentence definition from a sociology text be adequate?

Social control is the process of applying sanctions to obtain social conformity.

At first reading, this definition may raise images of control mainly by law enforcement agencies. This would be an inaccurate impression of what sociologists mean here. The definition also contains within it other terms that may need to be explained; for example, "social conformity" raises such questions as:

Who determines the standards of social conformity?

Are they always the same for all members of society?

Other questions may arise:

Why do most societies demand some level of social conformity?

At what stages of an individual's development are social controls imposed?

What kinds of sanctions are applied to assure social controls?

Are some more effective than others?

Can you think of other questions that the one-sentence definition raises? Below is an extended definition of social control from the same text.

Social Control

Social control is the process of applying sanctions to obtain conformity. Conformity to social norms is generally explained in terms of two social control processes. *Internal controls* cause members of society themselves to want to conform to the norms of society. *External controls* are pressures or sanctions that are applied to members by others. The two types of control tend to operate simultaneously.

   *Internal controls are those that exist inside individuals. They include a wide range of factors: positive self-image, self-control, ego strength, high frustration tolerance, and a sense of social responsibility, among others. These theories explained how we internalize norms, learn the expectations of others, and develop a desire to conform to them. Some types of deviance, such as criminality and mental illness, are widely believed to be caused by inadequate socialization, especially in early childhood.

   Most social control is directly related to a person's social self — our definitions of who we are in relation to the society we live in. Internal motivations to conformity result not from a fear of being caught or fear of punishment but because people have been socialized to see themselves in a certain way and to believe that stealing, cheating, murder, and certain other behaviors are wrong. In a study of deterrents to shoplifting, for example, Kraut (1976) concluded as follows: "People's definitions of themselves and of deviant behavior seem to act as internal constraints on shoplifting. When respondents explained why they hadn't stolen the last time they bought an item in a store, the two most important reasons they gave were their own honesty and their belief that shoplifting was unacceptable behavior."

   Our feelings about right and wrong are sometimes referred to as our conscience. The saying "Let your conscience be your guide" assumes that you have internalized certain notions about deviant and nondeviant behavior. For most people, the conscience develops as a direct result of socialization experiences in early childhood and later in one's life. Social institutions such as the family and religion are significant in internalizing social norms. Once social norms are internalized, deviations produce feelings of guilt, remorse, or conflict. The relatively high prevalence of conformity in comparison to deviance is due largely to internal controls.

   *External controls are those that come from outside an individual. They can be either informal or formal. *Informal external controls* involve peers, friends, parents, or the other people one associates with regularly. These persons or groups apply pressure to encourage individuals to obey the rules and conform to social expectations. The same techniques can be used to encourage conformity to deviant norms. In the shoplifting study just mentioned, Kraut (1976) found that external constraints are also very important and that informal sanctions are a stronger deterrent than formal sanctions. Shoplifting was strongly correlated with the subjects' perception of their friends' involvement in and approval of shoplifting. In other words, subjects whose friends shoplifted or approved of it were more apt to shoplift than subjects whose friends disapproved of it, which suggests that friends have a powerful influence on the acceptance or rejection of deviant behavior.

Informal social controls have been found to be the major cause of the low rates of alcoholism found among Jews. Glassner and Berg (1980) found that American Jews avoid alcohol problems through four protective social processes: (1) they associate alcohol abuse with non-Jews; (2) they learn moderate drinking norms, practices, and symbolism during childhood through religious and secular rituals; (3) they form adult relationships primarily with other moderate drinkers; and (4) they use a repertoire of techniques to avoid excessive drinking under social pressure. These techniques included reprimands by the spouse, developing reputations as nondrinkers by making jokes, avoiding many drinking situations, and finding rationalizations for not drinking. Alcoholism is a common form of deviance, but the low rate of alcoholism among Jews indicates that informal social controls can exert a powerful influence in controlling it.

Formal external controls, the systems created by society specifically to control deviance, are probably the least influential. Courts, police officers, and prisons are formal external controls. Unlike internal controls and informal external controls, formal controls are supposed to be impersonal and just. In actuality, however, the legal system tends to favor certain groups of people, as conflict theory suggests. Even in prisons, guards tend to overlook rule violations by certain prisoners and enforce rules with others. The discretionary power of police officers, prosecutors, judges, and other officials in arresting, prosecuting, and convicting people is often used arbitrarily. It may be highly dependent on factors other than deviance per se. Age, race, sex, social status, prior deviations, and other factors have all been shown to affect the nature and outcome of formal control mechanisms.

If we analyze the way this passage is developed, we can see that the first paragraph is devoted essentially to one-sentence definitions of terms. The first sentence provides the overall definition of social control and then, by breaking down the concept into sub-categories, the authors present one-sentence definitions of internal and external controls. The rest of the passage takes each of these sub-categories in turn and further elaborates upon them. Look at the two sentences marked by asterisks. Why did the authors use a variant of the one-sentence definitions given in the first paragraph as topic sentences?

Notice, too, that in the paragraphs devoted to external controls the authors further subdivide the concept by discussing two types of external controls, informal and formal.

Throughout the passage, examples are used to illustrate the definitions. Note in particular that to illustrate how both internal and external controls operate, the authors refer to the same study by another sociologist about deterrents to shoplifting. Why?

An entire paragraph is devoted to a discussion of the low rates of alcoholism among Jews and the way informal external controls tend to make Jews moderate drinkers. By providing this extended example, the authors have clarified the definition, made an abstract idea vivid and concrete, and increased our understanding of the concept. Might they have been equally successful if they had used several short examples to illustrate the definition? Using examples, whether a series of brief ones or one or two extended ones, is one of the more common techniques for explaining a definition.

In the section on formal external controls in the last paragraph, the first sentence not only provides a definition, "the systems created by society specifically to control deviance," it also makes a judgment about their overall ineffectiveness. Is this claim supported?

The paragraph also states that although these formal controls are meant to be "impersonal and just," they in reality tend to "favor certain groups of people." The paragraph thus represents a bias on the part of the authors. Do you think that this is an "informed" bias? Does it have a place in this introductory sociology text? Have the authors supplied enough substantiated detail to support their view?

Despite the bias indicated in the last paragraph, is the overall definition of social control sufficiently clear and extensive to communicate the idea to an audience of college freshmen?

Let us analyze another definition of a term as sociologists use it, the term *social role*. A one-sentence definition is "the collection of activities regularly performed by the occupant of a specific social position." For an audience of students in an advanced-level sociology course, this definition might suffice in that it would serve as a reminder of concepts covered previously. If the idea were being presented for the first time in an introductory course, however, it would be hopelessly confusing to students. Moreover, if your sociology instructor asked you to discuss the nature of social roles (a definition topic) on an essay examination, the one-sentence response would be inadequate because it would fail to reveal your understanding of the idea. The following excerpt from a sociology text gives a fuller explanation.

The Nature of Social Roles

Most of us understand *social roles* in a general way to mean the "parts" people play in society — like actors' roles in a drama. We learn a number of roles — for instance, those of student, teacher, wife, husband, police officer, comic, plumber, medical technician, lover, town drunk (or skid-row wino, depending on location). That's simple enough, but by leaving it at that, we run the risk of confusing roles with the people who play them. We observed this confusion among Richard Nixon and some of his supporters during the Watergate affair. President Nixon, the individual, was accused of misconduct by substantial segments of the press, the Congress, and the American public. Nixon and his supporters, however, repeatedly protested that those who attacked this particular president were, in fact, attacking *the presidency itself*. In other words: they claimed that the *role*, not the *individual*, was being threatened. His accusers, however, did not attack the presidency of pre-Nixon days, and they left the office unchallenged after his resignation, even though the charges against him proved essentially correct. Nixon the individual resigned that office — he had not performed the role according to its norms. That role is defined in the Constitution, and this, not the actions of a particular individual, is the basis for its existence.

A role cannot rest on the fortunes of a single individual because it is rooted in the social structure. We can easily miss this fact in casual observation because we only see roles in the form of the people playing them. But a role is not a person; rather it is a collection of activities regularly performed by the occupant of a specific social position (like that of president).

PRACTICE

After reading the model definition just above, answer the following questions.

1. What example did the author use to develop his explanation?

2. Why do you think he used one example?

3. Can you think of any other examples he might have used?

4. Where in the excerpt is the formal definition of the term? What was the advantage of this placement?

5. Does the article answer all your pertinent questions? What new questions occur to you?

Definitions, no matter how extensive, will probably not touch upon all the questions that might be raised about the term being defined; they should, however, make the overall idea clear to the specific audiences for which they are intended. Writers should focus on what they believe are the sources of people's difficulties in understanding the concept. Although the first passage on social controls broke down a single complex idea into several more manageable components (sub-categories), the second passage on social roles used a dramatic example to explain the difficult distinction between a role and the person performing it. Neither definition was totally *comprehensive*, but both managed to make *comprehensible* to their audience of beginning students in the field some premises upon which the discipline of sociology is based.

A Student at Work: The Role of Men in the Year 2000

One sociology instructor, as part of a unit on roles, asked her students if they could, out of their general knowledge, define the role of men in the year 2000. After a lively discussion, they attempted a formal definition. Since the discussion had focused largely on the position of men within the family, the first part of the definition, giving the general class, was: The role of men in the year 2000 will be that of equal partners with women in family life. The particular characteristics used to complete the definition were (1) sharing economic responsibilities and (2) sharing the responsibility for fulfilling physical and emotional needs of the children. The completed definition was:

> The role of men in the year 2000 will be that of equal partners with women in family life, sharing both economic responsibilities and the physical and emotional needs of the children.

The professor then asked why this definition was insufficient, why it would fail to satisfy the curiosity of anyone concerned with the problem. In the discussion, several students pointed out that the definition by itself lacked an explanation for the change in men's role, lacked an explanation of the phrase "sharing economic responsibilities," and was not detailed enough in describing how the "physical and emotional needs" would be allotted.

The logical step, then, was for the instructor to give the following assignment:

> Write an essay in which you define the role of men in the year 2000.

To broaden the students' understanding of the issue and problems involved, the instructor also provided two readings.

Before looking at the readings, one student asked the following subsidiary questions. Add any you can think of.

1.   What factors are causing the change in roles?

2.   In what ways have men's economic responsibilities been diminished?

3. In what ways have women's economic contributions been increased?

4. How will child care be shared?

5. What happens when role changes occur?

6. _____

7. _____

Below are the two readings.

Role Change

Sometimes we may be required to create totally new roles or to change the norms that govern old ones. This is called *role making*. Role making can occur for various reasons. New roles are sometimes created in response to unexpected or emergency situations. For example, increased delinquency in city schools, which was more than teachers could possibly handle, created the need for a new position, that of nonteaching assistant (NTA), whose sole job is discipline. Changes in technology have also spurred the development of new roles (such as computer programmer) and the revision of older ones. Thus when Henry Ford rearranged his Ford plant workers onto an assembly line, where each laborer worked on only part of the product, he not only made automobile production more efficient in his factory, but he revolutionized the role of worker throughout the world economic system.

Like role taking, role making begins in an awkward way, with our being consciously aware of our odd place and of our different ways of acting. Eventually, the new position or new interpretation will probably be recognized and accepted by other members of the role set, and we will become familiar with playing it.

Role making can signify a change for the better, but it can also be a strain because people are expected to abandon or modify roles that may have been central to their self-identity. Modern society, in particular, requires that its members be able to adapt to new roles with some frequency. In recent years, for instance, Americans have had to make substantial changes in the way they play some of their most important roles. The current controversy about sex roles is perhaps the most apparent example, but there have been others. Fathers are told to spend more time with their children, mothers less time than traditionally prescribed, and new guides to childrearing contradict the Dr. Spock gospel that guided a generation of parents.

The burden of adjusting to potential or actual loss of role has perhaps been most widespread in the economic sphere. In recent years, as many businesses have reorganized, many workers' positions have been eliminated — either through automation or because of "modifications in work methods [which] break down or regroup old craft lines . . . into altered, or even new, occupations" (National Center for Productivity and Quality of Working Life 1977, p. 8). Many labor unions have noticed this trend and have begun demanding provisions in their contracts to guarantee retraining for workers whose jobs are eliminated. Not so long ago, people could reasonably expect to perform the same economic role throughout their lives. Now, flexibility is necessary in case economic roles have to be changed.

The Future of American Sex Roles

Social necessity has always been a prime agent for change. During both world wars, for example, American women suddenly became capable of performing work they were thought unsuited for a year or two earlier: they "manned" the nation's defense plants. In the past most religions emphasized the procreative role of both men and women. After all, life was precarious, and many children did not survive infancy. Except for priests and other celibates, family and sex roles were interdependent. The moral/religious formula read: female = potential wife and mother; male = potential husband and father. However, the threatening possibility of standing room only on this planet and the easy availability of reliable birth-control devices have diminished the importance and desirability of reproduction. Procreation is no longer an imperative and while sexual relations are still necessary for conception (although artificial insemination can now be used), the reverse is less and less true; conception is no longer the typical outcome of sexual relations.

Other changes are also apparent. Women are breaking into occupations that used to be labeled "men only" (such as the priesthood), and men are entering areas once dominated by women (such as nursing and teaching in elementary schools). New attitudes toward sex and innovative family styles are also chipping away at the traditional roles. Of late we have seen men winning paternity leaves and alimony suits and numerous changes in the laws concerning adoption and in people's attitudes about divorce.

Both to those who applaud them and to those who deplore them, these changing styles and attitudes are symbolized by the equal rights amendment, better known as the ERA, a piece of legislation first written in 1923 and finally approved by the House in 1971 and by the Senate a year later. The ERA, which would be the Twenty-seventh Amendment to the Constitution, states that "Equality of rights under the law shall not be denied or abridged by the United States or by any state on account of sex." As of July 1977, thirty-five state legislatures of the thirty-eight needed for the amendment's passage had ratified the ERA. However, three of those thirty-five — Tennessee, Nebraska, and Idaho — followed their decision to ratify with a decision to rescind their ratification (a move that, some said, the U.S. Constitution did not permit). Indeed, even before the amendment's fate was decided, the ERA had already served to highlight the profound ambivalences, uncertainties, and misunderstandings that surround the issue of sexual equality in the United States. But despite its political future, ERA has changed American culture. As Martha Weinman Lear wrote in 1976, at the height of the ERA controversy, "Today, even people who call themselves antifeminist insist upon equal pay for equal work. It has passed into the national consciousness as a basic principle, not of feminism — as it clearly was (in the early 1960s) — but of pure justice" (*The New York Times*, April 11, 1976, p. 120).

Today sexual stereotypes and traditional attitudes coexist alongside the new, emerging patterns. Whether the old beliefs will change even more profoundly in the near future, or whether we will stand still for a while to evaluate recent changes, will reflect the capacity and desire of our society to change some of its most fundamental values.

But what are the far-reaching consequences of the changes in sex roles that have been occurring in recent decades? The gains of women have reached into every aspect of life: new laws and regulations govern pay, promotions, and job qualifications, as well as marital property and divorce. Even the mass media have altered their messages somewhat so that women in television serials now play other roles besides those of homemaker and mother. The other side of this new awareness in society is resistance to it. In general, earnings of women continue to be far lower than those of men, and the highest ranks of business and politics, despite the token admission of a few women, are still virtually all-male preserves. The traditional stereotypes of women as mothers and wives first, and of men as worker-breadwinners, persist. For many women, this means they must graft new responsibilities onto the old, becoming not more equal, only more tired.

The following are the steps that one student took as he planned and wrote his essay.

After the student had finished the readings, he first had to find out how he felt about the issue. Did he think that the role change would in fact occur? Doing a brief focused freewriting revealed that he did indeed believe that the work men and women do was changing rapidly so that by the year 2000 the distinctions between their work would be less clear.

The next step was to see if he had the material to support his position. What parts of the problem should he consider? What kinds of information should he supply? What examples could he use? He decided to do a few minutes of listing — enumerating all the ideas on the topic that came to mind. His list, containing ideas from the readings and from his own experience, is printed below:

> different jobs — women lawyers, male nurses — women want to work outside home — college educated — who cooks — men can as well, better — great chefs — housecleaning — no reason why men can't play with children, my dad always did even before — men won't have to be so competitive on jobs — crying child, only mother can comfort? Not true —

dirty diapers, ugh — take child to doctor?, lose time at work, but can take turns — 19th century men the strong support, women dependent, soft

Looking at the list and at his freewriting, the student decided that he had enough ideas to support the opinion that the role of men would change in the next fifteen years. He did have a sense that he could investigate the matter still further, but decided that since he had enough to write a competent essay, further investigation was unnecessary.

The next step was to find some sort of grouping or classification system that could be used and to create a thesis. The one-sentence definition that had been created in class might be used, but he wanted to write his own. Looking at the list, he saw that some of the items dealt with economic factors, others dealt with child care, while still others considered problems with running the house. His first tentative breakdown was:

economic   emotional and nurturing

He created the following tentative thesis statement and notes on the organization of his paper.

In the year 2000, the role of men will be more as partners in family life; economic and emotional and nurturing functions will be shared.

1. Economic — women as main providers, educated working wives, less need for men to succeed

2. Emotional and nurturing — cook, clean, men able to care for children

The organizational notes represented an important step, but the student still had to decide how he would present his ideas. He first thought of writing the essay about himself. He rejected that idea, however, because he had given no thought to the way he would feel about his role in the year 2000. Instead, he decided to write in general terms using generalized examples of situations that might occur.

His idea for the introduction came from the note in the list about the nineteenth century. Setting up the contrast between the Victorian role and the developing one could be interesting to read and would highlight the point he was going to make. When he started writing his first draft, he was still unsure about how he would conclude it, but by the time he got to the end, he remembered all the problems raised in the article on role change and used some of them to round off his paper.

After several drafts, his final essay looked like this:

Men in the Year 2000

Sex roles in the United States are in a period of transition. The Victorian era had a very clear set of expected behaviors that defined the position of the ideal man in his family. The man was the one who was the economic provider, necessarily competitive in order to give his family the best life possible. He was the strong, reliant one on whom the women and children depended, carefully concealing his own emotions so that his family could count on his rational judgment. As a result of these responsibilities, he appeared at all times to be contained and controlled. Since World War II, that definition has come increasingly under attack as women have sought to expand their own opportunities. Today women are found working side by side with men, holding jobs with equal responsibility and often with equal pay. At the same time, with the rising divorce rate and the increasing prevalence of fatherless homes, women have had to learn to cope with problems and act as the source of strength for their children. By the year 2000, the ideal of the man will have undergone a significant change. He will become more of a partner in family life by sharing the economic responsibilities and also sharing the emotional and nurturing functions.

By the year 2000, man's role as the main economic provider will be changed. Women have already assumed an important part of this function, to such an extent that the most recent statistics show that 49% of women over 16 are presently employed. Such a trend will clearly continue, and men are beginning to expect that women will help them by sharing the burdens of economic support. In some cases the woman may even become the dominant wage earner, especially if she has a career in business or one of the professions. Even though men will still dominate the professions and managerial positions, the tremendous pressure on men to be competitive and to succeed will have diminished.

Relieved of the pressure of having his worth measured in terms of his economic achievement, the American man will be able to develop aspects of his personality which have presently been inhibited or given only minimal attention. His normal emotional responses will no longer have to be curbed; rather he can be as responsive and as sensitive as he wishes. Such a change will not only be desirable, but it will, in fact, be necessary. If his wife and the mother of the family is actively involved in a career, there will be many instances in which the husband and father will have to take over the tasks of reassuring a frightened child, comforting a sick one, or soothing the feelings of an angry one. And, of course, if the wife is delayed at her office, the husband may well be in charge of preparing meals and cleaning up afterwards.

The difference between the ideal definition and the actual functioning of men is, of course, very wide now and will continue to be in the future. There will continue to be households where the man is the breadwinner and the woman stays home to cook, clean and raise the children. And there will be households where the woman is the sole economic support while the man manages the home. But for the most part, the definition of man's role by the year 2000 will include a lessened responsibility as economic provider and a larger role in the nurturing and emotional support of children.

This essay is certainly adequate in that it creates a workable definition of a potential role and provides evidence for such a prediction through convincing analysis of present conditions and a series of illustrations to support the claims of the thesis. The student looked up the current statistics of female employment and listed a number of ways in which a husband might assume nurturing functions. There is even a measure of humor in the last sentence of the third paragraph.

Despite these good points, the essay seems somewhat superficial. Even though the author is careful to indicate in the conclusion that there is a difference between the ideal definitions he is providing and the reality that may exist in the year 2000, there is no reason given in the body of the paper for this disparity. What emerges, therefore, is an unintended impression that by the year 2000 many men will have no difficulty adjusting to their new role. Perhaps the writer, in planning his essay and in creating his subsidiary questions, had not yet investigated the disparity between the ideal and the real, or failed to see the implications of the reading on role change that mentions "the burden of adjusting to potential or actual loss of role," or had not delved into his personal responses to such a change. After all, he is a college student in the 1980s and will more than likely be a wage earner in the year 2000. How will he feel, for example, if his wife should earn more than he does? if his wife has a more prestigious career? if he has to take care of the children after a long day's work? Would the training provided by his parents, his school, his peers, and the media prepare him to accept these changes easily? If he had included some of these considerations (and some others as well), his essay of definition, adequate as it is, would probably be more thoughtful.

Below is a reworking of the first section about the changing economic responsibilities of men in the year 2000. As you read it, think of the ways it differs from the original.

By the year 2000, man's role as the main economic provider will probably be considerably changed. Women have already assumed an important part of this function, to such an extent that the most recent statistics show that 40% of women over 16 are presently employed. Such a trend will clearly continue, and men are beginning to expect that women will help them by sharing the burdens of economic support. In some cases the woman may even become the dominant wage earner, especially if she has a career in business or in one of the professions.

Intellectually, I think, this is all for the best. After all, much of the differences between the behavior of men and women can be traced to the social environments in which they function. There was never a question of whether my grandmother should earn money although she did maintain a garden which supplied most of the vegetables. And often, I'm told, my grandfather would have sleepless nights worrying about layoffs at the plant or what to do if there was a strike. On the other hand, my mother having gone to college became an elementary school teacher and supported my father through law school, but once the children arrived she stopped working full time and devoted her energies to bringing us up. She is a very capable women and I often wonder how far she would have gone professionally if the society she lived in sanctioned mothers' working to their full capacity. Although she did economically contribute to the household by substitute teaching, the money she made was essentially for luxuries, like vacations. My father still assumes the major economic burden, and has become a workaholic desiring as he does to shine among his peers. His ulcer is a sign of the toll all this takes.

The young woman I am seeing and hope to marry plans to be a doctor and feels very strongly about continuing her career even after we have children. I agree that she should, but I often have second thoughts. I want to get a Ph.D. in history and teach in a university. Certainly it will be nice to be able to depend on the higher earnings of my wife, and a lot of pressure will be removed, but won't I feel somewhat lessened by assuming a secondary economic role? After all, my father, ulcers and all, is quite successful, and I do admire his achievements. I think I will be able to adjust to this potential reality, but not without considerable difficulty. If my situation is typical, I do think men will be less anxious in the year 2000 about their responsibility to provide, their need to compete, and their desire to succeed, but the remnants of the traditional definition of men as the sole economic support of their families may continue to influence their images of themselves as men.

Why did the writer choose to write three paragraphs instead of the original one? Why did the writer include several examples from his personal history? When is this sort of inclusion appropriate for a college essay?

Reread the third paragraph of the original model essay (the second section). Considering the readings, the discussion of the model, and the revision of the first body paragraph, what suggestions can you make for a revision of this section?

PRACTICE

Write an essay defining the role of women in the year 2000. You will now be creating your own definition, but the readings and the model essay might help you to develop this definition into a complete and thoughtful essay.

PRACTICE

With the permission of your instructor, you might want to write an essay of definition about another issue. In this case, you can select from the anthology (see Part 3 of this book) an article that interests you and write your essay on one of the definition questions provided there.

Combining Definition with Other Patterns of Questioning

Although many of your instructors will frequently ask you to write essays that focus on defining key terms, you will also most likely be asked to supply extended definitions as part of essays in answer to other kinds of controlling questions. In a psychology course, for example, you might be asked, "How is Carl Jung's theory of the collective unconscious an outgrowth of the work of Sigmund Freud on the unconscious?" This is essentially a comparison/contrast question in which you would indicate how one psychoanalytic theory emerges from another; you would probably first tell the ways that the two theories are similar, and then you would explain how they diverge. In order to do so, you would be wise to define what Jung meant by the "collective unconscious" and present definitions to explain Freud's ideas on the "unconscious." In essence, then, your answer would be a comparison and contrast of two sets of definitions.

In a history course on the labor movement in the United States you might be given this assignment: "Trace the growth of labor unions in the United States, focusing particularly on what led to the merger of trade unions (the American Federation of Labor) with industrial unions (the Congress of Industrial Organizations) to form the AFL/CIO in 1955." In this assignment you would have to define trade and industrial unions at some length before you could discuss the process by which they ultimately merged.

Knowing ways to integrate definitions into your essays is a useful skill. This section of the chapter will give you an opportunity to use definitions in the service of other forms of essays. To do so, we will further explore some additional concepts in sociology and trace the evolution of one student's essay in which definition was a key factor.

In order to help students see the connection between their personal values and the values of society, a sociology instructor made the following comments before asking his class to read a passage in their text.

> The various roles people play in our society and the general acceptance of these ways of behaving are due to *socialization*, the process through which we gain our sense of ourselves and learn the values of our society. This general acceptance, as you saw in our discussion of social control, is due less to the existence of threatening and punishing forces than to the fact that we have learned to control ourselves. But how and when did that learning take place? And how does that learning affect the values we hold as adults?
>
> Sociologists have examined this phenomenon and have isolated certain key institutions which, from earliest childhood, have been sending us messages that we have gradually accepted. The reading selection I am assigning summarizes the four major agencies of socialization in our society.

PRACTICE

Creating questions before you begin reading will guide your thinking. These are a few you might use; can you think of others?

1. What are the four agencies the writer will discuss?

2. Does he use examples to support his position? What ones does he give?

3. Can you think of any examples from your own life that are similar?

4. _____

5. _____

This is the passage the instructor asked his students to read for the next class session:

AGENCIES OF SOCIALIZATION

Socialization is found in all interaction, but the most influential interaction occurs in particular groups, which are referred to as *agencies of socialization*. Among the most important are the family, the schools, peer groups, and the mass media.

The Family

The family is the primary agency of socialization. It is the first socializing influence encountered by most children and affects them for the rest of their lives. A family that teaches children that their goals should be subjugated to those of the family teaches them a set of norms that will remain even after they learn elsewhere that their primary responsibility is to take care of themselves.

Families also give children their geographical location, as easterners or westerners, for example, and their urban or rural background. In addition, the family determines the child's social class, race, religious background, and ethnic group. Each of these factors can have a profound influence on children. They may learn to speak a particular dialect, to prefer certain foods, and to pursue certain types of leisure activities. The child's knowledge of appropriate work habits may be determined by the type of job the parents have. Some studies show that working-class parents emphasize obedience, which is necessary in working-class occupations, whereas middle-class parents emphasize exploration and experimentation, which develop the problem-solving skills necessary in middle-class jobs (Kohn, 1959).

Families also teach children values they will hold throughout life. They frequently adopt their parents' attitudes not only about work but also about the importance of education, patriotism, and religion. Even a child's sense of worth is determined, at least in part, by the child's parents.

One of the values instilled in the children of most American families concerns the worth of the unique individual. We are taught that we possess a set of talents, personality characteristics, strengths, and weaknesses peculiar to ourselves and that we are responsible for developing these traits. This view of the value of the individual is not found in all cultures, however. Many people who emigrated from southern Europe, for example, believe that one's primary responsibility is to the family, not to oneself. The son of a European farm family is expected to be loyal and obedient to the family, to work for its benefit, and someday to take over the farm, but in our culture, staying with the family is often regarded as a sign of weakness or lack of ambition. Both beliefs are just two of the many values that people learn primarily through the family.

The Schools

In some societies, socialization takes place almost entirely within the family, but in highly technical societies children are also socialized by the educational system. Schools in the United States teach more than reading, writing, arithmetic, and other basic skills. They also teach students to develop themselves, to test their achievements through competition, to discipline themselves, to cooperate with others, and to obey rules, all of which are necessary if a youngster is to achieve success in a society dominated by large organizations.

Schools teach sets of expectations about the work children will do when they mature. They begin by learning about the work roles of community helpers such as firefighters and doctors, and later they learn about occupations more formally. They take aptitude tests to discover their unique talents, and, with the help of guidance counselors, they set occupational goals.

Schools also teach citizenship in countless ways: they encourage children to take pride in their communities; to feel patriotic about their nation; to learn about the country's geography, history, and national holidays; to study government, explain the role of good citizens, urge their parents to vote and to pledge allegiance to the flag; to become informed about community and school leaders; and to respect school property.

It has been suggested that learning at home is on a personal, emotional level, whereas learning at school is basically intellectual. Evidence suggests, however, that learning at school also involves personal factors, such as a student's self-image and the teacher's perceptions of the student. In other words, students form a looking-glass self and perform in response to teacher expectations. In one experimental study in the classroom (Rosenthal and Jacobson, 1968), students were randomly divided into two groups. The teacher was told that those in the first group were bright and that those in the second group were not. The students believed to be highly intelligent by the teacher performed significantly better than those believed to be less intelligent. The teacher's expectations of the students influenced their performance.

Most school administrators and teachers reinforce our cultural emphasis on the uniqueness of individuals. Thus they try to identify the unique talents of students through comparison and competition with other students and then attempt to develop these talents so that they will become useful to the larger society.

Peer Groups

Young people spend considerable time in school, and their *peer group*, people their own age, is an important influence on their socialization. Peer group socialization has been increasing in this century because young people have been attending school for a longer period. They no longer drop out at fourteen — most finish high school and about half go on to college.

Young people today also spend more time with one another outside of school. Unlike young people of earlier decades, few are isolated on farms. Most live in cities or suburbs, and, increasingly, they have access to automobiles so they can spend time together away from their families. Teenagers' most intimate relationships are often those they have with their peers, and they influence one another greatly. In fact, some young people create their own unique subcultures. Coleman (1974), who refers to these simply as cultures, lists as examples the cultures of athletic groups in high school, the college campus culture, the drug culture, motorcycle cults, the culture of surfers, and religious cultures. In part because teenagers are often unsure of themselves, the sense of belonging that they get from their subculture may be extremely important to them, although the pressures to conform to group expectations can be quite severe.

The Mass Media

The American *mass media* — television, popular magazines, and other forms of communication intended for a large audience — are paid for by advertising. When dress, music, and other aspects of the youth subculture became big business, advertisers began directing their programs to young people. Radio stations brought new kinds of music not only to youth but also to a wider audience, thus socializing other age groups to the music of the youth subculture. The media also advertised youthful styles of dress. Young people who rejected fashion in favor of blue jeans, however, were later socialized to buy high fashion blue jeans and other garments with designer names. This type of interaction occurs constantly in the socialization process. As young people develop their unique talents, they influence society. Society in turn socializes them to use their unique talents in ways consistent with the values and norms of the society.

Young people are socialized to pursue activities apart from the family. As a result, the movie industry can rely on them to attend movies in theaters and also at school. Because youngsters have learned to be active and competitive, they prefer movies that show action and competition, and movies in turn reinforce this aspect of socialization. Violent horror films have been particularly popular over the last few years. Movies with themes of violent revenge also draw a lot of young people to the theaters, and actors like Clint Eastwood and Charles Bronson have made their reputations by acting in this type of movie.

Television also uses violent programming to appeal to teenagers, but teenagers do not stay home as much as younger children, so they watch less television. Younger children, who watch an average of almost four hours of television a day, urge their parents to buy the cereals, snack foods, and toys they see advertised. The shows children watch reinforce the norms of the larger society.

Programs about the family teach children what an American family should be like. Children may develop their conception of the family from what they see on television rather than from the home they live in. They learn, for example, that families include both a mother and a father, even though one-fifth of children have only one parent, and that families live in houses, even though many children live in apartments. Some mothers on television often stay home and wear aprons, while many others work and wear jeans rather than aprons. We do not know precisely how much children learn about the ideal family from television, but these family shows are undoubtedly influential.

The effects of television violence cannot be measured accurately because children also learn competition and violence from other sources, and television both socializes and reinforces the socialization they receive elsewhere. Studies do indicate, however, that children can learn new techniques for being violent from watching a movie in an experimental situation, as shown in the classic experiment done by Bandura (1965). A group of children who watched a movie in which a doll was treated aggressively in unusual ways later imitated these unusual aggressive behaviors. Although the mass media are not the only teachers of violence in America, viewers can certainly learn about violence from the media just as they learn it from other experiences.

The next day in his lecture the instructor made the following comments in introducing a writing assignment:

> From the reading, you saw that much of the substance of our values — our definitions of good and evil, successful and unsuccessful, desirable and undesirable — are built up from the bits and pieces of knowledge we have gained from our parents and siblings, our teachers and schoolmates, ministers, rabbis or priests, our friends, and from the programs we watch on TV. This is not to say, however, that all people in any given society will all hold exactly the same views. The various agencies of socialization will influence each person in slightly different ways, and, more important, each person has the ability to resist those ideas that he or she finds incompatible with the sense of self. Nevertheless, our definitions of those words with which we express our values — courage, honor, loyalty, for example — will reflect the influence of the agencies of socialization. An awareness of how this influence affects our definitions can help us understand the relationship between our personal selves and the social world to which we belong. I want you, therefore, to write an essay in which you define what you personally mean by "loyalty to one's country" and explore how external influences helped you create that definition.

Here is the question:

> How have the various agencies of socialization played a part in the formation of your definition of "loyalty to one's country?"

In order to write an essay in response to this topic, one student went through the following steps:

Collecting the Data.   Using subsidiary questions was the student's first step. The questioning technique provided a series of questions that helped the student find ideas and information that might be used in the essay. Some of the questions were:

> What actions do I consider to be examples of loyalty?

What would I use for the general class of the definition?

What would the social characteristics be?

What actions would contrast with loyalty?

Then the student engaged in focused freewriting. The freewriting was done to help him search his memory for experiences from family, school, friends, and TV that might have to do with loyalty to one's country. As such, it was primarily an information-gathering technique. It was also useful, however, in helping the student recognize some personal biases. Even though this assignment was essentially a personal essay, the student realized that the instructor would want him to write about the subject with some degree of detachment.

Weighing the Evidence.   By creating a chart using the four agencies of socialization as the main categories, the student listed all the ideas he had developed from questioning and freewriting. Part of his chart looked like this:

Family	School	Peer Group	Media
Respect for flag	Saluting flag	Wearing protest buttons	War heroes on TV
My family against war	Celebration of holidays	Nader's Raiders	Old war movies opposed to individual protest
_____	National anthem	_____	
_____	Blind obedience	_____	_____

Organizing the Essay.   The student realized that the categories from the chart might be used as sections of the essay. He preferred, however, to organize his essay by formulating a thesis statement that would provide his basic definition of loyalty to one's country, and to use each one of the special characteristics as a category for a section in the body of the paper. The influence of each of the agencies of socialization would then be presented under these headings. Below are the notations he made to guide himself:

Family	School	Peer Group	Media
Respect for flag	Saluting flag	Wearing protest buttons	War heroes on TV
My family against war	Celebration of holidays	Nader's Raiders	Old war movies opposed to individual protest
	National anthem		
	Blind obedience		

Parts of my definition:

1st characteristic:

symbols to be honored — (really should)

Flag
buildings
T.V show war heroes

2nd characteristic:

responses to official policies — (you can still be loyal even though you protest!!)
anti -war
blind obedience (?)
Nader's Raiders

The thesis statement he developed from these notes was:

Loyalty to one's country as I define it requires that people honor its symbols, even though it also permits them to disobey particular policies.

The final essay, produced after several revisions based both on self-evaluation and feedback from friends, is printed below:

Loyalty to One's Country

The question of defining what is meant by loyalty to one's country is a more complex one than it appears to be on the surface. Of course, most citizens have a sense of love for their homeland, but the precise definition of how far they should go in supporting any particular governmental action is less clear. There will always be situations when concerned citizens object to supporting specific policies, and citizens have a right to express their feelings and to protest against those policies. But the right to protest does not include the right to be disrespectful. Loyalty to one's country, as I define it, requires that people honor its symbols, even though it also permits them to disobey particular policies.

Loyalty to one's country is most easily expressed by showing respect for its symbols. People should remain quiet when the national anthem is being played or join in the singing. They should be careful in the treatment of the flag and avoid using it in ways that would soil it or denigrate its importance. Many of those who opposed the American involvement in the Vietnam War expressed their disapproval by ripping up the flag or burning it. Regardless of their feelings about the war, such treatment of the flag is inexcusable. The flag stands for more than just this one policy; it stands for the nation as a whole, the good things as well as the bad. By treating the flag with such disrespect, these protesters suggested that everything about the country was bad. The very fact that they were able to perform such actions without being subjected to long-term jail sentences proves how much freedom existed — and was symbolized by the flag they were destroying.

My belief in this view has its source in my family, in my schooling, and in part from my watching TV. When I was a child, my parents frequently discussed the war protesters while we had dinner. Although they themselves were against the war, they often expressed their sense of outrage at the way the protesters were behaving. Their dismay at the sense that the good qualities of this nation were being lost sight of in the protesters' actions made a great impact on me. This impact was reinforced by my school experiences which emphasized the triumphs of our country, in celebrations for presidents' birthdays, Thanksgiving Day, which included parading the flag and singing "The Star Spangled Banner" at our weekly assemblies. Even though the television news often showed the protesters in a favorable light, the many old movies I saw about World War II gave me a sense of responsibility to my country.

Although respecting our country is a basic requirement, it does not mean that blind obedience is required. Many of the policies of our government are opposed by various citizen groups — environmentalists seek to preserve our natural resources, and civil rights groups want to expand the government's enforcement of equal opportunities. These people have the right to present their positions and to argue with those in power in order to persuade them to change their policies. Some day our nation may again face the problem of going into a war that some citizens regard as unnecessary and unjust, and, here too, they have a right to express their feelings. In doing so, they are giving an even more fundamental support of the United States by living up to its basic principles of equality and justice, rather than accepting a current policy.

It was my family that encouraged me to believe in this way through their discussions about the Vietnam War. My friends, many of whom are actively involved in consumer rights groups, also are responsible for this feeling. But my teachers in school did not seem to support this position, for they were always saying that we had to be obedient even when we did not know the reason for an action. The old war movies on TV also seemed to oppose the principle of obedience by constantly showing soldiers following orders regardless of their own feelings.

Loyalty to one's country can be, for some people, an automatic response, and perhaps my sense of respect for the symbols of my country, particularly the flag, reflects some of that reflex quality derived from my elementary school experience, my family, and from television. But my sense that loyalty does not mean blind obedience to all my country's actions suggests that other factors, particularly those learned from my friends and my family, have made me less extreme. The combination of these two qualities has given me, I feel, a moderate position that allows me to judge my country's actions in a rational way.

Take time to analyze this student's essay on the basis of the following questions:

1. What is the thesis statement? Is it a suitable one for a definition?

2. What determined the categories for the body paragraphs?

3. What example does the writer give to support his position?

4. In addition to restating the thesis, what else does the conclusion do?

PRACTICE

Select one of the following concepts:

1. courage

2. responsibility for the less fortunate

3. honesty

4. thrift

Write an essay in which you: either give a definition of the term, and/or explain how the four agencies of socialization have influenced your decision.

The steps that the writer of the model essay followed may serve as a guide in planning and writing your essay. Be sure to allow for revision through self-evaluation and feedback from others. The guidelines for judging an essay, given in Part 1, Chapter 2, can help in evaluating your essay.

PRACTICE

Choose an article that interests you in the Anthology (Part 3 of this book) and write an essay answering one of the definition questions.

4

Questions of Comparison/Contrast

THINKING

Why Compare? Why Contrast?

The making of comparisons (finding similarities) and contrasts (seeing differences) is almost automatic in all our thoughts and actions. We say to ourselves, "There's a really good picture at the mall, and I can do my term paper for economics tomorrow," unaware of the steps that our thinking has taken. Behind the decision lies the question, "Should I go to the movies tonight or do my homework?" and behind that question lie a number of prior comparisons and contrasts, such as comparing the movies with other forms of entertainment like bowling or a concert, or contrasting recreational use of time with writing a term paper for economics. Because we are so accustomed to this form of thinking, we rarely articulate it to ourselves. Instead, we note one or two factors and arrive at a conclusion that will support our action.

While such a cursory review of the facts is sufficient for most of our daily activities, the kinds of thinking you will be called upon to do in college require that you give more explicit consideration to all the facts involved on both sides of a comparison or contrast. This way of investigating is particularly valuable for understanding new experiences. When we are faced with a situation that seems totally unfamiliar, we try to find something within our previous experience to which we can relate it. When you entered college for the first time, you probably compared and contrasted your first days there with your first days in high school. In the same way, scholars use their knowledge of the past as a way of understanding the present. Even the space scientists who analyzed the satellites orbiting Saturn compared them to the moon and its orbiting of the earth in order to begin to comprehend what they were looking at.

Although comparisons and contrasts frequently lead to a conclusion, your college instructors will often ask you simply to discuss similarities or differences in a piece of writing. What they hope is that by closely examining what makes one item (for example, a rose, a painting by a seventeenth-century Dutch master, an economic system like communism) *similar to and/or different from another item* (for example, an iris, a painting by a twentieth-century Dutch artist, an economic system like capitalism), you will observe each more closely and so gain a more comprehensive understanding of both. In addition, by fully examining the comparisons and contrasts between items in an isolated thinking and writing activity, you will have a sounder basis for intelligent judgment. When Voltaire, an eighteenth-century French philosopher, wrote, "Nations that do not learn from history are doomed to repeat it," he was in essence urging nations and their citizens to compare and contrast present circumstances with past circumstances and, by avoiding repetition of catastrophic error, to change the course of the future. Your instructors ask you to write comparison/contrast papers in order to point out connections between events and processes that you might not have considered, and also so that you will see likenesses when only differences are immediately apparent. This chapter, therefore, will deal with paragraphs and essays for which the question of comparison/contrast is the controlling one.

Making a Systematic Comparison

Although the language of comparison/contrast is familiar to you and reflects a thinking process that is carried on constantly on an intuitive level, the thinking and writing you will do in college require a much more conscious and systematic application of this approach. For this kind of thinking and writing you need to collect all the evidence, weigh your evidence, and organize your material into a coherent plan.

There are a few principles that you need to keep in mind as you think and write in this form. First, the items to be compared or contrasted need to have some relationship to each other. You can, in economics for example, compare communism with capitalism, but you cannot compare the *man*, Karl Marx, with the *theory* of laissez-faire. Students sometimes appear to be making this mistake because they word their statements imprecisely. The statement, "There are significant differences between the theory of laissez-faire and Karl Marx," would state the issue correctly only if it were reworded to read, "There are significant differences between Adam Smith's theory of laissez-faire and Karl Marx's theory of communism."

A far more important problem is deciding which points in a comparison and/or contrast should be considered significant and which should be regarded as superficial. In many instances, your instructors will give assignments that require you to discuss either similarities or differences, one or the other. In those cases, you will have to decide which of a number of points of likeness or difference plays the most important role, and even to focus your attention on similarities where you had considered only differences. A biology instructor, after having lectured extensively on the similarities between plant and animal life, might ask an exam question that calls upon you to discuss their differences. Questions of this sort are given in order to sharpen your powers of observation and analysis.

Frequently, however, you are given assignments in which the decision on whether to discuss similarities or differences is left to you. In these cases, you need to take care not to jump to a conclusion based on your feelings alone. You will rarely find in your college work that there are only similarities or only differences to be considered, or that only one feature can be thought significant. Rather, you need to make sure that you have considered all the information, both the obvious and the less-apparent, to see if the sheer weight of the evidence supports your intuitive response. Occasionally the evidence appears to be overwhelmingly in favor of one position or the other. You might, for instance, have ten items of difference and only two of similarity. Even so, you cannot rely on the numbers alone. You need to examine the relative importance of the particular aspects of the subjects that are being compared or contrasted. You may, with the guidance of your instructors, your textbooks, and your personal feelings, decide that the two items of similarity are significant and that the ten items of difference are only superficial. These decisions, which are often the most challenging to make, are also often the most rewarding. Once arrived at, they need to be justified either through reference to experts in the field or to the evidence you have found.

The final point to consider before you actually begin your writing is the finding of groupings that will be most useful in presenting your material. Often these groupings will become apparent as you collect your information; sometimes you will begin to see them as you weigh the evidence; frequently you will have to try out a number of different groupings or categories before you are ready to begin writing your first draft. Here, you need to be concerned that the main points of your argument are given proper emphasis rather than being buried.

A thorough application of the techniques for planning and writing a comparison/contrast paper will be presented in the main part of this chapter by using material from art history. First, however, a brief review of the steps will be presented using an example from sociology, in which the data are collected from direct observation, and another from government, in which the information is collected from readings.

Using Direct Observation

An instructor in an introductory sociology class was interested in showing his students how sociologists go about collecting data and analyzing them. He asked his students to visit two kindergartens and compare or contrast them as forces for socialization. He had arranged two one-hour visits, one to a university-related school and the other to a city school. He asked the students to focus their attention on one controlling question: How is respect for the rights of others taught?

Since a one-hour visit is short and the notes need to be as complete as possible, the students prepared to observe the classes and to collect their data by asking themselves preliminary subsidiary questions about what they wanted to record. One student's questions included the following:

1. What is the room like — size, equipment, furniture?

2. What is the attitude of the teachers? How many? Age? Sex?

3. How many students are there? Sex?

4. What kinds of activities go on?

Can you add to the list?

5. _____

6. _____

7. _____

After the visit, one student's notes looked like this:

School #1

Old school, high ceilings, big windows, drab gray walls, but lots of posters, children's artwork.

Doll corner, blocks, 3 easels, chairs around 2 tables, book corner, chairs set in semi-circle.

School #2

New building, floor to ceiling windows, yellow walls cheerful, own outdoor play area.

Dolls, blocks, books, 3 double easels, chairs set around 2 tables, gym pads for indoor play.

continued

School #1

1 teacher — middle-aged, sense of control, 1 assistant, young, follows teacher's orders.

Schedule — students arrive, hang coats in cubbies on back wall, teacher supervising, insists clothes be hung neatly. Students sit in semi-circle, those who want to play, gently but firmly told to go to chairs. When bell rings, teacher greets, makes comment on weather, leads children in song. Children listen to story of Little Engine, class discussion, quiet, students who interrupt are told to wait, class acts out engine and train with teachers at beginning and end, 2 students jostle others, told to sit down.

Free play, but children assigned; 4 paintings, 2 books, 5 blocks, 5 dolls, 6 at table with crayons and paper, teachers give instructions at cleanup time, all toys replaced neatly.

Students: 24 — 14 girls, 10 boys.

School #2

1 teacher, 20's, smiles a lot. 1 assistant, young, works on her own.

Schedule — students arrive, go to play areas after hanging up clothes, student who dropped coat on floor spoken to quietly, goes with teacher to hang it up; one table set up with scissors, paper, paste, another set with crayons and paper, 6 children at each, 3 paint at easel, 1 at doll corner, teachers assist as needed, 20 minutes later cleanup, not supervised, but checked after. Teacher gets group together by making a chain of students as she goes around room singing "get together" song.

Group sits on gym mats, sings alphabet song, listens to story discussion, much talk, many interruptions, teacher puts finger to lip to get quiet, doesn't always work. One child continues to interrupt, assistant takes aside.

Students: 18 — 10 girls, 8 boys.

Although there seemed to be plenty of information, the student realized that she might have some data in her head that were not in her notes. She asked some subsidiary questions in order to search her memory:

What impression did I get of the two rooms? Why?

How did teachers react when there was a disruption?

What is my impression of the students?

She added to her lists the information that she remembered — that Class Number 1 was very neat, but the teachers seemed annoyed at disruption, and the children were mostly very quiet; Class Number 2 seemed somewhat messy, but the teachers were almost always cheerful, and the children seemed more exuberant than in Class Number 1.

Since the student was writing a comparison/contrast paper, she decided to weigh the evidence by listing all the similarities and all the differences together. This way she could see if the actual number could decide the issue for her. Grouping for comparison and contrast, she made the following chart and filled in the information.

Similarities	Differences	
	Class 1	Class 2
Both have 1 teacher, 1 asst.		
	Old	New
_____	_____	_____
_____	_____	_____
_____		

Fill in the chart, using the student's notes.

Having isolated the similarities and differences, the student could begin to assess her data. In order to do so, she asked herself some subsidiary questions:

1. How many similarities are there? How many differences?

2. Which ones are important in proving that respect for others is being taught?

3. What types of activity would show respect?

4. What is meant by respect?

5. Why did the children in Class Number 2 seem cheerful?

Answering some of these questions, the student saw a sharp contrast between the two classes. There were more differences than similarities — Class Number 1 seemed much more concerned with explicitly teaching neatness, politeness, and order, while Class Number 2 seemed to rely on indirect methods.

Although the material appeared to be assembled in a usable form, the student felt uneasy; her own feelings about the two classrooms did not jibe with the evidence. Taking a few minutes, she wrote out her thoughts by doing a focused freewriting.

Well, they sure seemed different, those two schools. That one in the city, in that old building, boy were they strict, those kids really toed the mark — not unkind, though, just very firm — nice orderly feel to things. But the one at the university, wow, there didn't seem to be any of that, real free and easy . . . but things moved pretty smoothly there too. no one was running around wild. In the city school you knew there were rules and what they were . . . and I was going to say there were none at the university school but that's not really true, it's just that they weren't so obvious about it all. Hey, maybe they weren't so different after all, maybe it was just the way they went about getting order, teaching respect for the rights of others . . . hey . . .

Because the student had gone through the listing process, the questioning and thinking, and the freewriting, she realized that her original thesis of contrast (that the two classes were different) was less precise and less significant than a thesis that would stress their similarity: Both classes were teaching respect, but they had differing approaches. Only after she had gone through these steps was she able to plan her organization.

The student's problem then was to decide how to organize her findings by deciding upon her categories. Her first inclination, the most natural one, was to tell the story of each of the visits, first describing one class, its teachers, and its pupils, and telling each event as it happened, and then doing the same for the second class. Luckily, she thought for a few minutes before writing and realized that in approaching her writing in that way her main point would be lost in the narrative. She rearranged her material so that the key issue, respect for the rights of others, was most apparent.

She perceived three groupings that might work. Table 4.1 shows her categories, with some of the information she intended to use.

This format, she realized, would work for both classes, and she could either write completely about one class and then the other, or cover both classes under each of the three points. She was finally ready to write her first draft.

TABLE 4.1 Teaching Respect for Rights of Others

Physical Setting	Activities	Teacher/Pupil Interaction
Both cheerful	#1 by accenting neatness	#1 close supervision protects rights of others
Both plenty of play equipment	#2 by emphasizing respect for individual	#2 less supervision, sense of responsibility

Drawing on Reading

An instructor in an introductory government course was analyzing the factors involved in the writing of the Constitution of the United States. As part of his approach, he distributed brief biographical sketches of two participants in the Constitutional Convention of 1787. He asked the students to analyze the sketches to see which controlling question would be more appropriate, one of comparison or one of contrast.

Even before reading the biographical sketches, the students asked a few preliminary subsidiary questions:

What factors are most important in determining how a person thinks — age, career, economic and social status, particular region?

What parts of the Constitution were easily agreed on?

Why would these two men have agreed to them?

What parts of the Constitution were sources of controversy?

Where would these two men have disagreed?

What other questions could you ask?

The two biographical sketches follow.

Edmund Randolph

Edmund Randolph (1753–1813), born at "Tazewell Hall," a plantation near Williamsburg, Virginia, was a member of a family that for generations had been prominent members of the colony, and as a boy he met the most distinguished men of the time at his family's home. Educated at the College of William and Mary in Maryland, as were his father and grandfather before him, he then undertook the study of law. When the break between the American colonies and the British government seemed imminent, his father fled to England, but young Randolph remained to serve as an aide to Washington during the grim first years of the Revolution. He became a prominent political leader in Virginia, serving as attorney general, representative to the Continental Congress, and governor of the new state. Displeased with the way the nation was faring under the Articles of Confederation, he supported the idea of a new constitution and served as a delegate at the convention. There he presented the famous Virginia Plan on which much of the final version of the Constitution was based and was active in committee work; however, he refused to sign the final version when it was presented, although he did later become an active supporter of the Constitution.

Robert Morris

Robert Morris (1734–1806), often called the financier of the American Revolution, was born in Liverpool, England, and emigrated to the American colonies at the age of 13. After a brief, scanty education in Philadelphia, he joined a firm of shipping merchants where his diligence and energy won him a partnership by the time he was 20. As an importer-exporter, shipowner and banker, he soon accumulated great wealth and respect as a leading merchant in the Colonies.

Although he had refused to sign the Declaration of Independence because he felt it was premature, Morris had been active in the resistance to British rule since 1765, and once the Revolution started, he became its major financial support. Through his efforts, munitions, naval armaments, and all necessary supplies for the army were obtained. Although the funds to pay for this equipment were supposed to be supplied by the various colonies, the failure of those governments to honor their commitments forced him to use his own credit to underwrite loans from France and the Netherlands and even to pay for the supplies out of his own pocket. During the darkest days of the Revolution, his actions provided Washington with the moral support and material assistance without which the army could not have survived. Serving as a member of the Pennsylvania delegation to the Continental Congress and as virtual financial dictator, he was often accused of using his position to increase his own wealth, but he was also responsible for eliminating waste in various departments of the government.

He felt that the national government under the Articles of Confederation was not functioning properly, and he was elected as a delegate to the Constitutional Convention. While he took little part in the debate or in committee work, his close association with many of the leaders suggests that his ideas would be given consideration.

PRACTICE

The usual steps of focused freewriting and listing were followed. Below is a list of all information given about Robert Morris; fill in the second column with information about Edmund Randolph.

Morris	*Randolph*
Immigrant	_____
Uneducated	_____
Self-made man	_____
Merchant, shipowner	_____
Leading citizen	_____
Against Declaration of Independence, active in resistance against British, financial support of Revolution, not in army	_____ _____

Aware that states would not voluntarily give money to federal government	_____ _____
Elected official	_____
Friend of leaders	_____
Unhappy with government under Articles of Confederation	_____

While the similarities and differences between these two men are accentuated by listing the information side by side, it is helpful to indicate them more strongly. This can be done by underlining with different colored pencils, such as using red for similarities and green for differences. Or, to group for comparison/contrast, new lists can be constructed, one giving comparable facts and another giving contrasts.

PRACTICE

Create two comparison/contrast lists in the space below:

Similarities		*Differences*	
_____	*Morris*		*Randolph*
_____	_____		_____
_____	_____		_____
_____	_____		_____
_____	_____		_____
_____	_____		_____

Additional questions will guide thinking. Some subsidiary questions are:

What would be Randolph's definition of a good national government? Morris's?

How would the fact that Randolph was a Southerner influence his opinion? Morris's as a Northerner?

In what areas would their wealth and prestige be most significant?

If your class took the time to discuss this topic, you might have been surprised to discover that there is a difference of opinion about whether these two men were alike or different. In fact, this issue of the differences and similarities among the Founding Fathers is still being debated by historians and political scientists. The reason for such disagreement comes down to a matter of judgment, the decision being based on which factors should be considered *significant* and which can be regarded as *superficial*. One scholar might point out that Robert Morris, as an uneducated immigrant, a self-made businessman from a Northern state, would hold values and opinions significantly different from those of a slave-owning, landholding, Southern aristocrat like Edmund Randolph, and that the differences between these two men at the Constitutional Convention could cause conflicts that would later divide the country during the Civil War. Another scholar, however, might point out that both Morris and Randolph were men of wealth and prestige, men accustomed to roles of leadership and dedicated to the new nation. Seen from this point of view, the similarities between them could be stressed to explain why so much of the Constitution was agreed to without controversy, and the differences could be shown to be superficial.

Two possible organizational patterns might be used on this material, as shown in the outline below.

<table>
<tr><td>

I. Randolph
  A. Wealth
  B. Region
  C. _____
  D. _____
II. Morris
  A. Wealth
  B. Region
  C. _____
  D. _____

</td><td>

I. Wealth
  A. Randolph
  B. Morris
II. Region
  A. Randolph
  B. Morris
III. _____
  A. Randolph
  B. Morris
IV. _____
  A. Randolph
  B. Morris

</td></tr>
</table>

The rest of this chapter will elaborate upon strategies for writing paragraphs and essays of comparison/contrast using an introductory-level course in art history as the illustration. It should be understood that the suggestions made here are generally applicable whenever you are asked to answer a controlling question of comparison/contrast, no matter what the academic discipline. Your instructor for this course may ask you to write the essays assigned in this chapter or may provide you with alternatives. The anthology at the end of this book includes comparison/contrast essay assignments in other subjects.

WRITING

Art history is a particularly good discipline for studying the process of composing essays of comparison and contrast. Works of art from different periods or different places can highlight some universal aspects of the human condition, and at the same time they can reveal significant cultural differences. The same two pictures can, for example, provide the basis for essays of both comparison and of contrast.

A College Class at Work: Bruegel's "Peasant Wedding" and Renoir's "Le Moulin de la Galette" — Comparison and Contrast

The two reproductions, Bruegel's "Peasant Wedding" and Renoir's "Le Moulin de la Galette," a scene of an outdoor dance, shown in black and white in Figures 4.1 and 4.2 were used by one instructor of art history in the opening weeks of the semester in order to help the students develop their perceptions before she undertook the traditional chronological survey. She asked the students to examine the two paintings carefully and to note both the similarities and the differences. Readings and an essay assignment would be provided later. Study Bruegel's "Peasant Wedding" in Figure 4.1 and Renoir's "Le Moulin de la Galette" ("The Outdoor Dance") in Figure 4.2.

Collecting the Data

The two practices below help in examining these works of art.

Figure 4.1   *Pieter Bruegel, "Peasant Wedding"*

Figure 4.2   *Pierre Auguste Renoir, "Le Moulin de la Galette" ("The Outdoor Dance")*

PRACTICE

First list all the observable features of each painting.

Bruegel	*Renoir*
Gathering of people	People at a dance
Indoors	People dressed up
Eating and drinking	_____
_____	_____
_____	_____
_____	_____
_____	_____
_____	

PRACTICE

Some questions that might help in analyzing the paintings are listed below. Add any others you think might help.

1. What key figures do I see at first glance? Later?

2. What is the general mood of the two paintings?

3. Does my eye move through the painting? In what direction?

4. _____

5. _____

6. _____

7. _____

Grouping Data

One student listed all the observable data and created subsidiary questions. He was able not only to gather additional information, but also to organize this information in usable groups. The completed list for this student looks like this:

	Bruegel	*Renior*
What strikes me immediately about these two paintings?	1. A gathering of people 2. Indoors 3. People eating and drinking 4. Sometime in the past 5. Waiters serving food 6. Musicians playing 7. Everyone painted in clear outline	1. A dance 2. People dressed up 3. Color and shapes seem to blend into each other 4. Not modern times 5. Outdoors 6. People flirting with each other
Which figures in the paintings are visually prominent?	8. Waiter carrying trays 9. Boy slurping drink 10. Man pouring drink 11. Woman in front of hanging basket 12. Man reaching for food	7. Woman at table in striped dress 8. Woman in dark dress with arm around woman at table 9. Couple on the left — she in white dress; he, tall with hat at cocky angle 10. Man at table with back to viewer engaged in conversation with the two women
What is the general mood of each painting? What in the paintings makes me feel this way?	13. Mood doesn't seem consistent with weddings as I know them 14. No one is smiling except the lady under the basket 15. Hardly any conversation except for the two men at the table who seem to be making arrangements	11. Mood is gay, carefree 12. People are touching each other 13. People seem curious about each other 14. People's faces are flushed with excitement
How does each painter direct my attention to the entire crowd scene?	16. My eyes move from the lower right hand corner to the upper left hand corner because of the prominent table	15. My eyes move from lower right to upper left

Weighing the Evidence

The subsidiary questions and the listing of the data guarantee that none of the data will be neglected. The information is, however, still too disorganized to provide a basis for judging the similarities and differences. To solve that problem the students can create a chart that will make the comparisons and contrasts more apparent.

Using the list provided on page 158, or one that you have created yourself, pair as many items of similarities or differences in the following chart.

Similarities	Differences	
	Bruegel	Renoir
1. _____		
2. _____	1. _____	_____
3. _____	2. _____	_____
4. _____	3. _____	_____
5. _____	4. _____	_____

Here is the chart that one student created:

Similarities	Differences	
	Bruegel	Renoir
1. Both paintings are of large gatherings, festive occasions.	1. little conversation	a lot of talking
2. Music is being played in both.	2. few people are smiling	many people smiling
3. People are drinking in both.	3. mood not festive	mood is gay carefree
4. Viewer's eyes move from lower right to upper left.	4. clear outlines	color and shapes blend
5. Both paintings are not of modern times		

Although the lists and the chart will make the specific items of comparison and contrast readily apparent, they will not indicate the relative significance of the items. To make those decisions, a student can engage in focused freewriting, which often uncovers intuitive responses that can be tested by further analysis.

PRACTICE

Take ten minutes or so and write out your thoughts on the similarities or differences in the preceding chart that you think are crucial.

Analysis. Another approach to freewriting, or a follow-up to it, is a step-by-step analysis of each item in the chart. Below is a record of one student's analysis, but before reading it look at your own lists, charts, and freewriting to see if you can isolate the key elements in your data. Along with the student's list of comparisons and contrasts are our comments on them.

Similarities

1. Both paintings are of large gatherings, festive occasions.

   This comparison is obvious. Once it is mentioned there would be little more to say. As a matter of fact, this similarity immediately underscores the mood difference between these two paintings.

2. Music is being played in both.

3. People are drinking in both.

   These similarities are details that support the obvious similarity mentioned in Point Number 1. Even though the list might be expanded, it would lead to no significant comparison beyond the obvious one that these two paintings are of festive occasions.

4. Viewers' eyes move from lower right to upper left.

   This seems like a significant comparison because different artists use similar techniques to focus the viewers' attention. Certainly there is much that could be discussed here, but would a student at the start of the basic course be expected to discuss such a technical matter? More than likely, the instructor would reserve such a discussion for a more advanced course. In any case, there are other aspects of the artists' technique that are mentioned in the differences *column. Perhaps these are more significant.*

5. Both paintings are not of modern times.

   Certainly this is so. This similarity would, however, lead to a discussion of ways in which the clothing and the setting differ from twentieth-century styles. In addition, this similarity leads to another contrast: the fact that these two paintings are depictions of different time periods. Beginning students know too little about the history of painting to discuss this issue.

Differences

1. Little conversation vs. a lot of talking.

   This contrast emphasizes a significant mood difference between the paintings. If people are not engaged in conversation at a party, it would appear that they are not really having a good time. Conversely, if they are engaged in conversation, they are at least displaying superficial indications of enjoyment. Are there other contrasting items on this list that would indicate this mood difference?

2. Few people smiling vs. many people smiling.

   Smiles at a party indicate pleasure; serious expressions might indicate the reverse.

3. Mood is not festive vs. mood is gay, carefree.

   This difference seems to be a conclusion that can be derived from many of the other contrasts. It seems to be an underlying contrast *between these two paintings, and therefore provides a wealth of material for further elaboration.*

4. Everything painted in clear outline vs. colors and shapes blend.

   The fact that each of the figures in the Bruegel are distinct helps to emphasize people's separation from each other. Once again, however, it is important to question whether this difference emerges because of the dissimilarity in mood or because these two paintings were rendered at different times.

Once the instructor believed that the students had thought through the problem for themselves, she gave the following assignment:

Even though Bruegel's "A Peasant Wedding" and Renoir's painting of an outdoor dance, "La Moulin de la Galette," both depict festive occasions, do they present two different views of life? Explain.

Since the student had already decided that the contrast was more significant, he was able to move directly to the creation of a tentative thesis. Often, however, an instructor's assignment will reflect a thinking pattern different from your own. When this occurs you will have to go back over your data and review them from this new perspective.

The student whose analysis was recorded on pages 160–161 created the following tentative thesis:

> Even though both these paintings are of festive occasions, they represent two different views of life — Bruegel's dismal attitude and Renoir's cheerful approach.

Because she wanted the class to develop their own skills of observation and analysis rather than rely on what others had said, the class instructor assigned no reading until the students had formulated their own responses. Even if your instructor assigns the reading at the same time as the writing assignment, you will learn more and enjoy the course more thoroughly if you try to think through the problem before you do the reading. Some subsidiary questions that will make the reading more valuable are the following:

1.   What details do the writers mention that I ignored?

2.   What background information do they supply that might add to my understanding of these two paintings?

3.   What concepts in art history do they mention? How do these concepts help in understanding the paintings?

4.   In what ways do the writers' analyses of the paintings support or contradict my decision?

Below are the readings the instructor assigned.

Bruegel
(Reading One)

Pictures in which the painters deliberately cultivated a certain branch or kind of subject, particularly scenes from daily life, later became known as 'genre pictures' (*genre* being the French word for branch or kind).
The greatest of the Flemish sixteenth-century masters of 'genre' was Pieter Bruegel the Elder (1525?–69). We know little of his life except that he had been to Italy, like so many northern artists of his time, and that he lived and worked in Antwerp and Brussels, where he painted most of his pictures in the fifteen-sixties.
The 'kind' of painting on which Bruegel concentrated was scenes from

peasant life. He painted peasants merrymaking, feasting and working, and so people have come to think of him as one of the Flemish peasants. This is a common mistake which we are apt to make about artists. We are often inclined to confuse their work with their person.

It was the custom at that time to regard the country yokel as a figure of fun. I do not think that either Shakespeare or Bruegel accepted this custom out of snobbery, but in rustic life human nature was less disguised and covered up with a veneer of artificiality and convention. Thus, when they wanted to show up the folly of humankind, playwrights and artists often took low life as their subjects.

One of the most perfect of Bruegel's human comedies is his famous picture of a country wedding. Like most pictures, it loses a great deal in reproduction: all details become much smaller, and we must therefore look at it with double care. The reproduction may give at least an idea of its gay colours. The feast takes place in a barn, with straw stacked up high in the background. The bride sits in front of a piece of blue cloth, with a kind of crown suspended overhead. She sits quietly, with folded hands and a grin of utter contentment on her stupid face. The old man in the chair and the woman beside her are probably her parents, while the man farther back, who is so busy gobbling his food with his spoon, may be the bridegroom. Most of the people at the table concentrate on eating and drinking, and we notice this is only the beginning. In the left hand corner a man pours out beer — a good number of empty jugs are still in the basket — while two men with white aprons are carrying ten more platefuls of pie or porridge on an improvised tray. One of the guests passes the plates to the table. But much more is going on. There is the crowd in the background trying to get in; there are the musicians, one of them with a pathetic, forlorn and hungry look in his eyes, as he watches the food being carried past; there are the two outsiders at the corner of the table, the friar and the magistrate, engrossed in their own conversation; and there is the child in the foreground, who has got hold of a plate, and a feathered cap much too large for its little head, and who is completely absorbed in licking the delicious food — a picture of innocent greed. But what is even more admirable than all this wealth of anecdote, wit and observation, is the way in which Bruegel has organized his picture so that it does not look crowded or confusing. Tintoretto[1] himself could not have produced a more convincing picture of a crowded space than did Bruegel with his device of the table receding into the background and the movement of people starting with the crowd at the barn door, leading up to the foreground and the scene of the food carriers, and back again through the gesture of the man serving the table who leads our eyes directly to the small but central figure of the grinning bride.

---

[1] Sixteenth-century Italian painter.

Bruegel
(Reading Two)

Such an occasion where the table serves as a meeting place for a segment of the community is the wedding feast, as presented in a painting by the Flemish artist Pieter Bruegel. Though not the first, Bruegel was the most gifted genre painter of his century in depicting the daily life of the Flemish peasants. The little available biographical material indicates that he himself was not a peasant but a rather highly educated townsman, whose paintings were bought and admired by kings and many of the intellectual elite of his day. A humanist, Bruegel regarded his art as a means of recording his study of man, not in terms of ancient writers and philosophers or the coordinate system of the Church, but in the light of advanced contemporary secular theories and his own empirical experience. Bruegel's art reflects his astuteness as an observer, not critism of nor compassion for the peasantry. He saw the peasant not as the symbol of a basic natural wisdom but as an unreasoning creature who passively submitted to forces greater than himself. The peasants are always involved in some hereditary activity — the dominant note in their work, customs, and traditions. Bruegel's figures are motivated by simple, uncomplicated drives and enact their existence automatically, often with great vigor if not with great cheer. (Smiling peasants are rare in his paintings.)

Bruegel's subjects, whether Biblical or genre, share the phenomenon of recurrence, as if the artist had sought and set down certain eternal constants in life. Not content with social reportage, Bruegel brought to art a gift of lucid analysis and a genius for storytelling that elevates his *Peasant Wedding* from a prosaic event to good theater. The earth was Bruegel's stage and those upon it his characters. In this painting the set is a grain-filled barn after the harvest. An overflow of guests comes to celebrate the personal harvest of the farmer's daughter, who sits both coyly and smugly beneath a symbolic crown hung on a green cloth. The full grain stacks and the ripe bride are meaningfully associated, as are the groom and the fertility symbol of the crossed sheaves hanging before his eyes. Art historians were unable to agree on identification of the groom, but the literary historian Gilbert Highet found him in the dark-clad, intoxicated figure in the center, just to the left of the rear figure holding the door being used as a serving tray. The ill-mannered groom and his glaring parents seated opposite are wealthy townspeople, and as Highet points out, Bruegel encourages our speculations on both the wedding night and the married life of the bridal couple — though the painting's evidence makes the future quite clear.

A few of the subthemes in the nuptial drama are the friar's earnest pleas for subsidy from the obdurate landlord at the far right, who seems to enjoy the occasion less than does his dog; the longing gaze of the bagpiper at the distant food; and the contrast between the bride's brother filling a jug at the left and the little girl cleaning her plate. The activity of the former figure recalls Christ's changing of the water into wine at the Marriage of Cana. In fact, the diagonal composition of the long table and triangular grouping in the left foreground can be found in sixteenth-century paintings of the Last Supper, as was seen in the painting by Tintoretto. These objects also assist in maintaining the viewer's detachment from the action. The ample figures are hard edged in their firm outlines, so that the pile of round jugs in the basket invites an ironic comparison with the peasants who emptied them and with the piled-up figures in the doorway at the upper left who also wait to be filled.

Renoir
(Reading Three)

Scenes from the world of entertainment — dance halls, cafes, concerts, the theater — were favorite subjects for Impressionist painters. Auguste Renoir (1841–1919), another important member of the group, filled his with the *joie de vivre* of a singularly happy temperament. The flirting couples in *Le Moulin de la Galette*, under the dappled pattern of sunlight and shadow, radiate a human warmth that is utterly entrancing, even though the artist permits us no more than a fleeting glance at any of them. Our role is that of the casual stroller, who takes in this slice of life as he passes.

Renoir
(Reading Four)

"The world knew how to laugh in those days! Machinery had not absorbed all of life: you had leisure for enjoyment and no one was the worse for it." With this happy, wonderful picture before us, Renoir's reminiscence seems a pallid understatement. The canvas is so rich in attractions, so full of enchanting details, that it becomes nothing less than an affirmation of the goodness of living.

The painting celebrates the triumph of youth: the women are radiantly beautiful, the men as dashing and debonair as young blades ought to be. Renoir has become famous as a painter of the nude; but what painter has clothed the human form more entrancingly? And with unbelievable virtuosity, he has animated his figures with an amazing variety of postures and activities — bold, relaxed, eager, withdrawn, flirtatious — all of them graceful and natural.

There are bits of still-life, shimmering patterns of the light fixtures, children — like the dainty blonde creature in the lower left — tucked in here and there. One even fancies that the buzz of voices, the shuffle of feet, and the gay dance tune are part of the composition.

This is one of Renoir's largest and most ambitious compositions; yet he was not to regard it as one of his best paintings. Despite its apparent crowding and turbulence, it reveals a studied organization. The triangular foreground group is related through silhouette and color to the group at the trees; and this group, through yellow and gold-brown tones, becomes part of a vertical unit which provides stability to the right of the canvas. The other side allows easy entrance into space over a ground dappled blue and pink — Renoir's way of creating the effect of sunlight and shadow without introducing neutral dark values. By emphasizing the verticality of the dancing figures through sharp color contrasts, Renoir echoes verticality again, and repeats it playfully in the posts in the background.

These are only a few of the linear relationships; varied curves set up another series of rhythms. Rich color is contrasted with plain, and each is developed into an independent sub-theme: reds, yellows, blues, greens, blacks. Light flickers across the scene, resting here and there for compositional emphasis. Subject and method have been completely integrated into a unity which is one of the great achievements in the art of painting.

The student whose notes are in the chart on page 159 underlined key ideas as he read along. Here are his general notes, some copied verbatim from the texts, some paraphrased (notice that this student circled words to look up in the dictionary).

Bruegel	*Renoir*
Scenes from peasant life "genre" painter	Flirting couples radiate warmth filled with "joie de vivre"
Country yokel as a figure of fun	They dance with "happy abandon"
People concentrate on eating and drinking	Dress painted with loose strokes
Figures drawn in firm outlines	Renoir enchanted by festive beauty
Bride: Utter contentment on her "stupid" face	Used his friends as models
Diagonal composition of the long table and triangular grouping in the left foreground	Renoir is an "impressionist"
Art historians unable to agree on identification of groom	Spirit of the place seems to exude from it
Peasants seen as unreasoning creatures	

These readings seem to corroborate the tentative thesis the student arrived at previously. He highlighted certain terms for vocabulary study and/ or for use in the paper. The readings certainly validate the impressions that Bruegel emphasized the separation of people, Renoir the attraction between people.

Organizing the Essay

Once the general point of view has been established, the next step is to consider how the tentative thesis can be developed. In order to do so, you have to break down the information into workable units. Look back at your notes and see what categories would work for you. (Refer to Chapter 2 on Organizing.)

The student described above began by grouping ideas. In regard to Bruegel's painting, for example:

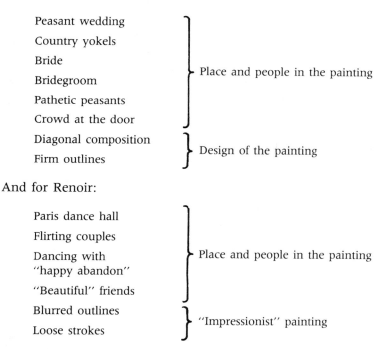

Peasant wedding
Country yokels
Bride
Bridegroom   } Place and people in the painting
Pathetic peasants
Crowd at the door

Diagonal composition } Design of the painting
Firm outlines

And for Renoir:

Paris dance hall
Flirting couples
Dancing with
"happy abandon"   } Place and people in the painting
"Beautiful" friends

Blurred outlines   } "Impressionist" painting
Loose strokes

From the groupings, the student saw two major similar categories for each painting: (1) what is going on, and (2) how the scenes are painted. He decided that these two categories could conveniently be labeled *content* and *technique*.

A chart of this information might look like this.

	Bruegel	*Renoir*
Content		
Technique		

In organizing the essay, the student could read the chart either vertically or horizontally. With a vertical reading, the essay would first consider all the information about Bruegel's content and technique and then follow with a discussion of Renoir's. Using a horizontal reading, the essay would first consider both Bruegel's and Renoir's content and follow with a presentation of both their techniques.

In-class Essay.   To begin the work of writing the essay, the instructor first asked the students to write a response in class, allowing them thirty minutes to complete it.

Below are two responses to the in-class writing assignments. One is a more adequate answer than the other. Which one? Why?

Example 1

Although Bruegel's painting of a country wedding and Renoir's of an outdoor dance both depict festive occasions, they are very different in mood. In Bruegel's painting almost every figure is involved in a separate activity or private musing. For example, the person sitting at the corner of the table picking up a few pies is handing it to someone who is looking elsewhere. The bride, the woman sitting in front of the hanging on the wall, is smiling smugly to herself. The bridegroom, the first man to her right, slurping his porridge, is oblivious to everything going on around him, particularly the occasion of his own wedding. Bruegel's technique reinforces this separateness in that the outline of each figure is painted with clear definition. In contrast, Renoir's painting of an outdoor dance indicates people's engagement with each other: people are dancing together; people are talking to each other; people are even touching each other. Renoir used design to reinforce this impression of people's engagement with each other. For example, the hand of the woman coming forward ultimately melts into the bright dress of her companion. It and the blurring of the dancing figures better convey the feeling of human contact and closeness. Bruegel painted a peasant wedding to illustrate his pessimistic view of life; Renoir painted an outdoor dance to show a considerably more optimistic image of the world. Not only do the activities of the people at these two parties reveal the perspectives of their painters, but so do the techniques each one used.

Example 2

In two paintings, one by Bruegel called the "Peasant Wedding" done in 1565 and one by Renoir "The Outdoor Dance" done in 1866, the first immediate impression is that both depict very similar festive occasions. If the canvas were to come alive and you were to enter either gathering you would probably feel, "Ah, a party, what fun!" There is plenty of food (look at those pie trays and drafts of ale); there is music (see the musician at left center with a medieval instrument); there are family members and friends (see the bride under the basket surrounded by her kin and the crowd at the door itching to join the festivities). But as you imagine yourself more and more in Bruegel's crowd you sense that something is not right. The people don't seem to be involved with each other; this is not such a joyous occasion. Therefore, a close examination of both paintings shows a sharp contrast. Bruegel looks at life in a comic — somewhat cynical — way, while Renoir sees the bright side of life. This difference can be seen in both content and style. For example, almost every figure in Bruegel's painting is involved in a separate activity or private musing. Notice the person who is sitting at the corner of the table, picking up a few pies, is handing them to someone who is looking elsewhere.

(Sorry, Professor Cooper, no more time.)

In Example 1, the opening sentence affirms a basic similarity between the two paintings and suggests a more significant difference between them that is not completed until the end of the essay. In this way the writer has provided a clear topic sentence without being dull and without following a formula too closely. The discussion within the paragraph has a clear sense of organization, covering pertinent information on Bruegel first and following it with a discussion of Renoir. The examples are specific, there are enough of them, and they are relevant and clearly presented.

Example 2 starts off quite well and in fact is quite imaginative in its effort to capture the reader's attention. Too much time, however, is spent discussing the festiveness in the Bruegel painting (an aspect that the writer will eventually contradict), so that there is no time left to cover all the significant aspects of the Bruegel painting and none at all for the Renoir. Despite the excellent start, the paper fails in the task it was supposed to perform. The limitations of time impose serious restrictions on what one can include in an in-class essay, so the emphasis should be on directness and clarity.

At-home Essay.   When the same assignment is given for an essay to be written at home, very different standards are used to judge the paper. Below is a student essay based on Example 2, now expanded to fully answer the question.

Bruegel and Renoir: Two Views of Life

In two paintings, one by Bruegel called the "Peasant Wedding" done in 1565 and one by Renoir "The Dance" done in 1866, the first immediate impression is that both depict very similar occasions. If the canvas were to come alive and if you were to enter either gathering, you would probably feel, "Ah, a party, what fun!" There's plenty of food, there's music, there are friends and there are even family members in the wedding party. But as you imagine yourself more and more in Bruegel's crowd you sense that something is not right. The people don't seem to be involved with each other; this is not such a joyous occasion. On the other hand, one could imagine having a delightful time within Renoir's crowd. Therefore, a close examination of both paintings shows a sharp contrast. Bruegel looks at life in a comic — somewhat satirical — way, while Renoir conveys the possibilities of life's gaiety. A close examination of both the content and style of these paintings make this difference evident.

In "A Peasant Wedding" by Pieter Bruegel, a "genre" painter of peasant scenes, we see a very close likeness to an actual 16th century wedding feast taking place in a barn. Almost every figure is involved in a separate activity or private musing. We might first notice the two large figures in the right foreground carrying the wooden tray of food pies. The figure nearest us stops for a moment for the person sitting at the corner of the table, picking up a few pies. Notice that he is handing a pie to someone who is looking elsewhere. We imagine that the pie will spill over on the table — one hand does not know what the other is doing. It also appears that the other pie carrier is ready to move on while his working partner is not. The man at the left pouring beer and the child licking her fingers appear separated from the central scene. The friar and the magistrate, intent on their private conversation at the right edge of the painting, reinforce the impression that these various activities contrast comically with the central purpose of the occasion, the celebration of a wedding.

There is more. The musician who looks longingly at the food going around the table does not seem to be interested in making music. The figure smack in the middle of the painting, clutching the pitcher, is looking agog. His bulging eye painted with such precision catches ours. What is he looking at? Is there anything really there, or is he stupified by too much Flemish beer? The bride, the woman sitting in front of the hanging on the wall, is smiling smugly to herself, and seemingly basking in her new role as wife. We may conclude that she is well suited for the bridegroom — the first man to her right (?) — slurping his porridge, oblivious to everything going on around him, particularly the occasion of his own wedding. That self-absorption, along with everyone else's, appears to be a central theme. This wedding scene was referred to as a "human comedy" by the art historian E. H. Gombrich since everybody's preoccupation has an element of satire about it. Here, in this symbolic act of joining together, no one is "together." Not one of the major figures is embracing another; not one person touches another.

Bruegel's technique reinforces his comical-satirical vision. The outline of each figure is painted with clear definition so that we see them separately. The bride's position in the painting is almost lost because of the large figures and the general activity in the foreground. We are diverted also by certain lines of the design. The triangular lines of the large food tray pull our eyes downward and to the right, and, with equal force, the long table directs us to the open door and the crowd to the left. Eventually, though, we do espy the bride sitting under the wicker basket against a prominent hanging on the wall.

In contrast, Renoir's painting of an outdoor dance indicates people's engagement with each other: people are dancing together; people are talking to each other; people are even touching each other. Probably our eyes momentarily settle first on the woman with the bright striped dress seated on the bench in the foreground. Her companion leans over, affectionately letting her hand fall on her friend's shoulder. Both their gazes fall upon a young man, mostly in shadow. To the right are two gentlemen; the one with the straw hat seems to be staring at the woman standing and stooping over. Ah, a possible flirtatious triangle: he likes her; she likes his companion. Just above this group, around the tree, are several people listening to the dance music. Perhaps the gentleman with the hat leaning toward the woman, who herself is leaning backward against the tree, is about to introduce himself. Like the group below, there is something suggesting an attraction. We cannot help notice the several couples dancing, especially the couple in the foreground in an amorous pose. The impact of the whole painting is light romantic sweetness, the romantic sweetness of people drawn to people.

Like Bruegel, Renoir also used design to reinforce his vision, but the vision is gay and carefree. The entire scene is awash in light. The softness of light is used to infuse the scene with romance. The outlines of Renoir's figures are not as clear as Bruegel's. For example, the hand of the woman leaning forward ultimately melts into the bright dress of her companion. It and the blurring of the dancing figures better convey the feeling of human contact and closeness. In this painting, the blurred figures help us sense the field of attraction between us all.

Although both these paintings present occasions that are usually thought of as happy, only Renoir captures the gaiety of the moment while the Bruegel undercuts it with a cynical view of life. It would be interesting to imagine Renoir painting the peasant wedding scene and Bruegel painting the outdoor dance. No doubt these scenes would have come out very differently, both in feeling and style. Every artist paints on canvas his view of the world and the people in it. Even though an artist paints in the style of his times, he uses that style in unique ways. Certainly Bruegel did; certainly Renoir did.

The first single-paragraph response and the essay reflect a common basic organizational scheme: They both contain a similar key sentence, and they both divide the discussion into content and technique. Both are basically similar responses to the analysis of the pre-writing process described above. There are, however, significant differences between them.

If Example 1, the paragraph done for an in-class assignment, had been handed in as the at-home essay, it would not have received a high grade.

The number of details is too limited, the description of them is quite sketchy, and all sense of the vividness of the experience of the two paintings is lost. Although the paragraph makes the contrast broadly apparent, it fails to achieve the impact and the nuances that are expected from an at-home essay.

In the full essay, we immediately get a sense of the reason these paintings in particular were chosen to be contrasted. By accentuating the close similarity in theme — that they are both depictions of festive occasions — the writer has enabled us to ferret out significant contrasts. The extensive use of detail emphasizes the contrast of the painters' world views. The essay's concluding paragraph, then, instead of merely summarizing, expresses an interesting supposition — that is, imagining each artist painting the other's scene. The implication is clear: no matter what the subject matter, a painter's vision comes through. This notion is a natural generalization resulting from the analysis of the two paintings.

Below is another version of the body of the model essay you have just read. Approximately the same material is presented, but in a different form.

> Bruegel's painting, "A Peasant Wedding," is a scene of a peasant wedding taking place in a barn, while Renoir's painting is a scene of an outdoor dance. Although each is a crowded scene, almost every figure in Bruegel's painting is involved in a separate activity or private musing, while in Renoir's scene most figures are involved in dancing or talking with another person or group. In the wedding scene, for example, the one pie carrier nearest the foreground stops for someone while the other carrier appears to be ready to move on. The person sitting at the corner of the table picking up a pie is ready to hand another one to someone who is looking elsewhere — one hand doesn't know what the other is doing. In contrast, the woman stooping and leaning over in Renoir's dance scene lets her hand fall affectionately on her friend's shoulder. She and her friend's gazes are riveted to the young man with his back to us. Again, in the wedding scene, the man to the left pouring beer, the child licking her fingers, the friar and the magistrate intent on their private conversation at the right edge of the painting reinforce the impression that these various activities contrast comically with the central purpose of the occasion, the celebration of a wedding. On the other hand, at the outdoor dance the two gentlemen to the right are intent on the conversation, the central activity in the foreground. The one with the straw hat seems to be staring at the woman standing and stooping over. Ah, a possible flirtatious triangle: he likes her; she likes his companion. Just above this group, around the tree are several people listening to the dance music. Perhaps the gentleman with the hat leaning toward the woman, who herself is leaning backward against the tree, is about to introduce himself. Like the group below, there is something suggesting an attraction.

There is more. The self-absorption of the musician in Bruegel's painting who looks longingly at the food going around the table, the figure in the middle of the painting holding a pitcher and looking agog, the bride (the woman sitting in front of the hanging) smiling smugly to herself, and her bridegroom (the first man to her right?) slurping porridge, oblivious to everything going on around him, contrast sharply with the several couples dancing in Renoir's painting, especially the couple in the foreground bathed in light. In the wedding scene, referred to as a "human comedy" by the art historian, E. H. Gombrich, there is the symbolic act of joining together, and yet no one is "together." Not one of the major figures is embracing another; not one person touches another. In the outdoor dance, instead, the impact of the whole painting is light romantic sweetness, the romantic sweetness of people drawn to people.

Both Bruegel's and Renoir's technique reinforce their visions, the one the comical-satirical vision, the other the gay and romantic vision. The outlines of Bruegel's figures are painted with clear definition so that we can see them separately; the outlines of Renoir's figures are not as clear. For example, the hand of the woman leaning forward ultimately melts into the bright dress of her companion. It and the blurring of the dancing figures better convey the feeling of human contact and closeness. Also the entire scene is awash in light. The softness of the light is used to infuse the scene with romance. The bride's position in the wedding scene dilutes whatever meaning she might have had. She is almost lost because the viewer is diverted by the large figures and the general activity in the foreground.

What pattern of organization does this version employ? A second way to write a comparison/contrast essay is to weave back and forth from one element to the other. In this particular case, the student discusses first the content of both paintings; then he considers the technique in both paintings, touching first on Bruegel, then on Renoir, and so on. If you look back to the chart on page 167, you will see that this essay is based on a horizontal reading of the chart.

PRACTICE

Figures 4.3 and 4.4 are black-and-white reproductions of a painting, "The Third Class Carriage," by Honoré Daumier and an aquatint etching, "In the Omnibus," by Mary Cassatt, respectively. Readings about each one follows its illustration.

Answer the following controlling question: What are the major differences between Honoré Daumier's "The Third Class Carriage" and Mary Cassatt's "In the Omnibus"?

Figure 4.3 *Honore Daumier (1808–1879), "The Third-Class Carriage." Oil on canvas, 25¾ × 35½". The Metropolitan Museum of Art, Bequest of Mrs. H. O. Havemeyer, 1929, The H. O. Havemeyer Collection. All rights reserved, The Metropolitan Museum of Art.*

The answer to this question could be written either as an in-class essay or as an at-home paper. Your instructor will specify the form you are to use.

Once again, you should use some or all of the pre-writing strategies covered in the previous discussion:

- Listing all observable items from both paintings with the aid of subsidiary questions

Figure 4.4   *Mary Cassatt, "In the Omnibus"*

- Freewriting and/or rearranging the lists by pairing items of similarity and difference

- Weighing the evidence to determine which of the comparisons or contrasts are significant

- Developing a preliminary thesis

- Reading the articles to add information and to validate or modify the preliminary thesis

- Grouping significant items into categories for organizational purposes

- Writing a tentative expanded thesis

Daumier

Most famous of all Daumier's paintings is *The Third Class Carriage*, a masterpiece preserved in three copies: the first is a watercolor, in the Walters Gallery, Baltimore; the second, copied from the first, is a squared canvas (the squaring lines quite visible) three times larger than the watercolor version, in oil on canvas, in the Metropolitan Museum, New York; and the third, also a canvas, is in the Toronto Art Gallery. The Metropolitan version is the most often seen and most frequently reproduced, and, indeed, perhaps deserves priority in excellence.

One of the finest touches in Adhémar's excellent book on Daumier is his photographic reproduction of twenty different studies, made in lithograph, sketch, and painting, of travelers squeezed together in a train compartment; it is a good selection of Daumier's variations on a theme which had fascinated him ever since the early 1840's with the first extensive building and expansion of the railroad in France. Many dozens of his cartoons exploit the infinite possibilities for comedy — smoke and cinders, crowding, open and unheated carriages, noise, etc. — inevitable to train travel, and the equally enchanting variations of the visual possibilities — slanting lines of cars and railroad tracks, faces and figures in new and frightening situations. *The Third Class Carriage* (Metropolitan) is the artistic culmination, the climax, of a long experience and deep interest in the railroad.

The Third Class Carriage was a difficult subject for a composition. What, exactly, can one do with three rows of people enclosed in a box? At least when Daumier had drawn the rows of parliamentarians in *The Legislative Belly*, the rows had been curving. Now he again mastered both the technical and symbolic problems confronting him. The foreground row of figures becomes a broad pyramid. The forms are conceived in vast contours (the Michelangelo allusion is inevitable and necessary), and as Meier-Graefe noted, "It still bears the mighty thumb-mark of the sculptor." The predominant colors are brown (always a favorite with Daumier), pink-rose, and gray, with touches of green or green-blue, and the figures are enclosed with subdued tones which enhance, or evoke, the visionary aspect and power of the painting. Daumier laboriously, slowly, built up his forms, as Marceau and Rosen showed in photographic analysis, in thin glaze upon thin glaze of watercolor-like paint. The effect is not lyrical but rather is massive and sensuous.

The literary interplay of meanings in the painting is as carefully contrived, but natural, as the composition itself. The painting is at once realistic and symbolic — potently symbolic because it is so firmly grounded in actuality. The central figure of the grandmother is both an old woman and Age.

Gnarled, worn, and weary, she stares neither at her family nor out of the canvas but into herself and down the years of her long life. She broods on the mystery of iniquity and goodness — for experience of both have lined her face — with the solemn grandeur of the lonely figure of The Adams Memorial. She is monumental in the manner of Daumier's sketch of *The Republic*, but more satisfactory to us because she is more real, not created in deliberate allegory. "This is mortality, this is eternity." She takes on symbolic extensions and can, as Josephine Allen says, "take her place beside other magnificent figures of old age — The Cumean Sibyl by Michelangelo or Rembrandt's Old Woman Cutting her Nails."

The sweet-faced mother nursing her baby is the maternal image, creativity, the life-force. The boy slumped on the bench asleep is innocence and childhood. The men and the women in the background are of various ages and professions. The rhythm of man's years is as clearly, if implicitly, expressed in these figures as in the words of Jaques on the seven ages of man.

Another counterpoint makes itself felt between foreground and background. The foreground voices the theme of loneliness. These four figures are, to borrow a word from Melville, "isolatoes." The grandmother is alone with her brooding memories, death is near her; the young mother and baby are absorbed, as one unit, with physical being and animal love, which oppose the age-death of the grandmother; the sleeping boy is alone in his world of dreams. The background voices the theme of the "socialities"; men and women talk together, for the moment friends in their life-voyage, not strangers. The entire composition, seen intellectually and unaesthetically, has the purity and force of a parable with the actuality of the physical world as well. It is firmly fixed in space and time and yet transcends them.

This serious and rich painting is by the greatest of all comic artists, and there is no paradox involved. The comic vision in our time is inextricably entangled with the tragic; Daumier's comic art shades off, even in cartoons, again and again into serious, even tragic, suggestions. Now, openly, profoundly, like the later Rembrandt, Daumier gives full expression in *The Third Class Carriage* to a somber but sure affirmation of life, good and evil, wrung from the infinite ambiguities of human experience.

Mary Cassatt

Three woman artists found favour in the eyes of Degas: Berthe Morisot, Suzanne Valadon and, above all, Mary Cassatt. In the case of the two latter, he especially admired their mastery of line. He paid Suzanne Valadon a compliment which, from him, was rare indeed when he told her, "You are one of us." His admiration for Mary Cassatt's work was equally genuine, though expressed, characteristically enough, in such grudging remarks as this one: "I cannot admit that a woman draws so well."

As a painter, Mary Cassatt saw a good deal of Pissarro, Marcellin

Desboutin and Degas in particular. It was inevitable that her friendship with these men should have led her to take an interest in graphic work, though it was chiefly at the urging of Degas that she took it up. He gave her technical instruction and helped her to pull impressions of her early attempts on his private press, which he afterwards placed at her disposal for the proofing of her prints.

In 1870, on the outbreak of the Franco-Prussian War, Mary Cassatt had left Paris and returned to Philadelphia with her parents and sister. In 1872 she came back to Europe and went first to Parma. There she worked with the painter-engraver Carlo Raimondi, who taught her the techniques of printmaking; but none of her prints of this period have survived. What she learned in Parma, however, proved very useful to her when, in Paris in 1877, she met Degas and he advised her to practise etching. In 1879 he asked her to contribute a plate to his projected publication *Le Jour et la Nuit*. She applied herself to etching assiduously and joyfully, deriving great satisfaction from it; some of Degas's letters describe her at work. But she followed the master's example, even to his working habits. The graphic art of Mary Cassatt accordingly remained private and confidential during her lifetime. Her one theme was that of the mother and child. She never married and never herself experienced the joys of motherhood. To that theme, by way of compensation, she devoted her career as an artist. Not a single landscape is to be found in her work. In this, too, she was at one with Degas, who liked to vent his spleen on open-air painters: "The police ought to fire on these landscapists who set up their easels in the countryside." But of course he was silenced when one of his friends countered that outrageous remark by saying: "Then you want them to fire on Corot?" For Corot, like Ingres, was one of Degas's gods. But his admirations never prevented him from expressing his views in striking and outspoken terms, and Degas had no use for landscape; it never provided the inspiration for any of his prints, no more than it did for Manet and Mary Cassatt. In this respect, all three stand apart from the other Impressionists, whose major theme was landscape.

Mary Cassatt told her biographer Achille Segard that when Degas, who with his friend Joseph Tourny had seen and admired one of her canvases, came to her and proposed that she should exhibit with the Impressionists, she accepted with alacrity: "At last I could work in complete independence without regard to the opinion of a jury. I had already recognized who were my true masters. I admired Manet, Courbet and Degas. I hated conventional art. I began to live." The collaboration between Degas and Mary Cassatt in graphic work reached a high point in 1879 when Degas was planning his publication *Le Jour et la Nuit*. But before that he had been struck by the skill and firmness of her drawings and had urged her to take up etching: "To have a pure line in drawing, learn to draw on copper. No pardoning there." Mary Cassatt followed his advice, and in order to gain a greater command of line, she made a point of drawing from the living model directly on the copper, and thus avoid any artifice or inaccuracy. Drawing with pencil or crayon no longer satisfied her. She preferred the needle on the copper plate. It betrayed the slightest errors and Mary Cassatt found that this medium was a rewarding school of discipline for the artist, exacting but effective in its results.

Degas was increasingly fond of aquatint — we have seen him writing at length to Pissarro about this technique — and for *Le Jour et la Nuit* he made his two aquatints of Mary Cassatt at the Louvre. She was then thirty-four and he urged her to take up aquatint in addition to etching, drypoint and soft-ground etching.

During the summer of 1880 she began to draw her subjects of family life directly on the copper in drypoint, representing her little nephews and nieces in the arms or on the lap of their mother or nurse. She made a series of twelve prints on this theme, plus a scene of repose, which were presented for the first time at her second one-man show in 1893 at Durand-Ruel's in Paris. This was an important exhibition, for in addition to these drypoints she showed fourteen colour aquatints, fifteen soft-ground etchings and aquatints in black and white, further drypoints, one lithograph, fourteen pastels and seventeen paintings on canvas. These included sets of studies of young women alone and mothers with their child.

As we have seen, the influence of Japanese prints on French artists in Paris goes back several decades before the great exhibition of 1890 held at the Ecole des Beaux-Arts, where hundreds of Japanese prints were on show. Mary Cassatt visited that exhibition repeatedly, often accompanied by Degas, Berthe Morisot and their friend Mallarmé. She was particularly attracted by Utamaro and purchased some of his prints. Not content with admiring, she went on to make a careful study of these woodblock prints whose technique was quite unfamiliar to her. She set herself to work out a means of expressing her own vision on copper by way of the Japanese woodcut techniques. She succeeded magnificently in the end, but her first attempts suffered from a certain discrepancy in the colours. The methods she worked out have been described by Adelyn D. Breeskin.

Exhibited in the Durand-Ruel galleries in both Paris and New York, this beautiful series of colour aquatints met with little success. With some bitterness she wrote: "I am very much disappointed that my compatriots have so little liking for any of my work." She persevered, however, and added to these a further series of five colour aquatints. For her lack of success never checked her output. Unlike some of her male associates in the Impressionist movement, she had the courage and faith to overcome indifference and produced more than two hundred and thirty prints. Blindness alone — another analogy with Degas — forced her to give up first printmaking, then painting. By about 1910 the glare of the copper plate as she worked over it in drypoint had become too much for her sensitive eyes and she had to abandon the medium entirely. From then until her death in 1926 failing eyesight prevented her from doing any further work: the same fate befell her as Degas in his last sad years.

The production of colour prints altered her vision as a painter, and she gradually came to paint her pictures with novel tones in terms of broad areas of colour. Her line too, as a result of the discipline imposed by etching, grew firmer and stronger. Great as her admiration was for Degas, Mary Cassatt maintained a complete independence of technique and inspiration with respect to her friend and mentor. Japanese prints had more influence on her and profoundly modified her art. In spite of the technical experiments that engrossed her, her work is dominated by emotion far more than by technique. The essential theme, the one overriding theme of her art, is motherhood. However hackneyed it may have been when she took it up, she treated it with a sincerity and freshness that were tantamount to a complete renewal. Some have seen in her choice of subject matter a tell-tale sign of suppressed desires and have imagined that she could not portray children with the authenticity of Renoir, Carrière or Suzanne Valadon, who painted their own children while she painted those of others. Such a view, whatever the apparent grounds for it, is belied by the great majority of Mary Cassatt's works. Just as Degas represented the natural movements of women bathing and dressing, without any artifice, so Mary Cassatt represented intimate scenes of women and children in all their simplicity, recording the commonplaces of daily life in the home, just as her fellow Impressionists recorded other commonplace aspects of daily life. Mary Cassatt was wholly in sympathy with their aims and outlook and made an important contribution of her own to Impressionist art.

A College Class at Work: Chrysler Building and Seagram Building — Comparison or Contrast?

In a unit dealing with the development of the twentieth-century sky-scraper, an art history instructor gave a lecture on the art deco and international styles in architecture. Art Deco, she said, was characterized by the addition of machine-made ornament to buildings. In contrast, proponents of the International style rejected decoration, maintaining that it was extraneous. For them, beauty was achieved by subtracting rather than adding, leaving only the basic structure of the building itself. To illustrate these two views, the instructor provided her students with photographs and readings on the Chrysler Building, a 1930 Art Deco skyscraper, and the Seagram Building, a 1958 example of the International style. She asked the students to write a paragraph contrasting these two New York City buildings, based on her lecture, the photographs, and the readings about the two buildings. Figures 4.5 and 4.6 are the photographs, first of the Chrysler Building and then of the Seagram Building.

Figure 4.5   *The Chrysler Building, New York City*

CHRYSLER BUILDING
405 Lexington Avenue, NE corner 42nd Street
William Van Alen, 1930

Is it silly or is it real? It is hard, even after years of looking carefully at this and so many other buildings, to answer that question. Chrysler *is* absurd, in a sense; the notion of a skyscraper topped by six levels of stainless-steel arches wrapping triangular windows, all culminating in a spire, and all on top of a tower ornamented by brick designs taken from automobile hubcaps and gargoyles modeled after radiator ornaments — of course that is silly.

Why, then, has it lasted? Chrysler is not rational, it is not profound, it is not subtle, it is not, even in the final analysis, very beautiful. But there is something that makes it wonderful, something that makes that odd silvery tower glimmer in the sun and thus bring a smile to our lips. The current rage for Art Deco has led to Chrysler's being overpraised, but even with the hyperbole put aside, this is a very good building indeed. Perhaps the reason is that it *does* express the romantic longings of a particular period, that it is, in its way, a more appropriate statement of what New York wanted to be about as the twenties turned into the thirties than any perfect box the International Style could dream of. The quality of Chrysler comes from its ability to be romantic and irrational and yet not quite so foolish as to be laughable; it stops just short, and therefore retains a shred of credibility amidst the fantasy — rather like New York itself.

The building changed hands not long ago — after several years as a property of the Goldman-DiLorenzo real estate empire, which treated it rather like a tenement in the South Bronx, the building is now in the hands of the Massachusetts Mutual Life Insurance Company, which seems to like it a bit more. A major rehabilitation is under way at this writing, and whether it cleans up the building or changes it is still unclear. The lobby, a fantastic triangle of African marble, and the richly paneled elevators are among New York's masterpiece Art Deco interiors, and they must be preserved at any cost.

SEAGRAM BUILDING
375 Park Avenue, 52nd to 53rd streets
Mies van der Rohe, Philip Johnson, 1958

"Reason," Mies van der Rohe used to quote St. Thomas Aquinas as saying, "is the first principle of all human work." Seagram is a temple to reason, a tower built to elucidate the Miesian principles of order, logic, and clarity in all things. It is not quite what it would seem, however — Mies was far more interested in having his buildings appear to be structurally simple than actually be structurally simple. But if the myth that has surrounded this building (and the rest of Mies's work) is not entirely accurate, that does not diminish Seagram's standing as one of the great buildings of the twentieth century. The bronze curtain wall is serene, the proportions are sublime, and the detailing — well, if not perfect here, then where? So meticulous was the care that lavatory fixtures and lettering on the lobby mailboxes were designed specially for use here.

Seagram is set back from Park Avenue on a deep plaza, with green Italian marble rails as benches along its sides and two great fountains in its foreground. It is all done to show off the tower, yet, curiously, the narcissistic plaza has ended up being one of New York's most relaxed and

Figure 4.6 *The Seagram Building, New York City*

welcoming public spaces. Mies conceived of it as a single spot of relief from the tight limestone canyons of Park Avenue; unfortunately, the brilliant success of Seagram led the city in its 1961 revision of the zoning code to encourage other tall towers on plazas. The result has been a slew of imitations, cheap Miesian buildings on uncomfortable, street-wrecking plazas.

The building is as good as it is largely as a result of the efforts of Phyllis Lambert, an architect and daughter of Samuel Bronfman, the late head of Joseph E. Seagram & Sons. She learned that her father had asked a routine commercial firm to design the building, and was so disturbed that she flew back from Paris to persuade him to hire an architect of international reputation instead. Father indulged daughter, putting her in charge of a search committee; she later wrote that she considered Frank Lloyd Wright but felt his work represented the frontier mentality of an America then gone, and that Le Corbusier's sculptural forms would not be a "good influence" in New York. Mies was the architect of the day, she felt: "Mies forces you in. You have to go deeper. You might think this austere strength, this ugly beauty, is terribly severe. It is, and yet all the more beauty in it."

All true — and yet. There may be few buildings in New York as beautiful as Seagram, and there are surely no postwar skyscrapers as truly exquisite, but it is not entirely the kind of beauty Mies intended it to be. Seagram is not only a bit of a trick structurally — Louis Kahn was fond of calling it "a beautiful lady with hidden corsets," for the "pure" Miesian skin hides lots of other kinds of supports — but it is, with its I beams running down the façade and its marble-paneled false windows on the sides, not a little mannered and ornamented. This is not the natural outgrowth of technology, as Mies pretended it was, and it is not the *Zeitgeist*. It was believed to be such, which led to wretched imitations and, even sadder, to a growing sense on the part of society at large that contemporary architecture was a faceless, styleless art.

In the end, Seagram, like all of Mies's work but like so little else the International Style produced, is true not to the rules of an abstract system but only to itself, like all great works of art.

Below is the paragraph written by one student who plans to major in art history.

Two 20th century architectural types represented in New York City are the Art Deco and International styles. Art Deco architecture is characterized by the use of ornament and contrasting textures and colors achieved by combining several materials such as stone, brick, teracotta and metal; the International Style rejects ornament altogether and is characterized by buildings of stark simplicity whose "beauty" is organic to the engineering and the functions of the structures themselves. Two famous examples of these styles, prominent in the skyline, are the Chrysler Building and the Seagram Building. The Chrysler Building, completed in 1930, rises 77 stories, 1048 feet above the ground; the Seagram Building, completed in 1958, is in contrast only 38 stories high. The Chrysler Building's most striking feature is its tower with its metal crestings at the top. Almost equally striking at the base of the tower are the brick frieze representing automobile hubcaps and the metal sculptures of winged creatures like those used on the 1929 Chrysler radiator caps. The Seagram Building, designed by Mies van der Rohe, in conjunction with Philip Johnson, rises starkly on stilts, a rectangular prism of dull bronze I-beams sheathed in gray-amber glass. Whereas the Chrysler Building occupies its entire plot and is thus enmeshed in the swarming activities of its surrounding streets, the Seagram Building is set back on a plaza 90 feet from the street, serenely aloof from the "hustle and bustle."

After returning the paragraphs to the students, the art history instructor asked them to read yet another selection and then to write a full essay on the following question:

Despite the fact that the Chrysler Building and the Seagram Building are quite different in appearance, in what ways can they be considered similar?

As you discovered in the pages on the development of the Bruegel/ Renoir contrast paper, it is often more fruitful to emphasize the differences between two similar entities. Conversely, it can also be enlightening to compare two dissimilar phenomena. In many instances during your studies in college, you will have to come to your own conclusion about whether to emphasize similarities or differences. As you read the following article and the full essay written by the student who plans to major in art history, you should consider why, in this instance, the instructor chose to stress the comparison.

Skyscrapers

During the first decades of the twentieth century, skyscrapers rose in our American cities like weeds at the sudden advent of spring. A great wave of speculation swept the land buoyed by an uncritical confidence in the serviceability of steel and of the mechanics of steel, of faith in the heroic destiny of modern industry — and when the wave had passed, the hearts of our cities were found ensnared in giant brambles of steel towers.

The drama was made possible not by economic circumstance alone but equally by that great advance in the science of building which accompanied our prosperity. I shall not pause here to disentangle cause and effect: I note merely that the skyscraper is an engineer's idea no less than the idea of the banker. It is not, like the temple and the cathedral, the product of social effort long sustained, or, like the dwelling, the intimate loved companion of men. It is a contrivance, a machine, the product of ingenuity and calculations.

Two inventions, the elevator and standardized steel construction, both arising from new technologies of iron and electricity, formed the materials out of which was built this the newest toy of our architects. We must understand these inventions if we are to understand the skyscraper.

By means of the elevator, operating in a shaft hundreds of feet in height, a building is transformed into an extension of a street. It becomes a vertical thoroughfare; a thoroughfare which draws a selected traffic from the street and returns it to the street. Around this thoroughfare we must imagine a steel cage; a cage endlessly divided by thin partitions into uniform compartments. A scaffolding composed of a thousand cells is raised around a cluster of elevator shafts. That is a skyscraper.

These veins are mechanized. A central core of elevator shafts, sometimes as many as fifty in one building, raises and lowers a stream of men smoothly, precisely, and without effort. The currents here are rapid, much more rapid than in the street, and yet they are more controlled. People move here, or are moved, without fatigue. They arrive at their destinations with a mechanical certainty. Three hundred places of business may open on that superhighway, the highway that is a machine.

Surrounding this machine is the steel cage which forms the second principle of its organization. Skyscrapers are, in effect, great skeletons, built of light rigid elements held together by rivets or by welding. The energy of their structures is not that of stone laid on stone, of solid arches pushing against each other: the structure presses only against the ground, its internal forces being inert. The interaction of weight and arrested force which is essential to the apprehension of stone architecture cannot be made accessible to the imagination here where no such interaction exists other than in the theory of engineers. We understand the building, if we understand it rightly, as a frame which, being clothed with thin membranes of masonry, may be made to define and shape a fragment of space; but that space, unlike the space within stone walls and under a masonry vault, is cellular and lightly contained.

Steel has set us free to create in buildings every shape and combination of shape which may be demanded by the complex movements of our civilization. The old materials — brick, stone, and wood — bound our buildings to convention and to geometry. Until our time the techniques of stone construction, confirming the laws of the academy, disciplined the forms of buildings within strict boundaries and imposed upon them a conformity to masterpieces completed, framed, set solidly upon the earth. The new materials release us — not always happily — from that constraint. The forms which buildings may now assume are limited only by practical resource and the daring of our imaginations.

The skyscraper assumed its thousand and one costumes gaily, innocently, supported by the vast naiveté of industrial corporations intent on the exhibition of their bigness. In a holiday spirit the colossal frameworks which rose almost overnight from the rocky bed of New York were encrusted one by one with the debris of the ancient civilizations; the libraries of architects yielded each day new discoveries, apt and rapturous spoil for the new art of 'exterior decoration'; and the campaniles of Italy and the cathedral towers of France were made to pierce the Manhattan sky with a hundred new felicities of form.

People are apt to overlook the skyscraper's very evident role as a channel of publicity. The Woolworth Tower made instantaneous and convincing this wide, if unorthodox, usefulness; thenceforth the great corporations built steel towers on conspicuous sites in order to call attention to their own importance. The medieval church had set them an example, imitated none too shyly by Louis XIV. Neither of these measured the success of their constructions in strictly financial terms; they were satisfied, as were often the builders of skyscrapers, with a certain prestige value difficult for us to appraise.

After reading the foregoing, the student planning to major in art history proceeded with the assignment by listing data, creating charts, freewriting, establishing a tentative thesis, and planning the organization of the essay. She decided that she would use the paragraph of contrast she had written for the first assignment as part of her opening. Why?

After several revisions, she submitted the following essay.

Chrysler and Seagram Buildings

The amalgam of architectural styles that make up Manhattan's skyline might leave the visitor with a sense of confused wonderment. Glass-sheathed skyscrapers dwarf spires of neo-gothic cathedrals; 19th century castiron warehouse fronts abut the twin towers of the World Trade Center; the Morgan library, a reconstruction of a 16th century Italian Renaissance palazzo, displays the wealth of a capitalist baron and stares at the blank masonry of "luxury" apartments, little boxes piled one atop the other. These contrasts are sharp and often disquieting, but help create the unique dynamic of the city.

Two twentieth century architectural types represented in New York City are the Art Deco and International styles. Art Deco architecture is characterized by the use of ornament and contrasting textures and colors achieved by combining several materials such as stone, brick, terra cotta and metal; the International Style rejects ornament altogether and is characterized by buildings of stark simplicity whose "beauty" is organic to the engineering and the functions of the structures themselves. Two famous examples of these styles, prominent in the skyline, are the Chrysler Building and the Seagram Building. The Chrysler Building, completed in 1930, rises 77 stories, 1048 feet above the ground; the Seagram Building, completed in 1958, is in contrast only 38 stories high. The Chrysler Building's most striking feature is its tower with its metal crestings at the top. Almost equally striking at the base of the tower are the brick frieze representing automobile hubcaps and the metal sculptures of winged creatures like those used on the 1929 Chrysler radiator caps. The Seagram Building, designed by Mies van der Rohe, in conjunction with Philip Johnson, rises starkly on stilts, a rectangular prism of dull bronze I-beams sheathed in gray-amber glass. Whereas the Chrysler Building occupies its entire plot and is thus enmeshed in the swarming activities of its surrounding streets, the Seagram Building is set back on a plaza 90 feet from the street, serenely aloof from the "hustle and bustle."

However, in a broader sense, these architecturally disparate structures both reflect twentieth century life. They both are, after all, skyscrapers; they both, albeit differently, present carefully planned images of their corporations to the world.

The development of steel and the invention of the elevator in the nineteenth century allowed for building up, up and ever further up. The skyscraper, however, is primarily a twentieth century phenomenon. It is the inevitable solution to the problems of an ever-expanding commercialism. Both the Chrysler Building (the world's tallest building until the Empire State Building was completed in 1931) and the Seagram Building accommodate hundreds of offices and thousands of workers. This high density of executive and clerical function centralizes in a single core structure the manifold activities of giant corporations. The actual manufacture of cars and whiskey is elsewhere; the decisions concerning their production and distribution are made here. Both buildings, therefore, represent the concentration of white collar skills characteristic of the modern city. With land values at a premium in New York City, what better solution than to build up? Despite their distinct styles, the Chrysler and Seagram Buildings both use essentially the same technology in the service of the same commercial god.

Like the absolute monarchs of France, who built such palaces as Versailles, and like the Catholic Church, that built the Vatican, giant corporations create through the edifices they raise images in the public's consciousness of their companies' prestige and power. The Chrysler Building, erected during the post-World War I boom, aggressively and somewhat brashly asserts its automotive mission through the proliferation of hubcaps, radiator caps and polished metal crestings. Art Deco, the fashionable architectural style of the period, was most appropriate because it allowed the Chrysler Corporation to create a visible emblem of the product it sells. The building and the corporation became synonymous in the public mind. The Seagram Building, a product of the post-World War II economic boom, creates another kind of association. Unless we equate the building's amber-colored glass curtain walls with whiskey bottles, there is very little to remind us of what the Seagram Corporation actually manufactures. Perhaps Seagram wanted to de-emphasize the evils of drink — alcoholism and revelry. Perhaps it wanted to connect its corporate name with dignity, clarity, rationality — qualities of moderation associated with "the one, but no more than two, drinks" man or woman of restraint. The International Style might have been chosen not only because it was finally gaining widespread acceptance in the United States, but also because it was perfect for the projection of such an image. The very coolness and reserve of the facade and the structure's placement on a relatively empty plaza certainly convey a remove from the excesses of sensuality. Both buildings communicate different messages, but both buildings were constructed, in part, to establish an image of their corporations for the world.

The Chrysler and Seagram Buildings, although different, reflect similar realities: the need to use the central city as the hub of economic activity and the desire to make an impression. To what extent could the same be said for many of the "clashing" architectural styles represented in New York City?

Even though this essay responds to a controlling question of comparison and is organized to indicate two basic similarities between the Chrysler and Seagram buildings, it does so by answering, in the development of its paragraphs, several other types of questions.

In the second paragraph, four subsidiary questions are considered. What type are they?

1.   What is the Art Deco style?

2. What is the International style?

3. How is the Chrysler Building representative of the Art Deco style?

4. How does the Seagram Building reflect the International style?

Examine the third and fourth paragraphs and re-create the questions they respond to. Identify them.

In this essay, the author presents the details about each building as part of the introduction. Unlike the notes about Bruegel and Renoir, these details are items of contrast rather than comparison. The body moves beyond these observable contrasts into aspects of architecture that deal with the way buildings reflect and affect the economic and social milieu of which they are a part. In making these comparisons, the architecture is placed within a cultural context.

PRACTICE

Answer the following questions about the introduction of the student essay.

- Why did the writer present a three-paragraph introduction?

- What is the purpose of the first paragraph?

- Why is a contrast made between the two buildings in the second paragraph of the introduction if the controlling question asks only for a comparison?

- How does the writer organize the information about the two buildings in the paragraph that discusses the contrast?

- What is the thesis statement?

Answer the following questions about the body of the essay.

- What are the topic sentences for the body paragraphs? How do they reflect the thesis?

- How does she organize the information in the paragraphs that discuss the similarities between these two buildings?

PRACTICE

The homes that people have created for themselves at different times and for different climates are all responses to the basic need for shelter. These various types of homes represent more than just the physical need for shelter, however; they are also attempts to express the human desire for beauty. The combination of this aesthetic goal with practical need makes architecture the most human of all art forms.

The four houses in Figures 4.7, 4.8, 4.9, and 4.10 and described below represent the efforts of different groups of people both to provide protection and to express their desire for beauty. Using any two of these examples, write an essay responding to the following statement:

> Although the physical needs for shelter vary from group to group and climate to climate, housing of all kinds shares certain similarities both in its provision for shelter and in their desire for beauty.

Follow the steps of collecting data, listing, charting, freewriting, weighing evidence, and creating a tentative thesis before you try to organize your essay. Your chart may divide the information on the basis of physical elements — walls, floors, ceilings, and so on — and discuss the aesthetic qualities of each, or it may separate the physical from the aesthetic and discuss each item separately. The two possibilities are charted below.

For the writing of the body of the essay, the charts could be read either horizontally, discussing each building separately, or vertically, discussing each element separately.

	Walls		Floor		Ceiling		Other	
	Phys.	Aesth.	Phys.	Aesth.	Phys.	Aesth.	Phys.	Aesth.
Structure #1								
Structure #2								
Structure #3								
Structure #4								

or

	Physical				Aesthetic			
	Walls	Floor	Ceiling	Other	Walls	Floor	Ceiling	Other
Structure #1								
Structure #2								
Structure #3								
Structure #4								

The Bedouin Tent

The Bedouin calls the tent *beit sha'r* — house of hair. The tent cloth is woven of pure goat hair or of a mixture of goat and sheep or camel wool. The woven cloth breadths are sewn together, the number and length depending on the wealth and status of the tent owner. A poor Arab may have only two breadths, twenty feet long for his tent, while a rich sheik may use six breadths, seventy feet long. Tension bands are sewn across the breadths, the number depending on the relative size of the tent. Each band is supported by three poles — a seven-foot-high center pole flanked by another on each side. The tent size is reckoned by the number of center poles (exclusive of the end ones) so that the poor tent has but one, while the sheik's tent has four. If the tent cloth is larger than eight breadths, it is made in two parts to keep each section within a camel's load. These large tents are only seen in semipermanent camps as the tent cloth is too difficult to move frequently.

Bedouin east of the Dead Sea sacrifice a sheep in the spot where they pitch the tent. The tent is always pitched by women: the ground is cleared of stones and shrubs and made as level as possible, then the tent is unrolled and spread over this place, and the ropes are pulled out and staked. From long experience the women can judge exactly where to place the stakes. A corner pole is then pushed up in place; next, the poles along one side, followed by the center poles. When all the poles are in place and the roof is aloft, the wall curtains are pinned in place and the carpets and other tent furnishings are brought in. Within an hour the tent is ready and the hearth fires are blazing.

Arabs pitch their tents facing either east toward Mecca or south so that the back wall is set against the northern winds and the men's side is toward the east. The direction of the tent depends on the particular tribal practice and the prevailing conditions at the time. In hot weather the tent is left completely open, the roof serving as a sunshade, but usually wall curtains (*ruag*) are pinned up for privacy and to keep out the wind and sand. These curtains can be moved to either side of the tent depending on wind direction and a variety of enclosures can be created by hanging them out on the ropes. The ruag, made of a looser weave than the roof cloth, are woven with red and black geometric designs. There is a piece of sack cloth at the bottom which can be buried in the sand or held down with rocks to seal out drafts. In Syria reed mats are often used for the outside walls. The dividing curtain (*qata*), separating the men's and women's sides, has the most elaborate designs woven into it — especially the end that extends out in front and is draped over the front ropes for all to see. In bad weather

Figure 4.7   *A Three-Pole Shammar Tent*

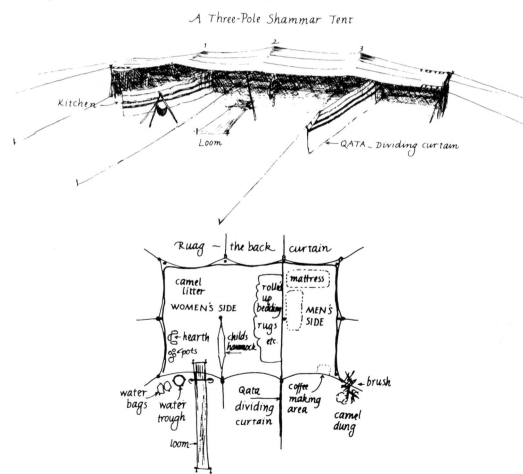

this end is brought across the front of the women's side, completely enclosing it.

The floor of the men's side is covered with carpets and mattresses for the guests to sit on. The host's camel saddle, covered with a sheepskin, is set on the rear mattress. This is a key piece of furniture — the host and guest of honor sit on either side of it and talk across it; the other guests sit in a semicircle facing them.

The women's side of the tent is bigger. It is the living and working area of the tent and is never seen by men other than the tent owner in accord with the traditional separation of sexes and seclusion of women. The women talk, cook, and weave on their side. In one corner of the women's side sits the camel litter in which they ride when the tribe migrates. The litter consists of a framework fastened to a camel saddle enclosed with cloth — a tent on camel back. Against the dividing curtain (qata) are stacked rugs and rolls of bedding, while near the far wall a bed of stones supports bags of grain and wool. The sleeping area is encircled with a border of stones. Saddlebags hang from tent poles and a hammock cradle may be stretched between them. The loom for weaving the tent cloth is set up with the warp running out the front of the tent. Outside the tent near the front corner goatskin water bags rest on a bed of bushes and a tripod suspends a goatskin churn. Nearby, the cooking hearth is made of three stones with iron bars set across to support cooking pots and bread pans.

Figure 4.8a   *A Courtyard House in Peking*

The Chinese Home

Illustrated here is a fairly recent Peking house which is typical enough to serve as a reference to some details of the Chinese house.

The exterior walls were of gray brick, the roof of gray half-round clay tiles. The entrance gateway, its doors and its roof timbers were bright with colour. These entrances were the only incidents in a street of houses where all rooms looked inwards. Guarded by servants as they were, no-one passed inside without permission. They were also the only point of contact from the inside to the outside world, and here the ladies sometimes used to come out to watch a procession or buy from pedlars.

Just opposite the entrance there was the familiar carved or coloured screen wall. The outer court was paved with stone slabs. A small pool with lotus growing in it was near the centre. A 'date tree' (*Zizyphus vulgaris*) and a crab apple tree grew in the courtyard, and many flowers were set out in pots round the edge. It was not a mere service courtyard; there were guest-rooms and some family-rooms in the side buildings. The kitchen and servants' rooms were in the suite on the south. But the long reception hall between the two courtyards marked a definite division between the outer half of the house, where acquaintances came and parties were held, and the inner half, where only relatives and intimate friends would normally penetrate.

This inner court, encircled by a verandah, was also stone-paved. There was a 'strangely shaped rock' in one corner, and two raised beds of shrub-peonies faced each other in the middle of the two sides. The columns of the buildings and verandah were all painted red, and the beams and other decorated woodwork other bright colours.

The use of the rooms was, of course, flexible, depending on the tastes and numbers of the family, of guests, dependants and so on. Traditionally the head of the family would occupy the main suite and a married son one of the side suites. The most private places in this very private house were the two little open-air courts surrounded by high walls, one at each end of the main suite. Neither was paved. One had a date tree growing in it; that was the special retreat of the father. The other, that of the mother and daughters, had just bare earth.

The floors of the rooms were stone slabs, and carpets were few. The whole window-wall of a room on the courtyard side was composed of a panel of windows and doors. Windows were of thick translucent paper, which had a certain amount of thermal resistance in winter. In spring they were rolled up, and the rooms opened to the outside air. Unlike the Japanese and the Indians, who continued to make more use of the floor, the Chinese, ever since T'ang times if not earlier, have used tables, chairs and bedsteads of similar heights to those in Europe.

The kitchen, the privy and the bathroom were more casually treated than in Europe and do not always appear on plans at all. The kitchen was sometimes in the open air on a verandah or in an outhouse. The privy, consisting of a narrow-lined rectangular pit about two feet deep with a narrow seat built over one end, was often built as a separate little shed in some convenient corner. Sewage disposal was by a system of carts, often run by private enterprise, which emptied the privies at night in a door-to-door collection and delivered the sewage outside the walls to the surrounding farms, where it was composted and used for fertilizer. As to the bathroom, it must be emphasized that all toilet arrangements in the houses of the better-off, including bathing and washing, were *mainly* provided for by means of basins, bathtubs, commodes, etc., brought to private rooms by servants. As in all civilizations until the industrial age, domestic comfort, even that of a comparatively modest house such as this example, let alone the luxury of a palace, depended not only on the buildings and equipment but on the cheap labor of servants.

  This detail of a courtyard shows a subsidiary suite of rooms, probably bedrooms, with, at the right, a lower gallery to join them to the principal living room. The court is paved and set with ornamental trees such as crab apple, and flowers in pots were set along the edges. Here celebrations were held, and in an outer courtyard a temporary stage might be set up when actors were hired for birthday parties.

  Roof and ground plan. These highly formal enclosures were so closely guarded that the doors themselves contained a deflectory arrangement of

Figure 4.8b *Floor Plan of a Courtyard House in Peking*

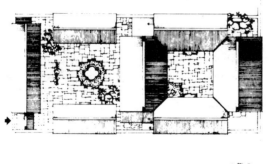

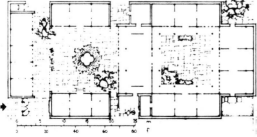

Figure 4.9 *Tom Watson's House, McDuffie County, Georgia*

barrier-screens. The outer court, surrounded by rooms for children, guests, the kitchen and servants, was paved with stone slabs with a small lotus pool in the centre. The inner court, separated from the outer by a long guest hall, was the parents' domain. In one corner of the inner court was an "artificial mountain," a strangely shaped stone, and two peony beds.

Tom Watson's House

A rear view of the house where the fiery populist Tom Watson was born. The house was built by Watson's grandfather in McDuffie County, Georgia, in about 1820. Watson, who was best known for establishing Rural Free Delivery when he was a U.S. Congressman (1891–1893) was a very fine writer. He described his birthplace in an autobiographical novel:

"Ours was just a plain house and none too large, not built of bricks brought over from England, but of timbers torn from the heart of the longleaf Georgia pine.

"The main body was made of logs hewed with the broad-axe, smoothed with the footadze, and joined powerfully at the ends — the four corners — by being interlocked into deep notches; upon these solid, heavy logs was laid, inside and out, a covering of plank: strong sleepers bore up the plank floor, stout rafters held the shingle roof. A partition, running from side to side nearest the western end, cut the main body of the original house into two parts, the smaller being a bedroom, the larger being the living room, where life on the homestead centered. Two stone chimneys, built outside, gave fireplaces to the living room and to the shed room. The house rested upon massive stone piers, two feet high, well-set in the ground . . .

"Such was my grandfather's house built for comfort, built to resist the storms of a hundred years . . .

"That old Southern homestead was a little kingdom, a complete social and industrial organism, almost wholly sufficient unto itself, asking less of the outer world than it gave."

Tom Watson ran unsuccessfully for president in 1900 as candidate of the People's party. He used his birthplace of logs as one of his appeals, following in the tradition of Andrew Jackson, Henry Clay, and William Henry Harrison.

Frank Lloyd Wright Project

For Wright these years were highly productive; they saw fruition of such masterpieces as the Isabel Roberts, Avery Coonley, Frederick Robie, and Mrs. Thomas Gale houses with their increasing emphasis on space-defining cantilevered planes and abstractly juxtaposed geometric masses. These houses had less appeal, though, among Wright's students than did his compact reinterpretation of the cube-shaped vernacular house, a form he revised in accordance with such non-residential designs as his Larkin Building and Unity Church. The resultant design he published in the *Ladies' Home Journal* in 1907 as 'A Fireproof House for $5000.'

To the crude, ungainly box Wright had imparted style. He flattened the roof, strengthened the cornice, ordered the window openings, and married the building to the ground. He vanquished the compartmentalized interior by opening the living and dining rooms as a single L-shaped space which pivoted around a central fireplace. To gain apparent breadth and horizontality he extended the entrance as a low, trellised terrace at the side. The design — in its traditional form or as revised by Wright — had many virtues. It was compact and economical to maintain and build. It required little land and its orientation was readily changed. And its appeal was broadened by identity with prevailing forms.

PRACTICE

You have learned about, and have had some practice in writing, paragraphs and essays in response to controlling questions of comparison/contrast in art history. For further practice you should go through the anthology and try your hand at writing a comparison/contrast essay in another discipline.

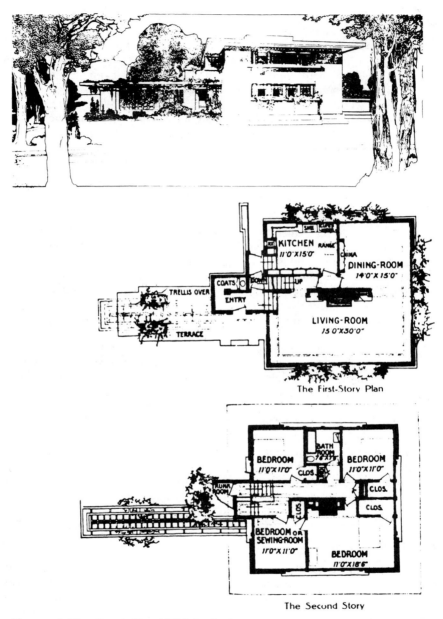

The First-Story Plan

The Second Story

Figure 4.10   *Frank Lloyd Wright Project*

chapter

5

Questions of Process

THINKING

What Is a Process?

The following account is a freshman's description of his first day at registration.

> As I arrived on campus, I realized I had left my registration notice at home, but I thought I remembered reading that the gym was the first stop.
> From a block away I could see a line that snaked out the double doors and spilled onto the walkway outside. Well, I placed myself at the end of the line and decided not to get rattled. I had heard about registration days from college friends of mine.
> The line was moving at a fairly good pace. At some point I noticed the students in front of me with official-looking cards, and a few students writing on them. I asked what they were.
> "It's the PL–220," the student in front of me said.
> "What's that?"
> "It's your registration data form, listing the courses you're planning to take this semester. You can't get your course cards in the gym without it. Pick one up in the auditorium."
> I guess I didn't remember reading that. 45 minutes later, after returning from the auditorium and waiting on line again, I was finally inside the gym. I wrote out the courses I wanted, including "History." I located the

199

History Department station first and confidently showed the gentleman my course card request. He looked up at me with exasperation:

"We offer 33 different courses — the Phoenicians, the Greeks, the Romans, the Middle Ages, the Renaissance" (he went on and on) ". . . you have to decide which one you want. You should read the descriptions in the catalog."

"Where do I get a catalog?"

"In the auditorium."

The anecdote above is presented not necessarily as a case of the usual experience at registration, though these incidents may be familiar to some of you; it is meant to convey the chaos of not having a plan of procedure. What the student has presented is his actual experiences, a *narrative*. It is not a guide that prescribes a series of steps to follow, a *process*. Obviously, there is a relationship between a narrative and a process. In a sense, process is a distillation of the major steps in a narrative. The following diagram highlights that relationship, using the same *narrative*. Alongside the narrative about registration is the account of the *process* of registration.

NARRATIVE

Steps in the Registration Process

As I arrived on campus, I realized I had left my registration notice at home, but I thought I remembered reading that the *gym was the first stop*.

From a block away I could see a line that snaked out the double doors and spilled onto the walkway outside. Well, I placed myself at the end of the line and decided not to get rattled. I had heard about registration days from college friends of mine.

1. Pick up registration materials in Clinton Auditorium.

The line was moving at a fairly good pace. At some point I noticed the students in front of me with official-looking cards, and a few students writing on them. I asked what they were.

Note: Catalogs are available at side exit upon request only.

"It's the PL–220," the one in front of me said.

"What's that?"

"It's your registration data form, listing the courses you're planning to take this semester. You can't get your course cards in the gym without it. Pick one up in the *auditorium*."

2. Fill out course cards PL–220. Write out section number and course title.

I guess I didn't remember reading that. 45 minutes later, after returning from the auditorium and waiting on line again, I was finally inside the gym. *I wrote out the courses I wanted*, including "History." I located the History Department station first and con-

3. Bring completed course

fidently showed the gentleman my course card request. He looked up at me with exasperation:

"We offer 33 different courses beginning with the Phoenicians, the Greeks, the Romans, the Middle Ages, the Renaissance" (he went on and on) ". . . you have to decide which one you want. You should read the descriptions in the catalog."

"Where do I get a *catalog*?"

"In the *auditorium*."

card to gymnasium and get approval from departmental stations.

to step 2
to step 1

The essential point to notice is that:

A *narrative* provides the unique experience of an individual or individuals through an event.

A *process* provides a generalized description of the steps that would be duplicated by all individuals going through the same event.

Narrative and process do, however, share some of the same features, notably in the way they impose order on the chaos of experience. The smooth flow of significant details in the student narrative was achieved by the elimination of a myriad of other minor events that he had considered unimportant. During registration he may have chatted with friends on his way to the auditorium, ducked into the cafeteria to buy a container of coffee and a doughnut, struck up one or more conversations with fellow students while standing on line, or spotted a particularly attractive woman he would like to meet. All these minor events were eliminated in order to concentrate on what he considered to be relevant details.

Describing a process presents additional problems because not all processes are so straightforward as this one. When you start thinking of the way humans behave, you will be struck by the confusion of our actual performances. Think for a moment of the contrast between the steps for writing an essay as outlined in this book with your actual practice. In writing this text we have presented a process in sequential steps, from deciding on a controlling question to editing the final draft. In actual practice, you may have jumped back and forth among these steps, perhaps modifying the controlling question after the first draft, brainstorming or freewriting for new ideas as late as the next-to-the-last draft. For the purposes of clarity, this text has isolated certain key steps in places where they might commonly occur, but as we have tried to show, writing is rarely so neat and orderly. Our book has tried to impose order on chaos; your process papers will often have to do the same.

It can thus be said that narrative imposes order through the judicious choice of relevant detail, while process imposes order through describing steps that can be duplicated.

Determining the Essential Steps in a Process

In the above example, the process was provided. During part of your academic writing experience — and more than likely in your future professional experience — you will yourself be required to write a process analysis or paper. In essence, what you will be doing in such an assignment is determining the number of significant steps to record or describe and establishing the boundaries of the process, the beginning and the end. Each of these conditions of a process requires some further consideration.

You have, more than likely, given directions for getting someplace. In attempting to give the clearest directions, you were attempting to provide the major steps, or markers, along the route. Your directions probably depended on special road features, on the number and clarity of signs, and on the kind of person who was to follow the instructions. In doing this you were choosing the number of significant steps in a process.

Suppose you had a friend, Lenny, who drives an old car, whose odometer (mileage gauge) is not working, who responds keenly to directions based on landmarks, and who often confuses left and right. What would be the best set of directions to your home, given the terrain features of the road map in Figure 5.1? The route is 5.5 miles from start to end point. Each *marker* (a dot) represents a potential step in the set of directions. The problem is to decide which markers are essential in the instructions to be given to Lenny.

After examining the map, you would probably agree that it is unnecessary to cite all the markers in the set of directions. Certainly, the marker designating Mark's Auto Body Shop is no aid, and indicating the High Lane (gravel road) intersection is not crucial. One problem in giving a set of directions, then, is the danger of over-explaining and thereby over-complicating matters.

On the other hand, citing too few markers, to *under-explain*, might present other problems, as in the following set of directions:

1. Turn left at fork of Route 41/Route 7.

2. Go 4.5 miles and turn right on Main Street.

3. Make two right turns on North and Cottage Streets.

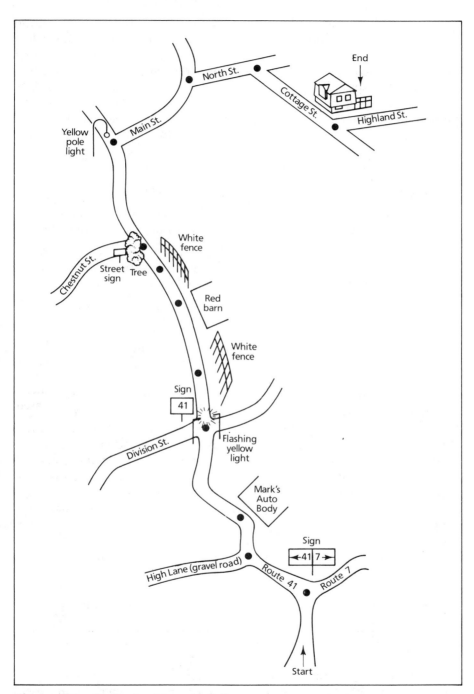

Figure 5.1 *Route for Lenny to Follow*

First of all, it is best to keep any *left* and *right* directions at a minimum, so Step 1 should be reworded. Lenny would be surprised by the flashing yellow light, a prominent feature on the way. Noting the exact mileage is a poor indication of the turnoff, especially since his odometer is not working. More important, he would be confused at the Chestnut Street intersection, since the street sign is partially obstructed and there is no other sign indicating the continuance of Route 41. Perhaps the best directions, the steps to follow, would be:

1.   Take Route 41 at fork of Route 41/Route 7.

2.   Continue straight after flashing yellow light.

3.   After second white fence, past the red barn, veer right — remember, not your watch hand — continuing on Route 41.

4.   At the overhead yellow pole light about a mile beyond the white fence, make a right onto Main Street. Don't worry about right and left here because only a right-hand turn is possible.

5.   Make two consecutive right turns, one on North and one on Cottage.

6.   Go to the last house on the left — your watch-hand side — with the large modern stained-glass window.

Notice the extreme importance of Step 4, the landmark for the turnoff. Also note that Steps 3 and 5 include other markers as well. Step 3 refers to both fences and the red barn at the same time and Step 5 to the two right turns. Often in indicating directions or presenting a process, several markers, or small steps, are grouped into larger ones. Because it is in the nature of process to group smaller steps into larger ones, such grouping can be seen as a function of classification.

Up to this point, it has been suggested that in describing a process it is necessary to:

- Trace the significant steps and eliminate unimportant ones.

- Group small steps into major ones.

- Consider the audience for whom the process is intended.

PRACTICE

Considering the discussion above, write a set of directions using the map in Figure 5.2. Your audience this time is another friend, Carol, who

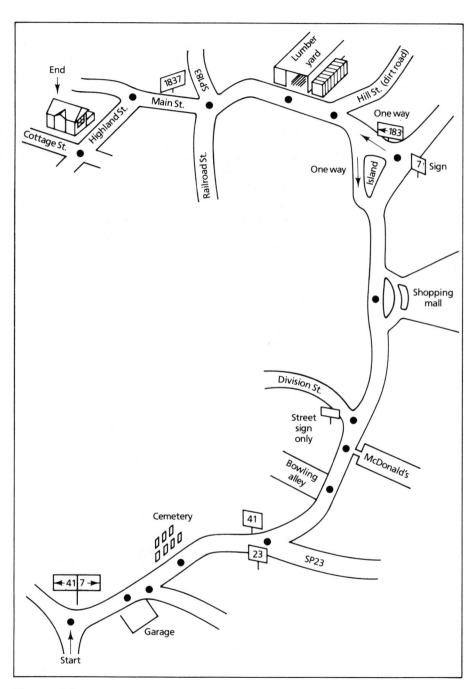

Figure 5.2   *Route for Carol to Follow*

depends heavily on road signs for directions, has been known to take the wrong fork in a road when given less-than-explicit directions, but has no trouble with left and right. The route is seven miles from start to end point.

Deciding Where to Begin

So far, we have considered processes with defined outer boundaries only — that is, clear markers for beginning and end. In analyzing some processes, you may be required to decide what the first step should be. Take the case of biographies and autobiographies of famous men and women and the authors' decisions on where and when to begin their stories. Although in the actual writing, a biography or autobiography may start at some crucial point in adulthood, a framework of significant events in chronological order underlies the presentation. Consider the early chapter headings of a biography of John Quincy Adams, the sixth president of the United States, the auto-biographies of Frederick Douglass, the abolitionist, and Agatha Christie, the famous writer of detective stories.

THE LIFE OF JOHN QUINCY ADAMS

Chapter I

The Ancestry, Birth, and Childhood of John
Quincy Adams   17

Chapter II

John Quincy Adams Studies Law — His Practice
— Engages in Public Life — Appointed Minister
to the Hague   45

Chapter III

Mr. Adams transferred to Berlin — His Marriage
— Literary Pursuits — Travels in Silesia — Nego-
tiates Treaties with Sweden and Prussia — Re-
called to the United States   63

Chapter IV

Chapter V

Etc.

THE LIFE OF FREDERICK DOUGLASS

THE LIFE OF AGATHA CHRISTIE

Unlike the other two, John Quincy Adams's story begins before he
was born. In fact, the author begins the biography with Adams's great-great-
grandfather, Henry Adams. Why does he begin so far back? The answer is
on the first pages, where the author includes an inscription from a monument
in memory of Adams's ancestor.

In Memory

of

HENRY ADAMS

This stone, and several others, have been placed in this yard, by a great-great-grandson, from a veneration of the piety, humility, simplicity, prudence, patience, temperance, frugality, industry, and perseverance of his ancestors, in hopes of recommending an imitation of their virtues to their posterity.

It is the qualities of character described in the inscription, the author believes, that have been passed on from generation to generation. He is suggesting that those qualities of character that helped Adams forge a successful road in life were contributed initially by his ancestors. This biography, therefore, begins four generations before Adams was born.

After a brief paragraph about the place of his birth, Frederick Douglass begins his story right at his birth:

The reader must not expect me to say much of my family. Genealogical trees did not flourish among slaves. A person of some consequence in civilized society, sometimes designated as father, was literally unknown to slave law and slave practice. I never met with a slave in that part of the country who could tell me with any certainty how old he was. . . . Masters allowed no questions to be put to them by slaves concerning their ages. Such questions were regarded by the masters as evidence of an impudent curiosity. From certain events, however, the dates of which I have since learned, I suppose myself to have been born in February, 1817.

These paragraphs leave quite an impression on the reader. Douglass's ancestry is unknown because of slavery — one of the grave wrongs that Douglass committed his life to correcting.

Unlike Frederick Douglass, Agatha Christie, the mystery writer, begins her autobiography not with her birth but with descriptions of her parents' personalities:

. . . of my father it could truly be said. "Oh what an agreeable man he is!" And the result was that the people in contact with him enjoyed a great measure of happiness.

• • •

I don't know what the quality was that he had. Yet he had no outstanding characteristics. He was not particularly intelligent. I think that he had a simple and loving heart, and he really cared for his fellow men.

He had a great sense of humour and he easily made people laugh. There was no meanness in him, no jealousy, and he was almost fantastically generous. And he had a natural happiness and serenity.

My mother was entirely different. She was an enigmatic and arresting personality — more forceful than my father — startlingly original in her ideas, shy and miserably diffident about herself, and at bottom, I think, with a natural melancholy.

• • •

As I was to realize many years later, my mother's ideas were always slightly at variance with reality. She saw the universe as more brightly coloured than it was, people as better or worse then they were. Perhaps because in the years of her childhood she had been quiet, restrained, with her emotions kept well below the surface. She tended to see the world in terms of drama that came near, sometimes, to melodrama. Her creative imagination was so strong that it could never see things as drab or ordinary. She had, too, curious flashes of intuition — of knowing suddenly what other people were thinking.

• • •

Her faculty for doing that sort of thing was always surprising her family. My sister said once: "Anything I don't want Mother to know, I don't even *think* of, if she's in the room."

Reading through the whole autobiography, one senses that Agatha Christie had a lovable disposition, and of course that she was a most imaginative person. It is interesting to note that her father and her mother, like the two detectives in her novels, Hercule Poirot and Miss Marple, were eccentric and intuitive. They had a knack for knowing what other people were about, and it was difficult to hide anything from them. Why, therefore, did Agatha Christie decide to begin her autobiography with descriptions of her parents' personalities?

Each of these authors used the opening chapter — the first major marker — for a particular purpose. Each wanted to convey a certain impression about themselves, a particular thesis: for Adams's biographer, Adams's desire to continue the great tradition of his ancestors; for Douglass, his sense of mission to make all men free; for Christie, her indebtedness to her family for a happy, productive life. Unless a process is bounded by the nature of a question or problem, the opening major marker, as well as all other significant markers, are determined by the overall purpose or thesis. If you were to write your autobiography, what general impression would you want to convey? Where would you begin?

WRITING

A Student at Work:
The Autobiography of Jules

You will shortly be asked to write an essay based on the following controlling question, "In the story of your life, what stages do you see as major?" In that assignment you will trace the major stages in your development to the present. You should examine your life to determine the impression you want to present to your audience. To help you decide upon this overall impression, you may want to consider one or more of the following categories: your academic, intellectual, emotional, social, or economic progress.

In preparing to write your essay, first examine the following process through which Jules, a 27-year-old Army veteran in a college composition class, tackled the assignment.

Collecting Data

In writing his paper Jules decided to focus on the steps leading to his decision to go to college. He had read the selections from Frederick Douglass, John Quincy Adams, and Agatha Christie; but since he was unsure where his essay should begin, he decided to construct the following chronological list of significant events in his life, as he remembered them.

BORN 1958

        1959: Took first steps

        1960: Fell in playground

        1961: Went to nursery school

        1962: Entered kindergarten

        1963: Sister born

        1964: Best friend moved away

        1966: Won school spelling bee

        1968: Joined Little League

        1969: Team won pennant

        1972: Entered high school

        1973: Parents divorced

        1973: Failed three major subjects

        1974: Got junior driver's license

1975: Arrested for drunken driving

1976: Graduated high school

1976: Entered Army (basic training,
      radio school, sent to Germany)

1978: Met Heidi in Munich

1979: Re-enlisted (sent for
      special training)

1980: Married Heidi

1981: Got discharged

1982: Got job at radio station

1982: Heidi joined me in the U.S.

1983: Nina born

1983: Decided to go to college

1984: Started college

PRACTICE

Since you will be asked to write an essay on this topic, list the events in your own life that you consider significant.

Weighing the Evidence

As Jules examined his chronological list, he found it difficult to decide which of the markers should be included in the essay. Where should he begin? That would depend on the purpose of his essay. Somehow, he wanted to communicate to his audience of mostly young men and women of 18 and 19 that entering college at the relatively late age of twenty-seven was the result of a process uniquely his own. If he simply divided his life into broad periods like early childhood, adolescence, young adulthood, and so on, would he be communicating the essence of this personal process? With this question in mind, he decided to explore the possibilities through a focused freewriting that would address the question, "What are the significant markers of my life?" Here are some of his thoughts.

I was born on July 23, 1957, a steamy hot day. My mother tells me that the delivery was normal and that I weighed a strapping eight pounds one ounce. Arriving home from the hospital, I was lovingly placed in my crib with a mobile of birds dangling delicately above me. STOP. This is stupid nonsense. I certainly don't remember this and anyway this probably happens to everyone.

The first day of nursery school was a trauma. I don't think my parents had ever really left me alone in strange surroundings before. This is also a pretty routine experience for most kids.

When Arnie moved away from the neighborhood, I was really upset. After all he was my first real buddy, and we shared our toys and got into a lot of mischief together. When he left, I moped around for a few days and got into fights with other kids. Maybe I should pursue this, but is it that significant in terms of my life? After all I did adjust pretty quickly and things went along smoothly until my parents broke up. That really started the ball rolling. Grades went down. Reckless driving. Hardly got out of high school. Went into Army. Got trained. Met and married Heidi. Nina born. Decided to make something of myself. College. I think that's it. I'll start with the divorce.

At this point Jules remembered reading about socialization and identity in his psychology text and how much the description of the eight stages of man's development as outlined by Erik H. Erikson had impressed him. The outline is shown in Table 5.1.

Jules really recognized himself in Erikson's depiction of the adolescent period reprinted below.

TABLE 5.1 Erikson's Eight Stages of Life

Age	Psychosocial Crises
Infancy	Basic trust vs. mistrust
Early childhood	Autonomy vs. shame and doubt
Four to five (play stage)	Initiative vs. guilt
Six to twelve (school age)	Industry vs. inferiority
Adolescence	Identity vs. role confusion
Young adulthood	Intimacy vs. isolation
Young adulthood and middle age	Generativity vs. stagnation
Old age	Integrity vs. despair

Identity vs. Role Confusion

Erikson believed that when one establishes a good relationship to skill and work, childhood proper comes to an end. Thus, as puberty begins, the child is starting to seek an identity that represents more than just accumulated childhood experiences. Ego identity, according to Erikson, is confidence that one's self is matched with others' perception of oneself, which ultimately becomes established in the promise of a career.

The danger in this stage is that the child can develop a role confusion. If the child is unsure of his or her skills, sexual identity, self-worth, and so on, he or she is also unlikely to be able to settle on an occupational identity. Given that in this culture we do not establish such an identity until later in adolescence or young adulthood, most adolescents "overidentify" with other people as a way of establishing themselves. Erikson believes that this is the reason that movie stars, rock stars, and so on are so popular with this age group. Moreover, he believes that "falling in love" is another way of finding one's identity, since adolescents often "project" themselves onto one another and are thereby better able to see themselves, as reflected in the other person. Thus, one's sense of identity can be clarified through one's relationship with another.

Jules believed that his parents' divorce had indeed inhibited his struggle for ego identity and resulted in role confusion. This, he felt, prevented him from making a smooth transition to the next stage, young adulthood. This reading, along with his focused freewriting, confirmed Jules's tentative decision to use as his first marker the period following his parents' divorce. Once this marker, his starting point, was in place, the other markers came easily as Jules continued his focused freewriting. The markers would be: the divorce, his Army experience, meeting and marrying Heidi, Nina's birth. Each marker would indicate a significant milestone on his journey to college, and within each marker he would group some of the significant events included in the same period.

PRACTICE

Using the chronological list of important events in your life that you have prepared, decide what the significant markers would be in your progress to the present. You might, like Jules, wish to do a focused freewriting. This writing might help you discover what you really want to communicate to your audience about the trends your life has followed.

Once Jules had decided upon his markers, he asked subsidiary questions to help him decide upon the details he might want to include. To generate them he used both the basic question patterns, the Who, Where, When questions, and combinations of the two. Below are some of his questions for his first marker, his parents' divorce:

1. Why did my parents separate?

2. Were my responses to the divorce similar to my sister's responses?

3. How was my behavior after the divorce different from before?

4. How did my anti-social behavior develop?

5. Who influenced me to behave this way?

6. Were my new friends like my old ones?

7. Why was I attracted to drop-outs?

8. What do I consider "anti-social" behavior?

9. Why did the fact that the divorce occurred when I was fifteen cause problems?

10. How do I fit in with Erik Erikson's description of adolescence? With the earlier stages he discusses?

Organizing the Essay

Once Jules had decided upon the markers he would use, planning the overall organization of the essay seemed easy. He would create a tentative thesis statement to include all the markers and then discuss each in some detail in a separate section of the body. He decided to create topic sentences for these markers in advance to guide him through his writing. Below is his general plan.

I. Introduction:
   Tentative thesis:
   Twenty-seven is an unusual age to start college, but being a freshman at this late date is the final result of a process that started with my parents' divorce, continued through a long stint in the Army, and culminated in my meeting and marrying a fine woman and having an adorable baby girl.

II. Body:

   A. Divorce of my parents
      Tentative topic sentence:

My parents' divorce when I was fifteen started a three-year downhill trend that almost ended in disaster.

B.   Army
Tentative topic sentence:
Serving in the military led me slowly but surely to a new-found confidence in myself.

C.   Meeting and marrying Heidi
Tentative topic sentence:
Meeting and marrying Heidi while I was in the Army also encouraged me to explore new territory.

D.   Birth of Nina
Tentative topic sentence:
The birth of my year-old baby girl, Nina, is the last link in a chain of events that catapulted me into being a college freshman at this late date.

PRACTICE

Using the markers you created for your own development in the previous exercise, devise an overall organizational plan for the essay you will be writing. In doing so, particularly in writing a tentative thesis, be aware of the message or impression you want your readers to come away with.

Jules wrote several drafts of the essay before submitting it to his English instructor. He asked a friend to help him correct the grammar, because he had had little experience with formal writing since high school and he was not yet feeling secure about his sentence structure. When he handed it in, he felt his paper was interesting and correct — the result of hard work. It was certainly a sincere effort to be honest with himself and his audience. He was, therefore, rather surprised and disappointed when the professor returned his paper with a *C* and the following comment:

Jules,
        I am impressed with your expressive use of language and the maturity of your perceptions about yourself and others. I do think, however, that the paper could use some revision. Rather than my telling you what I think, I would like you to read this essay in class to hear the possible reactions and suggestions of your real audience, your peers.

Below are the first four paragraphs of the paper Jules read.

The Rocky Road to Becoming an
Aging College Freshman

As a twenty-seven-year-old veteran, only now a freshman at college, I wander across campus aware of how young all the students seem. I am also equally aware that a number of my instructors are not the middle-aged men I had expected but rather men and women about my age. I look at these students and teachers and feel a little envious that their lives have progressed along the "normal" time frames for achievement, and I am often embarrassed about the fact that the way I got here does not conform to the usual patterns. Twenty-seven is perhaps an unusual age to start college, but being a freshman at this late date is the final result of a process which started with my parents' divorce, continued through a long stint in the Army, and concluded with meeting and marrying a fine woman and having an adorable baby girl. Through all this I slowly came to realize that life could offer more than I had ever thought possible.

As I learned in my sociology text, Erik Erikson, a famous psychoanalyst, defines adolescence as the period when young people integrate their experiences "to give a more permanent shape to who they are and where they are going as adults." However, Erikson also discusses the possibility of the adolescent not being able to integrate his or her personality "into a clear identity." My life during early adolescence probably was moving along toward this integration, but my "normal" development into an adult was abruptly halted by my parents' divorce when I was fifteen. This experience started me on a 3-year downhill plunge. I was a sophomore in high school at that time with better than average grades, and I was trying out for the junior varsity basketball team. The divorce came as a considerable shock to me since I was unaware of any serious disagreement between my parents. I guess they wanted to avoid involving my sister and me with their problems. Now that I think of it, they were on their best behavior with us, rarely disagreeing even about such small matters as what to have for dinner. Both my sister and I got a lot of expensive gifts at that time. I particularly remember the fancy stereo and color television they gave me for my room. The speakers really were something. I could fill the room with my rock albums and it sounded like actually being at a concert. I was probably the first kid on the block to have a color television, and my friends crowded into my room to watch the latest science fiction movies. Anyway, you can imagine my astonishment when my parents sat me down one Friday night and announced that Dad was moving out. I tried not showing any feeling, but I was really holding back my tears. For a long time Mom spent most of her time behind closed doors, but we could hear her sobbing away. When my father came every weekend to take Sandra and me out to dinner or to the movies, we all pretended that nothing was wrong. This kind of pretending really made my blood boil, but I didn't say anything. Anyway, everything turned sour for me at that point. I lost interest in school, spending most of my time in my room watching television or listening to the same album over and over and over again. I failed three majors that semester. Small wonder, since I hadn't even studied or paid attention in class. I was angry, and as a result I was bored with everything. But when I got my driver's license and Mom let me use the second car, things seemed to pick up a bit, but in reality that's when I got into real difficulty. My dropout-type friends and I would speed down the highway high on beer and other things. I guess we were openly displaying our contempt for any authority, our parents, our teachers, the community. Probably I should have joined the Army at seventeen and gotten the discipline I really needed. Sometimes I think the Army would be a good place for difficult teenagers; they would learn that they're not the big shots they pretend to be. They would learn the hard way that you've got to toe the line. And they'd learn a little respect for those people who had authority because they could control their behavior as I couldn't.

Anyway, we were finally arrested for drunken and reckless driving. My license was revoked, and I had to attend weekly group sessions with other delinquent types. By this time my parents were alarmed and switched their behavior from permissiveness to fairly rigid supervision. Even though this sometimes got me angry, I think I was relieved that controls were being placed upon me. Although it was too late to make up for my academic losses and graduate high school with respectable grades, I did pass, no small accomplishment. It was good to march down the aisle in my cap and gown. The shock of my parents' divorce made me lose control; the shock of getting into real trouble put me on firmer ground.

The next major period of my life was encompassed by the six years I spent in the Army. My anger and bitterness finally dissipated in the military and was reversed by the slow and steady progress I made there. There was boot camp which taught me endurance. The sergeant expected it of me, and after a while I expected it of myself. I was sent to Germany and when I reenlisted for another three years I was sent for advanced technical training in communications. After six years I decided it was time to resume civilian life.

PRACTICE

Rather than being told how Jules's class critiqued his paper, analyze the paper yourself, along with members of your class, and make appropriate recommendations for possible revision. Having covered a great deal of ground since group revision was first described in Chapter 1, you will probably now be able to do a more detailed analysis of Jules's essay. The procedure in the list below should help you do so.

1. Read Jules's paper to yourself again, jotting down some notes as you go along.

2. The paper should then be read aloud either in small groups or before the entire class.

3. The groups or the class should try to determine the basic idea Jules was trying to convey in his paper. Is this idea expressed in a thesis statement? Does the remainder of the introduction help to make the thesis clear? Does it help to arouse reader interest? Are the categories Jules has chosen to discuss appropriate for the explication of his thesis? Should Jules have started the process earlier? Later? Are there other markers he might have considered? Why or why not?

4. Examine the first body paragraph and decide whether Jules has adequately detailed the process he is describing. Is there too little information? Too much?

   Examine the second body paragraph. Is there too little information? Too much?

   Does Jules keep to the stage of his life he is describing in each paragraph, or does he digress? What do you think about Jules's including a reference to something he learned in psychology?

5. Do you agree with the professor's grade on the paper? Why, or why not?

PRACTICE

You are now ready to write your own essay. Here is the assignment.

Write an essay in which you describe the major markers in your development to the present. You should examine your life to determine what impression you want to present to your audience. To help you find this overall impression, you may want to consider one or more of the following categories: your academic, intellectual, emotional, social, or economic progress.

A suggested procedure to follow is:

1. Review the chapter headings (markers) you prepared earlier. Are they still the ones you want to consider? You might want to construct another list and decide on other markers, to do another focused freewriting, and/or create some additional subsidiary questions. What should be your first marker?

2. Establish a tentative plan for the entire paper. This might be no more than writing a thesis statement and appropriate topic sentences.

3. Consider the details you believe you should include. Before, during, and after you write your drafts, think about whether the details are necessary or superfluous to the support of your main idea. Think about what else might be included. Consider whether you are digressing.

4. Revise and edit your drafts.

5. Read a tentative draft to a fellow student or reading group.

6. Make the revisions you think would improve the essay, considering the suggestions of others.

7. Prepare a final edited copy for submission to your instructor.

A College Class at Work: Development of the Eye

Thinking and writing about process in the academic disciplines entails marking the beginnings and ends, grouping individual steps into usable segments, and, above all, showing the meaning of the process as a whole. Students in the natural sciences, for example, often encounter processes in their readings and must often provide the steps in a laboratory experiment as well as in writing essays that show their understanding of the course material.

The students in a course in human development faced these problems when their instructor was explaining the growth of the human fetus. She gave several lectures on the topic and also assigned readings. In order to help the students integrate the various strands, she gave them the following essay assignment:

> Relate the development of the eye to the general process of growth of the human embryo (first eight weeks).

Background Knowledge

The instructor provided the diagram of an embryo pictured below, and to guide the students' reading, she asked the following questions:

1. What sources of nourishment are available to the developing embryo? From the mother? From the ovum?

2. What is a blastocyst? How does it differ from the ovum?

3. What changes occur in the inner cell mass by the end of the second week? What are the three layers?

4. What are the steps in the sculpturing process?

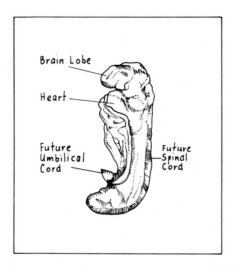

What follows is the reading assignment.

GROWTH[1]

The parents of a strapping teen-age son may find it hard to remember that their offspring was once a tiny seven-pounder. In less than a score of years, he has increased in height about three and a half times and in weight more than 20 times, at the same time changing from an infant to a man. But this visible growth and transformation are infinitesimal compared with those that take place in the first two months he spends in his mother's womb. There, in eight brief weeks, he increases in length about 240 times and in weight one million times; he grows from a single fertilized egg into a miniature baby.

---

[1] Life Science Library/*Growth* by James M. Tanner, Gordon Rattray Taylor and the Editors of Time-Life Books. © 1968 Time-Life Books Inc.

First come the more vital necessities. The most obvious of these is a nutritional system to supply the embryo with the raw materials for growth. This need the mother's body regularly anticipates. Every month the wall of the uterus grows a thick, spongy lining, rich in blood vessels. If the egg that has been released during this period is not fertilized by a sperm, the lining is sloughed off in menstruation. But if conception occurs, the lining remains and grows thicker, readying itself to receive the embryo and to supply it with nutrients from the mother's body.

The sperm and egg unite in one of the Fallopian tubes, the ducts that lead from the ovaries to the womb. The fertilized egg takes three or four days to drift down into its future home, dividing steadily all the time. By the time it arrives in the uterus, it has grown to a spherical cluster of several dozen cells. In the uterus it floats about for a few more days, continuing to divide. At the same time, its structure changes from a solid, spherical cluster of cells to a hollow ball, the blastocyst, with a tiny protuberance at one spot on its inner wall. Most of this little bump, known as the inner cell mass, is destined to become the embryo proper. But the cells that make up the greater part of the blastocyst play no direct part in building the baby. They, with bits of the inner cell mass, form the embryo's contribution to the structures that will protect and nourish it for the next nine months: the chorion, the outer membrane that surrounds the embryo; the amnion, the fluid-filled sac in which it floats; and the placenta, or afterbirth, where the exchange of materials takes place between mother and child.

About a week after conception, the blastocyst begins to burrow its way into the lining of the womb, attaching itself in such a fashion that the side on which the inner cell mass lies is in contact with the uterine lining. Almost immediately thereafter, its outer portion, which is known as the trophoblast, begins to grow rapidly. As it does it sends out fingerlike extensions, called villi, which also work their way into the wall; simultaneously the outer portion forms the chorion. Other trophoblast cells begin to join with part of the inner cell mass to produce the amnion, the fluid content of which serves to cushion the baby against shocks or pressure from the outside world.

The Genetic Blueprints

The gross structural changes that take place during the first eight weeks of embryonic life reflect equally profound alterations in the cells that make up the embryo. The blastocyst which first implanted itself in the uterine wall has not only expanded enormously, creating millions of cells from only a few dozen, it also has given rise to cells that are entirely different in appearance and in function both from one another and from the original fertilized egg. In the eight-week embryo, liver cells are clearly distinguishable from cells of the heart; muscle cells and blood cells are not interchangeable; bone cells cannot do the work of brain cells, or brain cells act as bone.

Yet all these cells contain exactly the same genes. Except for the sperm and the egg, every cell in the body has a full complement of hereditary material and thus is potentially capable of performing the functions of any kind of cell. As the embryo develops, however, the cells begin to specialize, "learning" to act on only one of these many possible sets of instructions. This process takes place gradually; little by little the possibilities are narrowed down until at last the cell achieves its permanent and, for the most part, irreversible character.

The Embryonic Sandwich

Cellular specialization progresses with a speed paralleling that of the structural changes. A mere two weeks after conception, the inner cell mass has already developed three distinct groups of cells, neatly arranged in a three-layered sandwich, which have, so to speak, divided up the body's structures among them. The top layer (the ectoderm) will give rise to the nervous system and all the outer coatings of the body: the epidermis, the hair, the fingernails. The middle layer (the mesoderm) will form the musculature, the bones and the cartilage, as well as the heart, veins and arteries. The bottom layer (the endoderm) will produce glands and the linings of such internal organs as the stomach and lungs.

Along with differentiation come two other equally basic cellular processes which shape the body's structures. Cells may change their position or migrate from one embryonic site to another; they may also multiply at different rates, producing a bulge at one place, a hollow at another. Like differentiation, these processes take place gradually. The shifting and multiplying of cells first block out rough shapes, then refine and elaborate them into finished organs.

The first step in this sculpturing process is the formation of the notochord. This structure, a rodlike primitive spine, develops from a group of mesodermal cells. Above the notochord, ectodermal cells multiply furiously to create a thickened strip, which then curls up into a tube that is the precursor of the spinal cord and brain. Meanwhile, cells from the mesoderm arrange themselves on either side of the notochord in paired blocks called somites, which will eventually develop into the vertebrae and muscles of the back. Together, these changes supply the embryo with a back and a front, as well as a fore-and-aft axis along which organ systems can arrange themselves. These, in turn, are formed by the same interweaving of processes of differentiation, movement and growth. The digestive system, for example, begins as a tube of mesodermal cells lined with cells from the endoderm. As the tube is forming, groups of cells along its length begin to specialize, giving rise to the esophagus, the stomach, the liver, the pancreas and the intestines. A pocket branching off from the same tube develops into the lungs and trachea.

By the ninth week of uterine life, the growing baby has moved so far along the road to birth that it can no longer be called by its original name. During its first two months in the womb, it was an embryo — a swelling within its mother. Now it has become a fetus — an offspring. The cartilage has begun to turn to bone, the skeleton is emerging, and all the vital organs have been outlined and formed. Much more growing remains to be done, and much refinement of structure is yet to be accomplished. But the emphasis has shifted radically. From here on, the development of function becomes the most important part of the process of growth. The seven months still separating the fetus from birth are primarily months of practice, months in which the baby's body learns to use all the intricate and delicate equipment it has been building as it grows.

After the students had completed their reading, the instructor lectured on the development of the embryo and the eye. One student's lecture notes on the embryo and on the eye looked like Tables 5.2 and 5.3.

TABLE 5.2   Lecture One: From Embryo to Fetus

Age (days)	Size (mm)	Development
1	.125	1 cell in ovarian tubes (oviduct) surrounded by thin temporary membrane — (zona pellucida) cell division
4	.115	Cells in oviduct — cells identical but smaller entering uterus
5	.095	Cell movement begins, forms outer ring and inner cell mass. Outer ring will become placenta, the inner cell mass will be embryo
7–8	.10	Beginning of implantation into wall of uterus
12	.7	Embryonic disc formed from inner cell mass — flat two layers
15	1.5	Two layers of disc grown to three a. ectoderm — (outer layer) — becomes skin, hair, nails, some brain, nerves b. mesoderm — (middle layer) — becomes skeleton, bone marrow, muscles, heart, blood, inner skin, kidneys, gonads c. endoderm (inner layer) — becomes lining of internal organs, lungs, trachea, pharynx, digestive tract, pancreas, liver. No visible difference in layers

continued

TABLE 5.2 *continued*

Age (days)	Size (mm)	Development
21	2.0	Differentiation starts, looks like backward C, brain lobe on top, heart sticks out under brain, start of spinal cord, start of umbilical cord
30–35	4.0–5.4	Growth of tail; arm and leg buds appear as solid lumps
35	6	Tail prominent, umbilical chord forming; eye, heart, liver, forming, jaws outlined, intestine changing from simple tube to loop, parts of lungs appearing, yolk sac separates, disappears
56	22–25	Fetus — head dominant in size, face and neck forming, back straightens, recognizable limbs, fingers and toes forming, tail regressing, body evenly rounded, mouth parts, intestines, lungs, heart, testes and ovaries distinguishable and developing, skeleton starts hardening, muscles forming, capable of some movement. Kidneys function. Formation of all body systems underway — respiratory, nervous, blood, digestion, etc.

One of the students in the class took the following steps as she planned her essay.

Collecting Data

Since she was working with three separate sets of data, the two sets of lecture notes and the reading, the student first needed to pull them together in some way. She decided to create one chart on which all the material could be entered. Part of her chart is reproduced in Table 5.4.

Weighing the Evidence

Once the information had been entered into the chart, the student realized she still faced a number of problems in planning her paper. In fact,

TABLE 5.3   Lecture Two: Development of the Eye

Age (days)	Size (mm)	Development
21–24	2.0–2.8	Swelling in forebrain forms bulge (optical vesicle) will become optic nerve, retina, iris, and coating of eyeball
30–35	4.3–5.4	Vesicle folds in on self, optic cup and lens pit forming cradle for future lens
35–37	6	Lens forming in pit
38–40	8–10	Lens developing, separation of parts, blood vessels developing, cornea begins, lens separated from surface of optic cup
42–44	12–14	Retina develops, eyes at 160° apart
56	22–25	Eyelids start, nerve fibers, iris developing pigment, main elements established, eyelids meet and fuse, do not open until 7th month. Eyes converge

TABLE 5.4   Student Chart Combining Lecture Notes and Reading

Age (days)	Size (mm)	Development
30–35	4.3–5.4	Eye — optic vesicle folds in on self (optic cup) — cradle for future lens
		Embryo — tail prominent, heart, liver forming, jaws outlined, intestine changing from simple tube to loop, parts of lungs appearing, yolk sac separates, disappears, limb buds evident
35–37	6	Eye — lens forming in pit
38–40	8–10	Eye — lens separated from surface of optic cup, blood vessels form, cornea begins to form
42	12–14	Embryo — upper jaw components prominent but separate; lower jaw halves fused — head dominant in size — external ear appearing, limbs recognizable

she did not even know what to do next. In order to clear up the confusion, she asked the question:

When does the process start?

Just as the biographers we discussed earlier had to decide where to begin, the student had to establish the point at which she should begin her discussion of the process. The assignment focused specifically on the eye, but if she began at that point, would she be able to show how its growth was connected with the earlier stages of development? How far back should she go, to the fertilized egg, or back further — to discuss the process of fertilization? Or even further back — to the development of mature reproductive organs? After some thought, her final decision was to begin with the fertilized egg, since she would be able then to concentrate her attention on the main point of the assignment: the growth of the embryo and the eye.

Once the chart was completed and the decision made on where to begin, the student wondered what she should do next. Would it be enough simply to write up her notes into sentences, using the chart as her reference? That would certainly cover all the information, but it seemed inadequate. Not only would it be a dull job to write and even duller to read, the paper would still be nothing more than a listing of events day by day. What should be the point of her paper?

Using Questions to Establish Significant Markers.   First the student used the basic question patterns to get the following questions. Add your own questions to the list.

1. Are there contrasts between the developments at different time periods?

2. What is the effect of cell multiplication?

3. _____

4. _____

Using the Who, What, Where, and When questions produced the following. Add your questions to the list.

5. When does movement start?

6. Where is the eye before and after movement?

7. _____

8. _____

Combining the two types produced the questions below. Add your own questions.

9. What effect does eye movement have on the general development of the face?

10. _____

11. _____

With Question 1 in mind, the student looked again at the chart. On closer inspection, she saw that in the earliest period, only cell multiplication occurred; then movement was added at the fifth day; differentiation occurred on the fifteenth day. Three separate stages of the process could thus be established.

Stage One: Cell multiplication (1–5 days)

Stage Two: Cell multiplication plus movement (5–15 days)

Stage Three: Cell multiplication plus movement plus differentiation (15–56 days)

Before the student proceeded, she engaged in focused freewriting:

> I just don't believe I can do this, way over my head, gotta try gotta try. Well what do I know . . . the big thing is first the cell multiplication . . . I never realized the embryo got smaller before it got bigger, how about that, what do I have to do? I've got to get some idea on how to put this together . . . those three stages seem to be a good idea, suppose I begin with just the cell division multiplication, funny they're the same thing here . . . that means a separate paragraph on just multiplication, then one on differentiation then one on movement . . . that means most of the essay won't be on target till the third paragraph . . . oh well . . . But the main point of the paper ought to pick up on the fact that it's cell differentiation that gets the whole thing started . . . Hey, that's ok.

Organizing the Essay

From her freewriting, the student found a focus for her paper: the fact that development of the eye and the development of the embryo both occurred when cell differentiation occurred. Her notes for the first draft are below:

Intro — Eye develops when cell differentiation occurs

Body — (1) Stage One: Cell multiplication

(2) Stage Two: Cell movement begins

(3) Stage Three: Cell differentiation
(a) Eye and embryo parts form
(b) Developments at end of 56 days

When the student looked at the draft, however, she realized that the two paragraphs on Stages One and Two had nothing to do with the eye, while the bulk of the important material that answered the instructor's question failed to be touched on until the fourth paragraph. Since Stages One and Two occurred before the development of the eye, the student revised her draft to place them in the introduction. The main part of the essay, the body, would then cover just the eye and the other kinds of growth that were occurring simultaneously.

Her new organization was:

Intro — Eye develops when cell differentiation occurs
(a) Stage One: Cell multiplication
(b) Stage Two: Cell movement
Body — Eye and Embryo at start of cell differentiation
(a) Changes
(b) Eye and embryo at 56th day

Her final draft, after revision and editing, looked like this:

Development of the Eye

The development of the eye is one of the many events that occur during the first nine weeks as the fertilized human egg (zygote) grows through the embryo stage to become a fetus. The first step in the process begins almost immediately with rapid cell multiplication during the first five days at the same time as the egg is traveling from the ovarian tubes to the uterus. In the second stage, the cells not only continue to multiply but now also realign themselves to form a new configuration called a blastocyst, part of which, the inner cell mass, will become the embryo and the rest of which will develop into the protective and nourishing parts. The blastocyst fastens itself to the wall of the uterus while the inner cell mass forms into a flat three-layered embryonic disc. It is not until the third stage, at about the fifteenth day when cells begin to differentiate, that specific parts of the body, such as the eye, can be said to develop.

At the beginning of the third week, the embryo is a soft lump of tissue that looks mostly like a letter C with a brain lobe on top, a bulge for the heart under that, the start of spinal and umbilical cords, the whole being about a tenth of an inch long. Sometime during the 21st to the 24th day, a swelling in the forebrain starts to form a bulge (the optical vesicle) which in the following two weeks gradually folds in on itself to become the optic cup for the developing lens. At the same time cells are lining up on either side of the proto spinal cord to start the process of becoming vertebrae and back muscles while others line up along a tube to start differentiating into the various parts of the digestive system.

By the 35th day, arm and leg buds have appeared as solid lumps; there is a clearly developing tail; the jaws are outlined; intestines and lungs start to appear, and the umbilical cord is becoming organized. At the same time the lens of the eye has been growing in the optic cup, and in the next two days it will separate itself while blood vessels and the cornea develop. In the sixth week, the head of the embryo contains the eye as a dark-rimmed circle just in front of a bulge that will become the nose, while under it a series of little folds are the start of the outer ear. The eyes are almost on opposite sides of the head, about 160° apart.

By the 50th day the iris develops pigment, the eyelids start to form, and all the main elements of the eye are established. Now the eyes start moving toward the front, the eyelids meet and fuse, not to open again until the seventh month. During these same weeks the changes in the rest of the body have transformed it into a recognizable human child. The head is dominant in size, the face and neck are forming, the back straightens, the limbs are recognizable as arms and legs with fingers and toes, the body is evenly rounded, the mouth, the intestines, lungs, heart, testes and ovaries are distinguishable, the skeleton is hardening and the fetus is capable of some movement.

The first nine weeks are a period of amazing growth during which the three stages of development — cell multiplication, cell movement, and cell differentiation — change the microscopic egg into a recognizable human fetus. All three steps are necessary, but it is not until cell differentiation occurs that the eye and other parts of the embryo begin to form into recognizable units.

The essay this student wrote involved making a number of decisions. She had to decide where to begin her discussion of the process, what significant markers she would use, and how much space to devote to each of these markers. The following questions will give you an opportunity to reconsider her thinking.

1. What arguments can you make for beginning the process at day 21 rather than day 1? Beginning the process with fertilization? What arguments can you make to support the student's position?

2. By putting Stages One and Two in the introduction the student omitted much of the information. Considering the assignment, do you think this was wise?

Using simple chronological steps to mark the process, the student could, however, have found other possibilities. She could have established stages of development for the embryo and fit the development of the eye into those steps. Such a breakdown might look like the one in Table 5.5. Or the student might have used the formation of the eye for her basic structure and related the changes in the embryo to these steps. Her organization would then be like the one in Table 5.6.

Which of these organizational patterns do you think is most useful?

A Student at Work: The Aging Process

Later in the same human development course, the instructor covered the process of aging. As she had done with the study of the developing embryo, she assigned reading and devoted two class hours to the issue. In a one-hour lecture she provided a general outline of the stages of growth, and then during the second hour provided the information on one woman's aging process by playing a taped interview.

Her assignment for the students was:

Write an essay in which you show how Madam X's personal aging process reflects the general aging process.

TABLE 5.5   Development of the Embryo and the Eye

Age (days)		Development
Stage 1	21	Embryo — first differentiation apparent — primitive structure Eye — optic cup
Stage 2	30–35	Embryo — parts begin to achieve mature form Eye — lens forms
Stage 3	42	Embryo — distinguishing features apparent Eye — retina forms
Stage 4	56	Complete embryo Eye — main parts established

TABLE 5.6 Formation of the Eye Related to Changes in the Embryo

Age (days)		Development
Stage 1	21	Optic cup forms
		Embryo structure primitive
Stage 2	30–35	Lens forms
		Embryo — start of mature form
Stage 3	42	Eye — retina forming
		Embryo — distinguishing features apparent
Stage 4	56	Eye — main parts established
		Embryo — complete

The reading assignment follows.

The Aging Process

One truth is now recognized to be universal among people and among animals that live long enough to become old. Aging never stems from a single cause, but develops through a multiplicity of changes.

For a while, the principal gains in gerontology were more detailed knowledge of what takes place as the years go by. The skin loses its smoothness because its inner fat tends to shift from its childish sites to locations deeper in the body. Usually the face grows thinner, the waist and thighs bigger. Anyone with a fat face appears younger, and so does a person with a slim waist. The placid individual gets fewer wrinkles by frowning less and rarely showing tension by corrugating the brow. Habitual gestures that crinkle the skin cause the fat to move and let the furrows deepen.

Sunlight may bleach the hair a little, but does not affect the color that is being formed in the hair follicles. Hair keeps its color so long as the special cells in the hair follicles continue to produce pigment. As we grow older they cease, one by one, intermittently at first, and then altogether. Usually the first white hairs appear on the temples and back of the neck, next in a scattering on the scalp and shoulders and chest, and much later elsewhere. It is as though a person were several ages at once in different areas.

We are much more inconvenienced when our eyes lose their youthful ability to change focus quickly from far to near. The loss comes gradually, as the lens in each eye gets stiffer. It fails to bulge out when the focusing muscles give it a chance to adjust for close vision.

At the same time that the lens is gaining weight, it is becoming more yellowish and less transparent. In consequence our eyes detect progressively less of the violet end of the spectrum as we grow older. Aging painters use less violet on their canvases. Even the blues they see are darker, the greens and yellows and oranges least affected by the filtering action of the lens. Everyone needs a little more light, particularly at night, to produce a recognizable image on the sensitive cells of the aging eye.

Some people are surprised to learn that they shrink by day and stretch at night. Erect stature decreases by almost an inch among most adults between arising in the morning and going to bed at night, because in our erect position our intervertebral discs become compressed. But as we age, these same discs of cartilage between one bone of the vertebral column and the next get thinner permanently. Even if we stand up straight to have our height measured first thing in the day, it is less after 40 than when we were 20. The arches in our feet get flatter too. By age 60 we are half an inch or more shorter than we were in youth.

Our nose and ears get stiffer, and our chest becomes more rigid, with less space for muscles between the ribs. Within the muscles all over the body, the contractile fibers tend to be replaced by fibrous connective tissue. Like old chickens we get tough. After age 80, we are likely to lose most of our fat, and to become as much as 30 pounds lighter by age 90 than we weighed at half that number of years.

The human brain, too, loses weight each year past the middle of an average life. The number of working nerve cells decreases. Fortunately, our reserves are so plentiful that we barely notice the change. In avoiding awkward situations we rely more upon experience than on reacting at high speed to save ourselves at the last moment. Although neuromotor control diminishes measurably, a healthy old person can still cope with most situations. Judgments, if slower, tend to be wiser.

A 30-year-old man in normal health can do enough work to raise a 36-pound weight 100 feet in a minute and still have his rate of heartbeat return to the resting frequency within two minutes. If the average 70-year-old is to recover as completely in this way, he must limit his output of work to raising the same weight 70 feet in the minute.

At the National Institutes of Health in Bethesda, Maryland, the favorite test is to ask men to turn a crank on a measuring machine. Dr. Nathan W. Shock, who is chief of the gerontology branch there, finds that for short assignments of this activity the maximum work rate without developing fatigue decreased by almost 60 per cent between ages 35 and 80. In the same years, the strength of a man's grasp in his dominant hand drops to about half, and his endurance in maintaining a firm grip for a minute or more diminishes by about a third. Curiously, although the subordinate hand is always the weaker one, it does not lose quite as much in either firmness or endurance of grip. By age 90, a right-handed oldster can grasp almost as well with his subordinate left hand as with his dominant right.

At any age, continued exercise requires extra oxygen and other materials carried by the blood, and produces acids as wastes that must be transported to the kidneys for disposal. After we are 14 or 15 years old, we pass the point at which the heart is most efficient, and gradually propel a smaller volume of blood per beat. To circulate the same amount of blood, in support of the same amount of muscular work, we need progressively faster heartbeats at the same time that the maximum of which we are capable decreases year by year.

The radioactive test is a good measure also of the arteries to the lungs, since if these are getting hard with deposits inside their walls, they are narrower and reduce the flow of blood out of the heart. A person who is 40 years old may need 50 or 60 seconds to get the solution through to the lungs, and is said to have an "arterial age" of 50 or 60. This same hardening of the arteries can be assumed to be widespread, limiting the flow of blood for vital needs. The loss of elasticity in the vessels becomes doubly dangerous because it decreases the cushioning effect on blood pressure in each cycle of the heart. The full vigor of the contracting heart may be felt in small arteries where the walls are increasingly fragile and liable to rupture. The person becomes liable to fatal bleeding internally, and to the vascular accidents that cause death so frequently by suddenly diminishing the supply of blood to brain and heart muscle.

The efficiency of the ventilating system in the lungs diminishes with age at a fairly regular pace. Both the amount of oxygen the blood can take up and carry to the tissues and also the amount of air moved into the lungs and out again decrease significantly. As we grow older, we take shallower breaths and feel discomfort if we force ourselves to breathe more vigorously. Consequently the maximum volume of air inhaled normally by a resting 75-year-old man is less than half as much as he took in without thinking about it at age 20. At the same time, the diffusion of oxygen from lungs into red blood cells becomes less efficient. For the same amount of blood going through the vessels in his lungs, an 80-year-old gets into his red cells only slightly more than a third as much oxygen as he did at age 20. To engage in comparable muscular exercise, he must breathe three times as hard.

During our youth, as much as a quarter of the blood pumped through the heart goes straightaway to the kidneys, where soluble wastes and water are removed to form urine. This permits the body to maintain the chemical nature of the blood extraordinarily constant — more constant than seems necessary, since a person can manage perfectly well with one healthy kidney instead of two. As we age, however, the proportion of the blood directed into the kidneys decreases steadily until, before age 80, it amounts to less than an eighth of the output of the heart. Correspondingly, the kidneys require more time to clear the blood of wastes, often six times as many hours. But given the time, they handle their tasks fully as well. So seldom do they develop degenerative difficulties themselves that kidney disease is only the fifteenth ranking cause of death in America, causing one death in each 145 among those tallied in the United States.

As more is learned about the safety features built into the human body, letting us continue life in satisfactory health although with a maturing pattern of behavior, we feel encouraged. We have no honest reason to view our later years as though watching a black curtain being pulled down over the world, shutting us in the dark. The kaleidoscopic adjustments in all our body functions are scarcely less wonderful than those that unfolded during the weeks and years after we arrived, squalling, red and wrinkled, for only our parents to really admire. Infancy and a sunrise have much in common, and so does the grace of age and a wondrous sunset. It is up to us to get the most from life at both ends.

A student who listened to the lecture on the issue of aging took the following lecture notes. Included in the notes are three graphs the instructor handed out.

Changes in general appearance a clue, but can be misleading. Need to decide which features are likely to give best indication of biological or physiological age rather than chronological.

1. Data on aging mostly done in terms of averages, not really accurate; also no longitudinal studies yet.

2. Do not know what causes aging. Best approach is in examination of cells. Two theories — wear and tear; genetic timetable.

3. Which of age-dependent changes provide a useful measure of aging?

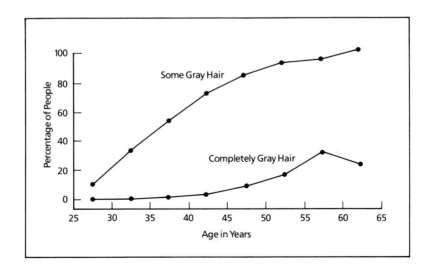

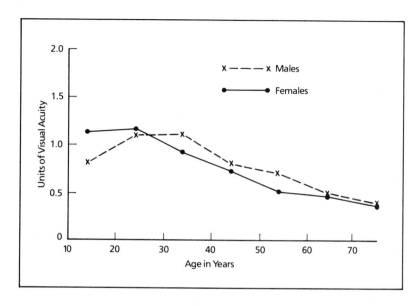

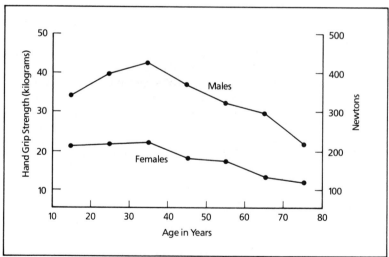

Specific Changes:

a. Hair — graying
b. Visual acuity lessened
c. Loss of strength — weaker
d. Blood pressure — rises after 40

   e. Lung capacity — declines after 40

   f. Incidence of disease increases — does not affect maximum life span

   g. Stress — old succumb more quickly than young

   h. Vision — need more illumination

   i. Hearing — diminishes, especially for tones of higher frequencies; less ability to separate sounds

   j. Verbal intelligence — unchanged, mild forgetfulness especially for names

   k. Brain — shrinks 10–12%, loss of gray matter after 50

   l. Physical size — shrink

Instead of giving a second lecture on aging, the instructor played the tape of the interview with Madame X, a 77-year-old woman who has been widowed for five years. She has two sons, both married, aged 56 and 53, and four grown grandchildren. The text of the interview follows.

Interviewer: Can you describe the process of growing old?

Madame X: Well, being old is no bed of roses, but it's turned out to be a lot less of a problem than I thought it would be. I've always been busy doing things all my life and although I've cut back some, I find I can still do quite a bit. I guess you could say I'm a vain woman, but I've always watched the way I looked — never was fat, exercised to keep my figure and all — and I remember all the signs of aging. Why, when I was 27 I noticed some gray hairs, especially above the temples, and by the time I was 32 there was a lot of gray, so I started dyeing it. I really don't know when I was all gray, but sometime in my early 50's I could see that the new hair was coming in all white. It was the skin changes, though, that were upsetting and they started early too. When I was 29, I could see the two frown lines between my eyebrows even when I wasn't frowning, and four or five years later I had "crow's feet" on either side of my eyes.

Interviewer: What is the difference between your skin now and before?

Madame X: The skin on my hands started getting visibly coarse in my late forties and at the same time the skin on my neck started sagging, like a double chin, though I still wasn't fat. About 55 I noticed that my underarms sagged and that was really discouraging. I did some special exercises for a long time and that delayed further sagging but it didn't correct the condition. Now, of course, I'm covered with wrinkles — arms and legs look like an alligator — and no matter what the ads say, those face creams and body lotions don't do a thing. And I sag all over.

Interviewer: How have these changes affected you?

Madame X: You know, I never found that these changes interfered with the way I felt or the kinds of things I wanted to do. Maybe people didn't make so many comments about how well I looked but I guess I was too busy to notice.

Interviewer: Can you tell me something about your vision and hearing?

Madame X: Oh they're not as good as they used to be, but I manage. I'm nearsighted, you know, so when I began having trouble reading — at about 45 — had to hold the book further and further away — I got bifocals. That was a disaster, never did learn to use them. Now I have two sets of glasses, one for distance and the other for close, and except for the fact that I keep forgetting where I put them, there's no problem. About 55–60, I started needing a lot of light when I read or sewed, more I think than I used to. The hearing isn't as sharp as it used to be; for the past 10 years I haven't found music as interesting as I used to. But the real problem which came up just 2–3 years ago is that when I go to a party, I have trouble following a conversation. All the sounds seem to jumble together. Even when I'm just talking to one other person, I sometimes have to ask him to talk up; people mumble more now than they used to. . . .

Interviewer: What about your general health — accidents, illnesses?

Madame X: Had the flu two years ago and it took almost six months before I felt my old self again. It didn't used to be like that. When I was younger, even in my 40's and 50's, I might get sick for a week or so, but I'd be out doing things in no time. And, well, there's a lot of aches and pains these days. And getting up in the mornings, I feel so stiff, it takes more than an hour to get myself going. That started in my mid-60's. But now, even the fingers don't move right, so buttoning my blouse takes forever. My doctor says my blood pressure is almost like that of a young woman — a bit higher but not much — and my heart is fine.

I guess the other thing to say is that my energy gives out sooner now. I've always liked to walk and still do a lot. When I was 50, I used to be able to walk for hours and now I find about 3/4 of an hour is tops. Just get out of breath if I try to go quickly, and lugging the vacuum cleaner when I houseclean is more of a chore than I remember even 5 years ago.

Interviewer: Would you call yourself an "old" woman?

Madame X: Well, I guess I'm luckier than most — don't have any serious health problems. And I have a lot of things I like to do — work with the church, and the "foster grandparent" program, visiting with the children in the local school, and I play bingo and cards with friends, and of course my children and grandchildren come visit. Sometimes I think the biggest problem is not with me but with the rest of the world. People always act as if I'm decrepit, tell me to take it easy, afraid to let me do things myself, even sort of avoid being with me — you know, some of the young women in the church group shy away when they see me. I wish the rest of the world would realize I'm still a person, and even if I'm a little slower, I'm not ready for a wheelchair. I still can think and feel and like to be useful. I can still get around, I think clearly, I am useful — no, I'm not an old woman yet.

PRACTICE

Using the transcript of the interview with Madame X or interviewing an older person yourself, write an essay responding to the instructor's assignment.

> Write an essay in which you show how Madame X's personal aging process reflects the general aging process.

In order to organize your materials you should:

1. Reread the article on aging and review the lecture notes.

2. Create a chronological list of markers.

3. Decide when you would begin the aging process.

4. Select those markers you consider significant.

You may find that you will have a number of possibilities and will have to do several drafts before you find the one that works best for you.

PRACTICE

From Part 3 of this book (the Anthology) choose an article that interests you and write an essay answering one of the process questions provided there.

---

chapter

6

Questions of Cause and Effect

THINKING

Why Ask About Causes and Effects?

How many times a day do you say something like, "I can't go to the movies because I have to go to a family gathering," or "Since the bus station was closed, I had to wait on the street"?

In making such remarks, what you are doing is supplying a *cause* that has produced a certain *effect*. When you told your friend that you had to go to a family gathering, you were giving the *cause* that produced the *effect* of your not being able to go to the movies. And when you said that the bus station was closed, you were supplying the *cause* that resulted in waiting on the street.

In each instance the single cause of the action or decision was apparently clear. But consider the following questions:

What was, or what were, the cause or causes of World War II?

What causes an economic recession?

In pursuing answers to these questions, one would find that the cause-effect link is not as obvious because there is probably more than one causal factor. In their fields of study, natural and social scientists and other scholars have to examine and weigh the relative merits of several causes and decide which are the most important. This effort to find the *significant cause(s)* is one of the major endeavors in academic study.

In previous chapters, it has been explained that the critical thinking practiced in college is more orderly, more organized, and more substantial than is normally used. Yet this kind of thinking is also exhibited in important ways in everyday life. The following real-life incident is presented to begin our study. Imagine the following scene:

> Tom, a second-semester student at Grompton College, is dressed handsomely for an interview with the chairperson of Marketing and Advertising. He is applying for official acceptance into its program. His brown jacket and light beige trousers fit well and look well. He is a believer in the adage, "Clothes make the man." The interview is at 2:00 o'clock. He arrives at school and is in front of the elevator doors at 1:53. Two minutes pass and no elevator arrives. He fidgets and decides to go up the three flights of stairs to the chairperson's office. Being thin and long-legged, he bounds up the stairs two at a time, turns the first landing, and, as he wheels around, grasps the narrow wall supporting the bannister. "What the . . . !" He feels something sticky. With great apprehension he opens the palm of his hand and then looks down at his trousers. He gasps, "Oh, no!"
>
> Oh, yes. A sign dangling from the bannister reads "Wet Paint." Besides a sticky smear of blue paint on his palm, there is a wide blue smudge across one leg of his trousers. He blurts aloud, "The school should pay for these pants."

Should the college pay? Maybe. We cannot decide until we examine the incident more closely.

Determining the Significant Cause(s)

If Tom were asked to write an essay about his experience he would need to find answers to a number of questions. Why did the unfortunate incident happen? Who is essentially responsible? Tom? The elevator maintenance crew? The paint crew? The supervisor of buildings and grounds? These queries are really leading up to the controlling question, "What is or what are the causes of this mishap?" Of course, certain other probing questions immediately come to mind:

Is Tom usually clumsy?

Where was the sign placed?

Was the sign large enough to be seen?

Was there more than one sign?

An essay on this problem would need to supply sufficient information to support the answer to the controlling question. Subsidiary questions using the basic patterns plus the Who, Where, When questions will help. Several are suggested below; can you think of others?

1. Was the sign, or were the signs, large enough to be seen? Where were they placed? When were they put in place?

2. What were the actions of the student that led to this mishap? Of the maintenance crew? Of the supervisor?

3. _____

4. _____

The answers to such questions should help resolve the issue of who was primarily responsible and why Tom thinks he is not.

In order to determine responsibility, all the facts leading up to the mishap must be gathered. One of the questions is an extremely important one:

What were the steps that led to this mishap?

It calls for a sequential series of incidents — a list of events — and a determination of possible causal links among them, *each of which is the effect of the previous one.* A model showing the cause-effect relationship in this story would help resolve the issue. Before examining Tom's predicament, a closer look at the cause-effect model in general is necessary.

The Causal Chain

A causal chain is, superficially, similar to the list of markers discussed in Chapter 5. Unlike the list, however, in which chronology provides the only links among the items in it, the causal chain provides a *reason* for the linkage. The cause of any event may have been preceded by a series of events that led up to it. Take Kevin, another college student, for example, who attempts to explain why he was fifty-five minutes late to a two-hour class. It's a bit of a story: The alarm clock failed to buzz, so he got up fifteen minutes later than usual; because of this he missed his 8:05 bus, having to take the 8:12, which took longer than usual because the bus driver stopped to get a container of coffee; because of this, he missed his usual 8:25 train, the next one taking a little longer than usual because it switched to a local track; because of this, he arrived at the college during a class change when the elevators were working to capacity, so he was further delayed.

You have to give Kevin credit. His story apparently has no holes in it. Like the list of events in Chapter 5, Kevin's explanation can be diagrammed, as in Figure 6.1.

What Kevin has presented is an instance of a *causal chain*. Causal chains resemble the lists of events discussed in Chapter 5 but differ from them in that a *reason* is necessary for connecting each item. Such chains link the causes for each succeeding event. Although there are several causes in the chain, there is, according to Kevin's analysis, one significant cause:

The circumstance of the malfunctioning alarm clock.

One difficulty we have in accepting Kevin's story, however, is the question whether the causes are significant enough to be considered the real ones. Yes, the alarm failed to buzz, but why? Did Kevin set it wrong before going to bed? If so, then does this not become the real cause of his lateness? And, if the clock was unreliable, should he not have gotten a new one? In either case, the suggestion is that there is a more significant *cause* than the

Figure 6.1 *Simple Causal Chain*

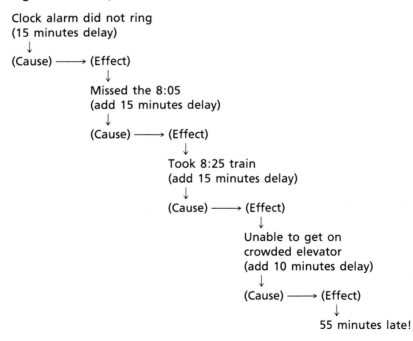

stated one. Perhaps the *significant cause* of his lateness, as psychologists might claim, is lack of motivation for going to class, and the less significant one is the failure of the alarm clock.

The Larger Context: Perspectives from Different Academic Disciplines

Although Kevin's explanation was orderly and the cause-effect links logically connected, his analysis may have been incomplete; the causal chain could have been extended. Other links could have been provided by seeing Kevin's behavior in a larger context, the perspective of psychology.

Psychoanalysis is a discipline that explores underlying or hidden motivation behind behavior. Sigmund Freud, the founder of this approach, examined his patients' slips of the tongue, forgetting of names, and loss of objects. Their explanations for such errors was something like "I had other things on my mind" or "I am absent-minded." Not so, says Freud. These explanations are merely symptoms of deeper causes. In most cases there is a purpose for such errors — that is, there is a more significant cause, unknown even to the patients themselves. And is Kevin (assuming our analysis of his behavior is correct) aware of his motivation? Probably not. The instructor, upon hearing Kevin's story, may respond with, "Uh-huh!" The instructor may very well believe that Kevin is telling the truth — the truth as Kevin knows it — but may assume that the real truth, the significant cause, is buried in Kevin's psyche.

The significant cause? Kevin's lack of motivation.

The interpretation of Kevin's story may be explored still further. Sociologists may analyze Kevin's situation from another point of view and therefore supply other significant links in the causal chain. Could it be that Kevin's background and group affiliation have an effect on his behavior? Kevin and his family may belong to an ethnic, religious, cultural, or social group that traditionally divides its activities in ways other than by the hands of the clock — by sun-up and sunset, long shadows and short shadows, high tide and low tide — natural occurrences that in some groups signal the time for work, for rest, and for play, as they do for farmers and fishermen. If Kevin's background is such, then setting an alarm clock has not been ingrained into his daily routine. The pattern of behavior learned from Kevin's background would impinge on his habits and non-habits. Sociologists might see Kevin's lateness as a cultural rather than a psychological phenomenon. In that case:

The significant cause? The mores of Kevin's cultural group.

A diagram of the causal chain reflecting the larger perspectives of the two disciplines, psychology and sociology, is in Figure 6.2.

Notice that the original first cause, the malfunctioning of the alarm clock, is now seen as being an *effect* of some previous cause.

Important social issues, too, can be examined from an interdisciplinary approach. The student who is asked in a health education course, "What are the major causes of alcoholism?" should be aware that psychologists, sociologists, and biochemists have all had their say in the matter. Psychologists would posit that alcoholic patients are individuals who exhibit certain traits: They have an unusual amount of stress and much deprivation in their lives. The significant cause of their drinking, according to this analysis, is primarily psychological.

But sociologists say that since there are substantial differences in the number of alcoholics among various groups, the causes must be other than psychological. The rate of problem drinking among men is five times higher than among women. Statistics show that the degree of alcoholism is different among various ethnic groups as well. The view here is that the major cause of alcoholism is a group's level of acceptance of drinking. The norms of a group determine the degree of alcoholism; the causes are sociological.

Yet another theory is the biochemists': Recent laboratory studies report

Figure 6.2 *Causal Chain Reflecting Perspectives of Psychology and Sociology*

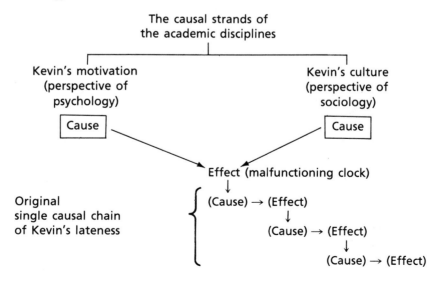

that certain problem drinkers metabolize alcohol differently from the way normal social drinkers do. These studies conclude that a major cause of alcoholism can be attributed to biological components of the body; the cause is physiological.

A diagram of the causal chain reflecting the discussion of alcoholism is in Figure 6.3.

From this it can be seen that the causes of alcoholism are not easily determined. Your decision as to the cause or causes that are the most significant will be based on your readings, your research, and your interpretation of the information. Writing on this subject will, as well, require attention to the needs of the particular audience. What would be the answers to the controlling question for a biochemistry class? a psychology class? a sociology class?

Of course, you should now expect that any attempt at establishing a significant cause through the perspectives of several academic disciplines will be complex. You might expect, then, that utilizing the perspective of only one discipline should be an easier undertaking. Not necessarily so. Usually, a discipline has several subsidiary perspectives, or what is known as schools of thought. In psychology, for example, there are both psychoanalytic and behaviorist schools of thought; in economics, supply-side and demand-side. Schools of thought arrive at different interpretations because of different assumptions.

Figure 6.3 *Causal Chain of Alcoholism from Several Viewpoints*

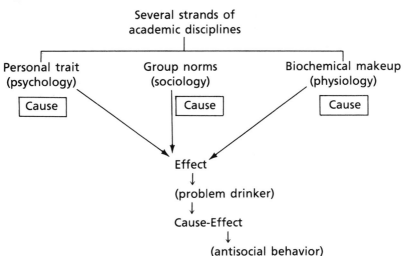

Historians determining the causes of the American Civil War, for example, are divided because of their different perspectives. One group of distinguished historians has emphasized the moral and ethical outrage against human slavery as the primary factor in the start of hostilities. This factor was considered important at the time; Lincoln, for example, called Harriet Beecher Stowe, the author of the antislavery novel, *Uncle Tom's Cabin*, "the little lady who started the big war." The war was fought primarily to eliminate slavery, say these historians.

Other historians disagree. They believe that the main issue was the question of states' rights vs. federal interference. These scholars look to the congressional debates prior to the war and point out that the Southern leaders, notably John C. Calhoun, focused their attention on the power of each state to make its own laws governing behavior within the state. For these leaders, the issue had nothing to do with moral considerations; it was concerned solely with the relationship between federal and state jurisdiction. Slavery, they claimed, was not an issue that could be decided by the federal government because the power to decide rested within each state. Since the election of Lincoln was considered a step toward increased federal interference, the South had to fire on Fort Sumter to protect its states' integrity, and historians who view these leaders as important see the issue of states' rights vs. federal interference as primary.

Historians of another persuasion have concentrated their attention on the economic differences between the North and the South prior to the war. They point out that while the South had remained primarily an agricultural region, producing cotton that was exported to England, among other countries, the North was rapidly becoming industrialized, manufacturing products that would compete with the industrial nations of Europe. The economic consequence of such a difference was immense. Historians who are concerned with economic matters, then, see a major cause for the Civil War in the opposing needs of the two antagonists; since their economic interests were in conflict, war was inevitable.

This discussion is, of course, oversimplified, for careful historians will take all of these factors into consideration. Different groups of historians, will, however, emphasize certain causes more than others. They will, like scholars in other disciplines, interpret the same information differently and therefore the causal chains they construct will show variations.

When new information is discovered, new causal chains are generated. Consider what was thought to be the cause of the plague, "The Black Death," during the fourteenth and fifteenth centuries. The whole of western Europe was swept by the most widespread and deadly epidemic in its history, killing at least a third of the total population. At that time medicine was not advanced enough to provide either a remedy for the disease or a reason for its occurrence. Today we know that the cause was fleas that bit infected animals, especially rats, and then passed on the infectious disease to humans. Without such knowledge and with a need to make sense of such devastation, many people believed the plague was punishment for past sins. They found the major cause to be somewhere in their past lives; we know now that the cause was more immediate, the fleas and infected rats scurrying around in homes and barns.

Establishing significant causes and effects is a complex matter. Despite this complexity, an examination of a problem from several perspectives offers the best possibility of arriving at an acceptable truth.

Post Hoc Reasoning:
A Possible Trap

Here are two major events in our country during this century:

Event A: The repeal of prohibition passed by Congress in 1933, allowing public drinking again

Event B: The onset of drought in the midwest in 1936

Some might argue, therefore, that since Event A preceded Event B, Event A caused Event B. Of course, the reasoning here is absurd. As you can see, the argument suffers from an illogical assumption. This kind of thinking is called *post hoc reasoning.*

Post hoc reasoning is the kind of reasoning in which one assumes that because Event A preceded Event B, Event A must be the cause of Event B. Post hoc reasoning equates a chronological sequence with causality. This assumption is often false.

Mystery writers have many of their characters display post hoc reasoning. In a typical scene, several people are witnesses to two people quarreling, let us say two partners in a firm. One says to the other in the heat of an argument, "I'll kill you." That very night one of the partners is found murdered. The witnesses — and some readers — believe at first that one partner murdered the other. After all, they reason, the suspect's threat (Event A) preceded the murder (Event B), did it not? It is at this point in such mystery stories that a private detective is hired — Perry Mason, Sam Spade, Nick Carter — who finds the real murderer to be someone else, thereby exposing the post hoc reasoning of the witnesses.

What the investigator does is examine the problem from several other vantage points, establishing other possible causal chains. Would the victim's secretary have reason to kill him? the victim's wife? the security guard? In your attempt to discover significant cause-effect links, you should, like the private investigator, see the problem from multiple perspectives, examining all the possibilities and thereby avoiding post hoc reasoning.

From the foregoing it is clear that the examination of the causes and/or the effects of any event or phenomenon is a complex undertaking. A distinction must be made between significant and less significant causes. To help make that distinction, causal chains should be constructed. In addition, in order to interpret findings, you should examine the issue from as many perspectives as you can.

PRACTICE

1. Remember Tom, whom we left at the beginning of this chapter staring at his ruined trousers? The controlling question was, "What is the cause(s) of this mishap?" With the considerations of the above discussion in mind, draw a causal chain and determine the links that are significant causes. The diagrams in Figures 6.2 and 6.3 can serve as models. To help you do this, a list of appropriate data regarding the persons involved in the incident is provided below. Not all the data are given in chronological order.

   Supervisor:
   - Assigned two men to paint the stairwells; one of the men was newly-hired.
   - Told the veteran painter (twenty years on the job) to break in the new worker.
   - Asked the veteran painter whether the necessary signs were put up in the stairwell.
   - After considering what the veteran painter told him, decided not to cordon off the area.
   - Was urged by the Dean of Students a week earlier to keep the stairwell open if possible.
   - Put in a request two weeks earlier to have elevators checked because it was reported that the doors were opening and closing a bit slowly.

   Maintenance crew:
   - Started painting the first landing of the stairwell on Wednesday.

- Painted the second and third landings on Thursday morning.

Veteran painter:

- Put the signs up on Wednesday, one large sign on the entrance door and two small signs, one dangling from the lower bannister and another from the upper bannister at the half-landing.
- Asked the newly-hired painter to put similar signs on the second and third landings, and was told it was done.

Wall sign on the second floor:

- Fell down after the men left at noon and went on to work in another part of the campus.

Tom:

- Grabbed the wall as he turned the landing.
- Arrived at school at 1:53.
- Waited two minutes for the elevator.
- Spoke with friends outside of school for fifteen minutes before entering.

2. What possible thesis statement would you write to answer the controlling question, "What is the cause(s) of this mishap?" Remember, it need not be solely one person's fault.

Below is a short story, part of a collection called *Dubliners*, by James Joyce, a famous early twentieth-century Irish novelist. The events are presented in chronological order. As you read, think about whether the events depicted could indeed establish a causal chain.

Counterparts

The bell rang furiously and, when Miss Parker went to the tube, a furious voice called out in a piercing North of Ireland accent:

— Send Farrington here!

Miss Parker returned to her machine, saying to a man who was writing at a desk:

— Mr Alleyne wants you upstairs.

The man muttered *Blast him!* under his breath and pushed back his chair to stand up. When he stood up he was tall and of great bulk. He had a hanging face, dark wine-coloured, with fair eyebrows and moustache: his eyes bulged forward slightly and the whites of them were dirty. He lifted up the counter and, passing by the clients, went out of the office with a heavy step.

He went heavily upstairs until he came to the second landing, where a door bore a brass plate with the inscription *Mr Alleyne*. Here he halted, puffing with labour and vexation, and knocked. The shrill voice cried:

— Come in!

The man entered Mr Alleyne's room. Simultaneously Mr Alleyne, a little man wearing gold-rimmed glasses on a cleanshaven face, shot his head up over a pile of documents. The head itself was so pink and hairless that it seemed like a large egg reposing on the papers. Mr Alleyne did not lose a moment:

— Farrington? What is the meaning of this? Why have I always to complain of you? May I ask you why you haven't made a copy of that contract between Bodley and Kirwan? I told you it must be ready by four o'clock.

— But Mr Shelley said, sir —

— *Mr Shelley said, sir.* . . . Kindly attend to what I say and not to what *Mr Shelley says, sir.* You have always some excuse or another for shirking work. Let me tell you that if the contract is not copied before this evening I'll lay the matter before Mr Crosbie. . . . Do you hear me now?

— Yes, sir.

— Do you hear me now? . . . Ay and another little matter! I might as well be talking to the wall as talking to you. Understand once for all that you get a half an hour for your lunch and not an hour and a half. How many courses do you want, I'd like to know. . . . Do you mind me, now?

— Yes, sir.

Mr Alleyne bent his head again upon his pile of papers. The man stared fixedly at the polished skull which directed the affairs of Crosbie & Alleyne, gauging its fragility. A spasm of rage gripped his throat for a few moments and then passed, leaving after it a sharp sensation of thirst. The man recognised the sensation and felt that he must have a good night's drinking. The middle of the month was passed and, if he could get the copy done in time, Mr Alleyne might give him an order on the cashier. He stood still, gazing fixedly at the head upon the pile of papers. Suddenly Mr Alleyne began to upset all the papers, searching for something. Then, as if he had been unaware of the man's presence till that moment, he shot up his head again, saying:

— Eh? Are you going to stand there all day? Upon my word, Farrington, you take things easy!

— I was waiting to see . . .

— Very good, you needn't wait to see. Go downstairs and do your work.

The man walked heavily towards the door and, as he went out of the room, he heard Mr Alleyne cry after him that if the contract was not copied by evening Mr Crosbie would hear of the matter.

He returned to his desk in the lower office and counted the sheets which remained to be copied. He took up his pen and dipped it in the ink but he continued to stare stupidly at the last words he had written: *In no case shall the said Bernard Bodley be . . .* The evening was falling and in a few minutes they would be lighting the gas: then he could write. He felt that he must slake the thirst in his throat. He stood up from his desk and, lifting the counter as before, passed out of the office. As he was passing out the chief clerk looked at him inquiringly.

— It's all right, Mr Shelley, said the man, pointing with his finger to indicate the objective of his journey.

The chief clerk glanced at the hat-rack but, seeing the row complete, offered no remark. As soon as he was on the landing the man pulled a shepherd's plaid cap out of his pocket, put it on his head and ran quickly down the rickety stairs. From the street door he walked on furtively on the inner side of the path towards the corner and all at once dived into a doorway. He was now safe in the dark snug of O'Neill's shop, and, filling up the little window that looked into the bar with his inflamed face, the colour of dark wine or dark meat, he called out:

— Here, Pat, give us a g.p., like a good fellow.

The curate brought him a glass of plain porter. The man drank it at a gulp and asked for a caraway seed. He put his penny on the counter and, leaving the curate to grope for it in the gloom, retreated out of the snug as furtively as he had entered it.

Darkness, accompanied by a thick fog, was gaining upon the dusk of February and the lamps in Eustace Street had been lit. The man went up by the houses until he reached the door of the office, wondering whether he could finish his copy in time. On the stairs a moist pungent odour of perfumes saluted his nose: evidently Miss Delacour had come while he was out in O'Neill's. He crammed his cap back again into his pocket and re-entered the office, assuming an air of absent-mindedness.

— Mr Alleyne has been calling for you, said the chief clerk severely. Where were you?

The man glanced at the two clients who were standing at the counter as if to intimate that their presence prevented him from answering. As the clients were both male the chief clerk allowed himself a laugh.

— I know that game, he said. Five times in one day is a little bit. . . . Well, you better look sharp and get a copy of our correspondence in the Delacour case for Mr Alleyne.

This address in the presence of the public, his run upstairs and the porter he had gulped down so hastily confused the man and, as he sat down at his desk to get what was required, he realised how hopeless was the task of finishing his copy of the contract before half past five. The dark damp night was coming and he longed to spend it in the bars, drinking with his friends amid the glare of gas and the clatter of glasses. He got out the Delacour correspondence and passed out of the office. He hoped Mr Alleyne would not discover that the last two letters were missing.

The moist pungent perfume lay all the way up to Mr Alleyne's room.

Miss Delacour was a middle-aged woman of Jewish appearance. Mr Alleyne was said to be sweet on her or on her money. She came to the office often and stayed a long time when she came. She was sitting beside his desk now in an aroma of perfumes, smoothing the handle of her umbrella and nodding the great black feather in her hat. Mr Alleyne had swivelled his chair round to face her and thrown his right foot jauntily upon his left knee. The man put the correspondence on the desk and bowed respectfully but neither Mr Alleyne nor Miss Delacour took any notice of his bow. Mr Alleyne tapped a finger on the correspondence and then flicked it towards him as if to say: *That's all right: you can go.*

The man returned to the lower office and sat down again at his desk. He stared intently at the incomplete phrase: *In no case shall the said Bernard Bodley be* . . . and thought how strange it was that the last three words began with the same letter. The chief clerk began to hurry Miss Parker, saying she would never have the letters typed in time for post. The man listened to the clicking of the machine for a few minutes and then set to work to finish his copy. But his head was not clear and his mind wandered away to the glare and rattle of the public-house. It was a night for hot punches. He struggled on with his copy, but when the clock struck five he had still fourteen pages to write. Blast it! He couldn't finish it in time. He longed to execrate aloud, to bring his fist down on something violently. He was so enraged that he wrote *Bernard Bernard* instead of *Bernard Bodley* and had to begin again on a clean sheet.

He felt strong enough to clear out the whole office singlehanded. His body ached to do something, to rush out and revel in violence. All the indignities of his life enraged him. . . . Could he ask the cashier privately for an advance? No, the cashier was no good, no damn good: he wouldn't give an advance. . . . He knew where he would meet the boys: Leonard and O'Halloran and Nosey Flynn. The barometer of his emotional nature was set for a spell of riot.

His imagination had so abstracted him that his name was called twice before he answered. Mr Alleyne and Miss Delacour were standing outside the counter and all the clerks had turned round in anticipation of something. The man got up from his desk. Mr Alleyne began a tirade of abuse, saying that two letters were missing. The man answered that he knew nothing about them, that he had made a faithful copy. The tirade continued: it was so bitter and violent that the man could hardly restrain his fist from descending upon the head of the manikin before him.

— I know nothing about any other two letters, he said stupidly.

— *You — know — nothing.* Of course you know nothing, said Mr Alleyne. Tell me, he added, glancing first for approval to the lady beside him, do you take me for a fool? Do you think me an utter fool?

The man glanced from the lady's face to the little egg-shaped head and back again; and, almost before he was aware of it, his tongue had found a felicitous moment:

— I don't think, sir, he said, that that's a fair question to put to me.

There was a pause in the very breathing of the clerks. Everyone was astounded (the author of the witticism no less than his neighbours) and Miss Delacour, who was a stout amiable person, began to smile broadly. Mr Alleyne flushed to the hue of a wild rose and his mouth twitched with a dwarf's passion. He shook his fist in the man's face till it seemed to vibrate like the knob of some electric machine:

— You impertinent ruffian! You impertinent ruffian! I'll make short work of you! Wait till you see! You'll apologise to me for your impertinence or you'll quit the office instanter! You'll quit this, I'm telling you, or you'll apologise to me!

·   ·   ·   ·   ·   ·   ·   ·   ·   ·   ·

He stood in a doorway opposite the office watching to see if the cashier would come out alone. All the clerks passed out and finally the cashier came out with the chief clerk. It was no use trying to say a word to him when he was with the chief clerk. The man felt that his position was bad enough. He had been obliged to offer an abject apology to Mr Alleyne for his impertinence but he knew what a hornet's nest the office would be for him. He could remember the way in which Mr Alleyne had hounded little Peake out of the office in order to make room for his own nephew. He felt savage and thirsty and revengeful, annoyed with himself and with everyone else. Mr Alleyne would never give him an hour's rest; his life would be a hell to him. He had made a proper fool of himself this time. Could he not keep his tongue in his cheek? But they had never pulled together from the first, he and Mr Alleyne, ever since the day Mr Alleyne had overheard him mimicking his North of Ireland accent to amuse Higgins and Miss Parker: that had been the beginning of it. He might have tried Higgins for the money, but sure Higgins never had anything for himself. A man with two establishments to keep up, of course he couldn't. . . .

He felt his great body again aching for the comfort of the public-house. The fog had begun to chill him and he wondered could he touch Pat in O'Neill's. He could not touch him for more than a bob — and a bob was no use. Yet he must get money somewhere or other: he had spent his last penny for the g.p. and soon it would be too late for getting money anywhere. Suddenly, as he was fingering his watch-chain, he thought of Terry Kelly's pawn-office in Fleet Street. That was the dart! Why didn't he think of it sooner?

He went through the narrow alley of Temple Bar quickly, muttering to himself that they could all go to hell because he was going to have a good night of it. The clerk in Terry Kelly's said *A crown!* but the consignor held out for six shillings; and in the end the six shillings was allowed him literally. He came out of the pawn-office joyfully, making a little cylinder of the coins between his thumb and fingers. In Westmoreland Street the footpaths were crowded with young men and women returning from business and ragged urchins ran here and there yelling out the names of the evening editions. The man passed through the crowd, looking on the spectacle generally with proud satisfaction and staring masterfully at the office-girls. His head was full of the noises of tram-gongs and swishing trolleys and his nose already sniffed the curling fumes of punch. As he walked on he preconsidered the terms in which he would narrate the incident to the boys.

— So, I just looked at him — coolly, you know, and looked at her. Then I looked back at him again — taking my time, you know. *I don't think that that's a fair question to put to me,* says I.

Nosey Flynn was sitting up in his usual corner of Davy Byrne's and, when he heard the story, he stood Farrington a half-one, saying it was as smart a thing as ever he heard. Farrington stood a drink in his turn. After a while O'Halloran and Paddy Leonard came in and the story was repeated to them. O'Halloran stood tailors of malt, hot, all round and told the story of the retort he had made to the chief clerk when he was in Callan's of Fownes's Street; but, as the retort was after the manner of the liberal shepherds in the eclogues, he had to admit that it was not so clever as Farrington's retort. At this Farrington told the boys to polish off that and have another.

Just as they were naming their poisons who should come in but Higgins! Of course he had to join in with the others. The men asked him to give his version of it, and he did so with great vivacity for the sight of five small hot whiskies was very exhilarating. Everyone roared laughing when he showed the way in which Mr Alleyne shook his fist in Farrington's face. Then he imitated Farrington, saying, *And here was my nabs, as cool as you please,* while Farrington looked at the company out of his heavy dirty eyes, smiling and at times drawing forth stray drops of liquor from his moustache with the aid of his lower lip.

When that round was over there was a pause. O'Halloran had money but neither of the other two seemed to have any; so the whole party left the shop somewhat regretfully. At the corner of Duke Street Higgins and Nosey Flynn bevelled off to the left while the other three turned back towards the city. Rain was drizzling down on the cold streets and, when they reached the Ballast Office, Farrington suggested the Scotch House. The bar was full of men and loud with the noise of tongues and glasses. The three men pushed past the whining match-sellers at the door and formed a little party at the corner of the counter. They began to exchange stories. Leonard introduced them to a young fellow named Weathers who was performing at the Tivoli as an acrobat and knockabout *artiste.* Farrington stood a drink all round. Weathers said he would take a small Irish and Apollinaris. Farrington, who had definite notions of what was what, asked the boys would they have an Apollinaris too; but the boys told Tim to make theirs hot. The talk became theatrical. O'Halloran stood a round and then Farrington stood another round, Weathers protesting that the hospitality was too Irish. He promised to get them in behind the scenes and introduce them to some nice girls. O'Halloran said that he and Leonard would go but that Farrington wouldn't go because he was a married man; and Farrington's heavy dirty eyes leered at the company in token that he understood he was being chaffed. Weathers made them all have just one little tincture at his expense and promised to meet them later on at Mulligan's in Poolbeg Street.

When the Scotch House closed they went round to Mulligan's. They went into the parlour at the back and O'Halloran ordered small hot specials all round. They were all beginning to feel mellow. Farrington was just standing another round when Weathers came back. Much to Farrington's relief he drank a glass of bitter this time. Funds were running low but they had enough to keep them going. Presently two young women with big hats and a young man in a check suit came in and sat at a table close by. Weathers saluted them and told the company that they were out of the Tivoli. Farrington's eyes wandered at every moment in the direction of one of the young women. There was something striking in her appearance. An immense scarf of peacock-blue muslin was wound round her hat and knotted in a great bow under her chin; and she wore bright yellow gloves, reaching to the elbow. Farrington gazed admiringly at the plump arm which she moved very often and with much grace; and when, after a little time, she answered his gaze he admired still more her large dark brown eyes. The oblique staring expression in them fascinated him. She glanced at him once or twice and, when the party was leaving the room, she brushed against his chair and said *O, pardon!* in a London accent. He watched her leave the room in the hope that she would look back at him, but he was disappointed. He cursed his want of money and cursed all the rounds he had stood, particularly all the whiskies and Apollinaris which he had stood to Weathers. If there was one thing that he hated it was a sponge. He was so angry that he lost count of the conversation of his friends.

When Paddy Leonard called him he found that they were talking about feats of strength. Weathers was showing his biceps muscle to the company and boasting so much that the other two had called on Farrington to uphold the national honour. Farrington pulled up his sleeve accordingly and showed his biceps muscle to the company. The two arms were examined and compared and finally it was agreed to have a trial of strength. The table was cleared and the two men rested their elbows on it, clasping hands. When Paddy Leonard said *Go!* each was to try to bring down the other's hand on to the table. Farrington looked very serious and determined.

The trial began. After about thirty seconds Weathers brought his opponent's hand slowly down on to the table. Farrington's dark wine-coloured face flushed darker still with anger and humiliation at having been defeated by such a stripling.

— You're not to put the weight of your body behind it. Play fair, he said.

— Who's not playing fair? said the other.

— Come on again. The two best out of three.

The trial began again. The veins stood out on Farrington's forehead, and the pallor of Weathers' complexion changed to peony. Their hands and arms trembled under the stress. After a long struggle Weathers again brought his opponent's hand slowly on to the table. There was a murmur of applause from the spectators. The curate, who was standing beside the table, nodded his red head towards the victor and said with loutish familiarity:

— Ah! that's the knack!

— What the hell do you know about it? said Farrington fiercely, turning on the man. What do you put in your gab for?

— Sh, sh! said O'Halloran, observing the violent expression of Farrington's face. Pony up, boys. We'll have just one little smahan more and then we'll be off.

A very sullen-faced man stood at the corner of O'Connell Bridge waiting for the little Sandymount tram to take him home. He was full of smouldering anger and revengefulness. He felt humiliated and discontented; he did not even feel drunk; and he had only twopence in his pocket. He cursed everything. He had done for himself in the office, pawned his watch, spent all his money; and he had not even got drunk. He began to feel thirsty again and he longed to be back again in the hot reeking public-house. He had lost his reputation as a strong man, having been defeated twice by a mere boy. His heart swelled with fury and, when he thought of the woman in the big hat who had brushed against him and said *Pardon!* his fury nearly choked him.

His tram let him down at Shelbourne Road and he steered his great body along in the shadow of the wall of the barracks. He loathed returning to his home. When he went in by the side-door he found the kitchen empty and the kitchen fire nearly out. He bawled upstairs:

— Ada! Ada!

His wife was a little sharp-faced woman who bullied her husband when he was sober and was bullied by him when he was drunk. They had five children. A little boy came running down the stairs.

— Who is that? said the man, peering through the darkness.

— Me, pa.

— Who are you? Charlie?

— No, pa. Tom.

— Where's your mother?

— She's out at the chapel.

— That's right. . . . Did she think of leaving any dinner for me?

— Yes, pa. I —

— Light the lamp. What do you mean by having the place in darkness? Are the other children in bed?

The man sat down heavily on one of the chairs while the little boy lit the lamp. He began to mimic his son's flat accent, saying half to himself: *At the chapel. At the chapel, if you please!* When the lamp was lit he banged his fist on the table and shouted:

— What's for my dinner?

— I'm going . . . to cook it, pa, said the little boy.

The man jumped up furiously and pointed to the fire.

— On that fire! You let the fire out! By God, I'll teach you to do that again!

He took a step to the door and seized the walking-stick which was standing behind it.

— I'll teach you to let the fire out! he said, rolling up his sleeve in order to give his arm free play.

The little boy cried *O, pa!* and ran whimpering round the table, but the man followed him and caught him by the coat. The little boy looked about him wildly but, seeing no way of escape fell upon his knees.

— Now, you'll let the fire out the next time! said the man, striking at him viciously with the stick. Take that, you little whelp!

The boy uttered a squeal of pain as the stick cut his thigh. He clasped his hands together in the air and his voice shook with fright.

— O, pa! he cried. Don't beat me, pa! And I'll . . . I'll say a *Hail Mary* for you. . . . I'll say a *Hail Mary* for you, pa, if you don't beat me. . . . I'll say a *Hail Mary*. . . .

PRACTICE

Figure 6.4 is an outline of a causal chain derived from the story, "Counterparts." Can you complete it? The first two items and the last item of the chain are filled in for you.

Figure 6.4   *Causal Chain of Events in* Counterparts

Farrington, a clerk in a law office, fails to
make a copy of the contract.
　　↓
(Cause) → (Effect)
　　　　　↓
　　　　Mr Alleyne, his boss, reprimands him
　　　　for shirking his duties.
　　　　　　↓
　　　　(Cause) → (Effect)

　　　　　　　(and so on)

　　　　　　　(Cause) → (Effect)
　　　　　　　　　　↓
　　　　　　　　Farrington beats his son.

Establishing the causal chain from the events of the story was probably easy, and with some imagination you could, no doubt, even create incidents that might have occurred prior to and following the story in order to extend that chain. Trying to determine significant causes for Farrington's beating his son, however, may be a bit more difficult, and because you have only the story itself as data for your deliberations, the real cause can only be speculative. Nevertheless, a work of literature can enrich your understanding of the human condition if you try to determine why people behave the way they do. Below are some cause-effect questions that might help you discuss this story in class.

1. How can conditions in the workplace affect the behavior of the individual in other aspects of his or her life?

2. Why does Farrington feel compelled to impress his cronies in the bar?

3. What is the most significant cause of Farrington's cruelty to his son?

4. What other factors could have caused Farrington's actions?

5. Is there any reason to feel sympathy for Farrington's cruel behavior toward his son?

WRITING

A Student at Work: Making a Purchase and the Law of Demand

The problems of isolating causes and analyzing effects are common concerns of all academic disciplines. The importance of this kind of thinking can be illustrated if we examine how economists use this process. When they analyze a situation like the Great Depression of 1929, they are attempting to isolate the main causes so that steps can be taken to prevent such events in the future. Their decisions about which causes to emphasize, therefore, will affect the lives of all of us. Businessmen, union leaders, and other individuals need to examine their own economic activities in order to establish the events in the past that caused their current situations — whether bankruptcy or prosperity — in order to continue those activities that brought economic health and to avoid those that brought economic disaster.

Basic Concepts: How a Market Economy Operates

In this section of the chapter you will read passages from economics texts that deal with some of the basic concepts of the discipline; you will see how essays of cause and effect are planned and written; and you will have an opportunity to develop your own essay using this pattern.

Basic to any understanding of economic theory is an understanding of the way our particular system works. The reading, called "Market-price Systems," will provide a brief overview. Below are some discussion questions to think about as you read.

1. Have you ever attended an auction, or read or heard about auctions? What actions do you think sellers of rocking chairs would take if they discovered that many people are interested in buying them?

2. What would be the economic effect of an announcement from a reputable health authority that eating carrots will prevent cancer? What would many people do in planning their menus in the future? How would that affect the buying decisions of supermarket owners? What other groups of people would be affected?

Market-price Systems

Economic systems based on prices and the bargaining that occurs between buyers and sellers are **market-price systems**. When the price is agreed upon and a sale is made, the three questions are answered. The buyer's agreement to pay determines what is produced, how it is produced, and, of course, for whom it is produced. Each buyer and seller represents an economic unit (individual, family, business firm, government agency, or foreign country) which is motivated by self-interest to make the best deal (or profit) it can for itself.

When buyers and sellers come together to agree on a purchase or sale, the transaction takes place in what economists call a **market**. The term "market" describes any method by which, or place at which, buyers can communicate with sellers. A good or service is purchased or sold for a price, and the price helps to determine what kinds of economic activity will take place in a market-price system.

The decisions made by buyers and sellers help to determine prices. And the prices in turn signal the ways our society decides what to produce, how to produce and for whom to produce. The quantity and quality of lettuce on hand in Los Angeles, for instance, is determined by hundreds of freely made producing and buying decisions. Each one of these decisions involves someone's conscious or unconscious assessment of opportunity cost. The farmer may wonder whether to grow lettuce or beets, the buyer may wonder whether to buy lettuce or spinach.

Many observers liken market-price systems to an *auction*, because somewhere behind the scene, buyers bid among themselves for the goods and services sellers want to sell. When you go to the supermarket, no bidding is apparent. The prices of everything are shown. You decide to buy or not to buy, or how much to buy, depending partly on price.

Where, then, is the auction? Your buying decisions cause changes in the store's inventory (often stored in a computer memory). When the inventory drops below desired levels, those who buy for the store must then *bid* (against other stores) for supplies offered by farmers (or brokers).

Your buying decisions will also influence farmers in their decisions about what crops to grow and how much land to devote to each crop, leading to decisions about what fertilizers, insecticides, delivery systems, and machinery they will need; those decisions will in turn influence the production decisions of firms that supply farmers.

While the United States is more nearly a market-price system than anything else, it is a mixture of systems just as it is a blend of capitalism and socialism. And while a market-price system is inevitably found in capitalistic countries, it is found also in traditional and in socialistic countries. Primitive tribes have primitive markets where exchange occurs. Often the method of exchange is barter, or trade, but money (shells, animals, skins) is also used to facilitate exchange. In socialist countries like the Soviet Union or China, private enterprise (small shops, private plots on farms) and private markets are still alive.

PRACTICE

If you look back at question 2 on p. 259, you will see that the causal chain is based on the situation described there. The first few items in the chain in Figure 6.5 are supplied; how far can you go in completing it?

Figure 6.5 *Causal Chain Reflecting Economic Effects of a Health Announcement*

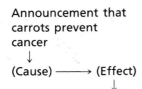

Announcement that
carrots prevent
cancer
    ↓
(Cause) ⟶ (Effect)
    ↓

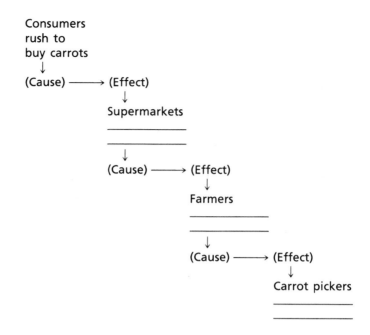

PRACTICE

Another way of looking at the effect of medical discoveries on the economy is to ask the question, "What would happen if health authorities announced that excessive consumption of sugar causes cancer?" If substantial numbers of people cut back on their use of sugar, how would that affect storeowners, shippers, sugar plantation owners, and workers on the plantations? Construct a causal chain to show these effects.

PRACTICE

If aspartame were shown to be a safe substitute, a different causal chain might result. What would that causal chain look like?

This description of the market-price system has been greatly simplified in order to get across the basic concept. In fact, the market-price system is vastly more complex. If you are taking or planning to take a course in economics, you will learn how the workings of the market-price system are affected, among other things, by the existence of a few dominant buyers or sellers, or by government regulations that seek to compensate for the potential inequities of our economic system. You should be aware, however, that economists, like all social scientists, usually construct such simplified models as in the illustrations on these pages in order to analyze a situation. By restricting a problem to just a few key factors and ignoring the multitude of complicated variables that determine human action in the real world, they hope to be able to determine the fundamental causes and effects and what can be done about them.

Understanding the market-price system is a necessary first step toward understanding and writing about the way the free enterprise system operates. You were probably already familiar with the basic concept in a general sort of way. Certainly, you are all too familiar with the fact that when an item is in short supply and many people want to buy it, the price goes up. If everyone rushed out to buy carrots before the farmers had a chance to plant more, harvest them, and get them to the market, the price of carrots would probably go up. And if people stopped buying sugar when supermarket shelves were full, the store owners would probably lower the price to attract new customers. This change in price as a result of the change in demand — a seemingly inevitable relationship of cause-effect — is a fundamental aspect of our economic system, so much so that it is given the status of a law. Below is an excerpt that more fully explains the law of demand.

THE ECONOMIC WAY OF THINKING

The Concept of Demand

Economists distrust the word *need* for reasons that should now be apparent. They prefer to use the concept of *demand*. Demand is a concept that *relates amounts that are purchased to the sacrifices that must be made to obtain these amounts.*

Ask yourself the following questions: How many records do you want to own? How many times do you want to go out to dinner in a year? What grade do you want from this course?

If you can answer any of those questions, it is because you have assumed some price in each case. Suppose you said you want an A from this course and plan to get one. What difference would it make if the price of an A went up? The teacher isn't taking bribes, the price of an A *to you* (that's what counts) is the sacrifice you must make to obtain it. Would you still want an A if it required twenty hours of study a week, while a B could be had for just one hour a week? You might still want it — who does not want A's? But you would probably not be willing to buy it at such a high price when a fairly good substitute, a B, is so much cheaper. And that is what counts. Human wants seem to be insatiable. But when a want can only be satisfied at some cost — that is to say, by giving up the satisfaction of some other wants to obtain it — we all moderate our desires and accept less than we would like to have.

The phenomenon of which we're speaking is so pervasive and so fundamental that some economists have been willing to assign it the status of a law: the law of demand. This law asserts that there is a negative relation between the amount of anything that people will purchase and the price (sacrifice) they must pay to obtain it. At higher prices, less will be purchased, at lower prices, more will be purchased.

On the basis of this reading you could construct very simple causal chains:

$$20 \text{ hours' work} \longrightarrow A$$

$$1 \text{ hour's work} \longrightarrow B$$

On the basis of these chains, you could also decide what actions you wish to take. But such simplifications leave out a great many factors that would probably play a role in your thinking — the desire to attend a concert the night before an exam, or the wish to impress the instructor.

Although the model is useful for a basic understanding, it needs to be expanded before it can be applied with any validity to the real world. Economists have therefore revised their explanation of the law of demand to include factors in addition to price that influence decisions. As with the discussion of Kevin and his alarm clock in the first part of this chapter, it was clear that such additional factors provide new perspectives on the situation, thus enabling us to view it from different angles. It is also similar to the problem mentioned earlier of historians trying to isolate the causes of the Civil War.

Below is the complete discussion of the law of demand, from the same source as the shorter extract above. This time it goes on to include factors other than price that need to be considered.

The Concept of Demand

Economists distrust the word *need* for reasons that should now be apparent. They prefer to use the concept of *demand*. Demand is a concept that *relates amounts that are purchased to the sacrifices that must be made to obtain these amounts.*

Ask yourself the following questions: How many records do you want to own? How many times do you want to go out to dinner in a year? What grade do you want from this course?

If you can answer any of those questions, it is because you have assumed some price in each case. Suppose you said you want an A from this course and plan to get one. What difference would it make if the price of an A went up? The teacher isn't taking bribes; the price of an A *to you* (that's what counts) is the sacrifice you must make to obtain it. Would you still want an A if it required twenty hours of study a week, while a B could be had for just one hour a week? You might still want it — who does not want A's? But you would probably not be willing to buy it at such a high price when a fairly good substitute, a B, is so much cheaper. And that is what counts. Human wants seem to be insatiable. But when a want can only be satisfied at some cost — that is to say, by giving up the satisfaction of some other wants to obtain it — we all moderate our desires and accept less than we would like to have.

The phenomenon of which we're speaking is so pervasive and so fundamental that some economists have been willing to assign it the status of a law: the law of demand. This law asserts that there is a negative relation between the amount of anything that people will purchase and the price (sacrifice) they must pay to obtain it. At higher prices, less will be purchased; at lower prices, more will be purchased.

Would you agree that this generalization can be called a *law?* Or can you think of exceptions? Genuine exceptions are rare at best. Why would anyone be indifferent to the sacrifices he must make? Or prefer more sacrifice to less? Which is what a person would be doing if he took more of something as the cost of obtaining it increased.

Alleged exceptions to the law of demand are usually based on a misinterpretation of the evidence. A masochist, for example, would not provide an exception, because pain is for him a good and not a sacrifice. But what of the familiar case where the price of something rises and people increase their purchases in anticipation of further price rises? If you think about it carefully you will see that this is not an exception to the law of demand. The expectation of higher prices in the future, created by the initial price rise, has increased people's current demand for the item. It is not the higher price but the changed *expectations* that have caused people to buy more. We would observe something quite different if the initial price increase did *not* create those changed expectations.

It has sometimes been argued that certain prestige goods are exceptions to the law of demand. For example, people supposedly buy mink coats because their price is high, not low. No doubt there are people who buy some items largely to impress others with how much they can afford to pay. And people sometimes, in the absence of better information, judge quality by price, so that over a limited range, at least, their willingness to purchase may be positively rather than negatively related to price.

Even these seeming exceptions can be explained in a way consistent with the law of demand. People may be purchasing prestige rather than mere mink, or economizing in the presence of limited information. But we are not interested in rare curiosities or subtle exercises in the definition of terms. Whether or not you are willing to call it a law, the fact is undeniable and extremely important: increases in the price of goods will characteristically be followed by decreases in the total amount purchased, and decreases in price will characteristically be followed by increases in the amount purchased. It is a serious mistake to overlook this pervasive fact.

Money Costs and Other Costs

The price in money that must be paid for something is not a complete measure of its cost to the purchaser. Sometimes, indeed, it is a very inadequate measure, as in the case of the student who wanted an A. Economists know this at least as well as anyone else. The concept of demand definitely does not suggest that money is the only thing that matters to people. Confusion about this point has done so much to create misunderstanding that we might profitably take a moment to clarify the matter.

Consider the case of a man buying soft drinks. Assume that he can purchase them in either returnable bottles or throwaway bottles, and that a six-pack of throwaway bottles is priced at 60 cents, while a six-pack of returnable bottles is priced at 50 cents plus an 18-cent deposit. Which will he buy? Which is cheaper?

It depends on the cost to him, of which the retailer's price is only one element. If he doesn't mind saving and returning bottles — that is, if the cost to him of doing so is low — he will probably find the returnable bottles cheaper and will buy them. On the other hand, if he lives in an apartment with very limited storage space, gets to the store rarely, consumes large quantities of soft drinks, and has a waste-disposal chute a few steps from his door, he may well find the throwaway bottles cheaper and will purchase them in preference to returnable bottles.

Now suppose that our hypothetical apartment dweller with a passion for pop attends an ecology conference and comes away convinced that we must recycle to survive. The cost to him of using throwaway bottles suddenly jumps, for now he suffers pangs of guilt every time he tosses a bottle in the waste-disposal chute. The added cost in moral regret may be sufficient to induce him to switch to returnable bottles.

Or it may not. Suppose that he is going on a camping trip and wants to take along a dozen bottles of pop. He must backpack them in to his camp site, and backpack the empties out again if he returns the bottles. The added cost of carrying a dozen empties may be enough to overcome the added cost of an uneasy conscience so that, in this case at least, he reverts to throwaway bottles. (Hopefully he throws them in a trash can.)

But let's change the last situation. Suppose the price of throwaway bottles is not 60 cents but 70 cents. Or 80 cents, or $1.80. At *some* price we may confidently expect that the cost of transporting empties will become less than the combined cost of buying throwaway bottles and living with guilt. (Unless he first decides to reduce his consumption or give up pop altogether on his camping trip.)

There ae several lessons to be drawn from this tale of the pop bottles. To assert that people purchase less of anything as the cost to them increases does *not* imply that people pay attention only to money, or that people are selfish, or that concern for social welfare does not influence economic behavior. It *does* imply that people respond to changes in cost and — a crucial implication — that a sufficiently large change in price can be counted on to tip almost any balance. When someone says that Americans won't give up the convenience of throwaway bottles and cans unless the government outlaws them, he overlooks several possibilities. A widespread change in attitude toward the environment could overcome the cost of being inconvenienced. And a sufficiently large tax on throwaway containers (call it a deposit if you wish) would make convenience a luxury too expensive to indulge in frequently.

The essential point in all this is that the money price of obtaining something is only one part, and occasionally even a very small part, of its cost. What the law of demand asserts is that people will do less of what they want to do as the cost to them of doing it increases, and do more as the cost decreases.

The reading selection on the law of demand indicates that considerations other than the price of an item can have a profound effect on buyers' decisions. These additional factors that can cause people to buy or not buy help explain why the cheapest item is not always the one that is sold. Without these additional factors, the basic law of demand seems to break down; with them, the law of demand fits more exactly with the actual operation of the marketplace.

Instead of the simple causal chain:

Cheapest price ⟶ item that is bought,

the causal chain is like the one in Figure 6.6.

Figure 6.6   *Causal Chain of Factors in a Purchase*

Cheapest price ⟶
Expectation of higher prices ⟶
Prestige ⟶   } item that is bought.
Convenience ⟶
Social responsibility ⟶

The value of this new causal chain for people in business is obvious; an understanding of it enables them to stock their shelves appropriately. But it is valuable for all consumers as well. By understanding the reasons for their own purchases, consumers may be able to avoid costly mistakes.

Although all the factors that were mentioned in the reading on the law of demand can play a part in any decision to purchase, any one of these factors may be the most important to a particular consumer at a particular time. Deciding on the factor that is the most significant cause and the one that is least significant is the crucial problem. It cannot be solved without careful investigation and thoughtful weighing of the evidence.

Writing the Essay: Isolating Causes

To help students become aware of this need to weigh various causes, an economics instructor gave his class the following assignment:

> Choose one major purchase you have made in the recent past and analyze your decision using the factors mentioned in the article on the law of demand. Write an essay explaining your purchase and indicate the factor that was most important in influencing your choice. Be sure to discuss all the factors — price, too — and explain why they were, or were not, significant for you.

The student knew as soon as she saw the assignment that she would focus on the new car she had just bought, a Horizon. It was certainly a major purchase and one she had agonized over for many months. Despite the long hours of comparison shopping she had really been unaware of the way the factors discussed in the reading had influenced her. She needed to review the purchase in a much more systematic way if she wanted to write a good essay. The controlling question for this student was, "Why did I buy the Horizon?" and some of the subsidiary questions she thought of are listed below. Can you think of others?

1. How did the Horizon compare with the three other cars I was considering?

2. What characteristics was I looking for when I considered cars?

3. What factors related to places and times I would be using the car were important to me?

4. _____

5. _____

Before proceeding, the student looked back at the reading to make sure she had understood it thoroughly. Her essay, no matter how carefully planned, would be incomplete if some significant aspect of the reading had been omitted. She wrote out the following summary:

> The law of demand states, "increases in the prices of goods will characteristically be followed by decreases in the total amount purchased and decreases in price will characteristically be followed by increases in the amount purchased." But it is necessary to take into consideration (1) the fact that people may buy more at higher prices if they expect further price rises, and (2) the fact that there are other factors besides money that are involved in a purchase. These other factors are (a) prestige, (b) convenience, and (c) social responsibility.

Re-creating her actions, the student thought, might help her see how she had arrived at her decision and provide the direction for her essay. She placed the events leading up to her purchase on a chronological list that looked like this:

Decided to buy a car

Father told me price range

Read *Consumer Reports*

Visited Chevette dealer

Jim told me front-wheel drive necessary

Visited Toyota dealer

Visited Honda dealer

Visited Horizon dealer

Read *Road & Track*

Talked to friends about repairs

Considered styling

Thought about problem

Decided to purchase Horizon

As she looked at her list, the student could see a few causal connections. Jim's statement about front-wheel drive had caused her to lose interest in the Chevette, and reading *Consumer Reports* had caused her to focus on four possible choices. For the most part, however, she could discern no clear pattern.

Writing the summary and making the list were helpful in focusing the student's thinking, and the questions had suggested another approach: to compare and contrast the possible choices. Realizing that part of the problem was a comparison/contrast, she used the technique she had learned to handle this way of thinking. She made a chart for each of the cars she had considered, listing under each one the factors mentioned in the essay on the law of demand as well as the qualities she had considered. Her chart looked like the one in Table 6.1.

Looking at her chart, the student could see that no one factor stood out. Each of the cars had both positive and negative points under the various

TABLE 6.1   Factors in a Car Purchase

Price	Prestige	Convenience	Social Responsibilities
		Toyota Tercel	
Cheapest	Import	Local dealer	Good gas mileage
	Well-styled	Parts may be difficult to get	
		Front-wheel drive	
		Chevette	
Next cheapest	Cute	Dealer nearby	Good gas mileage
		No front-wheel drive	American—helps American industry
		Horizon	
Middle of range	Dull design	Local dealer	Good gas mileage
Willing to pay	No glamour	No problem with parts	American car—support American industry
		Front-wheel drive	
		Honda Civic	
Highest price	Import	Dealer 25 miles away	Good gas mileage
		Front-wheel drive	

factors; there was no clear-cut distinction that pointed to the particular selection she had made. To help her focus her thoughts, therefore, she did the following focused freewriting:

> Well, why did I buy the Horizon? Price? Maybe to a certain extent, all the cars were in the same price category, but even with that category there were some significant differences, the Tercel was definitely the cheapest and the Honda cost a lot more, but really I would have been willing to pay that price if the car was exactly what I wanted. And it really came pretty close. Why didn't I? The Chevette, I guess I ruled that out because I really need front-wheel drive if I want to go skiing this winter. Jim told me that front-wheel drive is better on snowy roads. That's convenience. And I ruled out the Tercel because I worried about getting parts if anything broke. That's convenience too. But I'm not so sure I really worried about that so much, either on the Tercel or the Honda. I guess there was something about the Horizon being an American car that did count. I come from a town with a large auto factory and I remember how bad things were when the factory closed down. When push comes to shove I guess I just feel that Americans should support American business. . . .

The focused freewriting gave the student a chance to sort through her thoughts. She had been unaware of her sense of social responsibility and was surprised to see it emerge as a factor in her freewriting. Just to make sure that this was the factor she wanted to emphasize, she put her papers away for a few hours, had a soft drink, spoke to her friend on the phone, and did some other homework.

Writing the Essay:
Planning and Writing

The period of incubation that the student gave the problem was useful, for when she came back to it, she saw that the issue of social responsibility was still the most important in her choice. She wrote a tentative opening paragraph in which she expressed this idea.

> I bought the Horizon for reasons of social responsibility, because it was an American car and I believe that it is important to support American manufacturers. Convenience was the next most important factor; prestige didn't seem to matter. Nor did I expect prices to rise. Price was important in limiting the range of my selection, but once I had decided on a general figure, it didn't matter much at all.

The paragraph is so rough that many students would think it would have to be corrected before moving on. But the student knew that she was on the right trail, that as she continued to write and then to revise she would have a better idea of the paper's focus, and that a clearer thesis statement would emerge.

Next the student considered how to arrange the body paragraphs. In what order should the factors have been discussed? The student felt that putting the most important factor first or last would probably highlight it. She decided that she liked to build up to a climax, so she put social responsibility last. The order of the other paragraphs turned out to be more difficult than she had expected. As you read the model, see if you can understand the student's logic. She found that she needed to write not only a first draft but also a second, which she revised even further. After editing and recopying, her final version looked like this:

Social Responsibility — Buying American

Buying a new car is a major purchase for anyone, and when I had to make a choice I spent several weeks looking at models, reading about cars, and discussing them with my friends. Like other consumers, I was reacting to the law of demand, not in its simple terms, but as amplified by the factors mentioned by Paul T. Heyne in "The Economic Way of Thinking." In his discussion of the law of demand, Heyne states that "increases in the prices of goods will characteristically be followed by decreases in the total amount purchased and decreases in price will characteristically be followed by increases in the amount purchased." Heyne adds, however, the following modifications: that people will pay higher prices if they expect a price increase in the future, or if they feel they are getting prestige, convenience, or a sense of social responsibility. The expectation of higher prices was not a factor for me, and prestige received only a passing glance. Even though price, convenience and social responsibility were all significant considerations, I was not aware until I analyzed my decision how important social responsibility was to me. "Buy American" may sound corny, but for me it was a serious matter.

The price of the car played a part in my thinking, for it was the single most important factor in narrowing the range of cars that I would even consider buying. Since I was limited to $7,500, I could only afford to buy compact or sub-compact models. But even within that category, I discovered there was still a range of prices. The most expensive of the ones I looked at was the Honda Civic; the cheapest was the Toyota Tercel. Yet the difference in price between these two was over $800. The other two cars I considered — the Plymouth Horizon and the Chevrolet Chevette — were somewhere in the middle. I could conceivably have been influenced by price, have chosen the least expensive and saved a considerable sum. When I thought about the problem, however, I realized that the car I purchased would last for about five years. If I divided the total savings by five to find the savings per year, the amount I might save seemed much less important. Factors such as how well the car would hold up, the ease of servicing it, became much more important. As Paul T. Heyne says in "The Economic Way of Thinking," "The price in money that must be paid for something is not a complete measure of its cost to the purchaser." Certainly, it was not for me.

Prestige was another factor that might have influenced my decision, and perhaps if I could have afforded a Rolls-Royce or a Mercedes, it might have assumed greater weight in my thinking. I know that I would have enjoyed hearing my friends say, "Oooh look at that car!" when I drove up. But I also know that cars don't mean that much to me. I might spend more than I can afford on a great designer dress, because my sense of myself is more closely tied to what I wear. Cars, however, are not, for me, an extension of my identity.

Convenience played a considerable role in guiding my choice, and originally I thought it was the most significant factor. The Chevette was ruled out because it lacked front-wheel drive, a useful feature if I wanted to drive on the snowy roads in winter. And the lack of a Honda Service Center nearby made me question the advisability of purchasing it. I wondered, also, whether there would be any difficulty getting new parts for imported cars. Like the example Heyne gave with the soda-pop bottles, the convenience factor assumed great importance since the comparative costs were not sufficient to make a difference.

It was a sense of social responsibility that eventually led to my decision to buy the Horizon. I don't claim to be a "do-gooder" and, in fact, I was almost completely unaware of how important this factor was in my thinking while I was looking at the various models. But when I thought more carefully about my actions, I realized that supporting the American auto industry meant something to me. I grew up in a town that has a large auto assembly plant and I remember the economic problems when business fell off and the plant was closed. Not only were men out of work, but all the local businesses suffered as well. And I don't want to claim that if one of the imported cars had been considerably cheaper, or had substantial prestige, or some particular convenience that I could not get in an American car, that I would not have bought the foreign car and ignored my unconscious patriotic impulses. But since all the other factors were close enough, it was the sense of social responsibility that sealed my decision.

Understanding the various factors that cause people to choose one item to purchase instead of another has led me to an awareness of my own buying patterns and so, perhaps, to an awareness of others as well. In addition to price and prestige, convenience and social responsibility need to be considered. All of them played a part in my thinking when I bought my Horizon, but it was the concern with American business — my sense of social responsibility — that became the crucial factor.

In her introduction the student indicated that she would discuss the purchase of a car and that she would consider the way her final purchase reflected the modified law of demand explained in the reading. Notice that she quoted the basic law of demand from the article rather than paraphrasing it. Even though a summary in your own words is usually preferable, you can use a quote if the phrasing is particularly apt or if the material discussed involves a definition of a technical term. The thesis in the last two sentences is quite long because she wants to make sure that she has considered all the factors that influence demand.

The student worried about the order in which she would discuss the various factors in the body of the essay. The most significant issue was discussed last, thus giving a sense of climax to the paper, as the writer had felt it would. The earlier paragraphs, however, fail to follow the same sequence (least important to most important). The matter of price was discussed first because (1) the student writer wanted to show that price was the most important aspect of the law of demand, and (2) the discussion of price gave her a convenient way of covering the various models she had considered. Do you think the arrangement she used is justified?

One of the factors, the expectation of higher prices, is mentioned in the introduction but never discussed in the body. Why do you think the writer handled it this way? Do you think her decision to leave it out was a wise one? Why, or why not?

The conclusion of the essay restates the thesis and makes a brief mention of the value of such analysis. What other ways of ending it could you suggest?

An Academic Discipline at Work: Economic Decision-Making

Basic Concepts: Predicting Effects and Making Decisions

You have just followed a student writer weighing causes to evaluate the motivations for a major purchase. She applied information from an article in economics and, by using the cause-effect relationship, examined her past behavior. Conversely, the cause-effect relationship can be used predictively to help determine possible results and to provide an intelligent argument for a possible course of action. Since very few choices are as clear-cut as whether to open your umbrella during a rainstorm, when you make a decision you are usually considering several factors, the possible outcomes of alternative courses of action. If you asked, "Should I buy a Ford Escort, an American car, rather than a Honda, a foreign car?" you would be investigating the effects of both options. In short, you would be setting up several causal chains. A few possibilities are demonstrated in Figure 6.7.

Figure 6.7 *Several Causal Chains Relating to a Car Purchase*

Buying a Ford Escort, an American car
↓
(Cause) → (Effect)
　　　　↓
　　　More American automotive workers would be employed
　　　↓
　　　(Cause) → (Effect)
　　　　　　↓
　　　　　They would spend more money
　　　　　on goods and services
　　　　　↓
　　　　　(Cause) → (Effect)
　　　　　　　↓
　　　　　　The economy would be healthier
　　　　　　↓
　　　　　　(Cause) → (Effect)
　　　　　　　　↓
　　　　　　　and so on

Significant effect: One advantage of buying an American car

Buying a Honda, a foreign car
↓
(Cause) → (Effect)
　　　　↓
　　　Difficulty in replacing parts
　　　↓
　　　(Cause) → (Effect)
　　　　　↓
　　　　and so on

Significant effect: One disadvantage of buying the Honda, a foreign car

Buying a Ford Escort, an American car
↓
(Cause) → (Effect)
　　　　↓
　　　Fewer miles per gallon
　　　↓
　　　(Cause) → (Effect)
　　　　　↓

More disposable income spent on gas
↓
(Cause) → (Effect)

Significant effect: One disadvantage of buying the Ford Escort, an American car

Buying a Honda
↓
(Cause) → (Effect)
↓
Fewer repairs necessary, according to *Consumer Reports*
↓
(Cause) → (Effect)
↓
Relatively small investment on upkeep
↓
(Cause) → (Effects)
↓
and so on

Significant effect: A second advantage of buying a Honda

By constructing these and other causal chains you would be able to investigate both the positive and negative effects of a potential action — in this case, the kind of car you might buy. Your decision to purchase would then be based on a complete analysis of the situation. Causal chains allow you to pursue several lines of reasoning and therefore several perspectives. You can thus determine the significant positive and negative effects of your alternatives. Knowing these possible effects helps you weigh the evidence and therefore arrive at an intelligent decision. Schematically, your thought process would look like Figure 6.8.

PRACTICE

Select one of the following questions involving a personal economic choice. Set up the causal chains that would help you determine the significant economic effects of the two available options. The more lines of reasoning, (perspectives) you can consider, the more likely you are to discover the significant effects and the greater the possibility of making an informed decision.

1. Should I buy an expensive new winter coat, or should I purchase a cheaper one?

2. Should I continue to live in the dormitory at a fixed expense, or should I share an apartment with my roommate?

3. Should I borrow money in order to purchase a new car, or should I repair the old car?

4. Should I choose a career that might provide me with a large personal income but little job security, or should I select a career with limited financial gain but high job security?

5. Should I choose a career that requires considerable economic investment in graduate education, or should I choose one that I can pursue immediately upon graduation?

Whenever you are trying to arrive at a personal decision, you should probably weigh all the effects, both positive and negative, of all alternatives. Similarly, if you are trying to convince others to make a choice, it is important to consider all the effects. If a union leader, for example, urging workers to go on strike to rectify legitimate grievances neglected to present the dangers of doing so, he or she would be less than honest. If an officer of a large corporation failed to apprise the Board of Directors of the economic risks of investing profits in a new product, he or she would be subject to harsh

Figure 6.8 *How the Significant Effects of Causal Chains Relate to a Final Decision*

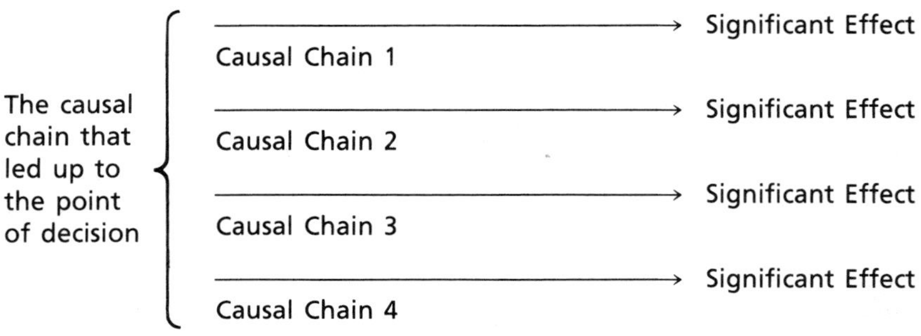

questioning. The officer would be wise, therefore, to consider the risks and indicate why the decision to reinvest should be made despite them — to try to convince his or her audience that the positive effects outweigh the negative consequences.

The main point of the union leader's speech could be expressed in this thesis statement:

> Even though you would lose a considerable amount of money during the strike period itself, the potential raises you will receive will ultimately more than compensate for your immediate losses.

The main point of the corporate officer's argument, the thesis statement, might be:

> Despite the fact that introducing the new product would necessitate considerable investment in new equipment and a higher marketing budget, the potentially high demand for it will eventually ensure us a larger profit.

Each thesis statement not only argues for a particular point of view but also makes a concession to the opposite position. Note that these thesis statements present only significant effects.

PRACTICE

Using the significant effects you devised in the previous practice, write two thesis statements, one favoring the decision and the other opposing it. Each of your thesis statements should consider both sides of the argument.

Look again at the thesis statement in the model essay:

> Even though price, convenience and social responsibility were all significant considerations, I was not aware until I analyzed my decision how important social responsibility was to me.

In this statement the student indicated that she would discuss several motivating factors (causes) in her purchase of a car, but that she would emphasize one. Similarly, the union leader mentioned a significant negative effect but emphasized that the significant positive effect would adequately compensate for it. Can you discern a similar pattern in the corporation officer's thesis? In the two you wrote?

These tentative thesis statements suggest the organization of an essay. The introduction would of course include the thesis. If the concession is significant and merits further explanation, it would be carefully considered in the paragraphs of the body, as would a full discussion of the arguments for the chosen position. Should the discussion of the concession appear before the discussion for the recommended choice? The conclusion would, in part, restate the point made in the thesis.

PRACTICE

Using the significant effects you devised in the previous practice, write two thesis statements, one favoring the decision and the other opposing it. Each of your thesis statements should consider both sides of the argument.

PRACTICE

Using one of the thesis statements you prepared in the previous practice, devise a plan for an essay you might write.

Case Study: Should a New Restaurant Be Opened?

Read the following case study about an important economic decision.

Doreen and Richard Potter met as undergraduates at Northern State University while they were both members of a food cooperative that supplied produce from local farms, as well as homemade breads and jams to students living off campus. As a result of this association they not only developed a romantic attachment and married at graduation, they learned a great deal about operating a business and preparing foods. Since both were still uncertain about their careers — Doreen had majored in marketing and John in organic agriculture — and both loved living in a university setting, they decided to open a small lunchroom on the business street just off campus, featuring a salad bar and homemade soups, breads, and pies. It was a simple, attractive establishment with eight tables, counter space for ten customers, red-checked plastic table cloths, dried flowers in small vases, travel posters on white walls, and taped folk-rock and classical music from Doreen's and John's personal collection.

After a slow start, business picked up considerably through word of mouth and advertisements in the campus weekly newspaper. It became a popular off-campus eatery attracting both students and faculty interested in natural foods. Doreen and Richard found that in order to meet the increasing demand, they had to hire a cook and a waitress. Although this necessitated a small rise in their prices, the number of customers continued to increase. John and Doreen managed to make a sufficient profit to maintain their needs and to have enough disposable income for other purposes. After four years they had accumulated about $10,000 in savings. They were certainly busy, but they were content.

When they had graduated four years earlier, John and Doreen had gone on a summer honeymoon trip to Europe, a wedding present given by Doreen's father, a successful lawyer from Omaha. During this vacation to France, Italy, and Spain they had expanded their gastronomic tastes by sampling many of the culinary specialties of these countries and had learned to enjoy wine with their meals. Upon their return, they still appreciated wholesome American cooking, but they became involved in learning how to make some of the dishes they had so much enjoyed in Europe. To this end they purchased a series of cookbooks and even took a course in continental cuisine at the university's extension division. They would occasionally introduce some of their more successful recipes as specials on their luncheon menu.

After four years, they began thinking of expanding their operation: (1) by acquiring more space, (2) by opening for dinner, and (3) by enlarging their menu to feature European cuisine. As luck would have it, a bookstore next door closed, making it possible for John and Doreen to put their thoughts into practice.

The decision to expand was a difficult one for the Potters. They had their savings and the promise of financial backing from Doreen's father. Their expertise in running a successful business put them in a favorable position to receive bank loans. Food supplies would be readily available from local farms. Of course, since the menu would now feature meats, fish, and poultry, they would have to pay considerably more for their supplies. They would have to make a considerable investment in establishing a wine cellar. Not only would they have the expense of enlarging their premises, but they would also have to hire a decorator to create a more suitable atmosphere for the leisurely dining experience they wanted to promote. Although their present cook was fine, they would have to hire a chef trained in the subtle arts of European cuisine. Of course, all these costs would have to be absorbed by their potential patrons.

Eastfield, the location of Northern State University, is a town of about 100,000 permanent residents with an additional temporary population of about 30,000 students during the academic year. In addition to the campus dining facilities there are the usual fast-food establishments around the university: four hamburger joints, a fried chicken takeout place, two pizzerias, four ''greasy spoon'' luncheonettes, and, since the Potters opened their lunchroom, three similar health food operations. There is one rather successful expensive steak and seafood restaurant for leisurely dining which, however, does not feature the kind of menu the Potters anticipate providing. This restaurant is popular with faculty, students on dates, and visiting parents taking their children out for a treat. It does not generally attract non-university customers, since the business center of the town has two such establishments. Just outside town overlooking a lake is a beautiful and elegant French restaurant, which definitely attracts the town's business and professional class as well as some university people. Although the menu the Potters are considering would be similar, their prices would be lower since their restaurant would be considerably less formal.

Although many of the student body struggle with tight budgets, a considerable number of them come from upper middle class families. Many students have traveled to Europe over summer vacations, and, as a matter of fact, the university sponsors a junior year abroad in Paris. Therefore a significant segment of the student body is familiar with the culinary pleasures of foreign places and would possibly pay to duplicate the experience around campus. Members of the faculty and the administration are always complaining about the dearth of charming dining facilities around the university and in the town generally.

Would a restaurant such as the Potters are contemplating be successful enough economically to warrant their investment? Should they go ahead, or should they maintain what they already have?

To help you analyze the problem and arrive at a reasonable decision, we present the following excerpt from an economics text dealing with some ways of anticipating demand. As you read, weigh the evidence by applying the information in the excerpt to the Potters' situation.

PRICE ELASTICITY DEFINED

Suppose a large department store drops the price of nylon jackets from $12 to $10. Sales thereupon increase from 100 jackets per month to 150. Revenue from sales increases from $1,200 ($12 × 100) to $1,500 ($10 × 150). Provided additional production costs or additional advertising and other selling expenses do not wipe out this gain, the sale is a success.

The demand for the product is thus described as being price-elastic. If the demand for something is price-elastic, entrepreneurs will take in more money if they lower the price because the increased volume of purchases will more than make up for lower unit prices. "Price-elastic" means the change in the *quantity* purchased is large relative to the *price* change, that the price change motivates consumers to increase their purchases by more than enough to offset price decreases.

Demand is also shown to be price-elastic when entrepreneurs raise the price and sales revenues fall. If, for instance, the department store raises its price on nylon jackets from $10 to

$12, and consumers respond by reducing purchases from 150 per month to 100 and sales revenue falls from $1,500 to $1,200, that demonstrates that demand is price-elastic. Again, consumer response is large relative to the price change.

If, however, the store lowers its price from $12 to $10 and sales increase from 100 jackets per month to 110, demand is price-inelastic. The sale has laid an egg. Total revenue — which is defined as price times quantity — has dropped from $1,200 ($12 × 100) to $1,100 ($10 × 110). The drop in price was not offset by a sufficient increase in the quantity demanded. Consumers were relatively indifferent to the price change.

PRICE ELASTICITY OF DEMAND

Now, let us see how the price elasticity of demand works in practice. There are four possibilities, which we'll call Situations I, II, III, and IV.

Situation I: Increase in quantity exceeds decrease in price

Suppose you are the owner of the Dazzle Toothpaste Company, and you decide to sell more toothpaste by lowering your price. You have been selling 100 tubes of toothpaste per week to retail stores at a price of $1 each. You try reducing the price 10 percent, to 90 cents. Thereafter, sales increase 20 percent to 120 tubes per week. Demand is elastic because the percentage increase in quantity exceeded the percentage decrease in price; buyers (the stores) are relatively responsive to your price change.

Notice an important point. You are taking in more money than before. Before the price change, you were taking in $100 per week (100 tubes at $1 each). After the price decrease, you are taking in $108 (120 tubes at 90 cents) — $8 more than before. The price drop has been more than offset by an increase in sales.

Situation II: Decrease in quantity exceeds increase in price

We can also tell the story in reverse. Suppose you have been selling 120 tubes per week at a price of 90 cents each. You try increasing the price to $1. What happens? Sales drop from 120 to 100 tubes per week, and you take in less money. Demand is elastic.

Situation III: Increase in quantity is less than the decrease in price

Consider another possibility. Assume again that you are selling 100 tubes per week at $1 each. You decide to lower the price to 90 cents. This time sales increase but only to 105 tubes per week. Total revenue falls from $100 per week to $94.50 (105 tubes at 90 cents). In this case, the price was dropped 10 percent, but quantity increased only 5 percent. Demand is now *inelastic:* consumers were relatively indifferent to the price decrease. They did not jump to buy.

Situation IV: Decrease in quantity is less than the increase in price

There is one more possibility. Suppose you increase the price from $1 to $1.10. Sales drop. As long as we assume that the law of demand is operating — that price and quantity are inversely related (the demand curve slopes down from left to right) — people will buy less when the price goes up. How much less? Suppose sales drop from 100 per week to 95, a drop of 5 percent. What happens to total revenue? Total revenue is now $104.50 (95 tubes at $1.10). Even though you sold fewer tubes, your total revenue went up. Why? Because this time, while price went up 10 percent, the number of tubes purchased went down only 5 percent. Consumers were relatively indifferent to the price increase — they wanted the toothpaste badly enough to go on buying almost the same quantity. Demand was inelastic.

Table 6.2 summarizes the four situations showing elasticity of demand.

What Conclusions Can We Make?

Our first conclusion is: When demand is *elastic,* the entrepreneur takes in more revenue from sales when the price is lowered and less revenue when the price is raised. (Again, keep in mind we are thinking only about changes in revenue, not about profit. We do not know what's happening to production costs when the volume of sales changes.)

Our second conclusion is: When demand is *inelastic,* the entrepreneur takes in less revenue when the price is lowered and more revenue when the price is raised.

TABLE 6.2   Elasticity of Demand: Four Situations

Situation	Price per tube	Quantity (sales per week)	Total revenue	Type of demand
I and II	$1.00	100	$100.00	
	.90	120	108.00	Elastic
III	$1.00	100	$100.00	
	.90	105	94.50	Inelastic
IV	$1.00	100	$100.00	
	1.10	95	104.50	Inelastic

A third conclusion: If you are a good entrepreneur, you should lie awake nights asking yourself whether the demand for your product is elastic or inelastic and what price changes will cause your total revenue to increase or decrease. But you must also think about the changes in costs, and, therefore, profits that occur with changes in sales volume.

FOUR TESTS OF PRICE ELASTICITY

No one can accurately forecast why people want what they want, or why they want something badly enough to be unaffected by price increases (inelasticity) or strongly motivated to buy more because of price decreases (elasticity). Nevertheless, economists are generally agreed that there are four important tests of the price elasticity of demand. Every good entrepreneur should consider these tests and try to relate them to his or her product. As we proceed through the tests, think about Dazzle Toothpaste. Is it elastic or inelastic with respect to each test? What do the results of all four tests reveal?

Test 1: Does the Product Have Many Substitutes?

The availability of close substitutes is by far the most important test of elasticity. If many substitutes are available, people will switch from Dazzle to Dentobrite or Glisten if Dazzle raises its price (assuming *ceteris paribus*, nothing else changes). In such a case, the percentage drop in Dazzle's quantity demanded would exceed the percentage increase in Dazzle's price; Dazzle's total revenue would fall. The more close substitutes there are, the greater the elasticity.

Remember also that if Dazzle lowered its price relative to the prices of competing brands, sales might increase more than enough to offset the price decrease. Why? Because people would stop buying Dentobrite, Glisten, and the like, and buy Dazzle.

On the other hand, if there are no close substitutes, consumers will buy about the same quantity regardless of price changes. Demand is inelastic.

Keep in mind also that old models (like old cars) are substitutes for new ones. If we can repair the old one, our demand for the new one will be elastic.

Test 2: How Expensive Is the Product Relative to the Buyer's Income?

What percentage of the buyer's annual income does the price of the product represent? If the product is very inexpensive, the chances are that the demand will be price-*in*elastic.

An example: There is a highly advertised brand of cupcakes, which are sold two to a package. A few years ago, a pair sold for 10 cents. In one jump, the price was raised to 13 cents — a 30 percent increase in price. Did anyone complain? Probably not. The point is that we tend to be indifferent to price changes of inexpensive items — paper clips, matches, bobby pins, and the like.

If, on the other hand, we are considering buying a car on a salary of $15,000 per year, a $5,000 car represents four months' work. A 10 percent change in the price of the car, $500, represents almost two weeks pay. The price change may affect us strongly. If the increase is $500, we may decide not to buy. Or, a $500 decrease may cause us to buy. We are strongly influenced by the price change either way.

Test 3: Is the Product a Luxury or a Necessity?

If the product is a necessity, demand will tend to be price-inelastic. Buyers will be relatively indifferent to price changes.

The demand for luxury goods will tend to be price-elastic — the more luxurious, the more elastic. Since we can take a luxury or leave it, we will be strongly influenced by price changes.

Test 4: To What Extent Are Consumers Habituated to the Product?

If one is hooked on heroin, heaven forbid, demand may be extremely price inelastic, almost vertical. (If the demand curve is absolutely straight up and down, it means that buyers will pay any price for a given quantity.) To a lesser extent, the same argument applies to people who insist on a certain brand of cigarettes, soap, deodorant, or toothpaste.

However, as time passes, a price difference may cause the habit to weaken. If a person is used to a particular brand of cigarettes, he or she may pay 5 cents more per pack for a while. But, as the time passes, the smoker may start wondering whether the brand is worth the extra 5 cents. Eventually, the person may drop the favorite brand and adopt another at a lower price. Thus, over time, demand becomes more price-elastic as the habit weakens.

Now, what about Dazzle Toothpaste? What does each test tell us about it?

Test 1: Are there substitutes? Yes, many. Vote: elastic.

Test 2: Percent of buyer's income? The toothpaste price is a small percentage of income. Vote: inelastic.

Test 3: Luxury or necessity?   To people who customarily brush their teeth, toothpaste is probably a necessity. But is any one brand like Dazzle a necessity? Probably not. Vote: elastic.

Test 4: Habit?   Probably relevant. Unless the price change is large, toothpaste users probably stick to a brand they are used to. Vote: inelastic.

Now, what is the overall result? We have two votes for elastic and two for inelastic. Are the elastic votes more important than the inelastic? Probably not. Thus, the overall vote is inelastic. What does this mean? Touchy question. If Dazzle Toothpaste, a relatively inexpensive item, is well established, with a fair number of customers habituated to using it, a price change of perhaps 10 percent one way or the other probably will not affect sales much.

What should you, the entrepreneur, do then? You might experiment with slightly higher prices. Chances are that sales will *not* drop by as large a percentage as your percentage increase in price. With increased prices, total revenue should rise.

We have completed our discussion of the price elasticity of demand. The four main points to remember are as follows:

1. If demand is price-elastic, total revenue will rise if the price falls, and fall if the price rises.

2. If demand is price-inelastic, total revenue will rise if the price rises, and fall if the price falls.

3. Elasticity should only be associated with small changes in price and quantity, since there will usually be different elasticities along any given demand curve or schedule.

4. If the coefficient is greater than one, demand is price-elastic; exactly one, elasticity is unitary; less than one, demand is price-inelastic.

Making the Decision

Consider the four tests of the price elasticity of demand as presented in the economics test. Then ask yourself the controlling question:

Would the Potters be successful if they changed the nature of their restaurant?

In answering this question, you will not only be weighing the evidence, providing the pluses and minuses of the situation, but you will be arriving at a judgment. Obviously, the situation is complex, and you cannot be certain that any advice you give would indeed work out as you predict. What is important is that your guess be an educated one, using as much of the information you have in order to substantiate your argument. Remember also that even though there may be non-economic factors worth investigating — the excitement and pleasure of opening such an establishment, or the reason the Potters are not pursuing the careers they had prepared for in college — the assignment limits you to economic factors.

As you read and reread the materials weighing the evidence, you will want to use some of the techniques described in this chapter to arrive at a decision and to support your argument. You could, for example, set up causal chains.

Cause: If the Potters open the new restaurant: If the Potters do not open the new restaurant:

_____ ✓   _____ ✓

_____ ✓   _____ ✓

_____ ✓   _____ ✓

_____ ✓   _____ ✓

_____ ✓   _____ ✓

_____ ✓   _____ ✓

_____ ✓   _____ ✓

In addition, you might want to take each of the tests of the price elasticity of demand in turn and apply it to the controlling question by forming and answering subsidiary questions like the following:

1. Are close substitutes to the proposed new restaurant available?

    Are there restaurants in town similar to the one the Potters already operate?

    Would the Potters be able to compete with the more expensive restaurants in town?

    _____

    _____

2. How expensive is the product relative to the buyer's income?

    _____

    _____

3. Is the product a luxury or a necessity?

    _____

    _____

4. Are consumers habituated to the product?

    _____

    _____

   In addition to these subsidiary questions, you might form others by combining basic patterns with Who, Where, When questions, such as the following:

1. Who would be the potential customers for the Potters' new restaurant?

2. _____

3. _____

PRACTICE

   After weighing the evidence and arriving at a decision, write a tentative thesis statement reflecting both points of view but favoring one. Using this statement as the basis for organizing an essay, decide on the extent to which you believe it beneficial to discuss the opposing arguments in the body. What would be the best sequence of paragraphs in the body? Your drafts should be as complete as possible. Furthermore, a good argument for a college essay, and for most life situations, considers all the available evidence.

PRACTICE

   Choose an article in Part 3 of this book, the Anthology, that interests you and write an essay answering one of the cause-effect questions provided there.

7

Research: Using Reading to Develop Insight

THE SETTINGS FOR RESEARCH

Imagine an English class studying utopian literature, descriptions of ideal societies. It is presently reading Aldous Huxley's *Brave New World*, a projection of a world six hundred years into the future, a world that controls reproduction for political and social ends. This theme is apparent at the outset of the novel:

> . . . the Director of Hatcheries and Conditioning entered the room. . . . A troop of newly arrived students . . . followed nervously, rather abjectly, at the Director's heels. Each of them carried a notebook, in which, whenever the great man spoke, he desperately scribbled. Straight from the horse's mouth. It was a rare privilege. The D. H. C. for Central London always made a point of personally conducting his new students round the various departments.
>
> • • •
>
> "I shall begin at the beginning," said the D.H.C. and the more zealous students recorded his intention in their notebooks: *Begin at the beginning*. "These," he waved his hand, "are the incubators." And opening an insulated door he showed them racks upon racks of numbered test-tubes.
>
> • • •
>
> "Bokanovsky's Process," repeated the Director, and the students underlined the words in their little notebooks.

One egg, one embryo, one adult — normality. But a bokanovskified egg will bud, will proliferate, will divide. From eight to ninety-six buds, and every bud will grow into a perfectly formed embryo, and every embryo into a full-sized adult. Making ninety-six human beings grow where only one grew before. Progress.

• • •

"Scores," the Director repeated and flung out his arms, as though he were distributing largesse. "Scores."

But one of the students was fool enough to ask where the advantage lay.

"My good boy!" The Director wheeled sharply round on him. "Can't you see? Can't you *see?*" He raised a hand; his expression was solemn. "Bokanovsky's Process is one of the major instruments of social stability!"

Major instruments of social stability.

Standard men and women; in uniform batches. The whole of a small factory staffed with the products of a single bokanovskified egg.

"Ninety-six identical twins working ninety-six identical machines!" The voice was almost tremulous with enthusiasm. "You really know where you are. For the first time in history." He quoted the planetary motto. "Community, Identity, Stability." Grand words.[1]

Did you note that the word *freedom* was not mentioned by the Director? Since this novel is a satire of a totalitarian state, Huxley wanted to point out the abuses of scientific investigations in such a government.

The discussion of the novel in class led inevitably to the issue of cloning today and its implications for free societies as well as totalitarian ones. Like the instructors who asked questions on cloning in Chapter 1, these students asked:

What exactly is cloning?

Why are scientists doing it?

Can I be cloned?

Would you accept my clone's taking your exam for me?

The English instructor's knowledge of the nature of cloning was limited. The students wanted to know more. This need to find out more about a subject — developing an informed opinion by reading authorities on the subject — is a major motivation for research.

Unlike the students in *Brave New World,* who felt intimidated by the Director, you are encouraged through your research to work independently.

---

[1]Aldous Huxley, *Brave New World* (New York: Harper & Row, 1969) pp. 1–4.

You are free to examine an idea wherever the research takes you. In the process you learn the primary skill of an emerging scholar: synthesizing information and ideas.

As in all the other writing assignments in this text, the research paper requires a focus of study, a controlling idea. Sometimes an instructor will provide a focus for you through a controlling question; sometimes not. In this connection, we will need to consider two possible situations:

A)   starting with a controlling question, and

B)   starting without a controlling question

If this were your first substantial research project, the task might seem overwhelming. Although most of you will experience ultimate satisfaction and reward in writing a research paper, there will be, in your solitary search, many moments of frustration in not knowing where to find material in the library. Without knowledge of a library's basic organization, a student could regard a library as a maze of shelves, cabinets, file drawers, and more shelves, all with indecipherable labels. There is also frustration in not knowing how to find related material within books or other library sources, and frustration in not being sure how much related material to include in your paper. To help you avoid some of these pitfalls, the discussion that follows will revolve around five interrelated steps in library research:

- searching for sources in the library

- identifying a focus

- scanning sources

- writing detailed notes

- preparing a research paper from notes

SEARCHING FOR SOURCES IN THE LIBRARY

In order to search for source material related to your general topic — whether you start with or without a controlling question — it is necessary to know the major parts of the library, as diagrammed in Figure 7.1.

Reference Works — Encyclopedias.   Usually, the first place to start is the shelves where the reference works are located. Encyclopedias are a good source from which to get an overview about a subject, especially a subject

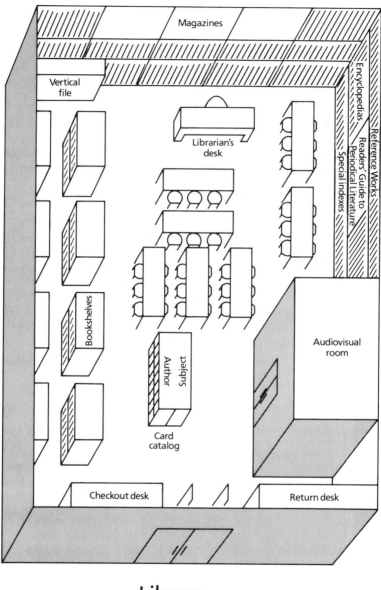

Library

Figure 7.1 *Diagram of a Library Showing Important Resources*

that you are starting out to research. Two encyclopedias considered by scholars to be among the best are the *Encyclopedia Americana* and the *Encyclopedia Britannica*.

Under each subject heading, the encyclopedias will more than likely make reference to other related subject headings. In beginning a research project, it is a good idea to read the material under all related headings in the encyclopedia. You will read more about this below under the heading *Cross-Referencing*.

Card Catalog.   As you probably know, the card catalog is organized by author, title, and subject. The library call number indicates the shelf on which a book is located.

A library uses one of two classification systems. Under the subject *cloning*, a student found two cards for the same book, one from a public library and the other from a college library. The two cards are reproduced in Figure 7.2.

The call number on the left-hand card is part of the Dewey Decimal classification system, and the one on the right-hand card is part of the Library of Congress system. If you use a particular library on a regular basis, it is a good idea to be familiar with its classification system. If you know, for example, that the call number 596.016 is subclassified as in Figure 7.3, you will have a clue to further research.

Figure 7.2   *Catalog Cards*

Public Library

```
                596.016
                  M

McKinnell, Robert Gilmore
   Cloning: a biologist
                   reports
Minneapolis: University of
Minnesota Press, C 1979,
VIII, 130 p.: ill., 24 cm.

   Includes index
   Bibliography: p. 119—121

   1. Cloning.  2. Cell
nuclei—transplantation.
3. Embryology, Experimental
(Title)
```

College Library

```
QH            Cloning
442.2
.M32
   McKinnell, Robert Gilmore



            (and so on)
```

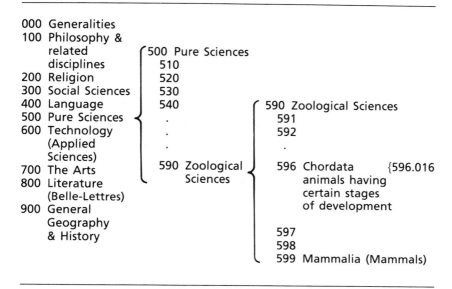

000 Generalities
100 Philosophy &
      related
      disciplines ⎰ 500 Pure Sciences
200 Religion   510
300 Social Sciences 520
400 Language   530
500 Pure Sciences   540
600 Technology   .
      (Applied   .
      Sciences)   .
700 The Arts   590 Zoological
800 Literature   Sciences
      (Belle-Lettres)
900 General
      Geography
      & History

590 Zoological Sciences
591
592
 .
596 Chordata   {596.016
      animals having
      certain stages
      of development

597
598
599 Mammalia (Mammals)

Figure 7.3 *Using a Dewey Decimal Call Number to Find Other Materials*

If you notice that the book by McKinnell was published in 1979, you may wonder whether scientists have learned more about the technology of cloning since that time. It may be worth your while to examine the upper range of numbers, from 597–599. You may discover, in the stacks for books bearing those numbers, later publications revealing that scientists have indeed been able to clone mice, the first mammals to be cloned. Without a familiarity with the library's classification system, you may not have searched further on adjacent shelves.

The same kind of search could be made in bookstacks using the Library of Congress system, as shown in Figure 7.4.

At the bottom of the catalog card are other related subject titles you may want to refer to. This cross-referencing is essential in searching out source material.

Reference Works — Abstracts and Indexes.   Two other kinds of references that help you locate sources are abstracts and indexes. Abstracts summarize and critique the sources listed. One general abstract that summarizes books from a broad range of subjects is the *Book Review Digest*. There are also specific reference books for broad fields of study, such as art, history, literature, and the social sciences. Students interested in the general topic of cloning would probably want to examine *Biological Abstracts*.

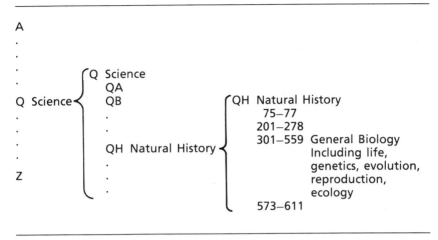

Figure 7.4   *Using a Library of Congress Call Number to Find Other Materials*

Although index references list only sources, they are extremely important. *The Readers' Guide to Periodical Literature* is the most popular index. It includes in its listing such periodicals as *Newsweek, Time, National Geographic, Commentary, Ebony, Foreign Policy, Congressional Digest,* and *Better Homes and Gardens.* As you gather, the *Readers' Guide* is quite comprehensive. For convenience in searching relevant material, it lists articles under author, title, and subject. For more scholarly journals there are specialized indexes; two related to the subject of cloning are *Applied Science and Technology Index* and *General Science Index.*

Magazines and Newspapers.   Each library has its complement of periodicals. Your college library may not carry a particular magazine listed in the indexes above. If the title of an article in an index indicates that the contents are essential to the preparation of your paper, you may have to look for that periodical in another library, or request it through an interlibrary loan. This delay in getting source material is one of the frustrations of library research.

Newspaper articles are important sources for research, and you should refer to them, particularly for the most current information. Articles in *The New York Times,* for example, are listed in *The New York Times Index.*

Audiovisual Room.   Your college library may have a specialized section or room for viewing films or listening to tapes and phonograph records. It usually has viewers for microfilm of important national newspapers, like *The New York Times*.

Vertical File.   Pamphlets, clippings, and pictures that come to the attention of the library are possible materials in a collection known as the vertical file. Its subject headings are usually the same as the classification system used in the library's catalog. In one of our own college libraries, several clippings from magazines and newspapers regarding the subject of cloning were available, including these two documents:

- a two-page "Position Statement on Recombinant DNA Technology" by a citizen group known as the Coalition for Responsible Genetic Research
- a one-page publication brief, "Impact of Applied Genetics," by the Office of Technology Assessment (OTA), an advisory arm of the United States Congress

Cross-Referencing.   Using these reference sources would be significantly easier if they all listed information under the same subject headings; unfortunately, they do not. The heading *Cloning* did appear in the card catalog, in *Readers' Guide*, and in the encyclopedias, but it was not used in the other indexes. Does a researcher, therefore, give up on those sources? Of course not. It takes a bit of detective work and some imagination, but almost all of these reference works will eventually yield some valuable materials.

Usually, editors of these indexes have substituted alternative subject headings for the expected one. A list of alternative subject headings can be found printed under the title "See also," which precedes or follows the listing of articles on a particular subject. *Readers' Guide*, for instance, and the card catalog at one college library include the following categories under *Cloning* in their "See also" column:

cell nuclei-transplantation

embryology

evolution

plants

genetic research

genetic engineering

Looking under these title headings in other references as well might be helpful. Using "genetic engineering" and "genetic research" as possible subject headings in *Book Review Digest* and *General Science Index* provides the key to unlocking their resources regarding the subject of cloning.

Sometimes it pays to spend a few minutes just thinking about possible alternative headings. A student doing research on cloning might realize that the topic is a branch of biology. By checking "Biology" in *The New York Times Index,* that student would be led to the heading "Biology and Bio-chemistry," where a number of useful articles are listed.

Not all of these alternative headings will always work, but this kind of investigation, called cross-referencing, is a necessary and valuable tool in research.

The Librarian.   If after a reasonable search of these references you seem to come to a dead end in attempting to get source material, then you should see your librarian. It is legitimate to ask him or her why a particular book may not be on a shelf, what other titles your subject could be under, which magazines the library subscribes to, and the location of certain references. Your librarian is there to help you use all the resources of the library.

IDENTIFYING A FOCUS

Knowing what the library has to offer is excellent preparation for research. This is especially true if one starts with only a general subject in mind. What is necessary at this point is to narrow down the general subject. Establishing a controlling question, therefore, is the next order of business.

Every research paper must have as its focus of study a controlling idea. The problem is to decide whether a particular controlling idea is worth pursuing and whether it is manageable, given the limitations of the assignment. Is the following controlling question regarding cloning an appropriate one for establishing a controlling idea?

How is cloning done?

Would this question seem appropriate in a humanities or a social science course? How is the perspective of such disciplines as English, sociology, or history better understood by pursuing this line of research? One might argue that knowing how cloning works would shed light on the possible effects it could have, both good and bad. True, but then the question is likely to take a different form such as:

How does understanding the scientific procedure of cloning help us better understand its social implications?

Both the focus and the original question have therefore changed.

Still, the original question does seem appropriate for a biology class — or does it? The cloning of plants and vegetable crops, of amphibians, and, of late, mammals each requires extensive development in order to answer the question fully. It is known, for example, that cloning is used in agriculture to produce uniform products: apples, potatoes, grapes, tomatoes, sugar cane, and garlic. The study of plant cloning itself may be enough for a research topic.

Appropriate . . . inappropriate . . . too narrow . . . too broad. . . . When is a controlling question good enough? This is a difficult decision but one that your instructors can help you with. They may advise you either to pursue the idea you have or to modify it depending on the nature of the source material found. Keep in mind that each of the controlling questions or ideas used as illustrations in the following section have come under the same kind of scrutiny.

Situation One: Starting with a Controlling Question

Let us assume that after reading *Brave New World* and a few essays regarding the probability of human cloning, the English class decided to do some research on the general topic. One student formulated for her research a focus that was approved by her instructor:

Why does cloning, genetic engineering, raise moral problems now and for future generations?

The value of a general search of the various facilities of the library applies in this case. This time, however, the search is focused on the *moral issues* regarding human cloning, so the search necessarily narrows.

Searching Subtopics in References.   Terms like "moral," "morality," "ethics," and "ethical" are added guideposts in researching the general topic. For these to be useful, the student has to look at the subtopics. Sometimes the exact guidewords will not appear, as in *Book Review Digest*:

Genetic engineering
     See also Recombinant D.N.A.
   Cherfas, J.   Man-made life
         Government policy
   Blank, R. H.   The political implications of
     human genetic technology
         Juvenile literature
   Snyder, G. S.   Test-tube life
         Social aspects

Krimsky, S.   Genetic alchemy
Rifkin, J.   Algeny

Nevertheless, one can reasonably infer that morality may be one of the issues included in the subheading "social aspects." Indeed, one title under it, *Genetic Alchemy*, suggests magic — to some people, a religious and moral issue. Since the *Readers' Guide* has no subtopic "ethics" or "moral issues" under the general topic *cloning*, the student used another approach. She turned to see if "ethics" were a general heading in the *Guide*. It was, and her search led her to the following entries:

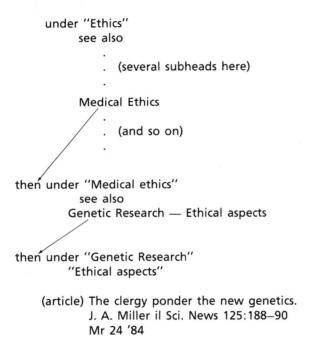

under "Ethics"
see also

  . (several subheads here)

Medical Ethics

  . (and so on)

then under "Medical ethics"
see also
Genetic Research — Ethical aspects

then under "Genetic Research"
"Ethical aspects"

(article) The clergy ponder the new genetics.
J. A. Miller il Sci. News 125:188–90
Mr 24 '84

A nice bit of hunting.

Another fruitful kind of exploration is to examine the titles of articles in the indexes. In *The New York Times Index* under "Biology and Biochemistry" this student spotted an article entitled "Playing God," and in *Applied Science and Technology* under "Genetic engineering" she found the article "Church seeks controls on gene research."

Searching Bibliographies and Suggested Reading Lists. Bibliographies list all the sources used by an author and are placed at the end of a book or article. Sometimes writers will replace the bibliography with a "Suggested Reading" list — works related to the subject. Both are excellent source references. The student found, for example, in McKinnell's book *Cloning* under "Suggested Reading," the title *The Ethics of Genetic Control* by J. Fletcher. Sometimes interesting related material is mentioned in the form of notes at the end of chapters. In another book this student found *In His Image: The Cloning of Man* by David Rorvik, and *Utopian Motherhood* by Robert Francoeur.

With her controlling question in mind, the student found her material efficiently. Some of her results can be seen graphically in Figure 7.5.

Library Research Information

①   Found in *The New York Times Index*

BIOLOGY and Biochemistry

Article by Sharon and Kathleen McAuliffe in support of genetic engineering; drawing (M), F1, 15:1

②   Found in the *Card Catalog*

```
                596.016
                  M

McKinnell, Robert Gilmore
     Cloning: a biologist
               reports
Minneapolis: University of
Minnesota Press, C 1979,
VIII, 130 p.: ill., 24 cm.

     Includes index
     Bibliography: p. 119—121

     1. Cloning.  2. Cell
nuclei—transplantation.
3. Embryology, Experimental
(Title)
```

③   Found at the end of a book

Suggested Reading

Fletcher, J. The Ethics of Genetic Control: Ending Reproductive Roulette. Garden City, New York: Anchor Press/Doubleday, 1974.

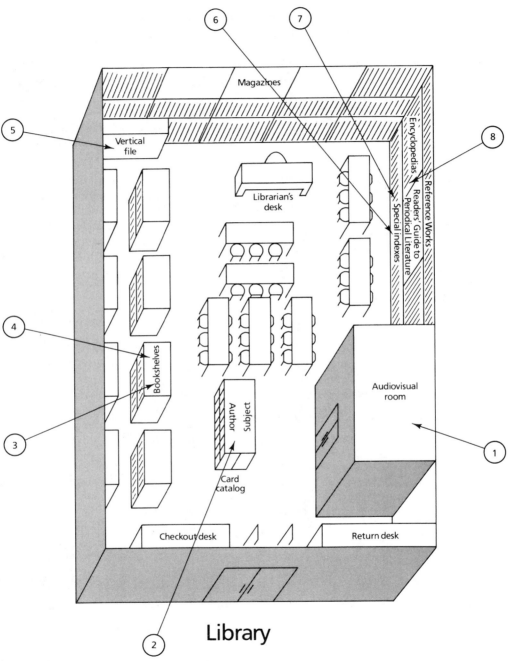

Figure 7.5 *Library Research*

Ramsey, P. Fabricated Man: The Ethics of Genetic Control. New Haven: Yale University Press, 1970.

④ Found at the end of a chapter in a book

Notes

2. Robert T. Francoeur. Utopian Motherhood. Garden City: Doubleday and Co., 1970.

4. David M. Rorvik. In His Image: The Cloning of Man. Philadelphia and New York: J.B. Lippincott Co., 1978.

⑤ Found in *Vertical File*

Coalition for Responsible Genetic Research

Position Statement on Recombinant DNA Technology

⑥ Found in *Applied Science and Technology Index*

Genetic engineering
    Church seeks control on gene research.
    Chem. Index p. 448, Je 20'83

⑦ Found in *Book Review Digest*

Blank, Robert H. The political implications of human genetic technology

"Blank is probably correct in assessing that the ethical and the moral implications of genetic engineering have received more general attention than the political implications . . ."
Choice 19, 399 N '81

⑧ Found in *The Readers' Guide to Periodical Literature,* March 1982 – February 1983

Raising the dead [cloning and back breeding of a vanished species] S. Webster, Sci Dig 90: 55 Jl '82

Scanning a Library Source. When potential source material is found, it is not always necessary for you to read it in its entirety to determine whether all or part of it is relevant to your subject. Scanning should usually be sufficient at this stage of your research. Scanning library source materials means letting your eye fall on its major headings: in a book, mainly its table of contents; in a long article, subheadings, if any.

Students with different controlling ideas who come across the same book would probably gravitate to different sections. Although the book *Cloning* by McKinnell is a useful source for most students, not every part is essential for everyone. Three students, an economics major, a biology major, and a political science major, had each formulated the following controlling questions:

Economics major	*Biology major*	*Political science major*
What would the relationship between labor and management be in a world of clones?	Is human cloning possible in our lifetime?	Who should make the decision to clone: the biologist/scientist? the clergyman? the politician? the artist? the businessman? the citizen? the philosopher?

Each student, scanning McKinnell's table of contents, was drawn to particular chapters. This idea is illustrated in Figure 7.6.

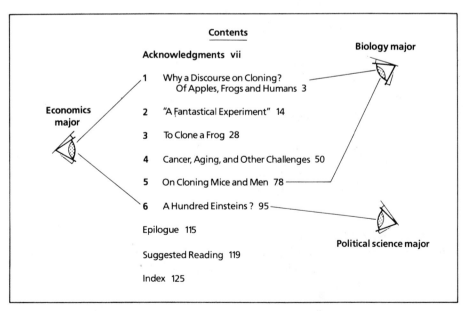

Figure 7.6 *Chapters Used by Students with Different Majors*

The economics major would certainly turn to Chapter 6, where the chapter heading suggests that the author will examine the question of who is to be cloned. This question has economic implications. The economics student wonders whether all clones should have extraordinary intellectual abilities, becoming leaders in education, in medicine, in industry, in government. Will our society, she wonders, have all leaders and no followers? She would probably also turn to Chapter 1 to see if McKinnell introduces any economic issues.

The biological sciences major would more than likely flip the pages to Chapters 1 and 5, which indicate that the author may discuss the state of cloning technology at the time of publication.

With a political science perspective, the third student would probably gravitate to Chapter 6. The question of who is to be cloned must involve the question, "Who makes the decisions to clone?" The process of deciding who should have this authority has political implications.

PRACTICE

These same three students, with their different controlling questions, came across another book entitled *Splicing Life*, and scanned its Table of Contents, part of which is reproduced below. What chapters and subsections within the chapters would each student be interested in?

Table of Contents for the book, *Splicing Life*

Situation Two: Starting without a Controlling Question

Let us assume another situation, a more likely one, in which most members of the class have not yet formulated a workable research topic. These students would find it difficult to explore the relevant sources until they have a tool at hand, a tentative controlling question or idea. But finding those ideas would be much easier if you first generated your own initial questions. Often this can be started without stepping into a library.

Formulating questions, as you recall, is a major piece of the thinking strategy explained in this text. In Chapter 1 we asked instructors from different disciplines to provide us with questions they would use if cloning were a topic in their introductory courses, and they came up with questions in the four basic patterns. Thinking of the four basic kinds of questions — process, cause-effect, comparison/contrast, and definition — and of the special considerations discussed in the separate chapters for each question, would be helpful at this initial stage of the research. Let us wed each type of question to the subject of cloning.

Questions that call for a sequence of steps are called process questions. This kind of question requires presenting the essential steps in the right order so that they can be duplicated by others. It also involves considering the number of steps that are necessary, and what the first step should be. Applying this analysis to the subject of cloning, some students came up with a few process questions. The first,

> Trace the historical development of cloning.

certainly involves determining the major first step: What was the first scientific cloning procedure? and the significant number of subsequent steps: from cloning plants, to cloning frogs, to cloning mice?

Many process questions naturally take the form, How is something done? Using this form of the question, therefore, and relating it to cloning, results in:

> How is cloning done?

This is a good beginning, but it would have to be modified, as discussed on page 296.

Chapter 6 discussed three major considerations regarding cause-effect. One is making distinctions between significant and less significant causes. The causes of the Civil War were judged in such a way in that chapter. The second consideration is linking all the connections in a causal chain. Remember Tom's awful smudge on his pants in the "Wet Paint" incident? All the pieces of the event had to be connected in order to find the real cause. Finally, causes must be viewed in the larger context of the various disciplines. The causes of alcoholism, as you might remember, could be psychological, sociological, or biological.

In light of these considerations, some questions emerge about cloning:

What would be the significant effect of cloning human beings?

Thinking of the causal chain, the second consideration, might generate this next question:

Why might the cloning of cancer cells lead to a cure for this disease?

Thinking about the larger contexts of the various disciplines, the third consideration might generate this question:

What would the effect of cloning be on religious, social, and political institutions?

Yet more questions can be generated by combining the basic question pattern with the Who? Where? When? question form. Something like that could be done with the last question. The result:

Who would be best able to evaluate the effects of cloning on society?

Now consider cloning from the point of view of comparison/contrast. In general, one aim of comparison and contrast, a method of analyzing likenesses and differences, is to make the unfamiliar more comprehensible by comparing it with something familiar. One obvious question regarding cloning, then, could be:

How does cloning differ from sexual reproduction?

Certain features are also explained better when compared or contrasted. In Chapter 6, the quality of human attraction in Renoir's painting ("people drawn to people") was made more apparent by contrasting it with Bruegel's painting of a wedding scene in which people were not paying much attention to each other. As to the features of cloning, another question could be:

What are the major similarities or differences between cloned frogs and sexually produced frogs?

Or, in terms of human cloning:

Would a cloned person be less human?

An obvious definition question would be "What is cloning?" and if you were writing a paper for your biology class, it could serve as the basis for further study. Such a controlling question could be answered by first providing an overall definition of cloning and then perhaps using the bulk of the paper to detail several methods of cloning plants and animals. Is this research question also appropriate for an English class?

Probably not, but suitable definition questions could emerge from the other question patterns. On reading *Brave New World*, for example, students would naturally be making comparisons between the clones and other characters in the novel. They may wonder, Can clones be considered the same as humans? or, to put it another way, Would a cloned person be less human? To answer this comparison/contrast question, they would have to answer a definition question:

What does it mean to be human?

This question could be the basis for interesting research.

SCANNING SOURCES

Usually, ideas for research papers can also be generated by scanning certain sections of a book. Certainly, the table of contents and beginnings of chapters come to mind. The blurb on the dust jacket, which summarizes the purpose and content of the book, is also a good source. Even a perusal of the index can generate ideas. As an example, note that several controlling questions can be developed by scanning the book *Cloning* by McKinnell, as shown in Figure 7.7.

Here are sample controlling questions derived from certain sections of the book on cloning by McKinnell. Try to write others

1. from jacket blurb:
   Why is cloning   _____
   misunderstood by   _____
   the public?   _____

2. from scanning
   introductions
   to chapters:
   Why is cloning   _____
   a subject of   _____
   controversy?   _____

Who are the

ideal people

to clone?

3. from Index:

What are the

advantages and

disadvantages of

the uniformity of

cloning with those

of the diversity of

sexual reproduction?

WRITING DETAILED NOTES

Gathering ideas and information from library sources needs to be done in some organized fashion, but finding and then reading these sources will probably follow in a less straightforward manner. In the early stages of your research, for example, you may come across material that you think could be used as part of a conclusion. What is the best way to store this material until you are ready to use it?

Writing *note cards* is a proven method in gathering and organizing information for research papers. Writing your notes on separate cards has the advantage of easily tabulating your sources. By making a category tab at the heading of each of your cards, you can better sort out your notes in preparation for the writing of your paper. A sample note card is in Figure 7.8.

Writing all the necessary bibliographical information somewhere on the note card assures that you will have it handy when you write your final draft. This information should include author, title, place of publication, publisher, date of publication, and page(s) of the passage quoted or paraphrased.

If you come across material that you are not sure will be used in your paper, it is still a good idea to write it on a note card and, if necessary, prepare a new category tab. You may ultimately discard such a card as irrelevant, or you may find it, in the end, to be quite useful and even be so important as to force a change in your original approach. Although you will be writing more cards than you will need, this method of writing note cards allows you to follow up on your initial hunches about the relevance of a source.

Scanning to Generate Controlling Questions

(blurb on jacket)

Robert Gilmore McKinnell
writes in this book:

Cloning is much in the news. The public has been bombarded with newspaper articles, magazine stories, books, television shows, and movies—as well as cartoons. Unfortunately, much of this information is incorrect. Inaccurate information plus an understandable public concern about whether a human has been or will be cloned, with all the ethical and moral questions that raises, have resulted in a very distorted view of what cloning is and why biologists choose to clone. The real story may seem less dramatic, but in a way it is more heartening. It is an account not of the production of carbon-copy dictators, millionaires, and Einsteins but of research that may provide answers to the very human problems of cancer and aging.

chapter **Why a Discourse**
1   on Cloning?

Cloning is much in the news. The public has been bombarded with newspaper articles, magazine stories, books, television shows, and movies—as well as cartoons. Unfortunately, much of this information is incorrect.

Index

chapter **Cancer, Aging, and**
4   Other Challenges

There are four major categories of cloning research: differentiation—much has been done in this area of research that stimulated the early cloning experiments; cancer—a much studied problem; immunobiology—only tentative, but promising probes have been made thus far; and aging—exciting work which is in its early stages.

AGING—NEW INSIGHT THROUGH CLONING?

Are the changes brought about because of continuous cell division? Is cell division *per se* a principal cause of aging?

Is there an alternative and feasible mode of examining the effect of many cell divisions on aging? If there is, can the data derived from the alternative mode be exploited to provide new and useful information about aging? The answer to that question is yes—and at least one alternative mode of study is, of course, cloning.

chapter **A Hundred Einsteins?**
6

SPARE PARTS—A REASON FOR CLONING?

It could be proposed that if one wished to utilize human cloning for spare parts, one should not make intact whole people, but should manufacture specific spare parts and then only as they are needed.

Figure 7.7 *Using the Jacket Blurb, Index, and Chapter Openings as Sources of Controlling Questions*

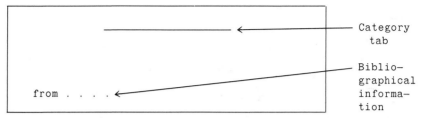

Figure 7.8 *Placement of Category Tab and Bibliographical Information on Note Card.*

Let us assume you came across the following passage in your research on cloning:

> In sum, the question of whether gene splicing will enable changes in human nature — and the ethical, social, and philosophical significance of such changes — cannot be determined until much more is known about human genetics, specifically the exact contribution of heredity to many human physical and, more important, behavioral traits. Indeed, one of the most important contributions genetic engineering could make to the science of behavioral genetics may be that it will help resolve the age-old controversy of nature versus nurture. If designed changes were possible, society would have to confront whether such changes should be made, and, if they should, which ones. The problems created by uncertainty are particularly notable here since any decision about what characteristics are "desirable" would depend on the world that people will be living in, which is itself unknowable in advance.[2]

You certainly would want to use part or all of the content of this source in writing your paper. There are four basic ways of doing this:

1. A *summary* is the shortest statement possible that presents the overall idea in your own words. Although it does not go into much detail, it forces you to understand the meaning of the passage. Figure 7.9 illustrates the summary on a note card.

2. A *paraphrase* is a restatement of the ideas, major examples, and supporting details in your own words and is presented in the same order as that of the author's. Since its aim is to force you to

---

[2] *Splicing Life*, President's Commission for the Study of Ethical Problems in Medicine and Biomedical and Behavioral Research (Washington, D.C.: Government Printing Office, November, 1982), p. 71.

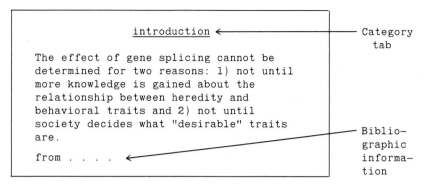

Figure 7.11 *Combined Paraphrase and Quotation on Note Card*

understand each part of the passage, it is longer than the summary. See the paraphrase in Figure 7.10.

3. A *direct quotation* is a word-for-word copy of the passage, used only if you think you will include the whole passage or a major portion of it because of its forceful and memorable language.

4. Very often, it is useful to employ a *combined paraphrase and quotation*, as in Figure 7.11.

Figure 7.10 *Paraphrase on Note Card*

```
                introduction

    The significance of gene splicing cannot
    be determined until more is known about
    the relationship between heredity and
    behavioral traits. Genetic engineering
    could help scientists resolve the
    argument whether we are born with
    characteristic traits or learn to have
    such traits (causes are either biological
    or environmental). If human nature could
    be changed, society would have to
    evaluate such changes. This is not easy
    because any desirable traits depend on
    future generations.

    from . . . .
```

```
                    introduction

        The significance of gene splicing cannot
        be determined until more is known about
        the relationship between heredity and
        behavioral traits. "Indeed one of the
        most important contributions genetic
        engineering could make to the science of
        behavioral genetics may be that it will
        help resolve the age-old controversy of
        nature vs. nurture." If human nature
        could be changed, society would have to
        evaluate such changes. This is not easy
        because any desirable traits depend on
        future generations.

        from . . . .
```

Figure 7.11 *Combined Paraphrase and Quotation on Note Card*

PRACTICE

For the following passage write three kinds of note cards: (1) summary, (2) paraphrase, and (3) combined paraphrase/direct quotation.

Where Expectation Exceeds Capability

The social environment of the human organism is far more complex and subtle than the physical environment. Although it is true that biologists can induce the replication of a genetic apparatus in certain instances, they do not have now nor are they ever likely to have the power to clone the social environment. The feature of development known as epigenesis prevents the creation of carbon-copy people. Thus expectation exceeds capability — even in the late twentieth century.

A boy baby reared as a girl baby acts like a girl baby. A contemporary American acts like a contemporary American. Had Mr. Einstein been cloned 20 years ago, that clone might be more concerned with sports cars, the ERA, in vitro fertilized babies, and rock music than with mathematics and physics. I would speculate that he might be consumed with concern about polluted air, polluted water, and over-refined and artificially preserved food. He might well think that mathematics and physics are not relevant (he might even fail to consider relevant or not relevant to what?). And so the argument goes. A cloned dictator could be a clerk-typist and a cloned assassinated president might become a professor. I know of no competent psychologist or behavioral biologist who could or would predict anything about what the expression of an individual's genes as a new person would be 20 years hence.[3]

PREPARING A RESEARCH PAPER FROM NOTES

The political science major mentioned earlier, after doing some research on his controlling question, *Who should make the decision to clone?* organized and classified his notes to create the following tentative outline:

> Controlling Question:
>   Who should make the decision to clone?
> Introduction:
>   Complicated decision factors
>   Refer to decisions in *Brave New World*
> Body:
>   I. Health factors
>   Decision makers
>   1. physicians
>   2. geneticists
>
>   II. Physique/Body type
>
> III. Psychological health
>   Psychologists
>
>   IV. Social role
>   A. Sociologists
>   B. Politicians
>
>   V. Economic status
>   A. Economic analysts
>   B. Executives
>
>   VI. Educational level
>   Educators
>
> VII. Employment possibilities
>   Government planners

---

[3]Robert Gilmore McKinnell, *Cloning: A Biologist Reports* (Minneapolis: University of Minnesota Press, 1980), pp. 102–103.

VIII. Ethnic balance
    A. Statisticians
    B. Citizen consensus
  IX. Moral conviction
      Clergymen
Conclusion

    After reading the passage on page 310 and writing a note card for it, the political science major realized that his original controlling question, Who should make the decision to clone humans? might have been premature. He might have to answer other questions first, like those suggested by the passage. Maybe the first question to answer would be:

> Now that human cloning may be possible, what kind of impact will it have on us?

Knowing the impact of human cloning on society will to a large extent determine those who should have the authority to clone humans. Given this new focus, he thought of a new organizational scheme for his paper.
    Remember how Chapter 2 helped in the organizing phase of the thinking strategy. We showed how a classification system is arrived at by:

dividing: separating a whole into its
                fundamental groups or parts
grouping: placing units (items) into
                categories

The student's note card helped him break down (divide) the impact of cloning into two considerations:

1. understanding the relationship of heredity and environment, and

2. knowing what a society would consider desirable traits.

Then in his revised outline he grouped his original list of factors more effectively:

Introduction:
    Discuss complicated decision factors.
    Refer to decisions in *Brave New World*
Thesis:
    In order to determine who should have the authority to clone humans, it is necessary first to determine the impact that human cloning will have on us and on further generations.

Body

I. Understanding of heredity and environmental factors
    A. Strictly hereditary factors
        1. health(?)
        2. physique
            and so on
    B. Strictly environmental factors
        1. social role
        2. education
            and so on
    C. So-called interrelated factors
            heredity ⟷ environment
        1. psychological (?)

II. Knowing desirable traits

Conclusion:
    Who should make decisions to clone?

This may not be the student's final outline; he may come across other readings that may alter his thinking — and, of course, his outline.

The illustration of the political science major's introductory section to his research paper in Figure 7.12 includes basic ideas from several relevant note cards.

Notice how the student writer culls from each note card the ideas he needs and how, if desirable, he rewords his own paraphrasing of the notes. He is not a slave to the exact wording of his notes. Indeed, not every word in the direct quote is used, and he even divides it into two parts for clearer presentation.

A glance at the footnotes indicates clearly why you should write all the bibliographical information somewhere on the note card. Remember, a footnote must be made for paraphrases as well as quotations. An author deserves credit for his or her ideas even though you have put them in your own words.

This chapter has examined several key features of the first phases of library research. It has shown how to generate controlling questions, establish a controlling idea, search and scan library sources, take notes, and incorporate notes into a paper. However, there is more to library research: organizing notes, writing a formal outline, writing and revising the paper. These organizing and composing skills have already been discussed in connection with the writing of essays; they apply to the writing of research papers as well. Of course, there is also the preparation of footnotes and a bibliography to consider, and the need to see what a final research paper looks like. A good handbook should be consulted for these features.

(Introduction to Research Paper)

   In his novel <u>Brave New World</u>,[1] Aldous Huxley describes a society of clones 600 years into the future, people who have been genetically reproduced from a single cell, test-tube style, not by the normal sexual union of two cells. Everyone was designed uniformly for the stability of society. Is this merely science fiction? Recently mice, the first mammals, were cloned by biologists in Switzerland.[2] Can the cloning of human beings be far behind?

   One researcher at the University of California answers the question this way:

      Down the line, people are going to have to face questions that have been addressed in <u>Brave New World</u> contexts . . . Yes, we're going to be able to design people . . .[3]

So, human cloning looks very possible. But he continues:

      . . . Society's going to have to take a hard look and make decisions about what to do.[4]

   The next question is, when human cloning becomes feasible, who in our society should make the decision to clone humans--philosophers? Clergymen? Biologists? Psychologists? Economists? Educators? Statisticians? Citizen consensus? If we don't want a <u>Brave New World</u> society, this question must be asked. It seems like a question worth pursuing and answering.

   The attempt at answering such a difficult question, however, must depend on first examining other significant factors closely . . .

---

   [1]Aldous Huxley, <u>Brave New World</u> (New York: Harper and Row, Perennial Classic, 1969).

   [2]"Closing in on Cloning," <u>Time Magazine</u>, Jan. 1981, p. 75.

   [3]Dr. John D. Baxter, UCLA, <u>Science Digest</u>, June 1980, pp. 20–21.

   [4]Baxter, p. 21.

---

introduction

Brave New World, a novel by Aldous Huxley (published in 1932) is a satire about a future society 600 years from now. It shows how the advancement in biology, physiology, and psychology affects individuals in a totalitarian state.

from Aldous Huxley, Brave New World New York: Harper and Row (Perennial Classics) 1969

(summary)

introduction

The first mammals, mice, were successfully cloned on January, 1981 in Switzerland by Karl Illmensee of the University of Geneva and Peter Hoppe of the Jackson Laboratory in Bar Harbor, Maine. Until recently, most animal cloning had been done with amphibians (frogs). Cloning mammals is more difficult because mammal eggs are microscopic.

from Time Magazine, Jan. 1981, "Closing in on Cloning," p. 75

(summary)

introduction

"Yes.. Down the line, people are going to have to face questions that have been addressed in Brave New World contexts... Yes, we're going to be able to design people and society's going to have to take a hard look and make decisions about what to do. I don't know what I would decide at that point."

from Science Digest, June 1980, p. 21. Dr. John D. Baxter, UCLA

(direct quote)

Figure 7.12 *How Note Cards Are Used in Writing a Research Paper*

PART 3

Anthology

Throughout this text you have been taught to write college-level essays responding to four types of controlling questions. As you worked through each chapter, however, you generally confined yourself to writing essays focusing on only one discipline; for cause-effect, for example, you wrote about economics.

The purpose of this anthology is to provide you with practice in responding to different types of essay assignments in several academic disciplines. This provision should reinforce the major point of this book:

> Even though a particular discipline involves viewing a subject from a
> certain perspective, such as economics, psychology, or sociology, the type of
> controlling question, which includes a distinct way of thinking critically,
> will largely determine the way the essay is finally written, no matter what
> discipline is being considered.

The readings in the Anthology are organized around two themes: work and human nature. For each theme the articles deal with the subject from the separate perspectives of several disciplines. After each article you will find essay assignments representing the controlling questions considered in the text. In addition, you will find controlling questions at the end of each thematic unit. They will allow you to consider and write about general issues relevant to the theme using several disciplines at once.

WORKING

In the early sections of an essay, "What Makes a Life Significant," William James, an American psychologist and philosopher of the late nineteenth century, contemplates the nature of heroism and bemoans its disappearance in modern life. Yet he recounts the following experience, which contradicts his initial premise.

> With these thoughts in my mind, I was speeding with the train toward Buffalo, when, near that city, the sight of a workman doing something on the dizzy edge of a sky-scaling iron construction brought me to my senses very suddenly. And now I perceived, by a flash of insight, that I had been steeping myself in pure ancestral blindness, and looking at life with the eyes of a remote spectator. Wishing for heroism and the spectacle of human nature on the rack, I had never noticed the great fields of heroism lying around about me, I had failed to see it present and alive. I could only think of it as dead and embalmed, labelled and costumed, as it is in the pages of romance. And yet there it was before me in the daily lives of the laboring classes. Not in clanging fights and desperate marches only is heroism to be looked for, but on every railway bridge and fire-proof building that is going up today. On freight-trains, on the decks of vessels, in cattle-yards and mines, on lumber-rafts, among the firemen and the policemen, the demand for courage is incessant; and the supply never fails. There, every day of the year somewhere, is human nature *in extremis* for you. And wherever a scythe, an axe, a pick, or a shovel is wielded, you have it sweating and aching and with its powers of patient endurance racked to the utmost under the length of hours of the strain.
>
> As I awoke to all this unidealized heroic life around me, the scales seemed to fall from my eyes; and a wave of sympathy greater than anything I had ever before felt with the common life of common men began to fill my soul.[1]

The authors, likewise, see the possibility of work as ennobling human nature. Besides the axe and the shovel, many other symbols from the modern work arena could be noted: the T-square, the syringe, the sales ledger, the computer, and the word processor. This part of the Anthology includes selections about work. They may be about job satisfaction, training for work, retirement from work, women working, or the status of minority employment.

---

[1] William James, "What Makes a Life Significant," from *Essays on Faith and Morals*, Cleveland, World Publishing Company, 1965.

Erich Fromm

Work

from *The Sane Society*

Erich Fromm, a psychoanalyst and social critic, in his book, The Sane
Society, *describes the alienation that people experience in industrial
societies. In the selection, "Work," reprinted from that book, he
maintains that work is necessary not only for people's economic survival
but also because it is man's "liberator from nature, his creator as a social
and independent being." Fromm believes that modern industrial society
has eliminated this second, most significant, aspect of work, with dire
consequences for the individual and, by extension, for society as a whole.*

What becomes the meaning of *work* in an alienated society?

We have already made some brief comments about this question in
the general discussion of alienation. But since this problem is of utmost
importance, not only for the understanding of present-day society, but also
for any attempt to create a saner society, I want to deal with the nature of
work separately and more extensively in the following pages.

Unless man exploits others, he has to work in order to live. However
primitive and simple his method of work may be, by the very fact of production,
he has risen above the animal kingdom; rightly has he been defined as "the
animal that produces." But work is not only an inescapable necessity for
man. Work is also his liberator from nature, his creator as a social and
independent being. *In the process of work, that is, the molding and changing of
nature outside of himself, man molds and changes himself.* He emerges from
nature by mastering her; he develops his powers of co-operation, of reason,
his sense of beauty. He separates himself from nature, from the original unity
with her, but at the same time unites himself with her again as her master
and builder. The more his work develops, the more his individuality develops.
In molding nature and re-creating her, he learns to make use of his powers,
increasing his skill and creativeness. Whether we think of the beautiful
paintings in the caves of Southern France, the ornaments on weapons among
primitive people, the statues and temples of Greece, the cathedrals of the
Middle Ages, the chairs and tables made by skilled craftsmen, or the cultivation

of flowers, trees or corn by peasants — all are expressions of the creative transformation of nature by man's reason and skill.

In Western history, craftsmanship, especially as it developed in the thirteenth and fourteenth centuries, constitutes one of the peaks in the evolution of creative work. Work was not only a useful activity, but one which carried with it a profound satisfaction. The main features of craftsmanship have been very lucidly expressed by C. W. Mills. "There is no ulterior motive in work other than the product being made and the processes of its creation. The details of daily work are meaningful because they are not detached in the worker's mind from the product of the work. The worker is free to control his own working action. The craftsman is thus able to learn from his work; and to use and develop his capacities and skills in its prosecution. There is no split of work and play, or work and culture. The craftsman's way of livelihood determines and infuses his entire mode of living."[a]

With the collapse of the medieval structure, and the beginning of the modern mode of production, the meaning and function of work changed fundamentally, especially in the Protestant countries. Man, being afraid of his newly won freedom, was overwhelmed by the need to subdue his doubts and fears by developing a feverish activity. The outcome of this activity, success or failure, decided his salvation, indicating whether he was among the saved or the lost souls. *Work, instead of being an activity satisfying in itself and pleasureable, became a duty and an obsession.* The more it was possible to gain riches by work, the more it became a pure means to the aim of wealth and success. Work became, in Max Weber's terms, the chief factor in a system of "inner-worldly asceticism," an answer to man's sense of aloneness and isolation.

However, work in this sense existed only for the upper and middle classes, those who could amass some capital and employ the work of others. For the vast majority of those who had only their physical energy to sell, work became nothing but forced labor. The worker in the eighteenth or nineteenth century who had to work sixteen hours if he did not want to starve was not doing it because he served the Lord in this way, nor because his success would show that he was among the "chosen" ones, but because he was forced to sell his energy to those who had the means of exploiting it. The first centuries of the modern age find the meaning of work divided into that of *duty* among the middle class, and that of *forced labor* among those without property.

The religious attitude toward work as a duty, which was still as prevalent

---

[a]C. W. Mills, *White Collar*, Oxford University Press, New York, 1951, p. 230.

in the nineteenth century, has been changing considerably in the last decades. Modern man does not know what to do with himself, how to spend his lifetime meaningfully, and he is driven to work in order to avoid an unbearable boredom. But work has ceased to be a moral and religious obligation in the sense of the middle-class attitude of the eighteenth and nineteenth centuries. Something new has emerged. Ever-increasing production, the drive to make bigger and better things, have become aims in themselves, new ideals. Work has become alienated from the working person.

What happens to the industrial worker? He spends his best energy for seven or eight hours a day in producing "something." He needs his work in order to make a living, but his role is essentially a passive one. He fulfills a small isolated function in a complicated and highly organized process of production, and is never confronted with "his" product as a whole, at least not as a producer, but only as a consumer, provided he has the money to buy "his" product in a store. He is concerned neither with the whole product in its physical aspects nor with its wider economic and social aspects. He is put in a certain place, has to carry out a certain task, but does not participate in the organization or management of the work. He is not interested, nor does he know why one produces this, instead of another commodity — what relation it has to the needs of society as a whole. The shoes, the cars, the electric bulbs, are produced by "the enterprise," using the machines. He is a part of the machine, rather than its master as an active agent. The machine, instead of being in his service to do work for him which once had to be performed by sheer physical energy, has become his master. Instead of the machine being the substitute for human energy, man has become a substitute for the machine. *His work can be defined as the performance of acts which cannot yet be performed by machines.*

Work is a means of getting money, not in itself a meaningful human activity. P. Drucker, observing workers in the automobile industry, expresses this idea very succinctly: "For the great majority of automobile workers, the only meaning of the job is in the pay check, not in anything connected with the work or the product. Work appears as something unnatural, a disagreeable, meaningless and stultifying condition of getting the pay check, devoid of dignity as well as of importance. No wonder that this puts a premium on slovenly work, on slowdowns, and on other tricks to get the same pay check with less work. No wonder that this results in an unhappy and discontented worker — because a pay check is not enough to base one's self-respect on."[b]

---

[b]Peter F. Drucker, *Concept of the Corporation*, The John Day Company, New York, 1946, p. 179.

This relationship of the worker to his work is an outcome of the whole social organization of which he is a part. Being "employed,"ᶜ he is not an active agent, has no responsibility except the proper performance of the isolated piece of work he is doing, and has little interest except the one of bringing home enough money to support himself and his family. Nothing more is expected of him, or wanted from him. He is part of the equipment hired by capital, and his role and function are determined by this quality of being a piece of equipment. In recent decades, increasing attention has been paid to the psychology of the worker, and to his attitude toward his work, to the "human problem of industry"; but this very formulation is indicative of the underlying attitude; there is a human being spending most of his lifetime at work, and what should be discussed is the *"industrial problem of human beings,"* rather than *"the human problem of industry."*

Most investigations in the field of industrial psychology are concerned with the question of how the productivity of the individual worker can be increased, and how he can be made to work with less friction; psychology has lent its services to "human engineering," an attempt to treat the worker and employee like a machine which runs better when it is well oiled. While Taylor was primarily concerned with a better organization of the technical use of the worker's physical powers, most industrial psychologists are mainly concerned with the manipulation of the worker's psyche. The underlying idea can be formulated like this: if he works better when he is happy, then let us make him happy, secure, satisfied, or anything else, provided it raises his output and diminishes friction. In the name of "human relations," the worker is treated with all devices which suit a completely alienated person; even happiness and human values are recommended in the interest of better relations with the public. Thus, for instance, according to *Time* magazine, one of the best-known American psychiatrists said to a group of fifteen hundred Supermarket executives: "It's going to be an increased satisfaction to our customers if we are happy. . . . It is going to pay off in cold dollars and cents to management, if we could put some of these general principles of values, human relationships, really into practice." One speaks of "human relations" and one means the most in-human relations, those between alienated automatons; one speaks of happiness and means the perfect routinization which has driven out the last doubt and all spontaneity.

The alienated and profoundly unsatisfactory character of work results in two reactions: one, the ideal of complete *laziness*; the other a deep-seated, though often unconscious *hostility* toward work and everything and everybody connected with it.

ᶜThe English "employed" like the German *angestellt* are terms which refer to things rather than to human beings.

It is not difficult to recognize the widespread longing for the state of complete laziness and passivity. Our advertising appeals to it even more than to sex. There are, of course, many useful and labor saving gadgets. But this usefulness often serves only as a rationalization for the appeal to complete passivity and receptivity. A package of breakfast cereal is being advertised as *"new — easier to eat."* An electric toaster is advertised with these words: *". . . the most distinctly different toaster in the world! Everything is done for you with this new toaster. You need not even bother to lower the bread. Power-action, through a unique electic motor, gently takes the bread right out of your fingers!"* How many courses in languages, or other subjects are announced with the slogan "effortless learning, no more of the old drudgery." Everybody knows the picture of the elderly couple in the advertisement of a life-insurance company, who have retired at the age of sixty, and spend their life in the complete bliss of having nothing to do except just travel.

Radio and television exhibit another element of this yearning for laziness: the idea of "push-button power"; by pushing a button, or turning a knob on my machine, I have the power to produce music, speeches, ball games, and on the television set, to command events of the world to appear before my eyes. The pleasure of driving cars certainly rests partly upon this same satisfaction of the wish for push-button power. By the effortless pushing of a button, a powerful machine is set in motion; little skill and effort is needed to make the driver feel that he is the ruler of space.

But there is far more serious and deep-seated reaction to the meaninglessness and boredom of work. It is a hostility toward work which is much less conscious than our craving for laziness and inactivity. Many a businessman feels himself the prisoner of his business and the commodities he sells; he has a feeling of fraudulency about his product and a secret contempt for it. He hates his customers, who force him to put up a show in order to sell. He hates his competitors because they are a threat; his employees as well as his superiors, because he is in a constant competitive fight with them. Most important of all, he hates himself, because he sees his life passing by, without making any sense beyond the momentary intoxication of success. Of course, this hate and contempt for others and for oneself, and for the very things one produces, is mainly unconscious, and only occasionally comes up to awareness in a fleeting thought, which is sufficiently disturbing to be set aside as quickly as possible. ■

QUESTIONS

Cause-Effect

Do you think Fromm's assessment is accurate, or do you think it is overstated? Why?

Comparison/Contrast

Compare and/or contrast the attitudes of two people of your acquaintance who work, one who considers his or her job to be interesting, the other who considers the job merely as a way to survive economically.

Cause-Effect

Erich Fromm asserts that "the alienated and profoundly unsatisfactory character of work results in two reactions: one, the ideal of complete *laziness*, the other a deep-seated, though often unconscious *hostility* toward work and everything and everybody connected with it." What effect would unsatisfactory work have on other aspects of a person's life?

Definition

What would you consider the essentials of a good job?

C. Wright Mills

Frames of Acceptance

from *White Collar*

C. Wright Mills, an economist, in this excerpt from the book White
Collar, *discusses the issue of job satisfaction. Whereas he generally agrees
with Erich Fromm that work in modern industrial society no longer
provides the gratification of a job well done, he believes that satisfaction is
now based on other factors: income, status, and power.*

Underneath virtually all experience of work today, there is a fatalistic
feeling that work *per se* is unpleasant. One type of work, or one particular
job, is contrasted with another type, experienced or imagined, within the
present world of work; judgments are rarely made about the world of work
as presently organized as against some other way of organizing it; so also,
satisfaction from work is felt in comparison with the satisfactions of other
jobs.

We do not know what proportions of the U.S. white-collar strata are
'satisfied' by their work and, more important, we do not know what being
satisfied means to them. But it is possible to speculate fruitfully about such
questions.

We do have the results of some questions, necessarily crude, regarding
feelings about present jobs. As in almost every other area, when sponge
questions are asked of a national cross-section, white-collar people, meaning
here clerical and sales employees, are in the middle zones. They stand close
to the national average (64 per cent asserting they find their work interesting
and enjoyable 'all the time'), while more of the professionals and executives
claim interest and enjoyment (85 per cent), and fewer of the factory workers
(41 per cent) do so.

Within the white-collar hierarchy, job satisfaction seems to follow the
hierarchical levels; in one study, for example, 86 per cent of the professionals,
74 per cent of the managerial, 42 per cent of the commercial employees,
stated general satisfaction. This is also true of wage-worker levels of skill:
56 per cent of the skilled, but 48 per cent of the semi-skilled, are satisfied.

Such figures tell us very little, since we do not know what the questions mean to the people who answer them, or whether they mean the same thing to different strata. However, work satisfaction is related to income and, if we had measures, we might find that it is also related to status as well as to power. What such questions probably measure are invidious judgments of the individual's standing with reference to other individuals. And the aspects of work, the terms of such comparisons, must be made clear.

Under modern conditions, the direct technical processes of work have been declining in meaning for the mass of employees, but other features of work — income, power, status — have come to the fore. Apart from the technical operations and the skills involved, work is a source of income; the amount, level, and security of pay, and what one's income history has been are part of work's meaning. Work is also a means of gaining status, at the place of work, and in the general community. Different types of work and different occupational levels carry differential status values. These again are part of the meaning of the job. And also work carries various sorts of power, over materials and tools and machines, but, more crucially now, over other people.

I. *Income:* The economic motives for work are now its only firm rationale. Work now has no other legitimating symbols, although certainly other gratifications and discontents are associated with it. The division of labor and the routinization of many job areas are reducing work to a commodity, of which money has become the only common denominator. To the worker who cannot receive technical gratifications from his work, its market value is all there is to it. The only significant occupational movement in the United States, the trade unions, have the pure and simple ideology of alienated work: more and more money for less and less work. There are, of course, other demands, but they can be only 'fixed up' to lessen the cry for more money. The sharp focus upon money is part and parcel of the lack of intrinsic meaning that work has come to have.

Underlying the modern approach to work there seems to be some vague feeling that 'one should earn one's own living,' a kind of Protestant undertow, attenuated into a secular convention. 'When work goes,' as H. A. Overstreet, a job psychologist writing of the slump, puts it, 'we know that the tragedy is more than economic. It is psychological. It strikes at the center of our personality. It takes from us something that rightly belongs to every self-respecting human being.' But income security — the fear of unemployment or under-employment — is more important. An undertow of anxiety about sickness, accident, or old age must support eagerness for work, and gratification may be based on the compulsion to relieve anxiety by working hard. Widespread unemployment, or fear of it, may even make an employee happily thankful for any job, contented to be at any kind of work when all around there are many workless, worried people. If satisfaction rests on relative status, there is here an invidious element that increases it. It is across this ground tone of convention and fear, built around work as a source of income, that other motives to work and other factors of satisfaction are available.

II. *Status:* Income and income security lead to other things, among them, status. With the decline of technical gratification, the employee often tries to center such meaning as he finds in work on other features of the job. Satisfaction in work often rests upon status satisfactions from work associations. As a social role played in relation to other people, work may become a source of self-esteem, on the job, among co-workers, superiors, subordinates, and customers, if any; and off the job, among friends, family, and community at large. The fact of doing one kind of job rather than another and doing one's job with skill and dispatch may be a source of self-esteem. For the man or woman lonely in the city, the mere fact of meeting people at the place of work may be a positive thing. Even anonymous work contacts in large enterprises may be highly esteemed by those who feel too closely bound by family and neighborhood. There is a gratification from working downtown in the city, uptown in the smaller urban center; there is the glamour of being attached to certain firms.

It is the status conferred on the exercise of given skills and on given income levels that is often the prime source of gratification or humiliation. The psychological effect of a detailed division of labor depends upon whether or not the worker has been downgraded, and upon whether or not his associates have also been downgraded. Pride in skill is relative to the skills he has exercised in the past and to the skills others exercise, and thus to the evaluation of his skills by other people whose opinions count. In like manner, the amount of money he receives may be seen by the employee and by others as the best gauge of his worth.

This may be all the more true when relations are increasingly 'objectified' and do not require intimate knowledge. For then there may be anxiety to keep secret the amount of money earned, and even to suggest to others that one earns more. 'Who earns the most?' asks Erich Engelhard. 'That is the important question, that is the gauge of all differentiations and the yardstick of the moneyed classes. We do not wish to show how we work, for in most cases others will soon have learned our tricks. This explains all the bragging. "The work I have to do!" exclaims one employee when he has only three letters to write. . . This boastfulness can be explained by a drive which impels certain people to evaluate their occupations very low in comparison with their intellectual aspirations but very high compared with the occupations of others.'

III. *Power:* Power over the technical aspects of work has been stripped from the individual, first, by the development of the market, which determines how and when he works, and second, by the bureaucratization of the work sphere, which subjects work operations to discipline. By virtue of these two alien forces the individual has lost power over the technical operations of his own work life.

But the exercise of power over other people has been elaborated. In so far as modern organizations of work are large scale, they are hierarchies of power, into which various occupations are fitted. The fact that one takes orders as well as gives them does not necessarily decrease the positive gratification achieved through the exercise of power on the job.

Status and power, as features of work gratification, are often blended; self-esteem may be based on the social power exercised in the course of work; victory over the will of another may greatly expand one's self-estimation. But the very opposite may also be true: in an almost masochistic way, people may be gratified by subordination on the job. We have already seen how office women in lower positions of authority are liable to identify with men in higher authority, transferring from prior family connections or projecting to future family relations.

All four aspects of occupation — skill, power, income, and status — must be taken into account to understand the meaning of work and the sources of its gratification. Any one of them may become the foremost aspect of the job, and in various combinations each is usually in the consciousness of the employee. To achieve and to exercise the power and status that higher income entails may be the very definition of satisfaction in work, and this satisfaction may have nothing whatsoever to do with the craft experience as the inherent need and full development of human activity. ∎

QUESTIONS

Definition

If you agree with C. Wright Mills's definition of work satisfaction, write an essay of definition, providing examples from your experience and/or observations to expand on the special characteristics of the definition provided by C. Wright Mills.

Cause-Effect

If you do not agree, explain why you think C. Wright Mills is either partially or totally wrong.

Marilyn Machlowitz

What Is Workaholism?

from *Workaholics*

*Workaholics is a study of the people who do not work to survive but
"live to work." Marilyn Machlowitz begins her book with an entire
chapter devoted to defining the term* workaholic. *Her concern here is to
consider the connotations of the word itself. After all, she says, the word
"owes its origin, as well as its negative overtones, to 'alcoholism.'" Unlike
Fromm, Machlowitz claims that a substantial number of us, even in our
industrial society, love work and think of work as the sustaining force.*

As retirees rapidly come to realize, a job provides a lot more than just
a paycheck. Jobs structure people's time. They permit regular interpersonal
interaction and provide a sense of identity, self-esteem, and self-respect. But
for all these positive effects attributed to working, alienated workers have
received far more of scholars' attention than have their highly absorbed
counterparts, the workaholics.

The popular press has paid some attention to work addicts. It's an
unusual business magazine that doesn't mention the word at least once per
issue. One career guide advises job applicants to answer the inevitable question
"What are your weaknesses?" with a quality that is apt to be attractive to
a prospective employer. It tells readers to say, "I'm such a workaholic that
I tend to get completely caught up in my work." And a women's magazine
told its readers to end a summer or vacation romance by warning men about
being a workaholic back at home.

But there is scant scientific research on workaholics. My own master's
thesis and doctoral dissertation were the first systematic studies of the phenomenon. My best estimate suggests that workaholics comprise no more
than 5 percent of the adult population. They probably make up a slightly
higher percentage of the workforce, since workaholics are the least likely to
be unemployed. Somehow, it seems, workaholics have overcome or averted
the difficulties and dissatisfactions that plague today's workers. Perhaps, once
workaholism is better understood, it will be possible to use the experience
of the work addict to enrich and enhance the working lives of others. But
first we need to dispel some of the negative attitudes we have about workaholics.

Most descriptions of the phenomenon do not define workaholism as much as they denigrate and deride workaholics. Lotte Bailyn of M.I.T. described the workaholic as the "victim of a newly recognized social disease presumably responsible for the disintegration of the family, [and] for severe distortion of full personal development." Likewise, a respected *New York Times* writer, Charlotte Curtis, portrayed the workaholic as someone who was "anxious, guilt-ridden, insecure, or self righteous about . . . work . . . a slave to a set schedule, merciless in his demands upon himself for peak performance . . . compulsively overcommitted."

The word "workaholism" owes its origin, as well as its negative overtones, to "alcoholism." What distinguishes workaholism from other addictions is that workaholism is sometimes considered a virtue, while others, such as alcoholism, or drug addiction, are invariably considered vices.

Yet workaholics are usually portrayed as a miserable lot. This bias stems from the ways we learn about them. The clergy hears their confessions; physicians and therapists, their complaints; and judges, their divorces. The few articles about workaholics that have appeared in scientific journals typically emphasize the psychosocial problems of specific patients. The workaholics that I interviewed had few such problems.

Another major bias against workaholics are the beliefs of nonworkaholics. People who work to live cannot understand those who live to work and love it. They watch in amazement and wonder about those who delight in what they do. Workaholics' unorthodox attitude — that their work is so much fun they'd probably do it for free — causes nonworkaholics to question their own situation. The latter group begins to worry "What's wrong with my job?" or, worse, "What's wrong with me?" To resolve these feelings, nonworkaholics resort to denouncing workaholics rather than running down themselves. They say, "Sure, workaholics are successful at work, but aren't they really ruining the rest of their lives?" This logic is akin to that of "Lucky in cards, unlucky in love" and equally untrue. Satisfaction with work and with life are more apt to be intertwined than mutually exclusive.

Workaholism is almost exclusively American, but it is also un-American. You are *supposed* to lead lives that are well-rounded, balanced, and more "normal" than those of workaholics. Sure, you should go to work weekdays, but you better not spend evenings and weekends at work, as well. Those times should be spent with the family or playing ball or seeing friends or gardening. Have you ever heard of a beauty pageant contestant who couldn't list at least half a dozen hobbies, from basket weaving to opera singing? In contrast, when faced with an employment application, a workaholic might have to leave that item blank. Workaholics are more willing to settle for excellence in one endeavor and to admit that they are inept and uninterested in anything else. As playwright Neil Simon said (italics mine), "I wish I *could* do other things well besides write, . . . play an instrument, learn other languages, cook, ski. My greatest sense of accomplishment is that I didn't waste time *trying* to learn those things."

Nor is it American to like your job that much, and those who do are suspect. To look forward to Monday instead of Friday is regarded as strange and even abnormal. Production workers attach posters to their machines that say "Hang in there; Friday's coming." In the executive suites such signs are understandably absent, but sentiments like "Thank God it's Friday" are frequently heard.

As a result, workaholics are often openly maligned. A top health insurance organization placed a full-page magazine ad warning of the alleged health hazards and related costs of working too hard. The photo featured an angry-looking man with a cigarette dangling from his lips and butts spilling out of an overflowing ashtray; his tie loosened, his collar undone, his shirt straining at his paunch, a styrofoam coffee cup in one hand and several others strewn about an incredibly cluttered desk. The headline read, "He's working twelve hours a day to increase the cost of health care." The copy continued, "In the Horatio Alger story the hero works day and night to get ahead and everybody looks up to him with admiration. Now, millions of Americans are following this example. . . . We're not asking you to stop working. Just try not to overdo it. And when you see someone who thinks he's Horatio Alger, don't think of him as a hero. Think of him as a villain."

Most workaholics won't admit that's what they are because the word has such negative connotations. In fact, so many of the people I interviewed objected to the word that I frequently substituted other phrases ("the role of work in the lives of successful hard workers") when talking to them. Everyone I interviewed acknowledged that they had been accused of being a workaholic. And almost all admitted that my characteristics of workaholism came a little too close for comfort. As television anchorwoman Jessica Savitch wrote me, "I do not like the label since it conjures up a negative addiction such as alcoholic. But the qualities you ascribe to a workaholic are qualities I seek and admire in others."

Not everyone, however, dismisses workaholics as dismal or dangerous. When a young mathematician heard I was writing a book about workaholics, he eagerly asked me, "Does your book tell how to become one?" And, indeed, in certain governmental, professional, and academic circles, work-aholism has managed to develop considerable cachet. In, say, Washington, D.C., New York City, or Cambridge, Massachusetts, you can hear quite a few people claim to be workaholics. I, for one, doubt that too many of them really are simply because they brag about it. Real workaholics will doubt, demur, or deny outright that that's what they are.

Then, too, workaholics do not necessarily recognize or realize just how hard they do work. But they don't mind working hard. While the masses may moan and grumble about having to work hard, workaholics enjoy and exult in it. In fact, Dr. John Rhoads, a psychiatrist on the faculty of Duke University, maintains that it is almost axiomatic that those who complain of being overworked are not. For example, Dick Vermeil, head coach of Philadelphia's pro football team, the Eagles, and a man who is invariably called a workaholic, told me, "I don't actually know what the word means, but I am tired of its being used in describing my personality. I do what I'm doing because I enjoy it very much and really don't consider it hard work."

While workaholics do work hard, not all hard workers are workaholics. I will use the work workaholic to describe those whose desire to work long and hard is intrinsic and whose work habits almost always exceed the prescriptions of the job they do and the expectations of the people with whom or for whom they work. But the first characteristic is the real determinant. What truly distinguishes workaholics from other hard workers is that the others work only to please a boss, earn a promotion, or meet a deadline. Moonlighters, for example, may work sixteen hours a day merely to make ends meet, but most of them stop working multiple shifts as soon as their financial circumstances permit. Accountants, too, may sometimes seem to work non-stop, but most slow down markedly after April 15th. For workaholics, on the other hand, the workload seldom lightens, for they don't *want* to work less. As Senator William Proxmire has found, "The less I work, the less I enjoy it."

Time spent working would be an appealing index of workaholism, but it would also be a misleading measure. Although workaholics may work from 5 A.M. to 9 P.M. instead of the more usual 9 A.M. to 5 P.M., the hours they work are not the *sine qua non* of workaholism. It is in fact preferable to view workaholism as an approach or an attitude toward working than as an amount of time at work. Workaholics will continue to think about work when they're not working — even at moments that are, well, inappropriate. One energy specialist recalls dreaming about Con Ed and seeing barrels of oil in her sleep. One research and development director mentally designs new studies while making love to his wife.

But numbers and totals do count: Workaholics are given to counting their work hours and especially their achievements. Dr. Denton Cooley, the founder and chief surgeon of the Texas Heart Institute of Houston, enclosed a six-page vitae and a two-page biography with his finished questionnaire, which was handwritten in the illegible scrawl for which physicians are famous. The vitae listed a string of international honors; the biography, his achievements: By 1978, Cooley had performed over 30,000 open heart operations, more than any other surgeon in the world. He and his staff perform 25 to 30 such operations a day. An aide explains:

I don't think you'll talk to anyone who likes to operate more than Cooley. People like him don't go into medicine for mankind. They do it because they like it. I mean he could relax, he doesn't need the money. His dad was a successful dentist who invested very wisely in Houston real estate. And Denton's surgical fees are more than one million dollars a year. But he just wouldn't be happy if he couldn't operate every day. Hell, I've seen him call in from a morning meeting in New York to set up an afternoon surgery schedule. The guy is hooked.

Dr. Cooley defended his dedication far more simply. He works as he does, he said, "because I enjoy it."

Workaholism is not restricted to hospital corridors, Congressional offices, or elegant executive suites. While we sneer at it in corporate executives, workaholism is something we've come to accept — and even admire — in artists, and it is what we expect of our personal physicians. It is also part and parcel of our image of most scientists, such as Edison and Einstein. As Wilfred J. Corrigan, former chairman of Fairchild Camera and Instrument Corporation told *Business Week*, "A lot of people in this industry are totally involved with their work. Everyone sees this as appropriate for an artist painting the Sistine chapel or an author writing a novel. But in science and technology, there are times when you just don't want to go home."

Although I interviewed far more white collar than blue collar workers, I found that workaholics exist in every occupation, from managers and doctors to secretaries and assembly line workers. One man had a combined M.D.–Ph.D.; another had only a high school diploma. A friend once described her apartment building's janitor as a workaholic. "I feel very fortunate," she said, "to have a super who's a compulsive worker. He won't even stop and talk. Occasionally, he'll have a conversation with someone while he's sweeping the sidewalk."

Nor is workaholism restricted to just one sex. While women have been almost completely overlooked in the little that has been written about workaholism, there have always been women workaholics. If housework, for instance, were rightfully regarded as work, generations of compulsive cleaners could be considered workaholics. And so would the tireless organizers of charity events. Today, women's workaholism is merely more apparent, since more and more women work outside their homes.

Dr. Helen De Rosis, associate clinical professor of psychiatry at New York University School of Medicine and the author of several books about women, cautions against confusing women workaholics with the so-called Superwomen. A Superwoman tries to be Supermom and Superwife as well as Superworker. Superwoman, according to syndicated columnist Ellen Goodman, is not only a Wonder Woman at work but an elegant dresser and an excellent cook as well. Her kids do not subsist on cold cereal: Superwoman gets up at the crack of dawn to make them a hot, nutritious, and nitrite-free breakfast. Her husband has a delicious dinner every night: She not only has time to get the groceries, but to whip up gourmet delights, courtesy of Julia Child and Cuisinart. Her relationship with her children is characterized, of course, by the *quality* — not by the quantity — of the time she spends with them. Similarly, her marriage can only be called a meaningful relationship. She and her husband are not only each other's best friend but also ecstatic lovers, because Superwoman is never too tired at night. Instead, she is, in the words of Ellen Goodman, "multiorgasmic until midnight."

According to Dr. De Rosis, whose books include *Women and Anxiety*, Superwomen and workaholics share a basic similarity: Both use their work as a defense against anxiety. While workaholics appear to enjoy their work, Dr. De Rosis explains that the enjoyment they experience is distinct from the pleasure felt by women who are able to shift their priorities for different occasions. "The workaholic can't do this. She can't say, 'Today I'll stay home because my child is sick.' She can't make that decision."

Nor should women workaholics be mistaken for women who must do double time to make up for sex-related obstacles in their careers. When Monica Bauer joined Xerox in 1966, she found that she "really did have to put in more time than my male associates just to get the information." Back then, Bauer was excluded from the "old boy network" and other informal channels of communication and had no "new girl network" to turn to. The times have changed, but Bauer's drive shows no decline. She continues to put in long days at Xerox, where she is now manager of low volume products and pricing, and recently completed an M.B.A. at the University of Rochester while working full-time.

So, despite the fact that workaholics come from all classes, sexes, and occupations, they all share one over-riding passion: work. After interviewing more than one hundred work addicts over several years, I have some good news and some bad news. The good news is that as a group, workaholics are surprisingly happy. They are doing exactly what they love — work — and they can't seem to get enough of it. If the circumstances are right — that is, if their jobs fit and their families are accommodating — then workaholics can be astonishingly productive. But here's the bad news: The people who work with and live with workaholics often suffer. Adjusting to the frenetic schedule of a workaholic is not easy and only rarely rewarding. At work these addicts are often demanding and sometimes not very effective. At home, well, you'll seldom find a workaholic at home. The tensions implicit in this rather unbalanced life-style cause very real dilemmas for those involved, and a good part of this book is about those problems. ∎

QUESTIONS

Cause-Effect

Would being a workaholic, as Machlowitz defines it, be detrimental to other aspects of a person's life? Explain.

Comparison/Contrast

Do you find any comparison between workaholics and other enthusiasts, such as people involved in political activity, sports fans, or community activists?

Definition

Define what you think would be an appropriate balance between work and leisure for you personally.

Robert L. Veninga and James P. Spradley

What Is Job Burnout?

from *The Work/Stress Connection: How to Cope with Job Burnout*

Behavioral scientist Robert L. Veninga and urban anthropologist James P. Spradley define job burnout as a "debilitating psychological condition brought about by unrelieved work stress." The excerpt in these pages elaborates upon this definition.

We wanted to identify the range of job pressures, trace out their consequences, and find out how people managed stress on the job.

One of the most important facts revealed by our data, though not new, struck us with new urgency. It is simply that *your job can be hazardous to your health.* Stress in the workplace can give you negative fringe benefits you never bargained for. Physical illness. Emotional exhaustion. Ulcers. High blood pressure. Drinking too much. Headaches. Depression. In short, your job can burn you out. It can leave you listless and angry, upset with your spouse and kids, unable to enjoy your evenings and weekends. Like a thief in the night, work stress robs millions of workers of their health and happiness, then goes scot-free while the blame is laid elsewhere.

But we learned an equally important lesson from the people we studied: *you can avoid job burnout.* You can prevent the damage caused by unrelieved work stress. You can find ways to release the pressure. It's possible to humanize the workplace, to match people with jobs, to equip workers to cope with stress. Again and again we talked with people who had learned to live with high levels of stress in their jobs. They knew how to identify and avoid the hazard and had discovered ways to renew themselves. They were workers who lived in pressure-cooker jobs from eight to five, yet remained free from job-burnout symptoms.

In this book we will have a great deal to say about both of these findings. Drawing on the data from our own studies of job burnout, we hope to provide you with a clear understanding of this malady, as well as show you how to avoid it altogether or recover if you become a casualty. From time to time we will draw on the literally thousands of recent scientific studies related to work, stress, and health. Let's begin with a definition of job burnout.

Job Burnout: A Definition

In this book job burnout refers to *a debilitating psychological condition brought about by unrelieved work stress, which results in:*

1. depleted energy reserves

2. lowered resistance to illness

3. increased dissatisfaction and pessimism

4. increased absenteeism and inefficiency at work.

This condition is debilitating because it has the power to weaken, even devastate, otherwise healthy, energetic, and competent individuals. Its primary cause is unrelieved stress, the kind that goes on day after day, month after month, year after year. It manifests itself in these four major symptom areas, ones we will look at briefly here.

Every kind of work creates some type of stress. You must work overtime to complete a report by a deadline imposed by someone else. You have to stand in the same two-by-three-foot area for eight hours a day, packaging tiny computer parts that come down the assembly line. You sit at your desk with nothing to do, watching the clock, unable to leave, unable to do what you would like. Each of these situations can place special demands on you — a stress to which you must respond. Some workers will find these stresses a challenge, even enjoyable, while others evaluate them in more negative terms.

For Sally Swanson, in her job as a bank teller, it was the unrelenting criticism of her supervisor that became a chronic irritant and stress. Bob Mackler's stress came, in part, from the fifty-five to sixty hours a week he spent at Wendy's. But more important, he continued to feel responsible even when not at work. On his day off he found himself calling in to see how things were going. The chronic nature of the pressure took its toll and, as Bob freely admitted, "I just burned out from that job." Both Bill Hansen and Liz Keifer felt the continuing stress that came from feeling trapped in jobs they had outgrown. Liz Keifer's frustration centered on an unchallenging job. Bill Hansen had come to doubt his own ability to find another church: "I feel used up here but don't see any hope of [being assigned to] another parish."

One of the first consequences of unrelieved work stress takes the form of depleted energy reserves. When people talk about burning out, they usually report feelings of exhaustion, weariness, loss of enthusiasm. They feel bone tired, when they go to bed and also when they wake up. A nurse told us, "I'm constantly preoccupied with the problems at work. I require more sleep and cannot drag myself out of bed in the morning." A purchasing agent confided, "I become emotionally exhausted and I just can't face going to work. I've even called in sick, just because I couldn't stand the thought of facing that place. I get depressed and forgetful." When your energy runs low, it can affect leisure-time activities. Bob Mackler loved to read books, but job burnout took away his interest, made his mind wander, and robbed him of his pleasure. "In three months I've only finished reading a couple chapters," he said, shaking his head.

Depleted energy reserves also can spoil your time with other people or wipe it out altogether. As the nurse mentioned above remarked, "I'm no fun to be with anymore." A middle-aged veterinarian said, "I used to enjoy playing with my son in the evening. Now I'm too tired. I get impatient with him. I just want to get alone."

The second result of the stress that causes job burnout is *lowered resistance to illness*. "I began to get more colds," said a school principal, reflecting on the start of his own experience of job burnout. This is a common complaint among those who suffer from job burnout, but more serious problems can follow. Dr. Carroll Brodsky, a physician at the University of California Medical School in San Francisco, studied the way work stress led to illness in prison guards and teachers. He found that two-thirds of those he studied suffered from diseases such as ulcers, hypertension, arthritis, and depression.

Dr. Walter Menninger, senior staff psychiatrist at the Menninger Foundation, Topeka, Kansas, believes there is a clear relationship between stress and the aches and pains of everyday life. He says, "A chronic backache may signal the load is getting too heavy; the ulcer may suggest dealing with a situation you can't stomach. . . . Some degree of exhaustion is observed along with the development of other symptoms such as migraine headache, gastrointestinal upset, canker sores, and flu."

The exact manner in which work stress lowers your resistance to illness and contributes to disease is not fully understood. Yet we do know that scientific studies have shown that stress is implicated in many serious illnesses. Take the nation's number-one killer: coronary heart disease. In one investigation, a group of experts rated overall stress of specialties in medicine, dentistry, and law, then studied the health records of professionals in these fields. They discovered that people in high-pressure jobs, such as trial lawyer and oral surgeon, not only smoked more (a stress-related activity), but had a higher incidence of coronary heart problems. In another study, tax accountants' cholesterol levels increased as the income-tax deadline drew near and their workloads increased. After work tapered off, cholesterol levels also declined. What they ate made little difference in this fluctuation. Another scientific study, this one of NASA personnel working on space flights, showed a direct relation between coronary-artery disease and stressful jobs. Researchers studied the health and work stress of managers, scientists, and engineers. The managers had to cope with the most work stress, especially in the form of conflict and overload. Among these three groups, the managers had a significantly higher incidence of coronary heart disease than the others.

The stress of job burnout also leads to *increased dissatisfaction and pessimism.* Again and again we found that as people lived with unrelieved stress, the jobs they once enjoyed turned sour. Many looked back wistfully to an earlier era of contentment with their work. A housewife suffering from job burnout said, "For the first five years I loved being a housewife. It was meaningful and fun, but that seems like a long time ago. Now when my husband comes home I'm ready to climb the walls. I get headaches almost every day. I feel guilty, but I just hate the feeling of being a trapped housewife." The head of personnel in a large company, who recognized his own symptoms of job stress, said, "I started noticing a definite change in how I felt about my job. Like staff meetings. I used to look forward to them eagerly, but now I dread them like the plague. I'm just too tired to put up with the hassles."

With amazing regularity we found that when people did learn to cope with work pressures, when they recovered from job burnout, their satisfaction level went up dramatically. A college professor is typical of many others. "I used to go around angry all the time at the administration of this college. I had lost my first love for students and for teaching. I came within a hair's breadth of giving it all up and trying some other career. I know now it was a case of burnout, and when I got that under control, my old enthusiasm returned. This college is a great place — and it really hasn't changed. But I sure have."

For many of those we studied, dissatisfaction had slowly turned to dark pessimism. We asked one sample of workers in a variety of occupations, "How would you feel if you had to continue your present job for the rest of your life?" Here are some of their candid answers, which reveal the tragedy of unrelieved stress:

— "I would be worn out at fifty."

— "Very depressed. Would probably require professional help."

— "I couldn't face it. I would be very depressed."

— "If my position were not to improve . . . I don't feel that I could stand it much longer, let alone for the rest of my life."

— "Horrible, I would feel pinned down, locked into a position where there would be very little sense of achievement."

— "I'd kill myself. I could not take it."

— "Totally defeated. There would be little to look forward to."

Finally, job burnout leads to *increased absenteeism and inefficiency at work.* This may occur because of actual stress-related illness or simply lowered morale. As Jerome Rosow, head of the Work in America Institute, says, "Workers who are turned off will stay out under any pretext." In 1976, the Bureau of Labor Statistics reported that Americans lose 3.5 percent of work hours through absenteeism. It has been estimated that one out of three workers on any particular day has called in sick because of a stress-related problem. And when job burnout sets in, even those days on the job are less efficiently spent. Workers under stress take longer coffee breaks, take longer to accomplish tasks, make more mistakes, and put off tasks that require immediate attention. Many observers see a direct link between job burnout and our national decline in worker productivity. ∎

QUESTIONS

Process

Short of changing jobs, what steps do you think could be taken to alleviate the condition of job burnout by the individual who suffers from it and/or by the company for which he or she works?

Cause-Effect

Choose a workplace with which you are familiar and where you feel job burnout is a common phenomenon, and discuss why you think burnout exists.

Cause-Effect

Job burnout not only affects the people suffering from its symptoms, but also the functioning of the organizations for which they work. Considering the definition provided in the article, describe some of these effects for a particular organization, such as a school, a manufacturing company, or a hospital.

Margaret Mead

The Education of the Samoan Child

from *Coming of Age in Samoa*

In the 1920s anthropologist Margaret Mead lived among the natives of the Samoan Islands off the coast of New Zealand, studying their culture. She published her findings in Coming of Age in Samoa, *a work that continues to be popular today. Through her close examination of Samoan society, Mead was able to isolate a number of elements that accounted for the particularly noncompetitive and peaceful life she found there. The excerpt included here from the chapter on the education of the Samoan child focuses primarily on the training of the adolescent boy.*

For the boy it is different. He hopes that some day he will hold a *matai* name, a name which will make him a member of the *Fono*, the assembly of headmen, which will give him a right to drink kava with chiefs, to work with chiefs rather than with the young men, to sit inside the house, even though his new title is only of "between the posts" rank, and not of enough importance to give him a right to a post for his back. But very seldom is he absolutely assured of getting such a name. Each family holds several of these titles which they confer upon the most promising youths in the whole family connection. He has many rivals. They also are in the *Aumaga*. He must always pit himself against them in the group activities. There are also several types of activities in one of which he must specialise. He must become a house-builder, a fisherman, an orator or a wood carver. Proficiency in some technique must set him off a little from his fellows. Fishing prowess means immediate rewards in the shape of food gifts to offer to his sweetheart; without such gifts his advances will be scorned. Skill in house-building means wealth and status, for a young man who is a skilled carpenter must be treated as courteously as a chief and addressed with the chief's language, the elaborate set of honorific words used to people of rank.

And with this goes the continual demand that he should not be too efficient, too outstanding, too precocious. He must never excel his fellows by more than a little. He must neither arouse their hatred nor the disapproval of his elders who are far readier to encourage and excuse the laggard than to condone precocity. And at the same time he shares his sister's reluctance to accept responsibility, and if he should excel greatly, not too obviously, he has good chances of being made a chief. If he is sufficiently talented, the *Fono* itself may deliberate, search out a vacant title to confer upon him and call him in that he may sit with the old men and learn wisdom. And yet so well recognised is the unwillingness of the young men to respond to this honour, that the provision is always made, "And if the young man runs away, then never shall he be made a chief, but always he must sit outside the house with the young men, preparing and serving the food of the *matais* with whom he may not sit in the *Fono.*"

Still more pertinent are the chances of his relationship group bestowing a *matai* name upon the gifted young man. And a *matai* he wishes to be, some day, some far-off day when his limbs have lost a little of their suppleness and his heart the love of fun and of dancing. As one chief of twenty-seven told me: "I have been a chief only four years and look, my hair is grey, although in Samoa grey hair comes very slowly, not in youth, as it comes to the white man. But always, I must act as if I were old. I must walk gravely and with a measured step. I may not dance except upon most solemn occasions, neither may I play games with the young men. Old men of sixty are my companions and watch my every word, lest I make a mistake. Thirty-one people live in my household. For them I must plan, I must find them food and clothing, settle their disputes, arrange their marriages. There is no one in my whole family who dares to scold me or even to address me familiarly by my first name. It is hard to be so young and yet to be a chief." And the old men shake their heads and agree that it is unseemly for one to be a chief so young.

The operation of natural ambition is further vitiated by the fact that the young man who is made a *matai* will not be the greatest among his former associates, but the youngest and greenest member of the *Fono*. And no longer may he associate familiarly with his old companions; a *matai* must associate only with *matais*, must work beside them in the bush and sit and talk quietly with them in the evening.

And so the boy is faced by a far more difficult dilemma than the girl. He dislikes responsibility, but he wishes to excel in his group; skill will hasten the day when he is made a chief, yet he receives censure and ridicule if he slackens his efforts; but he will be scolded if he proceeds too rapidly; yet if he would win a sweetheart, he must have prestige among his fellows. And conversely, his social prestige is increased by his amorous exploits.

So while the girl rests upon her "pass" proficiency, the boy is spurred to greater efforts. A boy is shy of a girl who does not have these proofs of efficiency and is known to be stupid and unskilled; he is afraid he may come to want to marry her. Marrying a girl without proficiency would be a most imprudent step and involve an endless amount of wrangling with his family. So the girl who is notoriously inept must take her lovers from among the casual, the jaded, and the married who are no longer afraid that their senses will betray them into an imprudent marriage.

But the seventeen-year-old girl does not wish to marry — not yet. It is better to live as a girl with no responsibility, and a rich variety of emotional experience. This is the best period of her life. There are as many beneath her whom she may bully as there are others above her to tyrannise over her. What she loses in prestige, she gains in freedom. She has very little baby-tending to do. Her eyes do not ache from weaving nor does her back break from bending all day over the tapa board. The long expeditions after fish and food and weaving materials give ample opportunities for rendezvous. Proficiency would mean more work, more confining work, and earlier marriage, and marriage is the inevitable to be deferred as long as possible. ∎

QUESTIONS

Comparison/Contrast

What similarities and/or differences do you see between the training for work of a Samoan adolescent boy and his American counterpart?

Process

Margaret Mead describes the process through which adolescent boys and girls are trained to assume their roles in Samoan society. Trace the steps through which various forces in the society in which you live have led you to select your proposed career goal.

Cause-Effect

From the point of view of the needs of the society at large, why are you being educated the way you are?

Kenneth B. Clark

The Dynamics of Under-Employment
from *Dark Ghetto*

It is illegal in most communities in the United States to deny work to anyone on the basis of racial, religious, or ethnic background; nevertheless, according to Kenneth B. Clark, an eminent black psychologist, it is a common practice. He describes in this excerpt from Dark Ghetto *the discouraging employment situation for blacks, particularly for black youth in Harlem during the 1960s.*

The roots of the pathology of ghetto communities lie in the menial, low-income jobs held by most ghetto residents. If the occupational level of the community could be raised, one would expect a corresponding decrease in social pathology, in dependency, disease, and crime.

With the growth of the civil rights movement, Negroes have won many footholds earlier forbidden to them, and it would seem logical to conclude, as many do, that Negroes are better off than ever before in this gradually desegregating and generally affluent society. But the fact is that in many ways the Negro's situation is deteriorating. The Negro has been left out of the swelling prosperity and social progress of the nation as a whole. He is in danger of becoming a permanent economic proletariat.

About one out of every seven or eight adults in Harlem is unemployed. In the city as a whole the rate of unemployment is half that. Harlem is a young community, compared to the rest of New York, and in 1960 twice as many young Negro men in the labor force, as compared to their white counterparts, were without jobs. For the girls, the gap was even greater — nearly two and one-half times the unemployment rate for white girls in the labor force. Across the country the picture is very much the same. Unemployment of Negroes is rising much faster than unemployment of whites. Among young men eighteen to twenty-four, the national rate is five times as high for Negroes as for whites.

An optimist could point to the fact that the average family income of Negroes has increased significantly within the two decades 1940–1960, but a more realistic observer would have to qualify this with the fact that the *discrepancy* between the average family income of whites and that of Negroes has increased even more significantly. The real income, the relative status income, of Negroes has gone down during a period when the race was supposed to have been making what candidates for elective office call, "the most dramatic progress of any oppressed group at any period of human history."

The menial and unrewarding jobs available to most Negroes can only mean a marginal subsistence for most ghetto families. The median income in Harlem is $3,480 compared to $5,103 for residents of New York City — a similar gap exists in the country as a whole. Half the families in Harlem have incomes under $4,000, while 75 percent of all New York City residents earn more than $4,000. Only one in twenty-five Negro families has an income above $10,000, while more than four in twenty-five of the white families do.

Nor do Negroes with an education receive the financial benefits available to whites. Herman P. Miller in his book, *Rich Man, Poor Man*,[a] states that Negroes who have completed four years of college *"can expect to earn only as much in a lifetime as whites who have not gone beyond the eighth grade."* This is true both in the North and in the South. The white high school graduate will earn just about as much as a Negro who has gone through college and beyond for graduate training. One young man in Harlem asked: "What is integration into poverty?" The question is not easy to answer.

Both the men and the women in the ghetto are relegated to the lowest status jobs. Sixty-four percent of the men in Harlem compared to only 38 percent of New York City's male population, and 74 percent of the women, compared to 37 percent for New York City, hold unskilled and service jobs. Only 7 percent of Harlem males are professionals, technicians, managers, proprietors, or officials. Twenty-four percent of the males in the city hold such prestige posts.

An eighteen-year-old Negro boy protested: "They keep telling us about job opportunities, this job opportunity, and that, but who wants a job working all week and bringing home a sweat man's pay?" Most of the men in the dark ghetto do work for a "sweat man's pay," and even *that* is now threatened by the rise of automation.

Many of the jobs now held by Negroes in the unskilled occupations are deadend jobs, due to disappear during the next decade. Decreases, or no expansions, are expected in industries in which more than 43 percent

---

[a] New York, Thomas Y. Crowell Co., 1964.

of the labor force in Harlem is now employed (i.e., transportation, manu-facturing, communication and utilities, and wholesale and retail trades). Employment in those industries and occupations requiring considerable education and training is expected to increase. As the pressure of unemployed white workers in the few expanding areas of unskilled jobs grows, the ability of ghetto residents to hold on to such jobs becomes doubtful. And by 1970 there will be 40 percent more Negro teen-agers (16–21) in Harlem than there were in 1960. The restless brooding young men without jobs who cluster in the bars in the winter and on stoops and corners in the summer are the stuff out of which riots are made. The solution to riots is not better police protection (or even the claims of police brutality) or pleas from civil rights leaders for law and order. The solution lies in finding jobs for the unemployed and in raising the social and economic status of the entire community. Otherwise the "long hot summers" will come every year.

By far the greatest growth in employment in New York City is expected in professional, technical, and similar occupations — some 75,000 to 80,000 jobs by the end of the present decade.[b] Of the 3 percent of Harlem residents in this group, the major portion are in the lower-paying professions: clergymen, teachers, musicians, and social welfare and recreation workers. A substantial increase of 40 percent in the number of managers, officials, and proprietors is expected in business and government, but the Negro has made few advances here. This will be offset by declines expected in retail business, where the trend toward bigness will result in fewer small store proprietors, another prophecy with grim implications for Negroes since the only business where Negro ownership exists in number is small stores. The number of clerical positions is due to grow in New York by 35,000 to 40,000 jobs. Approximately 14 percent of the residents of Harlem have such jobs, but most of them are in the lower-paying positions. Electronic data-processing systems will soon replace many clerks in routine and repetitive jobs, such as sorting, filing, and the operation of small machines — the kind of jobs Negroes have — while workers in jobs requiring contact with the public, such as claim clerks, complaints clerks, and bill collectors — usually white — will be least affected by office automation. The number of sales workers will decline as self-service increases, and here too, Negroes who have been successfully employed will lose out.

Jobs for skilled workers are due to grow in New York State by 28,000 yearly. Building trades craftsmen will be particularly in demand. But the

---

[b]*Manpower Outlook 1960–1970,* New York City Department of Labor, 1962, pp. 1 and 12, provides the projections that pertain to job expectations.

restrictions to apprenticeship training programs in the building trades industry have kept Negroes from these jobs. Semi-skilled and unskilled jobs (excluding service workers) will decrease by 70,000 to 80,000 jobs between 1960 and 1970. Thirty-eight percent of the Negro male workers living in Harlem have such jobs now. If present employment patterns persist, Negro and white workers who might ordinarily qualify for semiskilled jobs will undoubtedly be pushed into the unskilled labor force or become unemployed in the face of increasing competition with those who are better trained. Negro unemployment will rise as the unskilled labor supply exceeds the demand. The only jobs that will increase, and in which Negroes now dominate, are jobs as servants, waitresses, cooks — the traditional service jobs which have added to the Negro's sense of inferiority. But as the requirements for skilled jobs grow stiffer and as semiskilled jobs decline, Negroes will face strong competition from whites to hold even these marginal jobs.

It is illegal in New York to deny a job to anyone on the basis of skin color, but it is common practice anyway. First, Negro applicants are often said to lack the qualifications necessary for a particular job. Who can prove this to be disguised racial discrimination? Like any charge with some truth, the extent of the truth is hard to determine. Second, often working against the Negro applicant, though sometimes in his favor, are ethnic quotas applied to certain types of jobs, employed with the conscious intent of maintaining an "ethnic balance" in the work force. When the quota is filled, the Negro applicant, no matter how well qualified, is told that there are no openings. Third, and much more subtle, although no less discriminatory, is the practice employed by some unions of requiring that a member of the union vouch for an applicant. When the union has no Negro members, the possibility of finding someone to vouch for a Negro applicant is extremely remote.

Through historical processes certain ethnic or religious minority groups come to predominate in certain kinds of jobs: in New York, the waterfront for the Italians, the police force for the Irish, the school system for Jews, and the personal services for Negroes.[c]

A study by the Bureau of Social Science Research, Inc., showed a fourth technique of exclusion; that employers tend to label some jobs, usually the lowest, as "Negro jobs" — Negroes are hired by many firms, but at "Negro jobs," with menial status, minimum wages, and little if any security.

Furthermore, many Negroes are discouraged before they begin. Guidance counselors often in the past advised Negro students not to prepare for jobs

---

[c]A similar conception has been formulated by Eli Ginsberg in *A Policy for Skilled Manpower*, New York, Columbia University Press for the National Manpower Council, 1954, especially p. 249.

where employment opportunities for Negroes were limited. Doubtless they believed they did so in the best interests of the youth — better not to encourage him to pursue a career which is likely to end in bitter frustration and unemployment. There is some evidence that this form of root discrimination is now being reduced under persistent pressure from groups like the Urban League and the National Scholarship Service and Fund for Negro Students. The plethora of ineffective antidiscrimination and equal opportunities legislation — contrasted with the clear evidence of actual exclusion — leads one to suspect that this type of discrimination works in such a way as to be relatively immune to laws. It would appear that effective techniques for reducing discrimination in employment must, therefore, be as specific, subtle, and as pervasive as the evil they seek to overcome.

It has been charged over and over again that Negro youth lack motivation to succeed. To the extent that this is true, it is largely a consequence of ghetto psychology. Teen-age boys often help to support their families, and they have neither the time nor money nor encouragement to train for a white-collar job or skilled craft. Negroes often dread to try for jobs where Negroes have never worked before. Fear of the unknown is not peculiar to one racial group, and Negroes have had traumatic experiences in seeking employment. The Negro youth is caught in a vicious cycle: Poor preparation means poor jobs and low socio-economic status. Low status and poor jobs result in poor preparation for the next generation to come. ∎

QUESTIONS

Cause-Effect

What effects might the bleak employment statistics that Kenneth Clark presents have upon the emotional and social development of a minority group member?

Definition/Cause-Effect

What is your definition of a dead-end job? Examining your community, do you find any groups of people relegated to these jobs? If so, why?

Felice N. Schwartz, Margaret H. Schiffer, and Susan Gillotti

The Best and the Worst of Times

from *How to Go to Work When Your Husband Is Against It, Your Children Aren't Old Enough and There's Nothing You Can Do Anyhow*

The authors of the next selection present the dilemma of the woman who wishes to pursue a career but whose training has relegated her to being a wife and mother only. They claim that the idea of a woman's not working outside the home is relatively new, emerging when "industrialism had produced the first mass middle class." The authors assert that it is possible and desirable for women to function successfully both inside and outside the home.

This is the decade of the liberated woman.

An idea has come of age, and American women are standing up and demanding the end of a myth and the beginning of a new place in a new society. They are forcing America to reevaluate its concept of what is right for the female 53 percent of its population, a concept of support, submission, and dependency that has been merchandised so successfully for so long that women as well as men have accepted it as an eternal truth.

For the average woman today, raised to think that the only fulfillment is in marriage and children and that being a wife and mother is a full-time, lifetime career, these are both the best and the worst of times.

The best because the Women's Lib message reinforces and legitimatizes feelings she has already begun to articulate to herself. The worst because she is not yet emotionally convinced of the rightness of any alternative to the situation. A look at history can clarify the situation.

There is nothing unprecedented about women working outside their homes during and after childbearing and childrearing years. Throughout the history of the Western world, except for an aristocratic minority, women have worked alongside men. The concept of the stay-at-home wife is very much a product of nineteenth-century capitalism, for it was not until the industrial revolution that society was able to afford a large class of unemployed women. Even today, the middle-class, full-time wife and mother exists in numbers only in the United States and Western Europe. The Scandinavian countries accept her, but the trend there is decidely toward the woman who both works and raises a family, and social provisions are made to enable her to do so. In Russia and Israel we see the other extreme, as lacking in options as contemporary American society, but resulting from current economic necessity: women are expected to work full time throughout their lives.

There was a time when American women were needed in full-time jobs too. In pioneering years, they blazed the trails and fought the Indians side by side with their husbands and, as they settled in farms across the country, they tilled the soil, milked the cows, and harvested the crops beside their men. In that era of the extended family, there was a sharing of tasks, and family life depended on the combined efforts of its members, male and female, young and old.

By the beginning of the twentieth century, the picture began to change. Industrialism had produced the first mass middle class. The women of this group had no financial need to work and the economy did not require their services.

And so, except for a few pioneer, determined professional women and reluctant lady typists who needed the money, middle-class women did not work outside the home. There was a cultural factor involved, too. To the new middle-class men of the era, wives who did not work, a luxury formerly only available to the aristocracy, were a visible status symbol showing that they had arrived.

This pattern prevailed through the first three decades of the century. But with the increasing migration from the farm to the cities, a change began to take place. The extended family gave way to the nuclear family. Parents and children as an isolated unit became the rule rather than the exception. Families grew smaller as better contraceptive techniques became available; children were more closely spaced as medical advances reduced the number of miscarriages and stillbirths; the country was expanding its role in the education of the young and the care of the old. Yet still the middle-class wives stayed home, for society was not ready to accept the contribution they could make outside it.

In the 1930s, economic necessity brought many women into the job market at whatever work they could manage to get, and World War II made the defense plant working wife and mother a national heroine. Rosie the Riveter was not, in most cases, from the middle class, but she did much to dispel the notion that women were unsuited by nature for "men's jobs."

Then came the post-war era, and the trend reversed itself. The country needed to convert to a peacetime economy, from guns to washing machines, and a market for home equipment was highly desirable. The mood of the country fitted its economic needs. A long, grueling war was over. The returning G.I. was ready for a little quiet domesticity, and so was his wife. The simple joys of family life had overwhelming appeal.

Women's magazines got the message immediately and so, with the interlocking interests of women's editors, their advertisers, and their audience, "togetherness" was born. The old nineteenth-century image of the domestic woman as the social ideal was given another go-round. The woman who devoted herself to raising a large brood of children was glorified and she got extra points if they were delivered by natural childbirth.

There was a welter of books, magazine articles, and newspaper columns on the psychology of child raising. There was do-it-yourself home decorating and fancy cooking. For the "executive wife" there were formulas for enhancing one's husband's career and relieving the mounting pressures on the organization man.

The prevailing philosophy of liberal arts colleges of the time reinforced the image of women as the "culture bearers" for their children and community, giving women students both too much and too little: too much training in using their minds to be content as mere "culture bearers," and too little realistic guidance as to how they might use their education in the successive phases of their lives.

The educated woman gave in to social expectations, renounced career in favor of marriage, and remained hostage of the image, only slightly altered in deference to her education, of the woman who was charming, demure, frail, uncompetitive, essentially passive. (But capable — a woman who ran up curtains out of nothing, learned to do one hundred exotic things with hamburgers, was a prolific reader, comforted her husband in his professional tribulations, and found each day with her children filled with joy and excitement.)

But no matter how hard she tried, the glories of domestic life which she had envisioned began to fade. Cooking, child raising, and meeting the 6:10 were simply not enough. She was trapped at home all day as household help became less available and more expensive, or feeling unneeded and unproductive as the children moved into a life of their own. She wondered why she had bothered to earn a college degree if all she would do with her life would be diaper babies, wash the kitchen floor, or be a hostess to her spouse. She had little to offer her tired husband when he came home — except complaints.

She was caught in a double bind. While acknowledging her feelings of dissatisfaction, she often simultaneously felt guilty about having them.

When she complained about her frustrations, she felt that society might be right to label her "just another neurotic housewife."

If she was neurotic, there was good reason for it. The social pressures of the time conflicted directly with many of her emotional needs and no solutions were offered. She was legitimately unhappy and it is a credit to her intelligence and resilience that she kept any sense of perspective at all.

How could she plan realistically for the years after thirty-five if she had been conditioned all her life by the imperatives of motherhood?

How could she keep her education and skills alive unless she used them?

How could she create an atmosphere of warmth and stability and intellectual awareness in her home if she was restless, bored, and uncertain?

How could she foster independence in her children if she was herself dependent?

She simply could not.

With all the millions of words that were written about her and the concrete continuing education programs that were planned to meet her academic needs, the problems remained unsolved for the woman who wanted a full life, the complex balance of marriage, children, job, and leisure. Society had not yet adjusted its thinking to allow a woman to have a job without sacrifice to her family.

In the early 1960s, the picture began to change. Sociologists and psychologists began to realize that the educated family woman's dilemma was not a private problem and economists became aware that the demand for brainworkers was going to outstrip the supply.

The National Conference on the Status of Women led to a national study of the rights to which women are entitled and the wrongs to which they are prey. The conclusions, published in 1963, brought about the first wave of the current feminist movement. In that year, also, the instant rise to the best-seller list of Betty Friedan's *The Feminine Mystique* was a strong clue to the way the cultural winds were blowing.

The question of women's rights in employment and under the law, a matter of little interest to educated middle-class women during the fifties, surfaced in the sixties as a matter of general public concern. Women who, during the past decade, had been actively involved in the civil rights movements of others became aware that they were not being consulted on policy matters to a degree commensurate with their contributions. This was brought home dramatically to women students who were asked to bring coffee to their decision-making male colleagues during demonstrations.

Much was done during the 1960s to lay the groundwork for equitable treatment of women in pay, promotion, and hiring practices. The passage of equal employment legislation in 1963 was a milestone. President Johnson, declaring that women were our greatest untapped natural resource, announced his intention of making the federal government a showcase for female employment. Title VII of the Civil Rights Act of 1964 outlawed job discrimination on grounds of sex.

The barriers that have kept many women out of jobs are continuing to fall. Guidelines passed in 1970 by the Department of Labor to update the 1964 Civil Rights Act specifically prohibit such practices as making distinctions between married and unmarried persons of one sex unless the same distinctions are made between married and single persons of the opposite sex; denying employment to women with young children unless the same exclusionary policy exists for men; penalizing women in their conditions of employment because they require time away from work for childbearing.

But there is, of course, still much to be done. Despite the new technology, the new laws, and the new social attitudes, practice, as usual, lags behind theory. There are still hidden, and not-so-hidden barriers in many areas of employment because some employers pay lip service to the *de jure* rules, but resist changing the *de facto* situation.

Child care and tax adjustments remain problems for women who want and need to work. The day-care center has emerged as a social institution but, so far, it is in the pilot stage. A few experimentally minded organizations have created day-care centers for their employees or working mothers have formed them themselves, but if we are to utilize women fully as workers, for society's good as well as their own, corporations, local governments, public and private institutions must increase child-care facilities.

Tax adjustments must also be made for the wife who works. Under the present laws, a man may charge off expenses necessary to earn his living, but a single woman can deduct only $600 a year for the care of a child under twelve and nothing for household help. Married women can only take a deduction if the family's adjusted income is under $6900. Such laws seem to be saying that it is a luxury, not a necessity, for women to work outside their homes.

But the pattern of the future is clear. The cultural-lag time has almost elapsed, and the pressing demands of society will restructure the role of women in practice as well as in theory in an economy that needs her services. The jobs that will keep society running on an even keel are brainworker jobs that can be filled equally well by either sex and will call for the participation of all educated men and women.

Still, perhaps the one option that is most needed and least available to women today is the option to combine family and work. Part-time employment is a prerequisite for this option and, although society gives evidence of accepting as an idea the concept that women can be productive both at home and on the job, little or nothing has been done in the way of practical provisions for the realization of this combination of roles.

But the barriers are not insurmountable. The family woman who has a well-defined goal, motivation and initiative can overcome them with good planning and full use of the assets she already has in abundance. In doing so, she will not only find her own rewards, but she will have made it that much easier for the next woman in search of the good life. ∎

QUESTIONS

Cause-Effect

Many critics of the women's movement claim that it is undesirable for women with young children to work outside the home. Do you agree? Explain.

Comparison/Contrast

Choose a family of your acquaintance in which both parents work outside the home. Compare and contrast each parent's roles in terms of their jobs as well as their functions within the household.

Process

What steps in your opinion would make it feasible for women to pursue careers successfully and to still function adequately within the home? For your answer you might consider necessary changes within the home itself and in the society at large.

Definition

Considering several aspects of your personal aspirations (for example, family, career), write an essay in which you define a well-balanced life.

Juanita Kreps

The Economics of Aging

Life expectancy is higher now than at the beginning of the century, yet fewer men over 65 still work. "At the beginning of the century two out of three men 65 or over were in the labor force . . . now among the 65 or over males, only about one in four continue to work." Juanita Kreps, economist and Secretary of Commerce during the Carter administration, concerns herself in this article with the problems of maintaining adequate income after a lifetime of work.

If you were born in this century, you are likely to take your retirement for granted. For several years prior to retirement you have prepared for this new phase of life, and throughout your working years regular deductions from your paycheck have contributed to the retirement income you will receive.

However, this concept of retirement is relatively new. The possibility of living for eight or ten years on accumulated savings, annuities, and other assets was remote when your grandfather retired at 65. His life expectancy was lower than yours, so living to be 75 was less likely. Also, he probably had no monthly income from a pension fund or annuity. With no source of income except his earnings, he continued on the job as long as he could. Because a much larger proportion of the labor force was engaged in farming, most older men could find work for as many or as few hours as they wished.

During the first half of the twentieth century this picture changed markedly. The industrial pace quickened after the Civil War, gaining further momentum in the early decades of the new century to transform the nature of our economy — and the type of work men did. The transformation continued through two world wars.

By 1950 these changes were reflected not only in the way men worked but also in the way they did not work — that is, in their retirement from work. Between the beginning of the century — when two out of three men 65 or over were in the labor force — and its midpoint — when only one out of three older men worked — retirement came to be the established pattern. Now among the 65 and over males, only about one in four continue to work.

Other changes have taken place. The birth rate has declined and life expectancy has risen; the result is an aging population. This aging leads to new considerations of the special problems of older persons. The capacity to deal with these problems has emerged from another economic factor in the transformation: the increasing output and income of our economy. The first half of the twentieth century witnessed such vast improvements in national product level that the American economy can now "afford" to retire workers at 65 (or even 62) without jeopardizing output. In fact, our economy not only can afford retirement; it apparently requires it.

I

The practice of retirement, as well as the shortened workweek and later entrance into the labor force, are basically the result of increased productivity. Each development is made possible by the growth in output which enables man to produce enough goods and services to meet his family's needs in less than a 12-hour day and in a working life considerably shorter than that which began at age 14 and ended with death. It is possible, with modern production techniques and capital equipment, not only to provide for your current needs, but also to acquire claims against goods in the form of retirement income.

In a less productive economy, retirement is not possible. With lower productivity, it is not possible to subsist on the product earned in a short workweek, nor is it possible to keep children in school until 18. Output per manhour is so low that all persons are required to work practically all their lives. Leisure in any form invites starvation.

The contrast between these two extremes points up the advantages of living in a technologically advanced economy: higher productivity, hence higher living standard; a lowered workweek and thus more leisure; elimination of child labor and improved education. The dual effect in all cases is more goods and services and more free time in which to enjoy them.

But leisure time provided by retirement, although arising from the same set of circumstances that creates the shorter workweek and postpones age of entrance to the labor force, may not be greeted with quite the same enthusiasm. For many reasons, a sudden and complete withdrawal from work may prove a difficult adjustment. Full-time leisure may strike the new retiree as a dubious blessing, and the accompanying drop in income may restrict his leisure activities.

Ideally, if the retiree could balance his desire for leisure with his desire for earned income and continued participation on the job, he would probably retire gradually rather than suddenly at 65.

II

Complete withdrawal from work at age 65 — or earlier, in many cases (about half the men who have retired in recent years have done so before age 65) — presents one with an abundance of free time but often, also, a dearth of income. This sharp drop in income that accompanies retirement is hard to adjust to. For although living expenses may fall a bit, they surely will not decline as much as income.

Needless to say, many of the elderly who are now poor were poor during their working years as well. Their education and skill levels were low, their job opportunities scant. For those persons who are disadvantaged in their capacities to earn adequate incomes, society must make an important decision: how much will it contribute to their economic well-being? Are we willing to guarantee some minimum family income, in order to assure all persons the basic necessities, whether or not they "earn" these necessities by working? This question is one of the key domestic issues of the moment.

But such a minimum guarantee, even it if comes about, does not resolve the issues relating to income in retirement. Retirement income will be a problem to all of us. And there is no reassuring evidence that those of us now in middle age, and at the peak of our earnings, will be any better off, relative to these present incomes, when we retire. It is true we will all have a social security benefit, and that it will be higher. But in comparison with the standard of living we are now accustomed to, the contrast may well be just as extreme.

The problem lies, not just in low earnings during worklife, but in the allocation of one's total income throughout life. We are paid for working, and our tendency is to assume that all we earn in a year is available for consumption that year. We may save, true: we pay for homes, we save for children's education, for next summer's vacation (or more likely, for last summer's vacation). But we save very little, privately, for retirement and even when we do, we must have some investment know-how in order to have the savings grow with the rise in living costs.

Payroll taxes for social security purposes are a form of saving for retirement, of course. We pay for the benefits of today's retirees; in return our own benefits will be financed by those who work when we are in retirement. But the amount we save is limited, and the benefit is accordingly low. Moreover, we resist a higher payroll tax because we are reluctant to forego today's consumption in favor of tomorrow's.

Until we do smooth the income a good bit more, retirement incomes will continue to be substantially below earnings. The smoothing can occur in any one of several ways: by spreading work into the later years, particularly through part-time jobs; by private savings and annuities; by heavier contributions to public retirement benefits. Different people would elect different options. But they amount to the same thing in one sense. They all recognize the need for considering some reasonable balance of work and income through the lifespan, as opposed to a concentration of work and earnings in the middle years. Recognition of retirement as a relatively new lifestage, which requires its own financial arrangements, is obviously necessary, and just as obviously lacking. The implications of this lifestage for public policy have not been fully accepted; similarly, each of us needs to reexamine this perception of what lies ahead. In economic terms, the best summary of intergenerational relations comes from Kenneth Boulding: "One of the things we know for certain about any age group is that it has no future. The young become middle-aged and the middle-aged become old. . . . Consequently, the support which the middle-aged give to the young can be regarded as the first part of a deferred exchange, which will be consummated when those who are now young become middle-aged and support those who are now middle-aged who will then be old. Similarly, the support which the middle-aged give to the old can be regarded as the consummation of a bargain entered into a generation ago." It is this bargain that we made a generation ago that we are as a nation, sometimes guilty of neglecting.

III

Suppose we are concerned here with the handling of a man's own earnings through his worklife, and with making arrangements for these earnings to be apportioned in some optimal fashion, given the timing of his family's consumption needs. To make it simple (and to spread a bit of cheer), let us suppose that we are all young — so young, in fact, that we are just now entering the labor force. Suppose further that we are all male (which is a less cheerful assumption, at least to those of us who are not male; I trust it would be an equally unsatisfactory arrangement for those of you who are). This eliminates the sex difference in length of worklife, and allows us to speak of, say, a 40- to 45-year working period, from age 20 or 25 to 65.

The problem is one of accommodating the necessary variations in consumption that go with changes in family size and composition, and eventually, with retirement, subject of course to the overall constraint imposed by total earnings.

Imagine a two-dimensional diagram in which the vertical axis measures income, or consumption, in current dollars. Horizontally, visualize that we are indicating age, from the point of entry into the labor force, to death. By assumption, all of us are age 20, and have just taken our first jobs. You will see also that we all die promptly at age 80, thereby lending a certain order to things, which the actuaries may find reassuring.

What is the usual relationship between age and income level? We know from the data that the average income of the 30- to 40-year-old male in most any occupation or profession is higher than the average income of the 20- to 30-year-old; and that in most cases, the income of the 40- to 50-year-old is higher still. But alas, the average money income of males who are in the last decade of worklife, 55 to 65, is lower than that for the age group just younger. Thus, it is often pointed out that our incomes rise until we are in our 50s, then decline gradually until retirement, at which point they fall to perhaps one-half or a third.

But this conclusion is incorrect. It is true that at any point in time, a picture of average money income in an occupational group is an inverted U, that slopes upward more gently than it declines, then drops sharply and levels out for retirees. But this does not describe the usual behavior of a particular man's income through his lifetime. His income is likely to rise throughout his worklife, reflecting the impact both of experience and economic growth.

How, then, can we expect our money incomes to behave — those of us who are now a mere 20 — as we move through worklife? Not, surely, as the cross-sectional data indicate. Rather, we can reasonably expect that our highest incomes will accrue to us at the end of worklife. True, when we are receiving our highest income (at age 64, or thereabouts), that income will be lower than the income of our colleagues of age 60, if things continue as they are. But their incomes are higher than ours, on the average, not because ours have declined, but because they entered the labor force in a later, more productive era than we, and thus they will have higher incomes at any age, than we did at that age.

If our income does in fact continue to rise up to the point of retirement, what will happen to our consumption expenditures? Will we raise our living standards to absorb the rise in incomes as these increases occur? Turning to the two-dimensional diagram, will the consumption line follow along with the income line, rising gradually up to age 65, when both drop to some fraction — say, half, of their previous levels? Or is it more likely that a significant portion of the income in late worklife will be saved for consumption during the nonworking years?

The latter would seem reasonable, at first glance. In most families, the last child has finished school and left home by the time the father is in his early 50s, leaving a 10- to 15-year period of high earnings and somewhat reduced living costs. It would be possible to spread these earnings into the retirement period, thereby reducing the extent of the drop in consumption which now marks the withdrawal from the work force.

In model terms, we might suppose that the couple who has reached age 50, and sent their last child off to seek his fortune, might choose to hold their consumption levels fixed at the level reached at that age, in order to spread their next 15 years of earnings through the remainder of their lives. If one saved all increments in income after age 50 (in addition to whatever he was able to save during the earlier periods of heavier expenses), he would have approximately 15 years of saving and 15 years in which his income was supplemented by those savings, plus interest.

Depending on his time preference for consumption goods, he might elect to take an even more stringent position. He could say, for example: "My wife and I want to suffer no drop in our level of living at retirement; we want to expend our income in such a way as to allow the same standard during each of the last 30 years of our lives, even if we must reduce our expenditures at present. The question is then, what annual outlay is appropriate, given our projected earnings during the remaining 15 years of worklife, the expected level of social security benefits and private pensions, and the value of any equities, such as a home, on which we might draw?"

Long-range budgeting is indicated by a new consumption curve which rises along with income (although lying slightly below income) up to age 50. Then, whereas income continues to rise for another 15 years and then drop to one-half or one-third, where it is stable for the remainder of life, consumption levels off at age 50 (or even drops somewhat at that age), remaining constant through the remainder of the lifespan.

Needless to say, such an attempt would be impeded by many uncertainties. At what rate will earnings rise? What is a reasonable guess on the level of social security benefits? What of the differences in expenses as between working and nonworking years? How much must one allot to each successive year in order to offset pace change and thus allow real income to be stabilized? Perhaps most serious of all is the implied assumption that such a reallocation of consumption expenditures would solve the income problems of the low income elderly, whose earnings late in worklife are meager, as during their earlier years. No amount of retiming of consumption is effective in these cases; transfers of income, or improved job skills and job opportunities are the only alternatives.

None of us here are in that position. I suspect, moreover, that none of us expect to have any real income squeeze in our retirement years. This expectation may be borne out, of course. I would argue only that most people do in fact face such a crunch which, along with the other infirmities of old age, seems more than we should accept without protest.

Biologists and medical researchers are constantly improving the physical quality of life in the 60s and 70s. And despite the common complaint that they are merely keeping the very old alive longer and longer, thereby creating problems for the families of the aged, the primary thrust of their research would add life to years, not the inverse. Without adequate incomes in old age, however, physical stamina and intellectual vitality will have limited outlets. It follows either that worklife must be extended or some substantial reapportionment of the income earned in prior years must be arranged. ■

QUESTIONS

Process

Juanita Kreps says that "in most families, the last child has finished school and left home by the time the father is in his early 50s, leaving a 10- to 15-year period of high earnings and somewhat reduced living costs." By interviewing an individual or individuals in this category, your own parents perhaps, describe their plans for economic security during retirement.

Comparison/Contrast

What are the advantages and disadvantages of the two economic alternatives Ms. Kreps suggests for retirement: the extension of the working years or a "substantial reapportionment of the income earned in prior years"?

Cause-Effect

Juanita Kreps focuses particularly on the economic effects of retirement. Discuss some other problems that might result from quitting the work force at age sixty-five. Provide specific examples of these problems from your personal knowledge of older people.

Cause-Effect

Do you think older people look forward to retirement? Why, or why not?

Definition

What in your opinion would constitute a good life for the retired?

James Joyce

Counterparts

from *Dubliners*

The short story, ''Counterparts,'' by James Joyce, which appeared in Chapter 6, pp. 249–257, is part of a collection called Dubliners (1914). It is referred to in this section of the anthology because it describes the devastating effects upon its protagonist of work that neither stimulates nor provides self-respect. Reread it in order to consider the questions that follow here.

QUESTIONS

Comparison/Contrast

How does Farrington's job compare and/or contrast with one you have had in the level of interest, the possibility for advancement, and the attitude of the employer to the employee?

Cause-Effect

Discuss how dissatisfaction at the workplace may have ramifications in other areas of an individual's life. Use Farrington and either yourself or someone you know to illustrate your findings.

Definition (Cause-Effect)

What do you mean by self-respect? Does Farrington fit this definition? Why, or why not?

Cause-Effect

In protest against the humiliation he felt, Farrington insulted his boss. What, in your opinion, is an appropriate way to deal with problems between employer and employee? In answering the question you should evaluate Farrington's words and actions.

Questions for Essays Involving Several Readings

Following are general questions that apply to several of the foregoing selections at the same time. To answer each question, read or reread the selections referred to in parentheses below the question. Think about how you might use the information or ideas you gather in your answer.

CAUSE-EFFECT

Why is work a significant factor in a person's life?
(Fromm, Mills, Machlowitz, Veninga *et al.*, Schwartz *et al.*, Joyce)

DEFINITION

What is your definition of satisfactory work?
(Fromm, Mills, Machlowitz, Joyce)

CAUSE-EFFECT

Do you think it is necessary for work to provide satisfaction?
Explain.
(Fromm, Mills, Joyce)

CAUSE-EFFECT

Can men and women today be satisfied on their jobs?
(Fromm, Mills, Machlowitz, Veninga *et al.*, Schwartz *et al.*, Clark, Joyce)

CAUSE-EFFECT

The work ethic is broadly defined as acceptance of the desirability of working hard and belief in work as enhancing the dignity of the individual. What, in your opinion, is the status of the work ethic today? Provide reasons for your position.
(All selections apply)

PROCESS

Taking another look at the question above, trace the steps by which we train or fail to train our young to accept or reject the work ethic.
(All selections apply)

COMPARISON/CONTRAST

What comparisons and/or contrasts can be made between the problems of minorities and women in work?
(Clark, Schwartz *et al.*)

HUMAN NATURE

In the previous section of the Anthology, several articles were presented dealing with one of our major life experiences: work. Those articles not only examined what people actually do while they work, but also evaluated the quality of that work and the way it affects us. In pursuing these considerations, you may have asked yourself questions of a more universal nature: What should we do with our lives? What are we meant to do? and Who are we? This section, then, continues this exploration by examining the widest perspective possible, human nature itself.

Raymond Van Over, ed.

Sun Songs: Creation Myths from Around the World (excerpts)

The people who lived in the earliest period of our planet must have puzzled over the great paradoxes of the universe — life and death, the changing seasons, nature's bounty and calamities. They told stories to explain the contradictions and to reduce the chaos of life in the natural world. To some modern readers these myths may seem like absurd fictions, but the power they exerted for thousands of years and continue to exert in even the most highly developed nations suggests that they can contain in symbolic form some significant truths about ourselves and our relation to our world.

A group of myths of creation from many different cultures is presented here. You may be surprised to find similar patterns and themes in myths from widely-separated geographic locations. As you read them, think about the kinds of problems they were intended to solve, the mysteries they were meant to explain.

LENGUA CREATION MYTH OF PARAGUAY

The Creator, in the shape of a beetle, inhabited a hole in the earth, and he formed man and woman out of the clay which he threw up from his subterranean abode. At first the two were joined together, "like the Siamese twins," and in this very inconvenient posture they were sent out into the world, where they contended, at great disadvantage, with a race of powerful human beings whom the beetle had previously created. So the man and woman besought the beetle to separate them. He complied with their request and gave them the power to propagate their species. So they became the parents of mankind. But the beetle, having created the world, ceased to take any active part or interest in it.

A SIBERIAN-ALTAIC MYTH

In the beginning when there was nothing but water, God and the "First Man" moved about in the shape of two black geese over the waters of the primordial ocean. The devil, however, could not hide his nature, but endeavored ever to rise higher, until he finally sank down into the depths. Nearly suffocating, he was forced to call to God for help, and God raised him again into the air with the power of his word. God then spoke: "Let a stone rise from the bottom of the ocean!" When the stone appeared, Man seated himself upon it, but God asked him to dive under the water and bring land. Man brought earth in his hand and God scattered it on the surface of the water saying: "Let the world take shape!" Once more God asked Man to fetch earth. But Man then decided to take some for himself and brought a morsel in each hand. One handful he gave to God but the other he hid in his mouth, intending to create a world of his own. God threw the earth which the devil[a] had brought him beside the rest on the water, and the world at once began to expand and grow harder, but with the growing of the world the piece of earth in Man's mouth also swelled until he was about to suffocate so that he was again compelled to seek God's help. God inquired: "What was thy intention? Didst thou think thou couldst hide earth from me in thy mouth?" Man now told his secret intentions and at God's request spat the earth out of his mouth. Thus were formed the boggy places upon the earth.

---

[a]It appears that the devil and man are synonymous here.

HOPI CREATION MYTH

(Arizona)

In the beginning there was nothing but water everywhere, and two goddesses, both named Huruing Wuhti, lived in houses in the ocean, one of them in the east, and the other in the west; and these two by their efforts caused dry land to appear in the midst of the water. Nevertheless the sun, on his daily passage across the newly created earth, noticed that there was no living being of any kind on the face of the ground, and he brought this radical defect to the notice of the two deities. Accordingly the divinities met in consultation, the eastern goddess passing over the sea on the rainbow as a bridge to visit her western colleague. Having laid their heads together they resolved to make a little bird; so the goddess of the east made a wren of clay, and together they chanted an incantation over it, so that the bird soon came to life. Then they sent out the wren to fly over the world and see whether he could discover any living being on the face of the earth, but on his return he reported that no such being existed anywhere. Afterwards the two deities created many sorts of birds and beasts in like manner, and sent them forth to inhabit the world. Last of all the two goddesses made up their mind to create man. Thereupon the eastern goddess took clay and molded out of it first a woman and afterwards a man; and the clay man and woman were brought to life just as the birds and beasts had been so before them.

MICHOACAN CREATION MYTH

(Mexico)

The great god Tucapacha first made man and woman out of clay, but when the couple went to bathe in a river they absorbed so much water that the clay of which they were composed all fell to pieces. To remedy this inconvenience the Creator applied himself again to his task and molded them afresh out of ashes, but the result was again disappointing. At last, not to be baffled, he made them of metal. His perseverance was rewarded. The man and woman were now perfectly watertight; they bathed in the river without falling in pieces, and by their union they became the progenitors of mankind.

THE FOUR RACES OF MAN

(Greece)

In the beginning the Olympians under Kronos created the race of the Men of Gold. In those days men lived like gods in unalloyed happiness. They did not toil with their hands, for earth brought forth her fruits without their aid. They did not know the sorrows of old age, and death to them was like passing away in a calm sleep. After they had gone hence, their spirits were appointed to dwell above the earth, guarding and helping the living.

The gods next created the Men of Silver, but they could not be compared in virtue and happiness with the men of "the elder age of golden peace." For many years they remained mere children and as soon as they came to the full strength and statue of manhood they refused to do homage to the gods and fell to slaying one another. After death they became the good spirits who live within the earth.

The Men of Bronze followed, springing from ash trees and having hearts which were hard and jealous, so that with them "lust and strife began to gnaw the world." All the works of their hands were wrought in bronze. Through their own inventions they fell from their high estate and from the light they passed away to the dark realm of King Hades unhonored and unremembered.

Zeus then placed upon earth the race of the Heroes who fought at Thebes and Troy, and when they came to the end of life the Olympian sent them to happy abodes at the very limits of the earth.

After the Heroes came the Men of Iron — the race of these wild days. Our lot is labor and vexation of spirit by day and night, nor will this cease until the race ends, which will be when the order of nature has been reversed and human affection turned to hatred.

JUDEO-CHRISTIAN CREATION
GENESIS
CHAPTER 1

In the beginning God created the heaven and the earth.

2 And the earth was without form, and void; and darkness *was* upon the face of the deep. And the Spirit of God moved upon the face of the waters.

3 And God said, Let there be light: and there was light.

4 And God saw the light, that *it was* good: and God divided the light from the darkness.

5 And God called the light Day, and the darkness he called Night. And the evening and the morning were the first day.

6 And God said, Let there be a firmament in the midst of the waters, and let it divide the waters from the waters.

7 And God made the firmament, and divided the waters which *were* under the firmament from the waters which *were* above the firmament: and it was so.

8 And God called the firmament Heaven. And the evening and the morning were the second day.

9 And God said, Let the waters under the heaven be gathered together unto one place, and let the dry *land* appear: and it was so.

10 And God called the dry *land* Earth; and the gathering together of the waters called the Seas: and God saw that *it was* good.

11 And God said, Let the earth bring forth grass, the herb yielding seed, *and* the fruit tree yielding fruit after his kind, whose seed *is* in itself, upon the earth: and it was so.

12 And the earth brought forth grass, *and* herb yielding seed after his kind, and the tree yielding fruit, whose seed *was* in itself, after his kind: and God saw that *it was* good.

13 And the evening and the morning were the third day.

14 And God said, Let there be lights in the firmament of the heavens to divide the day from the night; and let them be for signs, and for seasons, and for days, and years: . . . .

AN EGYPTIAN GNOSTIC CREATION MYTH[b]

And the God laughed seven times. Ha-Ha-Ha-Ha-Ha-Ha-Ha. God laughed, and from these seven laughs seven Gods sprang up which embraced the whole universe; those were the first Gods.

When he first laughed, light appeared and its splendor shone through the whole universe. The God of the cosmos and of the fire. Then: BESSEN BERITHEN BERIO, which are magic words.

He laughed for the second time and everything was water; the earth heard the sound and saw the light and was astonished and moved, and so the moisture was divided into three and the God of the abyss appeared. The name is ESCHAKLEO: you are the OE, you are the eternal BETHELLE!

When the God wanted to laugh for the third time, bitterness came up in his mind and in his heart and it was called Hermes, through whom the whole universe is made manifest. But the one, the other Hermes, through whom the universe is ordered, remains within. He was called: SEMESILAMP. The first part of the name has to do with Shemesh, the sun, but the rest of the word is not explained.

Then the God laughed for the fifth time and while he was laughing he became sad and Moira (fate) appeared, holding the scales in her hand, showing that in her was justice. So you see justice comes from a state between laughing and sadness. But Hermes fought with Moira and said, "I am the just one!" While they were quarreling, God said to them, "Out of both of you justice will appear, everything should be submitted to you."

When the God laughed for the sixth time, he was terribly pleased and Chronos appeared with his sceptor, the sign of power, and God said to him that he should have the glory and the light, the sceptor of the ruler, and that everything present and future, would be submitted to him.

Then he laughed for the seventh time, drawing breath, and *while he was laughing he cried, and thus the soul came into being.* And God said, "Thou shalt move everything, and everything will be made happier through you. Hermes will lead you." When God said this, everything was set in motion and filled with breath.

When he saw the soul he bent down to the earth and whistled mightily and hearing this, the earth opened and gave birth to a being of herself. She

---

[b]This text has no exact date or origin. All that is known is that it comes from late antiquity, probably from Hellenized Egypt. The text begins with a list of angels and invocations to the godhead: "The first angel praises you in the language of birds, ARAI, ARAI. The sun praises you in the holy language LAILAM (Hebrew), with the same name." The 36-letter name means: "I go before you, I, the Sun, and it is through you that the sun boat comes up."

gave birth to a being of her own, the Pythic dragon, who knew everything ahead through the sound of the Godhead. And God called him ILLILU ILLILU ILLILU ITHOR, the shining one, PHOCHOPHOBOCH. When he appeared, the earth swelled up and the pole stood still and wished to explode. And God saw the dragon and was afraid and through his fright there came out Phobos (terror), full of weapons and so on.

SHILLUK CREATION MYTH

(*White Nile*)

The creator Juok molded all men out of earth, and . . . while he was engaged in the work of creation he wandered about the world. In the land of the whites he found a pure white earth or sand, and out of it he shaped white men. Then he came to the land of Egypt and out of the mud of the Nile he made red or brown men. Lastly, he came to the land of the Shilluks, and finding there black earth he created black men out of it. The way in which he modeled men was this. He took a lump of earth and said to himself, "I will make man, but he must be able to walk and run and go out into the fields, so I will give him two long legs, like the flamingo." Having done so, he thought again, "The man must be able to cultivate his millet, so I will give him two arms, one to hold the hoe, and the other to tear up the weeds." So he gave him two arms. Then he thought again, "The man must be able to see his millet, so I will give him two eyes." He did so accordingly. Next he thought to himself, "The man must be able to eat his millet, so I will give him a mouth." And a mouth he gave him accordingly. After that he thought within himself, "The man must be able to dance and speak and sing and shout, and for these purposes he must have a tongue." And a tongue he gave him accordingly. Lastly, the deity said to himself, "The man must be able to hear the noise of the dance and the speech of great men, and for that he needs two ears." So two ears he gave him, and sent him out into the world a perfect man.

KUMIS CREATION MYTH

(Eastern India)

God made the world and the trees and the creeping things first, and after that he made one man and one woman, forming their bodies of clay; but every night, when he had done his work, there came a great snake, which, while God was sleeping, devoured the two images. This happened twice or thrice, and God was at his wits' end, for he had to work all day and could not finish the pair in less than twelve hours; besides, if he did not sleep, "he would be no good," as the native narrator observed with some show of probability. So, as I have said, God was at his wits' end. But at last he got up early one morning and first made a dog and put life into it; and that night, when he had finished the images, he set the dog to watch them, and when the snake came, the dog barked and frightened it away. That is why to this day, when a man is dying, the dogs begin to howl; but the Kumis think that God sleeps heavily nowadays, or that the snake is bolder, for men die in spite of the howling of the dogs. If God did not sleep, there would be neither sickness nor death; it is during the hours of his slumber that the snake comes and carries us off.

BON PO AND TIBETAN CREATION MYTHS
Creating the Family of Man

There are on the earth three great families, and we are all of the great Tibetan family. This is what I have heard the Lamas say, who have studied the things of antiquity. At the beginning there was on the earth only a single man; he had neither house nor tent, for at that time the winter was not cold, and the summer was not hot; the wind did not blow so violently, and there fell neither snow nor rain; the tea grew of itself on the mountains, and the flocks had nothing to fear from beasts of prey. This man had three children, who lived a long time with him, nourishing themselves on milk and fruits. After having attained to a great age, this man died. The three children deliberated what they should do with the body of their father, and they could not agree about it; one wished to put him in a coffin, the other wanted to burn him, the third thought it would be best to expose the body on the summit of a mountain. They resolved then to divide it into three parts. The eldest had the body and arms; he was the ancestor of the great Chinese family, and that is why his descendents have become celebrated in arts and industry, and are remarkable for their tricks and stratagems. The second son had the breast; he was the father of the Tibetan family, and they are full of heart and courage, and do not fear death. From the third, who had inferior parts of the body, are descended the Tartars, who are simple and timid, without head or heart, and who know nothing but how to keep themselves firm in their saddles.

A CREATION MYTH
FROM NEW HEBRIDES

Taakeuta began, "Sir, I remember the voices of my fathers. Hearken to the words of Karongoa. . . ."

Naareau the Elder was the First of All. Not a man, not a beast, not a fish, not a thing was before him. He slept not, for there was no sleep; he ate not, for there was no hunger. He was in the Void. There was only Naareau sitting in the Void. Long he sat, and there was only he.

Then Naareau said in his heart, "I will make a woman." Behold! a woman grew out of the Void: Nei Teakea. He said again, "I will make a man." Behold! a man grew out of his thought: Na Atibu, the Rock. And Na Atibu lay with Nei Teakea. Behold! their child — even Naareau the Younger.

And Naareau the Elder said to Naareau the Younger, "All knowledge is whole in thee. I will make a thing for thee to work upon." So he made that thing in the Void. It was called the Darkness and the Cleaving Together; the sky and the earth and the sea were within it; but the sky and the earth clove together, and darkness was between them, for as yet there was no separation.

And when his work was done, Naareau the Elder said, "Enough! It is ready. I go, never to return." So he went, never to return, and no man knows where he abides now.

But Naareau the Younger walked on the overside of the sky that lay on the land. The sky was rock, and in some places it was rooted in the land, but in other places there were hollows between. A thought came into Naareau's heart; he said, "I will enter beneath it." He searched for a cleft wherein he might creep, but there was no cleft. He said again, "How, then, shall I enter? I will go with a spell." That was the First Spell. He knelt on the sky and began to tap it with his fingers, saying:

> Tap . . . tap, on heaven and its dwelling places.
> It is stone. What becomes of it? It echoes!
> It is rock. What becomes of it? It echoes!
> Open Sir Stone! Open, Sir Rock!
> It is open-o-o-o!

And at the third striking, the sky opened under his fingers. He said, "It is ready," and he looked down into the hollow place. It was black dark, and his ears heard the noise of breathing and snoring in the darkness. So he stood up and rubbed his fingertips together. Behold! the First Creature came out of them — even the Bat that he called Tiku-tiku-toumouma. And he said to the Bat, "Thou canst see in the darkness. Go before me and find what thou findest."

The Bat said, "I see people lying in this place." Naareau answered, "What are they like?" and the Bat said, "They move not; they say no word; they are all asleep." Naareau answered again, "It is the Company of Fools and Deaf Mutes. They are a Breed of Slaves. Tell me their names." Then the Bat settled on the forehead of each one as he lay in the darkness and called his name to Naareau: "This man is Uka the Blower. Here lies Naabawe the Sweeper. Behold! Karitoro the Roller-up. Now Kotekateka the Sitter. Kotei the Stander now — a great Multitude."

And when they were all named, Naareau said, "Enough. I will go in." So he crawled through the cleft and walked on the underside of the sky; and the Bat was his guide in the darkness. He stood among the Fools and Deaf Mutes and shouted, "Sirs, what are you doing?" None answered; only his voice came back out of the hollowness, "Sirs, what are you doing?" He said in his heart, "They are not yet in their right minds, but wait."

He went to a place in their midst; he shouted to them: "Move!" and they moved. He said again, "Move!" They set their hands against the underside of the sky. He said again, "Move!" They sat up; the sky was lifted a little. He said again, "Move! Stand!" They stood. He said again, "Higher!" But they answered, "How shall we lift it higher?" He made a beam of wood, saying, "Lift it on this." They did so. He said again, "Higher! Higher!" But they answered, "We can no more, we can no more, for the sky has roots in the land." So Naareau lifted up his voice and shouted, "Where are the Eel and the Turtle, the Octopus and the Great Ray?" The Fools and Deaf Mutes answered, "Alas! they are hidden away from the work." [Even then there were such people!] So he said, "Rest" and they rested; and he said to that one among them named Naabawe, "Go, call Riiki, the conger eel."

When Naabawe came to Riiki, he was coiled asleep with his wife, the short-tailed eel. Naabawe called him: he answered not, but lifted his head and bit him. Naabawe went back to Naareau, crying, "Alas! the conger eel bit me." So Naareau made a stick, with a slip-noose, saying, "We shall take him with this, if there is a bait to lure him." Then he called the Octopus from his hiding place: and the Octopus had ten arms. He struck off two arms and hung them on the stick as bait: therefore the octopus has only eight arms to this day. They took the lure to Riiki, and as they offered it to him, Naareau sang:

> Riiki of old, Riiki of old!
> Come hither, Riiki, thou mighty one;
> Leave thy wife, the short-tailed eel,

For thou shalt uproot the sky, thou shalt press down the depths.
Heave thyself up, Riiki, mighty and long,
Kingpost of the roof, prop up the sky and have done.
Have done, for the judgment is judged.

When Riiki heard the spell, he lifted up his head and the sleep went out of him. See him now! He puts forth his snout. He seizes the bait. Alas; they tighten the noose: he is fast caught, they haul him! he is dragged away from his wife the short-tailed eel, and Naareau is roaring and dancing. Yet pity him not, for the sky is ready to be lifted. The day of sundering has come.

Riiki said to Naareau, "What shall I do?" Naareau answered, "Lift up the sky on thy snout; press down the earth under thy tail." But when Riiki began to lift, the sky and the land groaned, and he said, "Perhaps they do not wish to be sundered." So Naareau lifted up his voice and sang:

Hark, hark how it groans, the Cleaving Together of old!
Speed between, Great Ray, slice it apart.
Hump thy back, Turtle, burst it apart.
Fling out thy arms, Octopus, tear it apart.
West, East, cut them away!
North, South, cut them away!
Lift, Riiki, lift, kingpost of the roof, prop of the sky.
It roars, it rumbles! Not yet, not yet is the Cleaving Together sundered.

When the Great Ray and the Turtle and the Octopus heard the words of Naareau, they began to tear at the roots of the sky that clung to the land. The Company of Fools and Deaf Mutes stood in the midst. They laughed; they shouted, "It moves! See how it moves!" And all that while Naareau was singing and Riiki pushing. He pushed up with his snout, he pushed down with his tail; the roots of the sky were torn from the earth; they snapped! The Cleaving Together was split asunder. Enough! Riiki straightened out his body; the sky stood high, the land sank, the Company of Fools and Deaf Mutes was left swimming in the sea.

But Naareau looked up at the sky and saw that there were no sides to it. He said, "Only I, Naareau, can pull down the sides of the sky." And he sang:

Behold I am seen in the West, it is West!
There is never a ghost, nor a land, nor a man;
There is only the Breed of the First Mother, and the
    First Father and the First Begetting;
There is only the First Naming of Names and the First
    Lying Together in the Void;

There is only the laying together of Na Atibu and Nei
  Teakea,
And we are flung down in the waters of the western sea.
It is West!

So also he sang in the east, and the north, and the south. He ran, he leaped, he flew, he was seen and gone again like the lightnings in the sides of heaven; and where he stayed, there he pulled down the side of the sky so that it was shaped like a bowl.

When that was done, he looked at the Company of Fools and Deaf Mutes, and saw that they were swimming in the sea. He said in his heart, "There shall be the First Land." He called to them, "Reach down, reach down-o-o! Clutch with your hands. Haul up the bedrock. Heave." ∎

QUESTIONS

Definition

What sort of definition of humanity would be developed out of myths that see people as created by animals?

Comparison

Surprising similarities exist among myths from many different areas. Discuss two or three significant similarities from among the myths you have read.

Contrast

Contrasts among myths indicate contrasts in views of people and the worlds in which they live. Discuss two or three significant differences from the myths you have read.

Cause-Effect

Myths continue to survive despite the nationalism of our age. What sociological and psychological factors are responsible for this tendency?

Cause-Effect (Definition/Process)

One scholar has suggested that our factual approach to the world is merely the creation of so-called scientific myths to replace the ancient irrational myths. How has this substitution affected our view of man and the world?

George Gaylord Simpson

The Future of Man and of Life

from *The Meaning of Evolution*

In the following excerpt from The Meaning of Evolution, *George Gaylord Simpson, a world-famous scientist, presents a synthesis of modern views of evolution. He states, in part, that "man has the power to modify . . . the direction of his own evolution."*

Man does broadly manipulate the environment and is learning how to do so more and more. He knows that evolution occurs and is fast learning exactly how it works. This must, if it continues, eventually make it possible for him to guide not only his own evolution but also that of any other organisms, if he so chooses. It is a decided possibility that he can really introduce finalism into organic evolution, which has conspicuously lacked a true goal in the past; the purpose and the end would, of course, be set and determined by man. He is rapidly coming to hold the power of life and death. He has casually caused the extinction of numerous other sorts of organisms and seems likely to devise means for causing extinction at will.

This awesome power includes the human prerogative of self-extinction. It is highly improbable that any organisms have ever become extinct as a result of their own activities alone and without some affliction unbidden and not determined wholly by their own natures. Man is probably quite capable of wiping himself out, or if he has not quite achieved the possibility as yet, he is making rapid progress in that direction.

If man does not exercise this, another of his unique capacities, or if in any case his extinction (ultimately inevitable) is long delayed, it is reasonably certain that he will evolve farther and will change more or less radically. It is hardly conceivable that even man's great powers will ever include the possibility of maintaining a frozen status quo in a changing universe. At present, in any case, cessation of human evolution is certainly not desirable or desired. By no standard of ethics whatever is human society now so good that any ethical man could wish it to persist unchanged or could fail to hope and to work for its improvement. On the biological side, few inhabitors of a human body can possibly think that it is perfect and that some change in it would not be highly desirable. Even those — movie stars, perhaps — who may think their own bodies incapable of improvement at the moment must deplore the approaching ravages of age and must, by the very contrast between themselves and others, perceive that the physical average for mankind needs changing. Whatever one may think of a possible future utopia in which man would be socially and biologically so perfect that any change would be for the worse, further human evolution now is obviously desirable provided, of course, that it is desirable in direction.

Man has the power to modify and within certain rather rigid limits to determine the direction of his own evolution. This power is increasing rapidly as knowledge of evolution increases. As regards biological evolution, this power has not as yet really been exercised systematically and consciously to any effective extent. Control of social evolution has also been much less in the past than it can be and is likely to be in the future, and has likewise been highly unsystematic and often not really conscious.

Invention by man of the new evolution, based on the inheritance of learning and worked out in social structures, has not eliminated in him the old organic evolution. The new evolution continues to interact with and in considerable measure to depend on the old. Guidance of the course of either will inevitably influence the other also, and can be most effective only by coordinated guidance of the two. This involves possible, although I think not necessary, conflict. Guidance of social evolution, to the extent that it is undertaken at all, necessarily follows some adopted ethical standards. That guidance becomes more difficult and its results slower if the ethical standards to be followed, like those discussed in the last chapter, hold that it is bad to impose regimentation or unnecessary compulsion on individuals.

The quickest and most effective guidance of biological evolution, too, could be achieved only by compulsion and therefore must here be held to be ethically bad. It is, nevertheless, possible for slower and less rigid but still, in the long run, effective guidance of both to be achieved in ways ethically good. It is each individual's responsibility to choose what he considers right directions for social and for biological evolution. With increase in knowledge and in its dissemination, there should eventually result sufficient unanimity on these points so that effective evolutionary motion would occur by voluntary individual actions. It is one of the known facts of organic evolution that a very minute incidence of natural selection will, under suitable circumstances, ultimately determine the direction of evolution. This involves the possibility that human evolution could be guided by united action of a small minority, although special conditions would be required for their action to become effective. It would, for instance, be ineffective if opposed by a different trend in the rest of the population, whether self-controlled or under the influence of natural selection only. It would be decisive if the direction of evolution were wholly random in the rest of the population or if it were about equally divided among different trends one of which coincided with that desired by the minority.

Under our ethics, the possibility of man's influencing the direction of his own evolution also involves his responsibility for doing so and for making that direction the best possible. Those ethics themselves define the best direction for social evolution. They also define in large measure the desirable directions for organic evolution, although the definition is indirect and less obvious.

The present organic structure of the human species is obviously consonant with far greater progress in the new evolution toward an ethical social ideal than has yet been achieved. Approach toward such an ideal must, however, also involve some physical evolutionary changes. Men differ greatly in intelligence, in temperament, and in various abilities that are in part, at least, hereditary. In some respects these differences are socially and ethically desirable. Differences in temperament are certainly desirable except for the relatively few temperaments that are incompatible with socially normal living. The good society would involve opportunities for the fullest development of every ethically good variety of temperament. Some differences in degree of intelligence may be desirable, but the point is debatable and in any case the raising of the average nearer to the present maximum is evidently desirable. Such changes as these would require provision of optimum environmental conditions, but could not be achieved by this means alone; genetic selection in the existing variability of the species would also be required. There is ample evidence that intelligence is if not strictly determined at least strictly limited as to potentialities by inheritance. Even temperament is apparently to some degree hereditary and correlated with physical structure, better knowledge of which would facilitate selection.[a]

Such changes, involving differences in distribution of existing characters within the human population, are evolutionary but they are of limited scope. Ultimate progress beyond these limits would necessarily involve the development of new characters in the human organism. Probably the new character most surely necessary for evolution beyond the present limits is an increase in intelligence above the existing maximum. Human progress depends on knowledge and learning, and the capacity for these is conditioned by intelligence. Most scientists are already aware that the progress of science is

---

[a]See, for instance, W. H. Sheldon, *The Varieties of Temperament* (New York and London, Harper, 1942). The evidence seems at present to be inconclusive and attempts to apply this knowledge now would be premature, but it does strongly suggest a future possibility.

being impeded by the fact that the most brilliant men simply do not have enough learning capacity to acquire all the details of more than increasingly narrow segments of the field of knowledge. Only a very stupid person can believe that mankind is already intelligent enough for its own good.

If and as it is achieved, this increase in intelligence will have other concomitants, among them a larger brain and changes to accommodate this, probably in the direction of making the adult more childlike in proportions.[b] Increase in length of life, besides corresponding with a nearly universal human desire, will also ultimately be necessary for intellectual and social progress, in order to allow for a longer juvenile learning period without subtracting from the period of adult life.

Many progressive changes which in other organisms would have to be physical, do not seem necessary or even desirable in man because they correspond with needs that he can supply more effectively and rapidly by technological means. There is no possible substitute for intelligence, but it can be greatly aided and supplemented. Organic development of new perceptual or, at least, sensory apparatus does not seem to be required for future human evolution. I am personally skeptical as to whether extrasensory perception, the other so-called psi phenomena, "group consciousness," and other such things dear to the hearts of many writers on the present and future of man really exist. Even if they do there is no reason to develop them because, as far as they might have any use, the same results can be achieved more fully and surely by mechanical means. It is, indeed, quite possible that development of such supposed phenomena would impede ethical progress.

The means of achieving biological evolutionary progress are already becoming clear, although it is doubtful whether we are yet ready to apply them well. The known avenues of such change are by environmental conditions of development, by selection, and by mutation (followed, of course, by selection). Control of environmental conditions is the only means now commonly in use and it is definitely advancing, although much remains to be done. It permits exploration of the full potentialities of the human organism in the way of healthier bodies, realization of more nearly the full life span, and so on, but it does not change those potentialities.[c]

---

[b]It is well known that man today resembles the young more than the adults of other higher primates. On this and other points pertinent to the present chapter, see Haldane's provocative paper, "Man's Evolution: Past and Future" (*Atlantic Monthly, 179* [1947], 45–51).

[c]"Control of environmental conditions" of course includes prevention and cure of internal diseases, proper diet, and other factors of health, as well as full and proper development of the mind and of social relationships.

Further steps, if and when taken, must involve selection, that is, some degree of control over differential reproduction. In principle this could be completely controlled by man, but even partially effective control is almost impossible in the present state of society and it is doubtful whether really full control could ever be exercised in an ethically good social system. The right to apply it must be voluntarily granted by the individuals concerned. Its effectiveness and the determination of the right direction in which to apply it will demand a great deal of knowledge that we do not now possess. Eugenics has deservedly been given a bad name by many sober students in recent years because of the prematurity of some eugenical claims and the stupidity of some of the postulates and enthusiasms of what had nearly become a cult. We are also still far too familiar with some of the supposedly eugenical practices of the Nazis and their like. The assumption that biological superiority is correlated with color of skin, with religious belief, with social status, or with success in business is imbecile in theory and vicious in practice. The almost equally naive, but less stupid and not especially vicious, idea that prevention of reproduction among persons with particular undesirable traits would quickly eradicate these traits in the population has also proved to be unfounded. The incidence of a few clearly harmful hereditary defects could be reduced by sterilization of the individuals possessing them, but they could not be wholly eliminated and in the light of present knowledge it is highly doubtful whether this means can produce any really noteworthy physical improvement in the human species as a whole.

Selection was, nevertheless, the means by which man arose and it is the means by which, if by any, his further organic evolution must be controlled. Man has so largely modified the impact of the sort of natural selection which produced him that desirable biological progression on this basis is not to be expected. There is no reason to believe that individuals with more desirable genetic characteristics now have more children than do those whose genetic factors are undesirable, and there is some reason to suspect the opposite. The present influence of natural selection on man is at least as likely to be retrogressive as progressive. Maintenance of something near the present biological level is probably about the best to be hoped for on this basis. The only proper possibility of progress seems to be in voluntary, positive social selection to produce in offspring new and improved genetic systems and to balance differential reproduction in favor of those having desirable genes and systems. As soon as we know what the desirable human genes and systems are and how to recognize them! The knowledge is now almost wholly lacking, but it seems practically certain that it is obtainable.

One thing that is definitely known now is that breeding for uniformity of type and for elimination of variability in the human species would be ethically, socially, and genetically bad and would not promote desirable evolution. This variability, with accompanying flexibility and capacity for individualization, is in itself ethically good, socially valuable, and evolutionarily desirable. It happens that the present human breeding structure is excellent for the promotion of adaptability and desirable variability and for control of evolution by selection. The theoretically ideal conditions in this respect involve a large population with wide genetic variety (reflected also in local polymorphism), divided into many relatively small, habitually interbreeding groups which are not, however, completely isolated but also have some gene interchange between them. This ideal is actually rather closely approached in the present breeding structure of the human species. Its continuance as a basis for effective selection and maintenance of desirable variability demands avoidance of both of two extremes. On one hand, a completely classless society or habitual general intermingling in marriage of all racial or other groups would be bad, from this point of view. On the other hand, effective segregation and prohibition of interbreeding between any two or more racial, religious, or other groups would be even worse.

Selection can in the long run make the most of the genetic factors now existing in the human species. Eventually its possibilities would be exhausted if there were not also new mutations. Mutations are known to occur in mankind at rates comparable to those in other animals and consistent with sustained evolution at moderate speed. Almost all of those known are disadvantageous and produce abnormalities definitely undesirable in present society and probably of no value for any desirable future development. We probably completely miss in study of human heredity the very small favorable mutations that are likely to exist and to be more frequent than these larger and generally unfavorable mutations. The ability to recognize these small mutations will be a necessary factor if man is to advance his own biological evolution by voluntary selection. At present we do not have the slightest idea as to how to produce to order the sort of mutation that may be needed or desired. We do not even know whether this is physically possible. If it is, and if man does discover the secret, then indeed evolution will pass fully into his control.

Now we cannot predict for sure whether the future course of human evolution will be upward or downward. We have, however, established the fact that it *can* be upward and we have a glimpse, although very far from full understanding, as to how to ensure this. It is our responsibility and that of our descendants to ensure that the future of the species is progressive and not retrogressive. The immediate tasks are to work for continuance of our species, for avoiding early self-extinction, settling ideological battles, and progressing toward an ethically good world state. The immediate means not only for these tremendous tasks but also for the future task of guiding human evolution lie within the ethic of knowledge. We need desperately to know more about ourselves, about our societies, about all of life, about the earth, and about the universe. We need to balance our knowledge better, to reverse the disparity in discovery in the physical, biological, and social sciences so that the social sciences shall be first and the physical last. We need to realize more fully and widely that technological advances and the invention and enjoyment of gadgets are not the most useful sort of knowledge and are relatively quite unimportant (occasionally downright harmful) for true human progress. We need to remember that cultural evolution proceeds only by interthinking, as organic evolution does only by interbreeding. The most brilliant of geniuses is an intellectual eunuch if his knowledge is not disseminated as widely as possible. It is immoral for any man, industry, or nation to reserve knowledge for its own advantage alone.

We need, too, to recognize the supreme importance of knowledge of organic and of social evolution. Such knowledge provides most of what we know of our place in the universe and it must guide us if we are to control the future evolution of mankind. ■

QUESTIONS

Definition

How would you define advancement in the human evolutionary process, and/or how would you define retrogression in the human evolutionary process?

Process

Trace the steps that might result in a human evolutionary decline, and/or trace the steps that would result in the advancement of the human evolutionary process.

Cause-Effect

Simpson states that man has the power of either "wiping himself out" or significantly improving his condition on earth. Considering your own sense of past and current history, can you hazard a guess as to whether the future course of human evolution will be upward or downward?

Robert Ardrey

Of Men and Mockingbirds

from *The Territorial Imperative*

Robert Ardrey, contemporary author and popularizer of certain evolutionary concepts, in the following excerpt from The Territorial Imperative *presents the thesis that man has retained and exercised a powerful animal instinct in securing and protecting the territory around him.*

A territory is an area of space, whether of water or earth or air, which an animal or group of animals defends as an exclusive preserve. The word is also used to describe the inward compulsion in animate beings to possess and defend such a space. A territorial species of animals, therefore, is one in which all males, and sometimes females too, bear an inherent drive to gain and defend an exclusive property.

In most but not all territorial species, defense is directed only against fellow members of the kind. A squirrel does not regard a mouse as a trespasser. In most but not all territorial species — not in chameleons, for example — the female is sexually unresponsive to an unpropertied male. As a general pattern of behavior, in territorial species the competition between males which we formerly believed was one for the possession of females is in truth for possession of property.

We may also say that in all territorial species, without exception, possession of a territory lends enhanced energy to the proprietor. Students of animal behavior cannot agree as to why this should be, but the challenger is almost invariably defeated, the intruder expelled. In part, there seems some mysterious flow of energy and resolve which invests a proprietor on his home grounds. But likewise, so marked is the inhibition lying on the intruder, so evident his sense of trespass, we may be permitted to wonder if in all territorial species there does not exist, more profound than simple learning, some universal recognition of territorial rights.

The concept of territory as a genetically determined form of behavior in many species is today accepted beyond question in the biological sciences. But so recently have our observations been made and our conclusions formed that we have yet to explore the implications of territory in our estimates of man. Is *Homo sapiens* a territorial species? Do we stake out property, chase off trespassers, defend our countries because we are sapient, or because we are animals? Because we choose, or because we must? Do certain laws of territorial behavior apply as rigorously in the affairs of men as in the affairs of chipmunks? That is the principal concern of this inquiry, and it is a matter of considerable concern, I believe, to any valid understanding of our nature. But it is a problem to be weighed in terms of present knowledge, not past.

How recently our information about animal territory has come to us is very well illustrated by reflections recorded only thirty years ago by the anthropologist Julian H. Steward, now of the University of Illinois. "Why are human beings the only animals having land-owning groups?" he wondered. And he brought together observations of twenty-four different hunting peoples so primitive that their ways differ little, in all probability, from the ways of paleolithic man. Their homes were isolated and far-spread — in Philippine and Congo forests, in Tasmania and Tierra del Fuego, in Canada's Mackenzie basin, in the Indian Ocean's Andaman Islands, in southwestern Africa's Kalahari Desert. So remote were they from each other that there seemed small likelihood that any one could have learned its ways from others. Yet all formed social bands occupying exclusive, permanent domains.

How could it be that such a number of peoples in such varying environments so remote from each other should all form similar social groups based on what would seem to be a human invention, the ownership of land? Steward came to a variety of conclusions, but one line of speculation was denied him. Even in 1936 he could not know that his assumption was false, since many animals form land-owning groups. Lions, eagles, wolves, great-horned owls are all hunters, and all guard exclusive hunting territories. The lions and wolves, besides, hunt in cooperative prides and packs differing little from the bands of primitive man. Ownership of land is scarcely a human invention, as our territorial propensity is something less than a human distinction.

Man, I shall attempt to demonstrate in this inquiry, is as much a territorial animal as is a mockingbird singing in the clear California night. We act as we do for reasons of our evolutionary past, not our cultural present, and our behavior is as much a mark of our species as is the shape of a human thigh bone or the configuration of nerves in a corner of the human brain. If we defend the title to our land or the sovereignty of our country, we do it for reasons no different, no less innate, no less ineradicable, than do lower animals. The dog barking at you from behind his master's fence acts for a motive indistinguishable from that of his master when the fence was built.

Neither are men and dogs and mockingbirds uncommon creatures in the natural world. Ring-tailed lemurs and great-crested grebes, prairie dogs, robins, tigers, muskrats, meadow warblers and Atlantic salmon, fence lizards, flat lizards, three-spined sticklebacks, nightingales and Norway rats, herring gulls and callicebus monkeys — all of us will give everything we are for a place of our own. Territory, in the evolving world of animals, is a force perhaps older than sex.

The survival value that territory brings to a species varies as widely as do the opportunities of species themselves. In some it offers security from the predator, in others security of food supply. In some its chief value seems the selection of worthy males for reproduction, in some the welding together of a group, and in many, like sea birds, the prime value seems simply the excitement and stimulation of border quarrels. And there are many species, of course, for which the territorial tie would be a handicap to survival. Grazing animals for the most part must move with the season's grass. Elephant herds acknowledge no territorial bond, but move like fleets of old gray galleons across the measureless African space. The gorilla, too, is a wanderer within a limited range who every night must build a new nest wherever his search for food may take him.

In those countless species, however, which through long evolutionary trial and error have come to incorporate a territorial pattern into their whole behavior complex, we shall find a remarkable uniformity. Widely unrelated though the species may be, a few distinct patterns are endlessly repeated. In the next chapter, for example, we shall examine arena behavior, in which solitary males defend mating stations to which females come solely for cop-ulation. It makes little difference whether the species be antelope or sage grouse, the pattern will be almost the same. And in the chapter after that we shall consider the pair territory, that portion of space occupied and defended by a breeding couple, as in robins and beavers and men. So we shall move along, surveying the territorial experience in the world of the animal as it has been observed by science in our generation.

It is information, all of it, which failed to enter your education and mine because it had not yet come to light. It is information, all of it, which yet fails to enter our children's textbooks or the processes of our own thought, through nothing but neglect. To me, this neglect seems a luxury which we cannot afford. Were we in a position to regard our knowledge of man as adequate in our negotiations with the human circumstance, and to look with satisfaction on our successful treatment of such human maladies as crime and war, racial antagonisms and social loneliness, then we might embrace the world of the animal simply to enjoy its intrinsic fascinations. But I find no evidence to support such self-satisfaction. And so this wealth of information concerning animal ways, placed before us by the new biology, must be regarded as a windfall in a time of human need.

If, as I believe, man's innumerable territorial expressions are human responses to an imperative lying with equal force on mockingbirds and men, then human self-estimate is due for radical revision. We acknowledge a few such almighty forces, but very few: the will to survive, the sexual impulse, the tie, perhaps, between mother and infant. It has been our inadequate knowledge of the natural world, I suggest, that has led us to look no further. And it may come to us as the strangest of thoughts that the bond between a man and the soil he walks on should be more powerful than his bond with the woman he sleeps with. Even so, in a rough, preliminary way we may test the supposition with a single question: How many men have you known of, in your lifetime, who died for their country? And how many for a woman?

Any force which may command us to act in opposition to the will to survive is a force to be inspected, at such a moment of history as ours, with the benefit of other than obsolete information. That I believe this force to be a portion of our evolutionary nature, a behavior pattern of such survival value to the emerging human being that it became fixed in our genetic endowment, just as the shape of our feet and the musculature of our buttocks became fixed, is the premise of this inquiry. Even as that behavior pattern called sex evolved in many organisms as nature's most effective answer to the problem of reproduction, so that behavior pattern called territory evolved in many organisms as a kind of defense mechanism, as nature's most effective answer to a variety of problems of survival.

I regard the territorial imperative as no less essential to the existence of contemporary man than it was to those bands of small-brained proto-men on the high African savannah millions of years ago. I see it as a force shaping our lives in countless unexpected ways, threatening our existence only to the degree that we fail to understand it. We can neither accept nor reject my premise, however, or even begin to explore its consequence, on any basis other than science's new knowledge of the animal in a state of nature. And since that knowledge has been acquired at the same time that radical changes have come to our understanding of evolution itself, we shall do well to defer until the next chapter our entrance to the field and our first specific inspection of territory. Before we inspect the behavior of the animal, let us inspect the behavior of that equally intriguing being, the scientist. ∎

QUESTIONS

Comparison/Contrast

Compare the behavior of two people you know who seem to be motivated by the so-called territorial imperative, or contrast the behavior of two people you know who you believe are markedly different in their need to secure and protect territory.

Process

Trace the steps in your upbringing that reflect either an exaggeration or a diminution of the territorial imperative.

Cause-Effect

Do you agree with Ardrey that humans, like other animals, secure and protect their territory through instinct rather than through learned behavior?

Process

Accepting Ardrey's definition of man's territorial imperative, can you say whether there are any methods that can be employed through which humanity can learn to live at peace?

Sigmund Freud

Life and Death Wishes

from *Civilization and Its Discontents*

Sigmund Freud, founder of psychoanalysis, wrote voluminously on the psychoanalytic technique, interpretation of dreams, and theories of sexuality. Another theory he developed later in his career in the book Civilization and Its Discontents *was that man has two basic opposing instincts, the life and death wishes.*

Starting from speculations on the beginning of life and from biological parallels, I drew the conclusion that, besides the instinct to preserve living substance and to join it into ever larger units, there must exist another, contrary instinct seeking to dissolve those units and to bring them back to their primaeval, inorganic state. That is to say, as well as Eros there was an instinct of death. The phenomena of life could be explained from the concurrent or mutually opposing action of these two instincts. It was not easy, however, to demonstrate the activities of this supposed death instinct. The manifestations of Eros were conspicuous and noisy enough. It might be assumed that the death instinct operated silently within the organism towards its dissolution, but that, of course, was no proof. A more fruitful idea was that a portion of the instinct is diverted towards the external world and comes to light as an instinct of aggressiveness and destructiveness. In this way the instinct itself could be pressed into the service of Eros, in that the organism was destroying some other thing, whether animate or inanimate, instead of destroying its own self. Conversely, any restriction of this aggressiveness directed outwards would be bound to increase the self-destruction, which is in any case proceeding. At the same time one can suspect from this example that the two kinds of instinct seldom — perhaps never — appear in isolation from each other, but are alloyed with each other in varying and very different proportions and so become unrecognizable to our judgement. In sadism, long since known to us as a component instinct of sexuality, we should have before us a particularly strong alloy of this kind between trends of love and the destructive instinct; while its counterpart, masochism, would be a union between destructiveness directed inwards and sexuality — a union which makes what is otherwise an imperceptible trend into a conspicuous and tangible one.

The assumption of the existence of an instinct of death or destruction has met with resistance even in analytic circles; I am aware that there is a frequent inclination rather to ascribe whatever is dangerous and hostile in love to an original bipolarity in its own nature. To begin with it was only tentatively that I put forward the views I have developed here, but in the course of time they have gained such a hold upon me that I can no longer think in any other way. To my mind, they are far more serviceable from a theoretical standpoint than any other possible ones; they provide that simplification, without either ignoring or doing violence to the facts, for which we strive in scientific work. I know that in sadism and masochism we have always seen before us manifestations of the destructive instinct (directed outwards and inwards), strongly alloyed with erotism; but I can no longer understand how we can have overlooked the ubiquity of non-erotic aggressivity and destructiveness and can have failed to give it its due place in our interpretation of life. (The desire for destruction when it is directed *inwards* mostly eludes our perception, of course, unless it is tinged with erotism.) I remember my own defensive attitude when the idea of an instinct of destruction first emerged in psycho-analytic literature, and how long it took before I became receptive to it. That others should have shown, and still show, the same attitude of rejection surprises me less. For 'little children do not like it' when there is talk of the inborn human inclination to 'badness,' to aggressiveness and destructiveness, and so to cruelty as well. God has made them in the image of His own perfection; nobody wants to be reminded how hard it is to reconcile the undeniable existence of evil — despite the protestations of Christian Science — with His all-powerfulness or His all-goodness. The Devil would be the best way out as an excuse for God; in that way he would be playing the same part as an agent of economic discharge as the Jew does in the world of the Aryan ideal. But even so, one can hold God responsible for the existence of the Devil just as well as for the existence of the wickedness which the Devil embodies. In view of these difficulties, each of us will be well advised, on some suitable occasion, to make a low bow to the deeply moral nature of mankind; it will help us to be generally popular and much will be forgiven us for it.

In all that follows I adopt the standpoint, therefore, that the inclination to aggression is an original, self-subsisting instinctual disposition in man, and I return to my view that it constitutes the greatest impediment to civilization. At one point in the course of this enquiry I was led to the idea that civilization was a special process which mankind undergoes, and I am still under the influence of that idea. I may now add that civilization is a process in the service of Eros, whose purpose is to combine single human individuals, and after that families, then races, peoples and nations, into one great unity, the unity of mankind. Why this has to happen, we do not know; the work of Eros is precisely this. These collections of men are to be libidinally bound to one another. Necessity alone, the advantages of work in common, will not hold them together. But man's natural aggressive instinct, the hostility of each against all and of all against each, opposes this programme of civilization. This aggressive instinct is the derivative and the main representative of the death instinct which we have found alongside of Eros and which shares world-dominion with it. And now, I think, the meaning of the evolution of civilization is no longer obscure to us. It must present the struggle between Eros and Death, between the instinct of life and the instinct of destruction, as it works itself out in the human species. This struggle is what all life essentially consists of, and the evolution of civilization may therefore be simply described as the struggle for life of the human species. And it is this battle of the giants that our nurse-maids try to appease with their lullaby about Heaven. ■

QUESTIONS

Cause-Effect

Examine one or two difficult periods in your life and determine to what extent the life and/or death wish was operative in your behavior.

Comparison/Contrast

Examine two couples that you know well and compare and/or contrast their relationship in light of Freud's theory of the life and death wish.

Cause-Effect

Do you think that a buildup of a military arsenal is an expression of the life wish, the death wish, or both?

Process

Discuss the steps through which an understanding of Freud's theory of the life and death wish could lead to a better world.

Henry David Thoreau

Spiritual and Temporal Values

from *Walden, of Life in the Woods*

Henry David Thoreau, nineteenth-century American essayist and poet, wrote Walden, of Life in the Woods *(1854), in which he examines man's spiritual and temporal values. This excerpt discusses the tendency of people to become so involved in the pressures of daily existence that life's "finer fruits cannot be plucked by them."*

Most men, even in this comparatively free country, through mere ignorance and mistake, are so occupied with the factitious cares and superfluously coarse labors of life that its finer fruits cannot be plucked by them. Their fingers, from excessive toil, are too clumsy and tremble too much for that. Actually, the laboring man has not leisure for a true integrity day by day; he cannot afford to sustain the manliest relations to men; his labor would be depreciated in the market. He has no time to be any thing but a machine. How can he remember well his ignorance — which his growth requires — who has so often to use his knowledge? We should feed and clothe him gratuitously sometimes, and recruit him with our cordials, before we judge of him. The finest qualities of our nature, like the bloom on fruits, can be preserved only by the most delicate handling. Yet we do not treat ourselves nor one another thus tenderly.

Some of you, we all know, are poor, find it hard to live, are sometimes, as it were, gasping for breath. I have no doubt that some of you who read this book are unable to pay for all the dinners which you have actually eaten, or for the coats and shoes which are fast wearing or are already worn out, and have come to this page to spend borrowed or stolen time, robbing your creditors of an hour. It is very evident what mean and sneaking lives many of you live, for my sight has been whetted by experience; always on the limits, trying to get into business and trying to get out of debt, a very ancient slough, called by the Latins *æs alienum*, another's brass, for some of their coins were made of brass; still living, and dying, and buried by this other's brass; always promising to pay, promising to pay, to-morrow, and dying to-day, insolvent; seeking to curry favor, to get custom, by how many modes, only not state-prison offences; lying, flattering, voting, contracting yourselves into a nutshell of civility, or dilating into an atmosphere of thin and vaporous generosity, that you may persuade your neighbor to let you make his shoes, or his hat, or his coat, or his carriage, or import his groceries for him; making yourselves sick, that you may lay up something against a sick day, something to be tucked away in an old chest, or in a stocking behind the plastering, or, more safely, in the brick bank; no matter where, no matter how much or how little.

The mass of men lead lives of quiet desperation. What is called resignation is confirmed desperation. From the desperate city you go into the desperate country, and have to console yourself with the bravery of minks and muskrats. A stereotyped but unconscious despair is concealed even under what are called the games and amusements of mankind. There is no play in them, for this comes after work. But it is a characteristic of wisdom not to do desperate things.

When we consider what, to use the words of the catechism, is the chief end of man, and what are the true necessaries and means of life, it appears as if men had deliberately chosen the common mode of living because they preferred it to any other. Yet they honestly think there is no choice left. But alert and healthy natures remember that the sun rose clear. It is never too late to give up our prejudices. No way of thinking or doing, however ancient, can be trusted without proof. What every body echoes or in silence passes by as true to-day may turn out to be falsehood to-morrow, mere smoke of opinion, which some had trusted for a cloud that would sprinkle fertilizing rain on their fields. What old people say you cannot do you try and find that you can. Old deeds for old people, and new deeds for new. Old people did not know enough once, perchance, to fetch fresh fuel to keep the fire a-going; new people put a little dry wood under a pot, and are whirled round the globe with the speed of birds, in a way to kill old people, as the phrase is. Age is no better, hardly so well, qualified for an instructor as youth, for it has not profited so much as it has lost. One may almost doubt if the wisest man has learned any thing of absolute value by living. Practically, the old have no very important advice to give the young, their own experience has been so partial, and their lives have been such miserable failures, for private reasons, as they must believe; and it may be that they have some faith left which belies that experience, and they are only less young than they were. I have lived some thirty years on this planet, and I have yet to hear the first syllable of valuable or even earnest advice from my seniors. They have told me nothing, and probably cannot tell me any thing, to the purpose. Here is life, an experiment to a great extent untried by me; but it does not avail me that they have tried it. If I have any experience which I think valuable, I am sure to reflect that this my Mentors said nothing about.

In any weather, at any hour of the day or night, I have been anxious to improve the nick of time, and notch it on my stick too; to stand on the meeting of two eternities, the past and future, which is precisely the present moment; to toe that line. You will pardon some obscurities, for there are more secrets in my trade than in most men's, and yet not voluntarily kept, but inseparable from its very nature. I would gladly tell all that I know about it, and never paint "No Admittance" on my gate.

• • •

For more than five years I maintained myself thus solely by the labor of my hands, and I found, that by working about six weeks in a year, I could meet all the expenses of living. The whole of my winters, as well as most of my summers, I had free and clear for study. I have thoroughly tried school-keeping, and found that my expenses were in proportion, or rather out of proportion, to my income, for I was obliged to dress and train, not to say think and believe, accordingly, and I lost my time into the bargain. As I did not teach for the good of my fellow-men, but simply for a livelihood, this was a failure. I have tried trade; but I found that it would take ten years to get under way in that, and that then I should probably be on my way to the devil.

• • •

In short, I am convinced, both by faith and experience, that to maintain one's self on this earth is not a hardship but a pastime, if we will live simply and wisely; as the pursuits of the simpler nations are still the sports of the more artificial. It is not necessary that a man should earn his living by the sweat of his brow, unless he sweats easier than I do.

• • •

Men think that it is essential that the *Nation* have commerce, and export ice, and talk through a telegraph, and ride thirty miles an hour, without a doubt, whether *they* do or not; but whether we should live like baboons or like men, is a little uncertain. If we do not get out sleepers, and forge rails, and devote days and nights to the work, but go to tinkering upon our *lives* to improve *them*, who will build railroads? And if railroads are not built, how shall we get to heaven in season? But if we stay at home and mind our business, who will want railroads? We do not ride on the railroad; it rides upon us. Did you ever think what those sleepers are that underlie the railroad? Each one is a man, an Irishman, or a Yankee man. The rails are laid on them, and they are covered with sand, and the cars run smoothly over them. They are sound sleepers, I assure you. And every few years a new lot is laid down and run over; so that, if some have the pleasure of riding on a rail, others have the misfortune to be ridden upon. And when they run over a man that is walking in his sleep, a supernumerary sleeper in the wrong position, and wake him up, they suddenly stop the cars, and make a hue and cry about it, as if this were an exception. I am glad to know that it takes a gang of men for every five miles to keep the sleepers down and level in their beds as it is, for this is a sign that they may sometime get up again.

Why should we live with such hurry and waste of life? We are determined to be starved before we are hungry. Men say that a stitch in time saves nine, and so they take a thousand stitches to-day to save nine to-morrow. As for *work*, we haven't any of any consequence. We have the Saint Vitus' dance, and cannot possibly keep our heads still. If I should only give a few pulls at the parish bell-rope, as for a fire, that is, without setting the bell, there is hardly a man on his farm in the outskirts of Concord, notwithstanding that press of engagements which was his excuse so many times this morning, nor a boy, nor a woman, I might almost say, but would forsake all and follow that sound, not mainly to save property from the flames, but, if we will confess the truth, much more to see it burn, since burn it must, and we, be it known, did not set it on fire, — or to see it put out, and have a hand in it, if that is done as handsomely; yes, even if it were the parish church itself. Hardly a man takes a half hour's nap after dinner, but when he wakes he holds up his head and asks, "What's the news?" as if the rest of mankind had stood his sentinels. Some give directions to be waked every half hour, doubtless for no other purpose; and then, to pay for it, they tell what they have dreamed. After a night's sleep the news is as indispensable as the breakfast. "Pray tell me any thing new that has happened to a man any where on this globe," — and he reads it over his coffee and rolls, that a man has had his eyes gouged out this morning on the Wachito River; never dreaming the while that he lives in the dark unfathomed mammoth cave of this world, and has but the rudiment of an eye himself. ∎

QUESTIONS

Definition

What is Thoreau's concept of man's connection with nature? Provide examples that would illustrate this.

Comparison/Contrast

Compare and/or contrast your reactions when you are in close contact with nature to your reactions when you are engaged in the busyness of daily life.

Cause-Effect

Thoreau believes that "the mass of men lead lives of quiet desperation." Is this an accurate evaluation of humanity? Why, or why not?

Cause-Effect

Many writers, unlike Thoreau, believe that the city is the pinnacle of civilization. Do you see the city as the best place for the expression of man's nature, or as a place where man's best characteristics are destroyed? Or do you see the city as doing both?

Cause-Effect

Is it possible for us to live in society according to Thoreau's precepts?

Jean Paul Sartre

Existentialism (excerpt)

Jean Paul Sartre, twentieth-century French philosopher, wrote Existentialism *(1946) in which he presented the idea that "existence precedes essence," meaning that there are no prescribed beliefs or ways to live. The human being, Sartre believes, is thrust into the world free to define himself.*

What is meant here by saying that existence precedes essence? It means that, first of all, man exists, turns up, appears on the scene, and, only afterwards, defines himself. If man, as the existentialist conceives him, is indefinable, it is because at first he is nothing. Only afterward will he be something, and he himself will have made what he will be. Thus, there is no human nature, since there is no God to conceive it. Not only is man what he conceives himself to be, but he is also only what he wills himself to be after this thrust toward existence.

Man is nothing else but what he makes of himself. Such is the first principle of existentialism. It is also what is called subjectivity, the name we are labeled with when charges are brought against us. But what do we mean by this, if not that man has a greater dignity than a stone or table? For we mean that man first exists, that is, that man first of all is the being who hurls himself toward a future and who is conscious of imagining himself as being in the future. Man is at the start a plan which is aware of itself, rather than a patch of moss, a piece of garbage, or a cauliflower; nothing exists prior to this plan; there is nothing in heaven; man will be what he will have planned to be. Not what he will want to be. Because by the word "will" we generally mean a conscious decision, which is subsequent to what we have already made of ourselves. I may want to belong to a political party, write a book, get married; but all that is only a manifestation of an earlier, more spontaneous choice that is called "will." But if existence really does precede essence, man is responsible for what he is. Thus, existentialism's first move is to make every man aware of what he is and to make the full responsibility of his existence rest on him. And when we say that a man is responsible for himself, we do not only mean that he is responsible for his own individuality, but that he is responsible for all men.

The word subjectivism has two meanings, and our opponents play on the two. Subjectivism means, on the one hand, that an individual chooses and makes himself; and, on the other, that it is impossible for man to transcend human subjectivity. The second of these is the essential meaning of existentialism. When we say that man chooses his own self, we mean that every one of us does likewise; but we also mean by that that in making this choice he also chooses all men. In fact, in creating the man that we want to be, there is not a single one of our acts which does not at the same time create an image of man as we think he ought to be. To choose to be this or that is to affirm at the same time the value of what we choose, because we can never choose evil. We always choose the good, and nothing can be good for us without being good for all.

If, on the other hand, existence precedes essence, and if we grant that we exist and fashion our image at one and the same time, the image is valid for everybody and for our whole age. Thus, our responsibility is much greater than we might have supposed, because it involves all mankind. If I am a workingman and choose to join a Christian trade-union rather than be a communist, and if by being a member I want to show that the best thing for man is resignation, that the kingdom of man is not of this world, I am not only involving my own case — I want to be resigned for everyone. As a result, my action has involved all humanity. To take a more individual matter, if I want to marry, to have children; even if this marriage depends solely on my own circumstances or passion or wish, I am involving all humanity in monogamy and not merely myself. Therefore, I am responsible for myself and for everyone else. I am creating a certain image of man of my own choosing. In choosing myself, I choose man.

This helps us understand what the actual content is of such rather grandiloquent words as anguish, forlornness, despair. As you will see, it's all quite simple.

First, what is meant by anguish? The existentialists say at once that man is anguish. What that means is this: the man who involves himself and who realizes that he is not only the person he chooses to be, but also a law-maker who is, at the same time, choosing all mankind as well as himself, can not help escape the feeling of his total and deep responsibility. Of course, there are many people who are not anxious; but we claim that they are hiding their anxiety, that they are fleeing from it. Certainly, many people believe that when they do something, they themselves are the only ones involved, and when someone says to them, "What if everyone acted that way?" they shrug their shoulders and answer, "Everyone doesn't act that way." But really, one should always ask himself, "What would happen if everybody looked at things that way?" There is no escaping this disturbing thought except by a kind of double-dealing. A man who lies and makes excuses for himself by saying "not everybody does that," is someone with an uneasy conscience, because the act of lying implies that a universal value is conferred upon the lie.

Anguish is evident even when it conceals itself. This is the anguish that Kierkegaard called the anguish of Abraham. You know the story: an angel has ordered Abraham to sacrifice his son; if it really were an angel who has come and said, "You are Abraham, you shall sacrifice your son," everything would be all right. But everyone might first wonder, "Is it really an angel, and am I really Abraham? What proof do I have?"

The existentialist does not think that man is going to help himself by finding in the world some omen by which to orient himself. Because he thinks that man will interpret the omen to suit himself. Therefore, he thinks that man, with no support and no aid, is condemned every moment to invent man. Ponge, in a very fine article, has said, "Man is the future of man." That's exactly it. But if it is taken to mean that this future is recorded in heaven, that God sees it, then it is false, because it would really no longer be a future. If it is taken to mean that, whatever a man may be, there is a future to be forged, a virgin future before him, then this remark is sound. But then we are forlorn.

To give you an example which will enable you to understand forlornness better, I shall cite the case of one of my students who came to see me under the following circumstances: his father was on bad terms with his mother, and, moreover, was inclined to be a collaborationist; his older brother had been killed in the German offensive of 1940, and the young man, with somewhat immature but generous feelings, wanted to avenge him. His mother lived alone with him, very much upset by the half-treason of her husband and the death of her older son; the boy was her only consolation.

The boy was faced with the choice of leaving for England and joining the Free French Forces — that is, leaving his mother behind — or remaining with his mother and helping her to carry on. He was fully aware that the woman lived only for him and that his going-off — and perhaps his death — would plunge her into despair. He was also aware that every act that he did for his mother's sake was a sure thing, in the sense that it was helping her to carry on, whereas every effort he made toward going off and fighting was an uncertain move which might run aground and prove completely useless; for example, on his way to England he might, while passing through Spain, be detained indefinitely in a Spanish camp; he might reach England or Algiers and be stuck in an office at a desk job. As a result, he was faced with two very different kinds of action: one, concrete, immediate, but concerning only one individual; the other concerned an incomparably vaster group, a national collectivity, but for that very reason was dubious, and might be interrupted en route. And, at the same time, he was wavering between two kinds of ethics. On the one hand, an ethics of sympathy, of personal devotion; on the other, a broader ethics, but one whose efficacy was more dubious. He had to choose between the two.

Who could help him choose? Christian doctrine? No. Christian doctrine says, "Be charitable, love your neighbor, take the more rugged path, etc., etc." But which is the more rugged path? Whom should he love as a brother? The fighting man or his mother? Which does the greater good, the vague act of fighting in a group, or the concrete one of helping a particular human being to go on living? Who can decide *a priori*? Nobody. No book of ethics can tell him. The Kantian ethics says, "Never treat any person as a means, but as an end." Very well, if I stay with my mother, I'll treat her as an end and not as a means; but by virtue of this very fact, I'm running the risk of treating the people around me who are fighting, as means; and, conversely, if I go to join those who are fighting, I'll be treating them as an end, and, by doing that, I run the risk of treating my mother as a means.

If values are vague, and if they are always too broad for the concrete and specific case that we are considering, the only thing left for us is to trust our instincts. That's what this young man tried to do; and when I saw him, he said, "In the end, feeling is what counts. I ought to choose whichever pushes me in one direction. If I feel that I love my mother enough to sacrifice everything else for her — my desire for vengeance, for action, for adventure — then I'll stay with her. If, on the contrary, I feel that my love for my mother isn't enough, I'll leave." ∎

QUESTIONS

Definition

What is meant by Sartre's term *existence*?

Comparison/Contrast

What comparisons can be made between the ethical elements of Sartre's philosophy and the ethical elements in traditional religions?

Cause-Effect

Would you rather believe in a reality with a prescribed set of beliefs, or in a reality such as Sartre describes? Why, or why not?

Perry LeFevre

Martin Buber and the Twofold Nature of Man

from *Understandings of Man*

Martin Buber, twentieth-century Jewish theologian, wrote I and Thou *(1923), espousing a belief in a twofold nature of man, who experiences himself and the world in two basic ways: the I-Thou, in which man relates to others as people, and the I-It, in which man relates to others as objects. The following excerpt is an explanation of Buber's ideas from Perry LeFevre's* Understanding of Man.

The reader of Martin Buber's classic work *I and Thou* will surely notice a difference in tone and direction in comparison with the work of our other authors. Buber, though he does not neglect the negative side of the human situation, seems much more interested in exploring the positive constructive dimensions of human experience. In this work he introduced the fundamental insight that permeates all his later work. This insight is that a man may be oriented to his world — to nature, to man, and to the products of human creativity — in two basic ways. The crucial question in individual life and in culture is which of these orientations will be dominant and controlling. Both are important and necessary for human fulfillment; but if one is dominant, human life will be impoverished; if the other is dominant, the fully human life becomes possible.

I. THE TWO BASIC ATTITUDES OR ORIENTATIONS

The two basic attitudes that one may take to what is other than himself Buber called *I-Thou* and *I-It*. An individual may regard the other as a "Thou" or as an "It." These are the crucial distinctions in Buber's understanding of man, and they lead to his further distinction between a life of monologue and a life of dialogue.

Perhaps the easiest way to get at the meaning of Buber's distinction is to look at your own experiences. How have you been treated by other individuals? Have you sometimes been treated as a thing and sometimes as a person? The first kind of treatment would belong to Buber's I-It dimension, the second to the I-Thou. A high school student once explained the difference in these terms: "My mother treats my dog like a dirty old shoe that gets in her way. I treat him like a member of the family."

Buber, of course, went much farther than pointing to the distinction. He analyzed it, showing the important differences between the two ways of addressing or responding to the other. For example, when I treat the other as an It, the relationship might be described as that of a subject to an object. The other is an object to me. This means, says Buber, that what happens in such a relationship really happens within me. I have the relationship, so to say, in my control, in my experience. I can ignore what I want to about the other. I control whatever of myself I let enter into the relationship. I may only be interested in the other with a part of my being — what I *see* in him, or what I *will* for him, or what I *think* about him. He is for my experience and my use. I act toward him with a part of my being and I am interested in only a part of his being. Furthermore, the relationship is one way — it goes out from me to him.

In the case of an I-Thou relationship I am related as a subject to a subject, as a person to a person. What happens in the relationship is not in me, or in him; it is in the "between." Further, the relationship is not one-way — it is mutual. I enter the relationship with the whole of my being and relate to the whole of his being. The experience is not just mine, it is "ours." I am not interested in "using" the other; the relationship is for itself.

Though the "I" is one of the poles in each of the relationships, for Buber they are really different kinds of "I." The I of the I-It relationship he calls the I of individuality. The I of the I-Thou relationship he calls the I of personality. Individuality makes its appearance simply by being differentiated from other individualities. A person comes into being, however, by entering into relations with other persons. Every man is both kinds of I. A man is more or less personal. Buber illustrated the difference by pointing to the kind of "I" that Jesus and Socrates were, in contrast to the kind of "I" that Napoleon possessed.

II. THE TWO CONSEQUENT WAYS
OF HUMAN LIFE

Depending upon which of the basic orientations to the other is dominant, a man leads a life of *monologue* or of *dialogue*. One of the elements in this contrast is the distinction between what Buber called "seeming" and "being." In dialogue the relationship proceeds from what one truly is. It is a relationship of "being." In monologue there is pretension and hypocrisy. One is interested in the impression he is giving to the other of what he is. In relationships of seeming the individual is concerned with the image the other is getting of him; he therefore contrives his looks, his speech, to create the image he wants the other to have. Here interaction is one of appearances. The individuals are not communicating their real being.

Another distinction important for differentiating monologue from genuine dialogue is that which Buber draws between the role of the propagandist and the educator. A relationship in which one tries to impose himself, his opinion, and his attitude on the other, even if he wants the other to think the result is really his own, represents the role of the propagandist. The kind of manipulation that is that of the advertiser or the salesman or the politician stands in the way of genuine dialogue. The attitude and action of the true educator is different. He too wants to affect the other, but he wants to do this by helping the other to unfold something that is really there in the being of the other. "He cannot wish to impose himself, for he believes in the effect of the actualizing forces — that is, he believes that in every man what is right is established in a single and uniquely personal way." Not imposition, but unfolding is the mark of dialogue.

In genuine dialogue I try to overcome the inadequacy of my perception of the other one. I try "to make him present." For Buber this means that one must regard the other as *the very one he is*. I try to become aware of him as different, essentially different, in the definite and unique way that is peculiar to him. And in so doing I *accept* him in his difference. I affirm him. I *confirm* him, even though I may think him wrong. I accept him for what he is and affirm his freedom to become what he would become.

All of this implies a heightening of the awareness of the other. I must try to experience him as a whole in his concreteness. This kind of awareness runs counter to an analytical dissection of the other. I do not try to reduce the other to an abstraction ("He is a neurotic") or to a stereotype ("He is a Jew"). Rather, I try to be aware of just this individual in his uniqueness and concreteness. The only way this can be done is through a cultivation of sensitivity to the other and through the use of one's imagination to "go over to the other side" and to put oneself in the other's place and see and feel the world from his perspective.

For genuine dialogue one must not only make the other present; one must be fully present in the relationship oneself. One must not hold a part of himself back from the relationship. One must be willing to express oneself without reserve. This does not mean, I think, that one always says everything; but dialogue is a relationship in which one is *willing* to be completely open. Sometimes silence itself is an important part of genuine dialogue. In dialogue the partners genuinely speak to each other; they intend to share out of the depths of their own being. In monologue, men talk past each other; they are centered in themselves, not in the relationship. ∎

QUESTIONS

Comparison/Contrast

Illustrate with personal experience and/or your observations of others the differences between the two basic attitudes (I-Thou, I-It) that Buber defines.

Cause-Effect

Is it possible to live a meaningful life in "dialogue" (I-Thou) in our modern society?

Cause-Effect (Definition)

Buber defines man by two kinds of primary relationships: I-Thou and I-It. Do you accept this distinction? Are there other significant ones?

Hannah Arendt

The Human Condition (excerpt)

from *The Human Condition*

Hannah Arendt, twentieth-century political theorist, in The Human Condition *reaffirms the three modes of man's "earthly" nature: "labor," our effort to continue the biological process of life; "work," our artificial remaking of the natural world of things; and "action," our relationship with other people.*

FROM THE PROLOGUE

In 1957, an earth-born object made by man was launched into the universe, where for some weeks it circled the earth according to the same laws of gravitation that swing and keep in motion the celestial bodies — the sun, the moon, and the stars. To be sure, the man-made satellite was no moon or star, no heavenly body which could follow its circling path for a time span that to us mortals, bound by earthly time, lasts from eternity to eternity. Yet, for a time it managed to stay in the skies; it dwelt and moved in the proximity of the heavenly bodies as though it had been admitted tentatively to their sublime company.

This event, second in importance to no other, not even to the splitting of the atom, would have been greeted with unmitigated joy if it had not been for the uncomfortable military and political circumstances attending it. But, curiously enough, this joy was not triumphal; it was not pride or awe at the tremendousness of human power and mastery which filled the hearts of men, who now, when they looked up from the earth toward the skies, could behold there a thing of their own making. The immediate reaction, expressed on the spur of the moment, was relief about the first "step toward escape from men's imprisonment to the earth." And this strange statement, far from being the accidental slip of some American reporter, unwittingly echoed the extraordinary line which, more than twenty years ago, had been carved on the funeral obelisk for one of Russia's great scientists: "Mankind will not remain bound to the earth forever."

Such feelings have been commonplace for some time. They show that men everywhere are by no means slow to catch up and adjust to scientific discoveries and technical developments, but that, on the contrary, they have outsped them by decades. Here, as in other respects, science has realized and affirmed what men anticipated in dreams that were neither wild nor idle. What is new is only that one of this country's most respectable newspapers finally brought to its front page what up to then had been buried in the highly non-respectable literature of science fiction (to which, unfortunately, nobody yet has paid the attention it deserves as a vehicle of mass sentiments and mass desires). The banality of the statement should not make us overlook how extraordinary in fact it was; for although Christians have spoken of the earth as a vale of tears and philosophers have looked upon their body as a prison of mind or soul, nobody in the history of mankind has ever conceived of the earth as a prison for men's bodies or shown such eagerness to go literally from here to the moon. Should the emancipation and secularization of the modern age, which began with a turning-away, not necessarily from God, but from a god who was the Father of men in heaven, end with an even more fateful repudiation of an Earth who was the Mother of all living creatures under the sky?

The earth is the very quintessence of the human condition, and earthly nature, for all we know, may be unique in the universe in providing human beings with a habitat in which they can move and breathe without effort and without artifice. The human artifice of the world separates human existence from all mere animal environment, but life itself is outside this artificial world, and through life man remains related to all other living organisms. For some time now, a great many scientific endeavors have been directed toward making life also "artificial," toward cutting the last tie through which even man belongs among the children of nature. It is the same desire to escape from imprisonment to the earth that is manifest in the attempt to create life in the test tube, in the desire to mix "frozen germ plasm from people of demonstrated ability under the microscope to produce superior human beings" and "to alter [their] size, shape and function"; and the wish to escape the human condition, I suspect, also underlies the hope to extend man's life-span far beyond the hundred-year limit.

This future man, whom the scientists tell us they will produce in no more than a hundred years, seems to be possessed by a rebellion against human existence as it has been given, a free gift from nowhere (secularly speaking), which he wishes to exchange, as it were, for something he has made himself. There is no reason to doubt our abilities to accomplish such an exchange, just as there is no reason to doubt our present ability to destroy all organic life on earth. The question is only whether we wish to use our new scientific and technical knowledge in this direction, and this question cannot be decided by scientific means; it is a political question of the first order and therefore can hardly be left to the decision of professional scientists or professional politicians.

While such possibilities still may lie in a distant future, the first boomerang effects of science's great triumphs have made themselves felt in a crisis within the natural sciences themselves. The trouble concerns the fact that the "truths" of the modern scientific world view, though they can be demonstrated in mathematical formulas and proved technologically, will no longer lend themselves to normal expression in speech and thought. The moment these "truths" are spoken of conceptually and coherently, the resulting statements will be "not perhaps as meaningless as a 'triangular circle,' but much more so than a 'winged lion' " (Erwin Schrödinger). We do not yet know whether this situation is final. But it could be that we, who are earth-bound creatures and have begun to act as though we were dwellers of the universe, will forever be unable to understand, that is, to think and speak about the things which nevertheless we are able to do. In this case, it would be as though our brain, which constitutes the physical, material condition of our thoughts, were unable to follow what we do, so that from now on we would indeed need artificial machines to do our thinking and speaking. If it should turn out to be true that knowledge (in the modern sense of know-how) and thought have parted company for good, then we would indeed become the helpless slaves, not so much of our machines as of our know-how, thoughtless creatures at the mercy of every gadget which is technically possible, no matter how murderous it is.

However, even apart from these last and yet uncertain consequences, the situation created by the sciences is of great political significance. Wherever the relevance of speech is at stake, matters become political by definition, for speech is what makes man a political being. If we would follow the advice, so frequently urged upon us, to adjust our cultural attitudes to the present status of scientific achievement, we would in all earnest adopt a way of life in which speech is no longer meaningful. For the sciences today have been forced to adopt a "language" of mathematical symbols which, though it was originally meant only as an abbreviation for spoken statements, now contains statements that in no way can be translated back into speech. The reason why it may be wise to distrust the political judgment of scientists *qua* scientists is not primarily their lack of "character" — that they did not refuse to develop atomic weapons — or their naïveté — that they did not understand that once these weapons were developed they would be the last to be consulted about their use — but precisely the fact that they move in a world where speech has lost its power. And whatever men do or know or experience can make sense only to the extent that it can be spoken about. There may be truths beyond speech, and they may be of great relevance to man in the singular, that is, to man in so far as he is not a political being, whatever else he may be. Men in the plural, that is, men in so far as they live and move and act in this world, can experience meaningfulness only because they can talk with and make sense to each other and to themselves.

Closer at hand and perhaps equally decisive is another no less threatening event. This is the advent of automation, which in a few decades probably will empty the factories and liberate mankind from its oldest and most natural burden, the burden of laboring and the bondage to necessity. Here, too, a fundamental aspect of the human condition is at stake, but the rebellion against it, the wish to be liberated from labor's "toil and trouble," is not modern but as old as recorded history. Freedom from labor itself is not new; it once belonged among the most firmly established privileges of the few. In this instance, it seems as though scientific progress and technical developments had been only taken advantage of to achieve something about which all former ages dreamed but which none had been able to realize.

However, this is so only in appearance. The modern age has carried with it a theoretical glorification of labor and has resulted in a factual transformation of the whole of society into a laboring society. The fulfilment of the wish, therefore, like the fulfilment of wishes in fairy tales, comes at a moment when it can only be self-defeating. It is a society of laborers which is about to be liberated from the fetters of labor, and this society does no longer know of those other higher and more meaningful activities for the sake of which this freedom would deserve to be won. Within this society, which is egalitarian because this is labor's way of making men live together, there is no class left, no aristocracy of either a political or spiritual nature from which a restoration of the other capacities of man could start anew. Even presidents, kings, and prime ministers think of their offices in terms of a job necessary for the life of society, and among the intellectuals, only solitary individuals are left who consider what they are doing in terms of work and not in terms of making a living. What we are confronted with is the prospect of a society of laborers without labor, that is, without the only activity left to them. Surely, nothing could be worse.

To these preoccupations and perplexities, this book does not offer an answer. Such answers are given every day, and they are matters of practical politics, subject to the agreement of many; they can never lie in theoretical considerations or the opinion of one person, as though we dealt here with problems for which only one solution is possible. What I propose in the following is a reconsideration of the human condition from the vantage point of our newest experience and our most recent fears. This, obviously, is a matter of thought, and thoughtlessness — the heedless recklessness or hopeless confusion or complacent repetition of "truths" which have become trivial and empty — seems to me among the outstanding characteristics of our time. What I propose, therefore, is very simple: it is nothing more than to think what we are doing.

FROM *VITA ACTIVA* AND THE HUMAN CONDITION

With the term *vita activa*, I propose to designate three fundamental human activities: labor, work, and action. They are fundamental because each corresponds to one of the basic conditions under which life on earth has been given to man.

Labor is the activity which corresponds to the biological process of the human body, whose spontaneous growth, metabolism, and eventual decay are bound to the vital necessities produced and fed into the life process by labor. The human condition of labor is life itself.

Work is the activity which corresponds to the unnaturalness of human existence, which is not imbedded in, and whose mortality is not compensated by, the species' ever-recurring life cycle. Work provides an "artificial" world of things, distinctly different from all natural surroundings. Within its borders each individual life is housed, while this world itself is meant to outlast and transcend them all. The human condition of work is worldliness.

Action, the only activity that goes on directly between men without the intermediary of things or matter, corresponds to the human condition of plurality, to the fact that men, not Man, live on the earth and inhabit the world. While all aspects of the human condition are somehow related to politics, this plurality is specifically *the* condition — not only the *conditio sine qua non*, but the *conditio per quam* — of all political life. Thus the language of the Romans, perhaps the most political people we have known, used the words "to live" and "to be among men" (*inter homines esse*) or "to die" and "to cease to be among men" (*inter homines esse desinere*) as synonyms. But in its most elementary form, the human condition of action is implicit even in Genesis ("Male and female created He *them*"), if we understand that this story of man's creation is distinguished in principle from the one according to which God originally created Man (*adam*), "him" and not "them," so that the multitude of human beings becomes the result of multiplication. Action would be an unnecessary luxury, a capricious interference with general laws of behavior, if men were endlessly reproducible repetitions of the same model, whose nature or essence was the same for all and as predictable as the nature or essence of any other thing. Plurality is the condition of human action because we are all the same, that is, human, in such a way that nobody is ever the same as anyone else who ever lived, lives, or will live.

All three activities and their corresponding conditions are intimately connected with the most general condition of human existence: birth and death, natality and mortality. Labor assures not only individual survival, but the life of the species. Work and its product, the human artifact, bestow a measure of permanence and durability upon the futility of mortal life and the fleeting character of human time. Action, in so far as it engages in founding and preserving political bodies, creates the condition for remembrance, that is, for history. Labor and work, as well as action, are also rooted in natality in so far as they have the task to provide and preserve the world for, to foresee and reckon with, the constant influx of newcomers who are born into the world as strangers. However, of the three, action has the closest connection with the human condition of natality; the new beginning inherent in birth can make itself felt in the world only because the newcomer possesses the capacity of beginning something anew, that is, of acting. In this sense of initiative, an element of action, and therefore of natality, is inherent in all human activities. Moreover, since action is the political activity par excellence, natality, and not mortality, may be the central category of political, as distinguished from metaphysical, thought.

The human condition comprehends more than the conditions under which life has been given to man. Men are conditioned beings because everything they come in contact with turns immediately into a condition of their existence. The world in which the *vita activa* spends itself consists of things produced by human activities; but the things that owe their existence exclusively to men nevertheless constantly condition their human makers. In addition to the conditions under which life is given to man on earth, and partly out of them, men constantly create their own, self-made conditions, which, their human origin and their variability notwithstanding, possess the same conditioning power as natural things. Whatever touches or enters into a sustained relationship with human life immediately assumes the character of a condition of human existence. This is why men, no matter what they do, are always conditioned beings. Whatever enters the human world of its own accord or is drawn into it by human effort becomes part of the human condition. The impact of the world's reality upon human existence is felt and received as a conditioning force. The objectivity of the world — its object- or thing-character — and the human condition supplement each other; because human existence is conditioned existence, it would be impossible without things, and things would be a heap of unrelated articles, a non-world, if they were not the conditioners of human existence. ∎

QUESTIONS

Cause-Effect

Which of the three elements in Hannah Arendt's definition of the human condition do you consider most important? Which least important? Why?

Comparison/Contrast

Compare and contrast Arendt's and Sartre's notions of the human condition.

Definition

If your view is significantly different from Hannah Arendt's, what is your definition of the human condition?

Niccolo Machiavelli

The Prince (excerpt)

Niccolo Machiavelli, 1469–1527, Italian statesman and author, wrote
The Prince, *in which he describes how political power is obtained: by
being "a great pretender and dissembler." There is in this work an
implied assumption about the nature of common folk.*

Upon this a question arises: whether it be better to be loved than feared
or feared than loved? It may be answered that one should wish to be both,
but, because it is difficult to unite them in one person, it is much safer to
be feared than loved, when, of the two, either must be dispensed with.
Because this is to be asserted in general of men, that they are ungrateful,
fickle, false, cowardly, covetous, and as long as you succeed they are yours
entirely; they will offer you their blood, property, life, and children, as is
said above, when the need is far distant; but when it approaches they turn
against you. And that prince who, relying entirely on their promises, has
neglected other precautions, is ruined; because friendships that are obtained
by payments, and not by greatness or nobility of mind, may indeed be earned,
but they are not secured, and in time of need cannot be relied upon; and
men have less scruple in offending one who is beloved than one who is
feared, for love is preserved by the link of obligation which, owing to the
baseness of men, is broken at every opportunity for their advantage; but
fear preserves you by a dread of punishment which never fails.

Nevertheless a prince ought to inspire fear in such a way that, if he
does not win love, he avoids hatred; because he can endure very well being
feared whilst he is not hated, which will always be as long as he abstains
from the property of his citizens and subjects and from their women. But
when it is necessary for him to proceed against the life of someone, he must
do it on proper justification and for manifest cause, but above all things he
must keep his hands off the property of others, because men more quickly
forget the death of their father than the loss of their patrimony. Besides,
pretexts for taking away the property are never wanting; for he who has
once begun to live by robbery will always find pretexts for seizing what
belongs to others; but reasons for taking life, on the contrary, are more
difficult to find and sooner lapse. But when a prince is with his army, and

has under control a multitude of soldiers, then it is quite necessary for him to disregard the reputation of cruelty, for without it he would never hold his army united or disposed to its duties.

Among the wonderful deeds of Hannibal this one is enumerated; that having led an enormous army, composed of many various races of men, to fight in foreign lands, no dissensions arose either among them or against the prince, whether in his bad or in his good fortune. This arose from nothing else than his inhuman cruelty, which, with his boundless valour, made him revered and terrible in the sight of his soldiers, but without that cruelty, his other virtues were not sufficient to produce this effect. And shortsighted writers admire his deeds from one point of view and from another condemn the principal cause of them. That it is true his other virtues would not have been sufficient for him may be proved by the case of Scipio, that most excellent man, not only of his own times but within the memory of man, against whom, nevertheless, his army rebelled in Spain; this arose from nothing but his too great forbearance, which gave his soldiers more licence than is consistent with military discipline. For this he was upbraided in the senate by Fabius Maximus, and called the corrupter of the Roman soldiery. The Locrians were laid waste by a legate of Scipio, yet they were not avenged by him, nor was the insolence of the legate punished, owing entirely to his easy nature. Insomuch that someone in the senate, wishing to excuse him, said there were many men who knew much better how not to err than to correct the errors of others. This disposition, if he had been continued in the command, would have destroyed in time the fame and glory of Scipio; but, he being under the control of the senate, this injurious characteristic not only concealed itself, but contributed to his glory.

Returning to the question of being feared or loved, I come to the conclusion that, men loving according to their own will and fearing according to that of the prince, a wise prince should establish himself on that which is in his own control and not in that of others; he must endeavour only to avoid hatred, as is noted.

CONCERNING THE WAY IN WHICH
PRINCES SHOULD KEEP FAITH

Every one admits how praiseworthy it is in a prince to keep faith, and to live with integrity and not with craft. Nevertheless our experience has been that those princes who have done great things have held good faith of little account, and have known how to circumvent the intellect of men by craft, and in the end have overcome those who have relied on their word. You must know there are two ways of contesting, the one by the law, the other by force; the first method is proper to men, the second to beasts; but because the first is frequently not sufficient, it is necessary to have recourse to the second. Therefore it is necessary for a prince to understand how to avail himself of the beast and the man. This has been figuratively taught to princes by ancient writers, who describe how Achilles and many other princes of old were given to the Centaur Chiron to nurse, who brought them up in his discipline; which means solely that, as they had for a teacher one who was half beast and half man, so it is necessary for a prince to know how to make use of both natures, and that one without the other is not durable. A prince, therefore, being compelled knowingly to adopt the beast, ought to choose the fox and the lion; because the lion cannot defend himself against snares and the fox cannot defend himself against wolves. Therefore, it is necessary to be a fox to discover the snares and a lion to terrify the wolves. Those who rely simply on the lion do not understand what they are about. Therefore a wise lord cannot, nor ought he to, keep faith when such observance may be turned against him, and when the reasons that caused him to pledge it exist no longer. If men were entirely good this precept would not hold, but because they are bad, and will not keep faith with you, you too are not bound to observe it with them. Nor will there ever be wanting to a prince legitimate reasons to excuse this nonobservance. Of this endless modern examples could be given, showing how many treaties and engagements have been made void and of no effect through the faithlessness of princes; and he who has known best how to employ the fox has succeeded best.

But it is necessary to know well how to disguise this characteristic, and to be a great pretender and dissembler; and men are so simple, and so subject to present necessities, that he who seeks to deceive will always find someone who will allow himself to be deceived. One recent example I cannot pass over in silence. Alexander VI did nothing else but deceive men, nor ever thought of doing otherwise, and he always found victims; for there never was a man who had greater power in asserting, or who with greater oaths would affirm a thing, yet would observe it less; nevertheless his deceits always succeeded according to his wishes, because he well understood this side of mankind.

Therefore it is unnecessary for a prince to have all the good qualities I have enumerated, but it is very necessary to appear to have them. And I shall dare to say this also, that to have them and always to observe them is injurious, and that to appear to have them is useful; to appear merciful, faithful, humane, religious, upright, and to be so, but with a mind so framed that should you require not to be so, you may be able and know how to change to the opposite.

And you have to understand this, that a prince, especially a new one, cannot observe all those things for which men are esteemed, being often forced, in order to maintain the state, to act contrary to fidelity, friendship, humanity, and religion. Therefore it is necessary for him to have a mind ready to turn itself accordingly as the winds and variations of fortune force it, yet, as I have said above, not to diverge from the good if he can avoid doing so, but, if compelled, then to know how to set about it.

For this reason a prince ought to take care that he never lets anything slip from his lips that is not replete with the above-named five qualities, that he may appear to him who sees and hears him altogether merciful, faithful, humane, upright, and religious. There is nothing more necessary to appear to have than this last quality, inasmuch as men judge generally more by the eye than by the hand, because it belongs to everybody to see you, to few to come in touch with you. Every one sees what you appear to be, few really know what you are, and those few dare not oppose themselves to the opinion of the many, who have the majesty of the state to defend them; and in the actions of all men, and especially of princes, which it is not prudent to challenge, one judges by the result.

For that reason, let a prince have the credit of conquering and holding his state, the means will always be considered honest, and he will be praised by everybody; because the vulgar are always taken by what a thing seems to be and by what comes of it; and in the world there are only the vulgar, for the few find a place there only when the many have no ground to rest on.

One prince of the present time, whom it is not well to name, never preaches anything else but peace and good faith, and to both he is most hostile, and either, if he had kept it, would have deprived him of reputation and kingdom many a time. ∎

QUESTIONS

Cause-Effect

Do you find Machiavelli's ideas to be utterly cynical or soberly realistic? Or both? Explain.

Definition

Define your notion of leadership.

Cause-Effect

Does modern political leadership pattern itself on Machiavelli's ideas? Why, or why not?

Comparison/Contrast (Definition)

Read the excerpt below, pp. 418–421, from Thomas Paine's *Rights of Man*. What are Machiavelli's and Paine's notions of the "rights of man"? Are they at complete variance, or are there some points of similarity?

Thomas Paine

Rights of Man (excerpt)

Thomas Paine, 1737–1809, American patriot and political theorist, wrote the Rights of Man *(1792). In this excerpt he defines man's inalienable rights and society's obligation to protect them.*

If any generation of men ever possessed the right of dictating the mode by which the world should be governed for ever, it was the first generation that existed; and if that generation did it not, no succeeding generation can show any authority for doing it, nor can set any up. The illuminating and divine principle of the equal rights of man, (for it has its origin from the Maker of man) relates, not only to the living individuals, but to generations of men succeeding each other. Every generation is equal in rights to the generations which preceded it, by the same rule that every individual is born equal in rights with his contemporary.

Every history of the creation, and every traditionary account, whether from the lettered or unlettered world, however they may vary in their opinion or belief of certain particulars, all agree in establishing one point, *the unity of man*; by which I mean, that men are all of *one degree*, and consequently that all men are born equal, and with equal natural right, in the same manner as if posterity had been continued by *creation* instead of *generation*, the latter being only the mode by which the former is carried forward; and consequently, every child born into the world must be considered as deriving its existence from God. The world is as new to him as it was to the first man that existed, and his natural right in it is of the same kind.

The Mosaic account of the creation, whether taken as divine authority, or merely historical, is full to this point, *the unity or equality of man*. The expressions admit of no controversy. 'And God said, Let us make man in our own image. In the image of God created he him; male and female created he them.' The distinction of sexes is pointed out, but no other distinction is even implied. If this be not divine authority, it is at least historical authority, and shows that the equality of man, so far from being a modern doctrine, is the oldest upon record.

It is also to be observed, that all the religions known in the world are founded, so far as they relate to man, on the *unity of man*, as being all of one degree. Whether in heaven or in hell, or in whatever state man may be supposed to exist hereafter, the good and the bad are the only distinctions. Nay, even the laws of governments are obliged to slide into this principle, by making degrees to consist in crimes, and not in persons.

It is one of the greatest of all truths, and of the highest advantage to cultivate. By considering man in this light, and by instructing him to consider himself in this light, it places him in a close connexion with all his duties, whether to his Creator, or to the creation, of which he is a part; and it is only when he forgets his origin, or, to use a more fashionable phrase, his *birth and family*, that he becomes dissolute. It is not among the least of the evils of the present existing governments in all parts of Europe, that man, considered as man, is thrown back to a vast distance from his Maker, and the artificial chasm filled up by a succession of barriers, or sort of turnpike gates, through which he has to pass. I will quote Mr Burke's catalogue of barriers that he has set up between man and his Maker. Putting himself in the character of a herald, he says — 'We fear God — we look with *awe* to kings — with affection to parliaments — with duty to magistrates — with reverence to priests, and with respect to nobility.' Mr Burke has forgotten to put in '*chivalry*'. He has also forgotten to put in Peter.

The duty of man is not a wilderness of turnpike gates, through which he is to pass by tickets from one to the other. It is plain and simple, and consists but of two points. His duty to God, which every man must feel; and with respect to his neighbour, to do as he would be done by. If those to whom power is delegated do well, they will be respected; if not, they will be despised: and with regard to those to whom no power is delegated, but who assume it, the rational world can know nothing of them.

Hitherto we have spoken only (and that but in part) of the natural rights of man. We have now to consider the civil rights of man, and to show how the one originates from the other. Man did not enter into society to become *worse* than he was before, nor to have fewer rights than he had before, but to have those rights better secured. His natural rights are the foundation of all his civil rights. But in order to pursue this distinction with more precision, it will be necessary to mark the different qualities of natural and civil rights.

A few words will explain this. Natural rights are those which appertain to man in right of his existence. Of this kind are all the intellectual rights, or rights of the mind, and also all those rights of acting as an individual for his own comfort and happiness, which are not injurious to the natural rights of others. — Civil rights are those which appertain to man in right of his being a member of society. Every civil right has for its foundation, some natural right pre-existing in the individual, but to the enjoyment of which his individual power is not, in all cases, sufficiently competent. Of this kind are all those which relate to security and protection.

From this short review, it will be easy to distinguish between that class of natural rights which man retains after entering into society, and those which he throws into the common stock as a member of society.

The natural rights which he retains, are all those in which the *power* to execute is as perfect in the individual as the right itself. Among this class, as is before mentioned, are all the intellectual rights, or rights of the mind: consequently, religion is one of those rights. The natural rights which are not retained, are all those in which, though the right is perfect in the individual, the power to execute them is defective. They answer not his purpose. A man, by natural right, has a right to judge in his own cause; and so far as the right of mind is concerned, he never surrenders it: But what availeth it him to judge, if he has not power to redress? He therefore deposits this right in the common stock of society, and takes the arm of society, of which he is a part, in preference and in addition to his own. Society *grants* him nothing. Every man is a proprietor in society, and draws on the capital as a matter of right.

From these premises, two or three certain conclusions will follow.

First, That every civil right grows out of a natural right; or, in other words, is a natural right exchanged.

Secondly, That civil power, properly considered as such, is made up of the aggregate of that class of the natural rights of man, which becomes defective in the individual in point of power, and answers not his purpose; but when collected to a focus, becomes competent to the purpose of every one.

Thirdly, That the power produced from the aggregate of natural rights, imperfect in power in the individual, cannot be applied to invade the natural rights which are retained in the individual, and in which the power to execute is as perfect as the right itself.

We have now, in a few words, traced man from a natural individual to a member of society, and shown, or endeavoured to show, the quality of the natural rights retained, and of those which are exchanged for civil rights. Let us now apply these principles to governments.

In casting our eyes over the world, it is extremely easy to distinguish the governments which have arisen out of society, or out of the social compact, from those which have not: but to place this in a clearer light than what a single glance may afford, it will be proper to take a review of the several sources from which governments have arisen, and on which they have been founded.

They may be all comprehended under three heads. First, Superstition. Secondly, Power. Thirdly, The common interest of society, and the common rights of man. ■

QUESTIONS

Cause-Effect

Paine claims that a "civil" right is, on the one hand, derived from a "natural" right and yet, on the other, is different from a "natural" right. Choose at least two "civil" rights (for example, the right to vote and the right to bear arms) and determine to what degree they are derived from "natural" rights.

Cause-Effect

To what extent are "natural" rights observed in America?

Comparison/Contrast

Compare and contrast Paine's and Marx's (or Paine's and Machiavelli's) ideas about the "rights" of men to determine their destinies.

Process

Trace the ways in which civil rights have been observed in the United States in the last twenty-five years.

Karl Marx and Friedrich Engels

The Communist Manifesto
(excerpt)

Karl Marx and Friedrich Engels wrote The Communist Manifesto
*(1850). This work has exerted enormous influence on the social fabric of
many nations. The excerpt from this work describes the basic struggle
between the bourgeoisie (those who control the means of production) and
the proletariat (the exploited).*

I. BOURGEOIS AND PROLETARIANS[a]

The history of all hitherto existing society[b] is the history of class struggles.

Free man and slave, patrician and plebeian, lord and serf, guild master[c] and journeyman, in a word, oppressor and oppressed, stood in constant opposition to one another, carried on an uninterrupted, now hidden, now open fight, a fight that each time ended either in a revolutionary reconstitution of society at large or in the common ruin of the contending classes.

In the earlier epochs of history we find almost everywhere a complicated

---

[a]By "bourgeoisie" is meant the class of modern capitalists, owners of the means of social production and employers of wage labor. By proletariat, the class of modern wage laborers who, having no means of production of their own, are reduced to selling their labor power in order to live. [Note by Engels to the English edition of 1888.]

[b]That is, all *written* history. In 1847 the pre-history of society, the social organization existing previous to recorded history was all but unknown. Since then Haxthausen discovered common ownership of land in Russia, Maurer proved it to be the social foundation from which all Teutonic races started in history, and by and by village communities were found to be, or to have been, the primitive form of society everywhere from India to Ireland. The inner organization of this primitive communistic society was laid bare, in its typical form, by Morgan's crowning discovery of the true nature of the *gens* and its relation to the *tribe*. With the dissolution of these primeval communities society begins to be differentiated into separate and finally antagonistic classes. I have attempted to retrace this process of dissolution in *Der Ursprung der Familie, des Privateigenthums und des Staats* [*The Origin of the Family, Private Property and the State*], second edition, Stuttgart, 1886. [Note by Engels to the English edition of 1888.]

[c]Guild master, that is, a full member of a guild, a master within, not a head of a guild. [Note by Engels to the English edition of 1888.]

arrangement of society into various orders, a manifold gradation of social rank. In ancient Rome we have patricians, knights, plebeians, slaves; in the Middle Ages, feudal lords, vassals, guild masters, journeymen, apprentices, serfs; in almost all of these classes, again, subordinate gradations.

The modern bourgeois society that has sprouted from the ruins of feudal society has not done away with class antagonisms. It has but established new classes, new conditions of oppression, new forms of struggle in place of the old ones.

Our epoch, the epoch of the bourgeoisie, possesses, however, this distinctive feature: it has simplified the class antagonisms. Society as a whole is more and more splitting up into two great hostile camps, into two great classes directly facing each other: bourgeoisie and proletariat.

From the serfs of the Middle Ages sprang the chartered burghers of the earliest towns. From these burgesses the first elements of the bourgeoisie were developed.

The discovery of America, the rounding of the Cape opened up fresh ground for the rising bourgeoisie. The East Indian and Chinese markets, the colonization of America, trade with the colonies, the increase in the means of exchange and in commodities generally, gave to commerce, to navigation, to industry an impulse never before known, and thereby, to the revolutionary element in the tottering feudal society, a rapid development.

The feudal system of industry, under which industrial production was monopolized by closed guilds, now no longer sufficed for the growing wants of the new markets. The manufacturing system took its place. The guild masters were pushed on one side by the manufacturing middle class; division of labor between the different corporate guilds vanished in the face of division of labor in each single workshop.

Meantime the markets kept ever growing, the demand ever rising. Even manufacture no longer sufficed. Thereupon steam and machinery revolutionized industrial production. The place of manufacture was taken by the giant, modern industry, the place of the industrial middle class by industrial millionaires, the leaders of whole industrial armies, the modern bourgeois.

Modern industry has established the world market, for which the discovery of America paved the way. This market has given an immense development to commerce, to navigation, to communication by land. This development has, in its turn, reacted on the extension of industry; and in proportion as industry, commerce, navigation, railways extended, in the same proportion the bourgeoisie developed, increased its capital, and pushed into the background every class handed down from the Middle Ages.

We see, therefore, how the modern bourgeoisie is itself the product of a long course of development, of a series of revolutions in the modes of production and of exchange.

Each step in the development of the bourgeoisie was accompanied by a corresponding political advance of that class. An oppressed class under the sway of the feudal nobility, an armed and self-governing association in the medieval commune[d]; here independent urban republic (as in Italy and Germany), there taxable "third estate" of the monarchy (as in France), afterwards, in the period of manufacture proper, serving either the semi-feudal or the absolute monarchy as a counterpoise against the nobility, and, in fact, cornerstone of the great monarchies in general, the bourgeoisie has at last, since the establishment of modern industry and of the world market, conquered for itself, in the modern representative state, exclusive political sway. The executive of the modern state is but a committee for managing the common affairs of the whole bourgeoisie.

The bourgeoisie, historically, has played a most revolutionary part.

The bourgeoisie, wherever it has got the upper hand, has put an end to all feudal, patriarchal, idyllic relations. It has pitilessly torn asunder the motley feudal ties that bound man to his "natural superiors," and has left remaining no other nexus between man and man than naked self-interest, than callous "cash payment." It has drowned the most heavenly ecstasies of religious fervor, of chivalrous enthusiasm, of Philistine sentimentalism in the icy water of egotistical calculation. It has resolved personal worth into exchange value and, in place of the numberless indefeasible chartered freedoms, has set up that single, unconscionable freedom — free trade. In one word, for exploitation, veiled by religious and political illusions, it has substituted naked, shameless, direct, brutal exploitation.

The bourgeoisie has stripped of its halo every occupation hitherto honored and looked up to with reverent awe. It has converted the physician, the lawyer, the priest, the poet, the man of science into its paid wage laborers.

The bourgeoisie has torn away from the family its sentimental veil, and has reduced the family relation to a mere money relation.

The bourgeoisie has disclosed how it came to pass that the brutal display of vigor in the Middle Ages, which reactionists so much admire, found its fitting complement in the most slothful indolence. It has been the first to show what man's activity can bring about. It has accomplished wonders far surpassing Egyptian pyramids, Roman aqueducts, and Gothic cathedrals; it

---

[d]"Commune" was the name taken, in France, by the nascent towns even before they had conquered from their feudal lords and masters local self-government and political rights as the "third estate." Generally speaking, for the economic development of the bourgeoisie, England is here taken as the typical country; for its political development, France. [Note by Engels to the English edition of 1888.]

has conducted expeditions that put in the shade all former exoduses of nations and crusades.

The bourgeoisie cannot exist without constantly revolutionizing the instruments of production, and thereby the relations of production, and with them the whole relations of society. Conservation of the old modes of production in unaltered form was, on the contrary, the first condition of existence for all earlier industrial classes. Constant revolutionizing of production, uninterrupted disturbance of all social conditions, everlasting uncertainty and agitation distinguish the bourgeois epoch from all earlier ones. All fixed, fast-frozen relations, with their train of ancient and venerable prejudices and opinions, are swept away, all new-formed ones become antiquated before they can ossify. All that is solid melts into air, all that is holy is profaned, and man is at last compelled to face with sober senses his real conditions of life and his relations with his kind.

The need of a constantly expanding market for its products chases the bourgeoisie over the whole surface of the globe. It must nestle everywhere, settle everywhere, establish connections everywhere.

The bourgeoisie has through its exploitation of the world market given a cosmopolitan character to production and consumption in every country. To the great chagrin of reactionists, it has drawn from under the feet of industry the national ground on which it stood. All old-established national industries have been destroyed or are daily being destroyed. They are dislodged by new industries, whose introduction becomes a life and death question for all civilized nations, by industries that no longer work up indigenous raw material, but raw material drawn from the remotest zones; industries whose products are consumed not only at home, but in every quarter of the globe. In place of the old wants, satisfied by the productions of the country, we find new wants, requiring for their satisfaction the products of distant lands and climes. In place of the old local and national seclusion and self-sufficiency we have intercourse in every direction, universal interdependence of nations. And as in material, so also in intellectual production. The intellectual creations of individual nations become common property. National one-sidedness and narrowmindedness become more and more impossible, and from the numerous national and local literatures there arises a world literature.

The bourgeoisie, by the rapid improvement of all instruments of production, by the immensely facilitated means of communication, draws all, even the most barbarian, nations into civilization. The cheap prices of its commodities are the heavy artillery with which it batters down all Chinese walls, with which it forces the barbarians' intensely obstinate hatred of foreigners to capitulate. It compels all nations, on pain of extinction, to adopt the bourgeois mode of production; it compels them to introduce what it calls civilization into their midst, i.e., to become bourgeois themselves. In one word, it creates a world after its own image.

The bourgeoisie has subjected the country to the rule of the towns. It has created enormous cities, has greatly increased the urban population as compared with the rural, and has thus rescued a considerable part of the population from the idiocy of rural life. Just as it has made the country dependent on the towns, so it has made barbarian and semi-barbarian countries dependent on the civilized ones, nations of peasants on nations of bourgeois, the East on the West.

The bourgeoisie keeps more and more doing away with the scattered state of the population, of the means of production, and of property. It has agglomerated population, centralized means of production, and has concentrated property in a few hands. The necessary consequence of this was political centralization. Independent, or but loosely connected provinces, with separate interests, laws, governments and systems of taxation, became lumped together into one nation, with one government, one code of laws, one national class interest, one frontier, and one customs tariff.

The bourgeoisie, during its rule of scarce one hundred years, has created more massive and more colossal productive forces than have all preceding generations together. Subjection of nature's forces to man, machinery, application of chemistry to industry and agriculture, steam navigation, railways, electric telegraphs, clearing of whole continents for cultivation, canalization of rivers, whole populations conjured out of the ground — what earlier century had even a presentiment that such productive forces slumbered in the lap of social labor?

We see then: the means of production and of exchange, on whose foundation the bourgeoisie built itself up, were generated in feudal society. At a certain stage in the development of these means of production and of exchange, the conditions under which feudal society produced and exchanged, the feudal organization of agriculture and manufacturing industry, in one word, the feudal relations of property, became no longer compatible with the already developed productive forces; they became so many fetters. They had to be burst asunder; they were burst asunder.

Into their place stepped free competition, accompanied by a social and political constitution adapted to it, and by the economic and political sway of the bourgeois class.

A similar movement is going on before our own eyes. Modern bourgeois society with its relations of production, of exchange, and of property, a society that has conjured up such gigantic means of production and of exchange, is like the sorcerer who is no longer able to control the powers of the nether world whom he has called up by his spells. For many a decade past, the history of industry and commerce is but the history of the revolt of modern productive forces against modern conditions of production, against the property relations that are the conditions for the existence of the bourgeoisie and of its rule. It is enough to mention the commercial crises that by their periodic return put on its trial, each time more threateningly, the existence of the entire bourgeois society. In these crises a great part not only of the existing products but also of the previously created productive forces are periodically destroyed. In these crises there breaks out an epidemic that in all earlier epochs would have seemed an absurdity — the epidemic of over-production. Society suddenly finds itself put back into a state of momentary barbarism; it appears as if a famine, a universal war of devastation had cut off the supply of every means of subsistence; industry and commerce seem to be destroyed; and why? Because there is too much civilization, too much means of subsistence, too much industry, too much commerce. The productive forces at the disposal of society no longer tend to further the development of the conditions of bourgeois property; on the contrary, they have become too powerful for these conditions, by which they are fettered, and as soon as they overcome these fetters they bring disorder into the whole of bourgeois society, endanger the existence of bourgeois property. The conditions of bourgeois society are too narrow to comprise the wealth created by them. And how does the bourgeoisie get over these crises? On the one hand, by enforced destruction of a mass of productive forces; on the other, by the conquest of new markets, and by the more thorough exploitation of the old ones. That is to say, by paving the way for more extensive and more destructive crises, and by diminishing the means whereby crises are prevented.

The weapons with which the bourgeoisie felled feudalism to the ground are now turned against the bourgeoisie itself.

But not only has the bourgeoisie forged the weapons that bring death to itself; it has also called into existence the men who are to wield those weapons — the modern working class — the proletarians.

In proportion as the bourgeoisie, i.e., capital, is developed, in the same proportion is the proletariat, the modern working class, developed — a class of laborers, who live only so long as they find work, and who find work only so long as their labor increases capital. These laborers, who must sell themselves piecemeal, are a commodity, like every other article of commerce, and are consequently exposed to all the vicissitudes of competition, to all the fluctuations of the market.

Owing to the extensive use of machinery and to division of labor, the work of the proletarians has lost all individual character and, consequently, all charm for the workman. He becomes an appendage of the machine, and it is only the simplest, most monotonous, and most easily acquired knack that is required of him. Hence the cost of production of a workman is restricted, almost entirely, to the means of subsistence that he requires for his maintenance and for the propagation of his race. But the price of a commodity, and therefore also of labor, is equal to its cost of production. In proportion, therefore, as the repulsiveness of the work increases, the wage decreases. Nay, more, in proportion as the use of machinery and division of labor increases, in the same proportion the burden of toil also increases, whether by prolongation of the working hours, by increase of the work exacted in a given time, or by increased speed of the machinery, etc.

Modern industry has converted the little workshop of the patriarchal master into the great factory of the industrial capitalist. Masses of laborers, crowded into the factory, are organized like soldiers. As privates of the industrial army they are placed under the command of a perfect hierarchy of officers and sergeants. Not only are they slaves of the bourgeois class, and of the bourgeois state; they are daily and hourly enslaved by the machine, by the overlooker, and, above all, by the individual bourgeois manufacturer himself. The more openly this despotism proclaims gain to be its end and aim, the more petty, the more hateful, and the more embittering it is.

The less the skill and exertion of strength implied in manual labor, in other words, the more modern industry becomes developed, the more is the labor of men superseded by that of women. Differences of age and sex have no longer any distinctive social validity for the working class. All are instruments of labor, more or less expensive to use, according to their age and sex.

No sooner is the exploitation of the laborer by the manufacturer over, to the extent that he receives his wages in cash, than he is set upon by the other portions of the bourgeoisie, the landlord, the shopkeeper, the pawnbroker, etc.

The lower strata of the middle class — the small tradespeople, shop-keepers, and retired tradesmen generally, the handicraftsmen and peasants — all these sink gradually into the proletariat, partly because their diminutive capital does not suffice for the scale on which modern industry is carried on, and is swamped in the competition with the large capitalists, partly because their specialized skill is rendered worthless by new methods of production. Thus the proletariat is recruited from all classes of the population.

The proletariat goes through various stages of development. With its birth begins its struggle with the bourgeoisie. At first the contest is carried on by individual laborers, then by the workpeople of a factory, then by the operatives of one trade, in one locality, against the individual bourgeois who directly exploits them. They direct their attacks not against the bourgeois conditions of production, but against the instruments of production themselves; they destroy imported wares that compete with their labor, they smash to pieces machinery, they set factories ablaze, they seek to restore by force the vanished status of the workman of the Middle Ages.

At this stage the laborers still form an incoherent mass scattered over the whole country and broken up by their mutual competition. If anywhere they unite to form more compact bodies, this is not yet the consequence of their own active union, but of the union of the bourgeoisie, which class, in order to attain its own political ends, is compelled to set the whole proletariat in motion, and is moreover yet, for a time, able to do so. At this stage, therefore, the proletarians do not fight their enemies, but the enemies of their enemies, the remnants of absolute monarchy, the landowners, the non-industrial bourgeois, the petty bourgeoisie. Thus the whole historical movement is concentrated in the hands of the bourgeoisie; every victory so obtained is a victory for the bourgeoisie.

But with the development of industry the proletariat not only increases in number; it becomes concentrated in greater masses, its strength grows, and it feels that strength more. The various interests and conditions of life within the ranks of the proletariat are more and more equalized, in proportion as machinery obliterates all distinctions of labor and nearly everywhere reduces wages to the same low level. The growing competition among the bourgeois and the resulting commercial crises make the wages of the workers ever more fluctuating. The unceasing improvement of machinery, ever more rapidly developing, makes their livelihood more and more precarious; the collisions between individual workmen and individual bourgeois take more and more the character of collisions between two classes. Thereupon the workers begin to form combinations (trade unions) against the bourgeois; they club together in order to keep up the rate of wages; they found permanent associations in order to make provision beforehand for these occasional revolts. Here and there the contest breaks out into riots.

Now and then the workers are victorious, but only for a time. The real fruit of their battles lies not in the immediate result, but in the ever expanding union of the workers. This union is helped on by the improved means of communication that are created by modern industry and that place the workers of different localities in contact with one another. It was just this contact that was needed to centralize the numerous local struggles, all of the same character, into one national struggle between classes. But every class struggle is a political struggle. And that union, to attain which the burghers of the Middle Ages, with their miserable highways, required centuries, the modern proletarians, thanks to railways, achieve in a few years.

This organization of the proletarians into a class, and consequently into a political party, is continually being upset again by the competition between the workers themselves. But it ever rises up again, stronger, firmer, mightier. It compels legislative recognition of particular interests of the workers by taking advantage of the divisions among the bourgeoisie itself. Thus the ten-hour bill in England was carried.

Altogether collisions between the classes of the old society further, in many ways, the course of development of the proletariat. The bourgeoisie finds itself involved in a constant battle. At first with the aristocracy; later on, with those portions of the bourgeoisie itself whose interests have become antagonistic to the progress of industry; at all times, with the bourgeoisie of foreign countries. In all these battles it sees itself compelled to appeal to the proletariat, to ask for its help, and thus to drag it into the political arena. The bourgeoisie itself, therefore, supplies the proletariat with its own elements of political and general education: in other words, it furnishes the proletariat with weapons for fighting the bourgeoisie.

Further, as we have already seen, entire sections of the ruling classes are, by the advance of industry, precipitated into the proletariat, or are at least threatened in their conditions of existence. These also supply the proletariat with fresh elements of enlightenment and progress.

Finally, in times when the class struggle nears the decisive hour, the process of dissolution going on within the ruling class, in fact within the whole range of old society, assumes such a violent, glaring character that a small section of the ruling class cuts itself adrift and joins the revolutionary class, the class that holds the future in its hands. Just as, therefore, at an earlier period, a section of the nobility went over to the bourgeoisie, so now a portion of the bourgeoisie goes over to the proletariat, and in particular a portion of the bourgeois ideologists, who have raised themselves to the level of comprehending theoretically the historical movement as a whole.

Of all the classes that stand face to face with the bourgeoisie today, the proletariat alone is a really revolutionary class. The other classes decay and finally disappear in the face of modern industry; the proletariat is its special and essential product.

The lower-middle class, the small manufacturer, the shopkeeper, the artisan, the peasant, all these fight against the bourgeoisie, to save from extinction their existence as factions of the middle class. They are therefore not revolutionary, but conservative. Nay, more, they are reactionary, for they try to roll back the wheel of history. If by chance they are revolutionary they are so only in view of their impending transfer into the proletariat; they thus defend not their present but their future interests, they desert their own standpoint to place themselves at that of the proletariat.

The "dangerous class," the social scum, that passively rotting mass thrown off by the lowest layers of old society, may, here and there, be swept into the movement by a proletarian revolution; its conditions of life, however, prepare it far more for the part of a bribed tool of reactionary intrigue.

In the conditions of the proletariat those of old society at large are already virtually swamped. The proletarian is without property; his relation to his wife and children has no longer anything in common with the bourgeois family relations; modern industrial labor, modern subjection to capital, the same in England as in France, in America as in Germany, has stripped him of every trace of national character. Law, morality, religion are to him so many bourgeois prejudices, behind which lurk in ambush just as many bourgeois interests.

All the preceding classes that got the upper hand sought to fortify their already acquired status by subjecting society at large to their conditions of appropriation. The proletarians cannot become masters of the productive forces of society, except by abolishing their own previous mode of appropriation, and thereby also every other previous mode of appropriation. They have nothing of their own to secure and to fortify; their mission is to destroy all previous securities for, and insurances of, individual property.

All previous historical movements were movements of minorities, or in the interest of minorities. The proletarian movement is the self-conscious, independent movement of the immense majority, in the interests of the immense majority. The proletariat, the lowest stratum of our present society, cannot stir, cannot raise itself up, without the whole superincumbent strata of official society being sprung into the air.

Though not in substance, yet in form, the struggle of the proletariat with the bourgeoisie is at first a national struggle. The proletariat of each country must, of course, first of all settle matters with its own bourgeoisie.

In depicting the most general phases of the development of the proletariat, we traced the more or less veiled civil war, raging within existing society, up to the point where that war breaks out into open revolution, and where the violent overthrow of the bourgeoisie lays the foundation for the sway of the proletariat.

Hitherto every form of society has been based, as we have already seen, on the antagonism of oppressing and oppressed classes. But in order to oppress a class certain conditions must be assured to it under which it can, at least, continue its slavish existence. The serf, in the period of serfdom, raised himself to membership in the commune, just as the petty bourgeois, under the yoke of feudal absolutism, managed to develop into a bourgeois. The modern laborer, on the contrary, instead of rising with the progress of industry, sinks deeper and deeper below the conditions of existence of his own class. He becomes a pauper, and pauperism develops more rapidly than population and wealth. And here it becomes evident that the bourgeoisie is unfit any longer to be the ruling class in society, and to impose its conditions of existence upon society as an overriding law. It is unfit to rule because it is incompetent to assure an existence to its slave within his slavery, because it cannot help letting him sink into such a state that it has to feed him instead of being fed by him. Society can no longer live under this bourgeoisie: in other words, its existence is no longer compatible with society.

The essential condition for the existence, and for the sway of the bourgeois class, is the formation and augmentation of capital; the condition for capital is wage labor. Wage labor rests exclusively on competition between the laborers. The advance of industry, whose involuntary promoter is the bourgeoisie, replaces the isolation of the laborers, due to competition, by their revolutionary combination, due to association. The development of modern industry, therefore, cuts from under its feet the very foundation on which the bourgeoisie produces and appropriates products. What the bourgeoisie, therefore, produces, above all, is its own gravediggers. Its fall and the victory of the proletariat are equally inevitable. ∎

QUESTIONS

Cause-Effect (Definition)

Are Marx's definitions of the bourgeoisie and the proletariat still applicable today? Explain.

Cause-Effect

Should we — can we — live in a classless society?

Cause-Effect

Marx defines man — economically, politically, spiritually — in terms of a class struggle. Do you agree or disagree?

Process (Cause-Effect)

Marx claimed in 1850 that all capitalist countries would evolve into communist societies. This has not happened in the United States or in most industrialized countries. Instead, what has emerged is a stronger middle class within these countries. How and why did this happen?

Carl Sagan

Can We Know the Universe? Reflections on a Grain of Salt

from *Broca's Brain*

Carl Sagan, a physicist and cosmologist, wrote this chapter in Broca's Brain *to show how our knowledge of the world is affected by the laws of nature.*

Science is a way of thinking much more than it is a body of knowledge. Its goal is to find out how the world works, to seek what regularities there may be, to penetrate to the connections of things — from subnuclear particles, which may be the constituents of all matter, to living organisms, the human social community, and thence to the cosmos as a whole. Our intuition is by no means an infallible guide. Our perceptions may be distorted by training and prejudice or merely because of the limitations of our sense organs, which, of course, perceive directly but a small fraction of the phenomena of the world. Even so straightforward a question as whether in the absence of friction a pound of lead falls faster than a gram of fluff was answered incorrectly by Aristotle and almost everyone else before the time of Galileo. Science is based on experiment, on a willingness to challenge old dogma, on an openness to see the universe as it really is. Accordingly, science sometimes requires courage — at the very least the courage to question the conventional wisdom.

Beyond this the main trick of science is to *really* think of something: the shape of clouds and their occasional sharp bottom edges at the same altitude everywhere in the sky; the formation of a dewdrop on a leaf; the origin of a name or a word — Shakespeare, say, or "philanthropic"; the reason for human social customs — the incest taboo, for example; how it is that a lens in sunlight can make paper burn; how a "walking stick" got to look so much like a twig; why the Moon seems to follow us as we walk; what prevents us from digging a hole down to the center of the Earth; what the definition is of "down" on a spherical Earth; how it is possible for the body to convert yesterday's lunch into today's muscle and sinew; or how far is up — does the universe go on forever, or if it does not, is there any meaning to the question of what lies on the other side? Some of these questions are pretty easy. Others, especially the last, are mysteries to which no one even today knows the answer. They are natural questions to ask. Every culture has posed such questions in one way or another. Almost always the proposed answers are in the nature of "Just So Stories," attempted explanations divorced from experiment, or even from careful comparative observations.

But the scientific cast of mind examines the world critically as if many alternative worlds might exist, as if other things might be here which are not. Then we are forced to ask why what we see is present and not something else. Why are the Sun and the Moon and the planets spheres? Why not pyraminds, or cubes, or dodecahedra? Why not irregular, jumbly shapes? Why so symmetrical, worlds? If you spend any time spinning hypotheses, checking to see whether they make sense, whether they conform to what else we know, thinking of tests you can pose to substantiate or deflate your hypotheses, you will find yourself doing science. And as you come to practice this habit of thought more and more you will get better and better at it. To penetrate into the heart of the thing — even a little thing, a blade of grass, as Walt Whitman said — is to experience a kind of exhilaration that, it may be, only human beings of all the beings on this planet can feel. We are an intelligent species and the use of our intelligence quite properly gives us pleasure. In this respect the brain is like a muscle. When we think well, we feel good. Understanding is a kind of ecstasy.

But to what extent can we *really* know the universe around us? Sometimes this question is posed by people who hope the answer will be in the negative, who are fearful of a universe in which everything might one day be known. And sometimes we hear pronouncements from scientists who confidently state that everything worth knowing will soon be known — or even is already known — and who paint pictures of a Dionysian or Polynesian age in which the zest for intellectual discovery has withered, to be replaced by a kind of subdued languor, the lotus eaters drinking fermented coconut milk or some other mild hallucinogen. In addition to maligning both the Polynesians, who were intrepid explorers (and whose brief respite in paradise is now sadly ending), as well as the inducements to intellectual discovery provided by some hallucinogens, this contention turns out to be trivially mistaken.

Let us approach a much more modest question: not whether we can know the universe or the Milky Way Galaxy or a star or a world. Can we know, ultimately and in detail, a grain of salt? Consider one microgram of table salt, a speck just barely large enough for someone with keen eyesight to make out without a microscope. In that grain of salt there are about 10^{16} sodium and chlorine atoms. This is a 1 followed by 16 zeros, 10 million billion atoms. If we wish to know a grain of salt, we must know at least the three-dimensional positions of each of these atoms. (In fact, there is much more to be known — for example, the nature of the forces between the atoms — but we are making only a modest calculation.) Now, is this number more or less than the number of things which the brain can know?

How much *can* the brain know? There are perhaps 10^{11} neurons in the brain, the circuit elements and switches that are responsible in their electrical and chemical activity for the functioning of our minds. A typical brain neuron has perhaps a thousand little wires, called dendrites, which connect it with its fellows. If, as seems likely, every bit of information in the brain corresponds to one of these connections, the total number of things knowable by the brain is no more than 10^{14}, one hundred trillion. But this number is only one percent of the number of atoms in our speck of salt.

So in this sense the universe is intractable, astonishingly immune to any human attempt at full knowledge. We cannot on this level understand a grain of salt, much less the universe.

But let us look a little more deeply at our microgram of salt. Salt happens to be a crystal in which, except for defects in the structure of the crystal lattice, the position of every sodium and chlorine atom is predetermined. If we could shrink ourselves into this crystalline world, we would see rank upon rank of atoms in an ordered array, a regularly alternating structure — sodium, chlorine, sodium, chlorine, specifying the sheet of atoms we are standing on and all the sheets above us and below us. An absolutely pure crystal of salt could have the position of every atom specified by something like 10 bits of information.[a] This would not strain the information-carrying capacity of the brain.

If the universe had natural laws that governed its behavior to the same degree of regularity that determines a crystal of salt, then, of course, the universe would be knowable. Even if there were many such laws, each of considerable complexity, human beings might have the capability to understand them all. Even if such knowledge exceeded the information-carrying capacity of the brain, we might store the additional information outside our bodies — in books, for example, or in computer memories — and still, in some sense, know the universe.

Human beings are, understandably, highly motivated to find regularities, natural laws. The search for rules, the only possible way to understand such

---

[a]Chlorine is a deadly poison gas employed on European battlefields in World War I. Sodium is a corrosive metal which burns upon contact with water. Together they make a placid and unpoisonous material, table salt. Why each of these substances has the properties it does is a subject called chemistry, which requires more than 10 bits of information to understand.

a vast and complex universe, is called science. The universe forces those who live in it to understand it. Those creatures who find everyday experience a muddled jumble of events with no predictability, no regularity, are in grave peril. The universe belongs to those who, at least to some degree, have figured it out.

It is an astonishing fact that there *are* laws of nature, rules that summarize conveniently — not just qualitatively but quantitatively — how the world works. We might imagine a universe in which there are no such laws, in which the 10^{80} elementary particles that make up a universe like our own behave with utter and uncompromising abandon. To understand such a universe we would need a brain at least as massive as the universe. It seems unlikely that such a universe could have life and intelligence, because beings and brains require some degree of internal stability and order. But even if in a much more random universe there were such beings with an intelligence much greater than our own, there could not be much knowledge, passion or joy.

Fortunately for us, we live in a universe that has at least important parts that are knowable. Our common-sense experience and our evolutionary history have prepared us to understand something of the workaday world. When we go into other realms, however, common sense and ordinary intuition turn out to be highly unreliable guides. It is stunning that as we go close to the speed of light our mass increases indefinitely, we shrink toward zero thickness in the direction of motion, and time for us comes as near to stopping as we would like. Many people think that this is silly, and every week or two I get a letter from someone who complains to me about it. But it is a virtually certain consequence not just of experiment but also of Albert Einstein's brilliant analysis of space and time called the Special Theory of Relativity. It does not matter that these effects seem unreasonable to us. We are not in the habit of traveling close to the speed of light. The testimony of our common sense is suspect at high velocities.

Or consider an isolated molecule composed of two atoms shaped something like a dumbbell — a molecule of salt, it might be. Such a molecule rotates about an axis through the line connecting the two atoms. But in the world of quantum mechanics, the realm of the very small, not all orientations of our dumbbell molecule are possible. It might be that the molecule could be oriented in a horizontal position, say, or in a vertical position, but not at many angles in between. Some rotational positions are forbidden. Forbidden by what? By the laws of nature. The universe is built in such a way as to limit, or quantize, rotation. We do not experience this directly in everyday life; we would find it startling as well as awkward in sitting-up exercises, to find arms outstretched from the sides or pointed up to the skies permitted but many intermediate positions forbidden. We do not live in the world of the small, on the scale of 10^{-13} centimeters, in the realm where there are twelve zeros between the decimal place and the one. Our common-sense intuitions do not count. What does count is experiment — in this case observations from the far infrared spectra of molecules. They show molecular rotation to be quantized.

The idea that the world places restrictions on what humans might do is frustrating. Why *shouldn't* we be able to have intermediate rotational positions? Why *can't* we travel faster than the speed of light? But so far as we can tell, this is the way the universe is constructed. Such prohibitions not only press us toward a little humility; they also make the world more knowable. Every restriction corresponds to a law of nature, a regularization of the universe. The more restrictions there are on what matter and energy can do, the more knowledge human beings can attain. Whether in some sense the universe is ultimately knowable depends not only on how many natural laws there are that encompass widely divergent phenomena, but also on whether we have the openness and the intellectual capacity to understand such laws. Our formulations of the regularities of nature are surely dependent on how the brain is built, but also, and to a significant degree, on how the universe is built.

For myself, I like a universe that includes much that is unknown and, at the same time, much that is knowable. A universe in which everything is known would be static and dull, as boring as the heaven of some weak-minded theologians. A universe that is unknowable is no fit place for a thinking being. The ideal universe for us is one very much like the universe we inhabit. And I would guess that this is not really much of a coincidence. ∎

QUESTIONS

Definition

What is science, according to Carl Sagan?

Cause-Effect

What are the effects of the limitations that the laws of nature impose on human learning?

Comparison/Contrast

What are the differences between our common sense expectations and the actual findings of scientists with regard to the following:

traveling at the speed of light, traveling in the direction of motion, and possible positions for atoms in a molecule of salt?

Process

What are the steps that a scientist goes through in order to "do science"?

Questions for Essays Involving Several Readings

Following are general questions that apply to several of the foregoing selections at the same time. To answer each question, read or reread the selections referred to in parentheses below the question. Think about how you might use information or ideas from the articles in your answer.

DEFINITION

What is man's purpose?
(Simpson, Buber, Thoreau, Myths, Sartre, Arendt, Marx, Paine, Sagan)

CAUSE-EFFECT (DEFINITION)

Is man a moral being?
(All articles)

DEFINITION (CAUSE-EFFECT)

Is man by nature a divided self? If so, how do you define the division?
(Freud, Buber, Arendt, Thoreau, Myths)

CONTRAST

What two perspectives of man described by authors in this section do you find to be in most opposition? Why?

COMPARISON

What two perspectives of man described by authors in this section are most similar?

CAUSE-EFFECT

Are there instincts that you wish were not part of man's nature? To what extent should society curb these instincts?
(Freud, Ardrey, Myths, Machiavelli)

PROCESS

If you believe man is evolving, what stages have already taken place in the process, and/or what stages must be followed to ensure man's progress?
(Sagan, Ardrey, Marx, Myths, Freud, Buber)

CAUSE-EFFECT

Can human nature change? Why, or why not?
(Sartre, Buber, Freud, Ardrey, Marx)

CAUSE-EFFECT (DEFINITION)

To what extent does man's civilization reflect man's nature?
(Freud, Ardrey, Paine, Machiavelli, Marx, Sartre, Sagan)

CAUSE-EFFECT

Should it be reason or emotion that controls man's existence?
(Freud, Sagan, Ardrey, Arendt, Paine, Marx, Machiavelli)

"Creating the Family of Man" from *A Cultural History of Tibet* by David Snellgrove and Hugh Richardson (New York: Frederick A. Praeger, 1968). Reprinted by permission of the publisher.

"A Creation Myth from New Hebrides" from *A Pattern of Islands* by Sir Arthur Grimble. Copyright 1952 by Sir Arthur Grimble. Reprinted by permission of John Murray (Publishers) Ltd.

"The Future of Man and of Life" from *The Meaning of Evolution: A Study of the History of Life and of Its Significance for Man* by George Gaylord Simpson. Copyright © 1949 by Yale University Press. Reprinted by permission of the publisher.

"Of Men and Mockingbirds" excerpted from *The Territorial Imperative* by Robert Ardrey. Copyright © 1966 by Robert Ardrey. Reprinted with the permission of Atheneum Publishers, Inc.

"Life and Death Wishes" reprinted from *Civilization and Its Discontents* by Sigmund Freud, translated by James Strachey. Copyright © 1961 by James Strachey. With the permission of W. W. Norton & Company, Inc., Sigmund Freud Copyrights ltd, The Institute of Psycho-Analysis, and The Hogarth Press.

From *Existentialism* by Jean-Paul Sartre, translated by Bernard Frechtman. Copyright 1947 by The Philosophical Library, Inc. Excerpted by permission of the publisher.

"Martin Buber and the Twofold Nature of Man" from *Understandings of Man*, by Perry LeFevre. Copyright © 1966 by W. L. Jenkins. Reprinted and used by permission of The Westminster Press, Philadelphia, PA.

From *The Human Condition* by Hannah Arendt. © 1958 by The University of Chicago. Reprinted by permission of The University of Chicago Press.

From *The Prince* by Niccolo Machiavelli, translated by W. K. Marriott (London: J. M. Dent, 1974). Reprinted by permission.

From *Broca's Brain* by Carl Sagan. Copyright © 1979 by Carl Sagan. Reprinted by permission of Random House, Inc.

Photo and Figure Credits

Figure 2.5: Reprinted by permission of Herbert H. Lehman College.

Figures 2.8 and 2.9: From *A Field Guide to Trees and Shrubs* by George A. Petrides. Copyright © 1958, 1972 by George A. Petrides. Reprinted by permission of Houghton Mifflin Company.   Figure 4.1: Courtesy of Kunsthistorisches Museum.   Figure 4.2: Courtesy of Réunion des musées nationaux.   Figure 4.4: Courtesy of the Library of Congress.   Figure 4.5: © 1985 by Sandra Baker.   Figure 4.6: © 1972 by Don Morgan, Photo Researchers.   Figure 4.7: From *Tents: Architecture of the Nomads* by Torvald Faegre. Copyright © 1979 by Torvald Faegre. Reprinted by permission of Doubleday & Company, Inc.   Figure 4.8 and floor plan: From "Chinese Architecture," by Andrew Boyd, in *World Architecture: An Illustrated History*, edited by Trewin Copplestone (London: Paul Hamlyn, 1963).   Figure 4.9: From *The Log Cabin: Homes of the North American Wilderness* by Alex W. Bealer (New York: Crown Publishers, 1978). Reprinted by permission.

Selected Excerpts

Page 48: Excerpted from *The Kinds of Mankind: An Introduction to Race and Racism* by Morton Klass and Hal Hellman. (Philadelphia: J. B. Lippincott, 1971).

Page 49: Excerpted from *Biology and Its Makers* by William A. Locy. (New York: Henry Holt & Co., 1908).

Page 50: Table derived from *Biology and Its Makers* by William A. Locy. (New York: Henry Holt & Co., 1908).

Page 117: Quotation from *Hard Times* by Charles Dickens. (New York: Harper & Brothers, 1960).

Page 165: Excerpted from *History of Art* by H. W. Janson. (New York: Harry N. Abrams, 1965).

Page 206: Chapter headings from *The Life of John Quincy Adams* by William Seward. (Derby, Miller & Co., 1849).

Page 207: Excerpted from *Life and Times of Frederick Douglass* (Hartford, Conn.: Park Publishing Co., 1881).

Page 208: From *The Life of John Quincy Adams* by William Seward. (Derby, Miller & Co., 1849).

Page 208: Excerpted from *Life and Times of Frederick Douglass* (Hartford, Conn.: Park Publishing Co., 1881).

Page 212: Table derived from *Identity, Youth, and Crisis* by Erik H. Erikson. (New York: W. W. Norton, 1968).

Page 303: Table of Contents from *Splicing Life: A Report on the Social and Ethical Issues of Genetic Engineering with Human Beings* by the President's Commission for the Study of Ethical Problems in Medicine and Biomedical and Behavioral Research. (Washington, D.C.: U.S. Government Printing Office, 1982).

Page 310: Excerpted from *Splicing Life: A Report on the Social and Ethical Issues of Genetic Engineering with Human Beings* by the President's Commission for the Study of Ethical Problems in Medicine and Biomedical and Behavioral Research. (Washington, D.C.: U.S. Government Printing Office, 1982).

Page 316: Excerpted from "Portents of Gene Cloning: Big Advances in Medical Enigmas" by Marvin Grosswirth in *Science Digest*, June 1980.

Page 318: Excerpted from "What Makes a Life Significant?" by William James in *Essays on Faith and Morals*, ed. Ralph Barton Perry (Cleveland: World Publishing Co., 1968).

Page 365: Excerpted from *Sun Songs: Creation Myths from Around the World*, edited by Raymond Van Over. (New York, New American Library, 1980).

Page 404: Quotation in "Martin Buber and the Twofold Nature of Man" from "The William Alanson White Memorial Lectures, Fourth Series," by Martin Buber in *Psychiatry*, Vol. XX, No. 2, (May, 1957).

Index